Introductory ECONOMICS

Fourth Edition

EIntroductory
ECONOMICS
Fourth Edition

Arleen J. Hoag
Owens Community College, Ohio

John H. Hoag
Bowling Green State University, Ohio

 **World Scientific**

NEW JERSEY · LONDON · SINGAPORE · BEIJING · SHANGHAI · HONG KONG · TAIPEI · CHENNAI

Published by

World Scientific Publishing Co. Pte. Ltd.

5 Toh Tuck Link, Singapore 596224

USA office: 27 Warren Street, Suite 401-402, Hackensack, NJ 07601

UK office: 57 Shelton Street, London WC2H 9HE

Library of Congress Cataloging-in-Publication Data
Hoag, Arleen J., 1944–   .
   Introductory economics / Arleen J. Hoag, John H. Hoag. -- 4th ed.
      p. cm.
   Includes bibliographical references and index.
   ISBN-13 978-981-256-891-5 (pbk)
   ISBN-10 981-256-891-3 (pbk)
    1. Economics.   I. Hoag, John H., 1944–   . II. Title.

  HB171.5.H67 2006
  330--dc22

                          2006049628

British Library Cataloguing-in-Publication Data
A catalogue record for this book is available from the British Library.

The first and second editions of this book were published by Prentice Hall.

First published 2006
Reprinted 2008

Printed in Singapore by Mainland Press Pte Ltd

For Howard,
For all you gave,

To Chris and Ann,
Who know the meaning of opportunity cost,

And Scott.

BRIEF OUTLINE

CONTENTS

PREFACE

To the Instructor

The objective of the survey course is to provide the student with an understanding of economic forces. In a scant forty or so hours of class time, the student is expected to gain an understanding not just of the economic problems of today but also of those that will be encountered in the future. The achievement of this nearly impossible goal involves the instructor, the student, and a textbook. A good text provides the student with a foundation on which the instructor can build. We believe that we have written a book that serves as this foundation and makes the classroom time more productive.

Our book contains thirty-one short chapters, each of which is devoted to a different economic concept. This format differentiates it from other texts that introduce another idea before the earlier one is taken in. The book is carefully structured to show the relation among the concepts introduced and to establish a comprehensive overview. We have stated the important economic principles clearly, always with the student in mind. The text is also designed to provide flexibility for the instructor. Another feature is that *Introductory Economics* concludes each chapter with a workbook section written by the textbook authors.

The text is organized in eight modules: The Economic Problem, Price Determination, Behind the Supply Curve, Measuring the Economy, The Level of Income, Money, Trade, and Conclusion. Each of the modules has an introduction, which provides an overview of the upcoming chapters and also establishes the relationship between the modules. Each chapter is designed to cover a single concept so that the student can easily read and digest the material in one sitting. Each chapter contains an introduction and a summary to help the student organize the material within the chapter and understand the connection between chapters. We help the student to see that economics is not just a collection of facts but a unified approach to thinking about the world. To encourage this thought process, there are questions for discussion at the end of each chapter. Each chapter also includes a self-review section composed of fill in the blanks and multiple choice questions to provide reinforcement of the chapter content.

We believe you will find that our text is clearly written. *Readability*, a Scandanavian PC Systems software, was used to enhance the reading level of the text. Our material is written at the level of a newspaper. Yet the essential concepts are carefully developed. *Introductory Economics* covers the basic economic concepts in detail. This means that not only are the basic principles stated, but the logic involved is also provided. In addition, examples are given to develop the student's intuition. We believe that the traditional principles can be expressed in a way that seems intuitive and makes sense.

To encourage the student to "think economics," we present a text that is readable, but with a difference. Not only is the text easy to read, but to accommodate the concentration span and comprehension of the average student, the concepts are presented in small chunks so that they can be digested. Specifically we employ the one-concept chapter. The student can comprehend one concept and obtain the satisfaction from the learning process before proceeding to another concept. This fosters positive reinforcement. The student can also cover a major concept easily within one sitting. For example, we have a chapter each on demand, supply, elasticity, and equilibrium, while other texts present the same material in one or two extensive chapters. At the same time, we take care that all the chapters become fully integrated into the book as a whole.

This text is written with the idea that the student will be alone while reading and must understand the written material without anyone's help. Critical definitions are in boldface, listed in the key concepts for each chapter, and included in a glossary. We have approached the text as if the reader is the student sitting next to our desk. Questions are asked and the student is induced to interact in the thought process. We have tried to be direct, personal, and patient. We lead and echo the student's thought process and encourage active learning. We want the student to see the logic in the subject and hope that the resulting enlightenment will encourage the student to read on. This is the essence of learning.

This text is flexible. If an instructor wishes to present deeper material, such as the Keynesian Cross, it is there — otherwise it can be easily skipped. The instructor, not the textbook, controls the course. The flexibility is enhanced by the "one-concept" chapters, which make it easy to leave out concepts by deleting whole chapters.

Introductory Economics provides a balance between micro and macro. And although micro precedes macro in this text, a reordering is made easy by changing the order of the one-concept chapters. The traditional problems in macro, including the unemployment and inflation trade-off, are discussed. A somewhat unusual chapter on economic policy, Chapter 29, shows the complexity of economic decision making. Here is a discussion of policy choices, pros and cons, with consideration given to the alternative approaches. Students are encouraged to think, not just be given "answers." The role that goals play in policymaking concludes the macro discussion.

In addition to the textbook, we have also written a study guide that is available on line in PDF format at http://www.cba.bgsu.edu/faculty_staff/hoag/studyguide.html. The study guide is free and does not require any registration. Each chapter of the text has a corresponding chapter in the study guide. There is also an introduction to graphs to help students understand and practice working with graphs. Each chapter of the study guide has a Matching section, an In The News section, and some more multiple choice questions to help the student review. Some chapters also have problems for the student to work out. Our experience is that the study guide provides the student with structured exercises to help cement the learning and to practice with the concepts. We believe it is an excellent addition to the course.

We have invested over sixty-five combined years in the classroom, and we have found some things that work for us. This text attempts to share some of those ideas. We hope that *Introductory Economics* can complement the special things you do in your classroom and make the classroom experience more productive for both you and your students.

INTRODUCTION

For the Student

You are beginning the study of a subject that surrounds your life. It is a subject of revolution. It helps to elect presidents, and it defeats them. It is a cause of wars, yet its main practitioners are not generals, statesmen, or leaders. Rather, the driving force for the subject originates with quiet professors. It is dry and dusty and has been called the "dismal science." Yet it is the cause of debates that border on violence. It has been important since the beginning of human activity and will be for all the foreseeable future. It is the frustrating and fascinating study of economics.

You will not be able to avoid the impact of economics even if you move to a remote wilderness area. Wherever you go, nature, for all its bounty, confronts you with one overwhelming truth. There is always something scarce. It is this scarcity that economics is about.

Economics is important. Economics is an essential part of your everyday living. And no doubt you will be affected by economic upheavals during your lifetime. Some industries may decline and lose their economic power. You may be unemployed. There may be a rapid increase in inflation. Now is the time for you to learn about economics so that you can understand the economic events that go on around you. But how do you study economics?

There are two important points. First is that the language of economics is important. You should be aware that the vocabulary is an essential part of economics. You will know that a term is being defined when it is in bold print in the text. These key concepts will be listed at the end of each chapter. A glossary of important terms is located at the end of the text. The terms must be understood. If you do not understand a term, you will not understand the discussion that uses the term. Economics is full of words, common to everyday speech, that have a special meaning to economists. You must carefully distinguish the common meaning from the economist's meaning, so be sure to learn the vocabulary.

The second important point is that economists have a fondness for asking "why?" We are not content to simply tell you that people buy more at a lower price. We want you to know why. So every chance we get, we are going to explain why something is true. You will want to pay attention to these explanations, as they are the heart of economics. We believe that hands-on experience is useful. At the end of each chapter, you will find questions for thought and discussion that will give you the opportunity to answer why. Also included is a self-review section consisting of fill in the blank and multiple choice. Use these to reinforce your vocabulary and general understanding. You will have a better grasp of the material.

So start by reading the text and paying close attention to the definitions. Also note when the explanations are being given. You should do this before the class discussion. The class will be much clearer if you do. Do not be shy about rereading. You will be surprised at how much you learn when you read the text again. You may also want to get out a pencil and some paper to work along with the text. While reading, stop and look at the tables and graphs that help to illustrate the point being made. They are not just there for their beauty! Let the discussion in the text guide you through the illustrations. If you understand these aids, you will have a better understanding of economics.

The book has eight modules. Each of the modules has an introduction followed by the chapters. The module introduction provides an overview of the upcoming chapters and also provides the relationship between the modules. Each chapter is designed to cover one concept. Each chapter includes an introduction and summary that will help you organize the material within the chapter and understand the connection between chapters. Economics is not just a collection of facts but a unified approach to thinking about the world. As you make your way through the text, you will develop this way of thinking.

In addition, there is a study guide available free online at http://www.cba. bgsu.edu/faculty_staff/hoag/studyguide.html in PDF format. You will find an introduction to graphs to help you review this important skill. The study guide also has one chapter for each chapter of the text. Each chapter has a set of Matching questions, a set of In the News questions, and some added multiple choice. Some chapters will also have some numerical problems for you to solve. The best way to learn economics and understand it is to practice. Our experience is that students who use a study guide are likely to do better in the course than those who do not. We strongly urge you to visit the web site http://www.cba.bgsu.edu/faculty_staff/hoag/studyguide.html.

What do we want you to be able to do when you are done with this book? Our main goal is for you to understand some basic economic concepts so that you can use economics to better understand the world around you. We believe that the economic principles you learn today will be just as applicable in four or even forty years.

It does not seem so long ago that we began our journey into economics as you are doing now. One thing we remember about the start of that journey is the prospect of discovering new ideas and gaining a deeper understanding of the world. We hope that through this book we can share in your discovery.

ACKNOWLEDGMENTS

No book is written without help from others. We are now aware of how extensive this help is. We would like publicly to thank those who have wittingly or unwittingly lent support to this venture and to us. The reviewers are James Aylsworth, Lakeland Community College; John Bockino, Suffolk County Community College; George Bohler, Florida Community College; Deidre V. Christie, Greenville Technical College; Roger Goldberg, Ohio Northern University; Raymond Mack, Boisce Community College of Allegheny County; John Megan, Milwaukee Area Technical College; Angela Nation, Santa Fe Community College; Harold J. O'Neil, Suffolk Community College; William Ruchensky, Western Iowa Technical Community College; Charles Wishhart, Indiana State University; and Richard Zuber, University of North Carolina.

We have also profited by suggestions from Professors M. Neil Browne, Randy LaHote, J. David Reed, Martha Terrie, and Brian Winters of Bowling Green State University and Dr. Ben Stevenson of Owens Community College. We are indebted to John Thompson for able research assistance. Portions of the manuscript were read by former graduate students Raja Kamal and Maria Solarez. Rich Douglas of Bowling Green State University and Mark Wheeler of Western Michigan University also read and commented on portions of the manuscript. In addition, we would like to thank Howard L. Hoag, who read the entire manuscript and offered extensive comments and criticisms. Nearly every page is improved because of his effort. Finally, we would like to thank our former students, for they ultimately shaped this book.

We have had excellent support from the editorial and production staff of World Scientific. Their professional efforts have made *Introductory Economics* an attractive and readable book.

In the final analysis, we must take responsibility for this book and whatever errors remain. There were two kinds of errors, those we found and those we did not. The ones that remain are honest and are not due to the lack of an eraser.

Module | 1 | THE ECONOMIC PROBLEM

The first four chapters in this book are a module. This book has seven modules. Each module focuses on a particular aspect of the economic problem. The first module introduces you to the economic problem. We will have more to say about the contents of this module in a moment. But first you should understand that each module consists of chapters containing topics that are closely related. We have grouped the chapters according to ideas which are most useful with each other. There will be an introduction such as this for each module to provide the basic framework that you will need for that module. Each chapter will reveal an important economic concept that is related to the other chapters in the module. The topics in one module are also related to ideas in other modules, so there is a strong common thread running throughout all the modules. You will continue to expand your knowledge as you progress through this textbook. Economics is not merely a collection of facts but is a unified approach to problem solving.

This introductory module involves two basic ideas. First, choices must be made among the different ways of using resources. Second is the idea that different societies may choose different ways of making these decisions. These decisions involve all aspects of our lives and are constantly being made and remade. Questions must be answered such as, How much land should be used for wheat production? If more wheat is grown, what will we give up? How much national defense should be provided? What are we willing to give up to get more defense? If we want more aid for the poor and disadvantaged, who will have to do with less? These questions, and others like them, are similar to those faced by our grandparents and those that will be faced by our grandchildren. These perpetual questions will constantly require our attention and will not go away. We cannot avoid making these decisions; one way or another, they will be made. How will they be made?

Decisions are made by the society and the individuals in the society weighing the costs of an action against the benefits of that action. This view — that weighing costs and benefits is an appropriate way to decide how the world will be — is what economics is about. You can think of economics as trying to answer those perpetual questions. But rather than providing answers, economics provides a method: ask what the costs and benefits are and upon whom they fall. Needless to say, what one thinks are benefits may be costs to another. So, economics cannot provide solutions to questions, but it can provide a stage on which the debate over the issues can be clearly understood. You cannot afford to sit back and let others attend the debate in your place. You have too much at stake to not listen and contribute.

We are surrounded by economic activity. In fact, it is so common that we may not recognize it when we see it. And even if we do not see them, economic forces are constantly shaping our lives.

In this first module, you can begin to look for and recognize economic forces and begin your orientation to economics. This module is largely an introductory overview of the economic problem. As you will learn, the challenge that each society faces is how to use the resources that are available to it. This is the economic problem. The meaning of economics is given in the first chapter. There the economic problem is fully discussed. Chapter 2 provides more detail, if desired, on the methods of economics. An example of the method used by economists is given in the third chapter, which also serves to unify and illustrate the preceding two chapters. The fact that every society must face certain decisions, and that every society has different ways to make these decisions, is the content of Chapter 4. One of the goals of this text is to provide you with the tools needed to understand the economic problem.

Chapter | 1 | THE MEANING OF ECONOMICS

Key Topics
  resources
  scarcity
  choices
  opportunity cost

Goals
  understand the scope of economics
  recognize the existence of scarcity
  examine the relation of scarcity, choice, and opportunity cost

What is economics? The subject matter of economics is introduced in this chapter. We want to give you an overview of the subject and an idea of how economists view the world. Of course, you should not expect to understand all of economics after just one chapter. However, let us see if by the end of this chapter you can achieve a basic understanding of the meaning of economics.

This chapter starts with a definition of economics. In each of the remaining sections, one concept in the definition will be discussed. We must take the definition apart before it can be put together in a meaningful way. The definition will be developed into a clear description of the science of economics. Every time you come to a new section, look back to the definition to see where and why the new material fits into the definition.

> ***Economics*** *is a social science that studies how society chooses*
> *to allocate its scarce resources, which have alternative uses, to*
> *provide goods and services for present and future consumption.*

The definition starts "Economics is," and that is what is being defined. So the remaining words need to be understood to make sense of economics. Let us start with "goods and services".

Goods and Services

What exactly are goods and services? A **good** is anything that satisfies a want. That is the purpose of production — to provide goods that satisfy wants. So goods are produced, and the consumption of those goods satisfies wants. Goods can be tangible or intangible. Tangible goods are physical items such as bulldozers or pizzas. Intangible goods such as medical care or education are called services. Both goods and services satisfy wants and therefore can be called goods.

Resources

The satisfaction of wants can only be accomplished by using up **resources**, the inputs, the so-called factors of production or means of production. These resources can be classified as land, labor, capital, and entrepreneurship.

Land is land itself and anything that grows on it or can be taken from it — the "natural resources." Imagine producing anything from a pizza to a medical doctor without the use of land somewhere along the productive process. **Labor**, another resource, is human effort, both physical and mental.

The resource capital is also known as capital goods. An economist's use of capital is not a reference to money but to a resource. **Capital** is a man-made tool of production; it is a good that has been produced for use in the production of other goods. Goods are produced for one of two purposes. A good may be a consumer good used for the satisfaction of wants, which is the ultimate purpose of production. Or a good may be a capital good produced not for consumption but for use in producing more goods, either consumer or capital. So capital goods, such as a mechanic's wrench or a school building, are resources that have been produced and that will combine with other resources, such as land and labor, to produce more output.

Some goods may be a consumer good in one use and a capital good in another use. For example, consider a personal computer. When the computer is used to play solitaire, it is a consumer good. On the other hand, when it is used as a word processor to write a textbook, it is a capital good. To tell whether a good is a consumer good or a capital good, ask yourself a question: Is the good going to be consumed directly or will it be used to produce more goods? If it is to be consumed directly and purchased by consumers, it is a consumer good; if it is to be used to produce other goods and purchased by business, it is a capital good.

Entrepreneurship is human effort again. Entrepreneurs are the risk takers. They are more than managers, although they use managerial ability. Entrepreneurs reap the profits or bear the losses of their undertakings. **Entrepreneurship** is the organizational force that combines the other factors of production — land, labor, and capital — and transforms them into the desired output. The output may be capital or consumer goods, but ultimately consumer goods are produced to satisfy wants.

Scarcity

Resources are scarce. Scarcity is a relationship between how much there is of something and how much of it is wanted. Resources are scarce compared to all of the uses we have for them. If we want to use more than there is of an item, it is scarce. Note that this meaning is different from the usual meaning of scarce, which is "rarely found in nature." How are they different? Consider this example. Is water scarce? How could anyone argue that water is scarce in the usual sense? Water covers nearly two-thirds of the earth's surface. Yet an economist would say that water is scarce. Why? The reason is that there are so many competing uses for water that more water is wanted than is available. If you find this hard to believe, ask farmers and ranchers in the West, where water rights are jealously guarded. As soon as someone is willing to pay for a good, or a resource, it is scarce by the economist's definition.

Consider scarcity from another point of view. What if scarcity did not exist? Then all goods would be free goods. **Free goods** would mean that you could have all you want of everything without having to give up something else you also want. Can you think of goods that are not scarce? There may be some. Take air, for example. Isn't it free? What do you have to give up to get air? In some locations, it probably is free. But, in other locations, it is not, especially if air means clean air. You could make a fortune if you could find a way to provide clean air on a smoggy day in Los Angeles. People pay to avoid the smog: they don't go out when the smog is bad, they car pool, and so on. So even air may not be free. In fact, it is hard to think of goods or resources that *are* free.

The production of goods to satisfy a want will reduce the amount of the available resources. Resources are limited. There is only so much land, labor, capital, and entrepreneurship in existence at any point in time. Resources are therefore scarce because there is not enough of them to go around to produce all the things that we would like to produce to satisfy all our wants. Hence goods are scarce, too. Scarce resources yield scarce goods.

On the one hand, resources are limited, but on the other hand, human wants are unlimited. Wants are unlimited or nearly so. How can that be? Everyone has wants, and if the truth were known, each individual has nearly unlimited wants. Examine my wish list. It certainly includes more goods and services than I have right now. I would like to live in some exciting places. Paris would be acceptable, but not all the time. I would also like a home in Hawaii or on the Monterey peninsula. And of course a place in the Alps for skiing. And because these places are far away from each other, and I do not want to depend on commercial airlines — a private jet would be nice. And probably a Rolls-Royce or a Mercedes for the family and a Ferrari or Porsche for me. Too, I would not want to spend all my time cleaning house or cooking, so each home would need a complete staff. The list is fairly long already, and I haven't gotten to my special passion — hats! You can easily see that if each member of society made up a wish list, the wants of all people added up would be enormous. Nearly unlimited. The point is that wants exceed what can be produced from our limited resources.

Unlimited wants alone are not a problem, but certainly a problem exists when unlimited wants are combined with a limited means of satisfying those wants. The production of any good on our wish list uses up resources. Then scarcity sets in. We can never satisfy all of society's unlimited wants with limited resources and the consequently limited goods.

Unlimited wants reflect human nature. The limitation of resources is imposed upon us by nature. Therefore, unlimited wants competing for limited resources creates the basic economic problem of **scarcity**. This is a difficulty that cannot be overcome by cleverness or good fortune. Scarcity, the interaction of unlimited wants with limited resources, has been called the economic problem.

In fact, you are starting the study of economics, which would not exist except for scarcity. If that makes you think that scarcity might be the cause of many of your problems, you are right. Scarcity is the economic problem. Therefore, choices must be made.

Choices

We must choose how to use our scarce resources. Scarcity forces choice. And economics, which deals with scarcity, is often called the study of choosing. We cannot have all we want of everything we want. Scarcity. Scarcity is imposed by limited factors of production yielding limited output of goods relative to unlimited wants. Choices must be made.

Now you see that since we do not have enough capital goods to assist in the production of all those consumer goods to satisfy our unlimited wants, capital is a scarce resource. And we must choose how to use capital. For similar reasons, we must choose how to use land, labor, and entrepreneurship. The fact that choices must be made in turn reflects the fact that scarcity does exist.

Alternative Uses

So far we see that society is faced with the problem of not having enough resources to provide for all wants. And thus choices must be made about how those resources will be used or allocated. **Allocate** means distribute. Society must make choices among the alternatives. Society must decide which goods will be produced, how to allocate resources to produce goods, and how to allocate the goods among the population. The method used to decide how these allocations will be made depends on the kind of economic system the society has chosen. Chapter 4 will expand on this topic.

Since resources have alternative uses and are scarce, it is necessary to choose among the alternatives. Land, labor, capital, and entrepreneurship may be used in one combination to produce pianos and in another to produce computers or psychiatric care. Yet we cannot have all the pianos, computers, and psychiatric care as well as all of everything else we might want. There are many alternative ways to use the resources, and choices must be made.

It makes no difference whether the problem is how government will use its resources or how individuals or business use theirs. In every case, resources are scarce, and choices must be made. So government chooses to use resources for medical research or expeditions to the Antarctic. Individuals choose how to spend their time and income. Entrepreneurs decide how to use land, labor, and capital. In each case, there are many alternative ways in which those choices could be made.

Sometimes, at first glance, there appears to be no alternative. But there are always alternatives. For example, what if there is a shortage of teachers in science and mathematics? Some might conclude that the only alternative is to train more teachers. There may be no other choice as attractive as that, but there are alternatives. We could require less math and science in our schools. We could employ teachers trained in other countries or in political science. The schools could be closed. Students could teach other students. Classes could be larger, or teachers could be drafted out of retirement. There are alternative ways that this problem of "scarce teachers" could be solved. We must choose among alternatives.

Scarcity imposes a limitation on the amount of output that society can produce. Because there are always alternative uses of the resources and because scarcity exists, society cannot produce all that it wants. It must therefore choose among the alternatives. Hence cost is imposed on society; economists call this cost opportunity cost. What is opportunity cost?

Opportunity Cost

Opportunity cost is a concept you did not see in the definition of economics. But not seeing it doesn't mean that it isn't there. There is yet more to say about the definition, but this is the logical place to introduce a related concept.

Opportunity costs are everywhere, due to scarcity and the necessity of choosing. Opportunity cost is not what you choose when you make a choice — it is what you did *not* choose in making a choice. **Opportunity cost** is the value of the forgone alternative — what you gave up when you got something.

Your brain is wrestling with the idea of opportunity cost now. You have temporarily given up the opportunity to think of food. But what about your stomach? If it is full, it has temporarily given up the opportunity to be empty. Or vice versa. You open your mouth to protest the existence of opportunity cost. You could have laughed or yawned or sung the *Star Spangled Banner* at full volume instead. All are opportunity costs. You buy the blue shirt rather than the green, or 1,700 pieces of bubble gum, or leave the dollars in your checking account. Opportunity cost. Your state uses its limited budget to build more roads rather than schools. Opportunity cost. Your government chooses more defense spending and sacrifices human services. You guessed it.

Look back at the scarcity discussion. It was concluded there that the concept of free goods is not a realistic concept. Economists are fond of saying that there is no such thing as a free lunch. Even if your friend buys your lunch, you give up something — namely, time. That time could have been used for some other purpose, so there is an opportunity cost associated with lunch, no matter who buys. From the point of view of society, resources are used up to provide the lunch. These resources are limited. Resources applied to this production cannot be applied to that production. Consequently, the production of a good to satisfy a want imposes an opportunity cost. So opportunity cost is why goods are not free, but scarce.

Well, we got a little carried away and introduced an unannounced concept — opportunity cost. But you can see how it happened. Scarcity results in choice; choice results in opportunity cost. For your dedication in this chapter so far, take the concept of opportunity cost as a free bonus. Or was it free?

Present and Future Consumption

Choice also imposes opportunity cost over time. The use of resources now means that those resources will not be available for future use. A decision must be made, an opportunity cost encountered, as to whether to allocate for present needs or future needs. Today versus tomorrow.

Some goods will be consumed today and some in the future. By reducing consumption today, future consumption may be increased. Isn't that one reason you are in school? If you are not working full time, you are not consuming all you could. You are postponing consumption. Why? Because you believe you could get a better job (and one with more pay) if you have more training and education. So you can consume even more later. Thus you postpone current consumption while building up your skills so as to increase consumption later. Again, a barrel of oil pumped from the ground now is a barrel of oil that will not be available for consumption any day in the future. So to use the oil today imposes forgone opportunities in the future.

Social Science

Economics is a science, a social science that studies how society chooses. Sciences are alike in their use of the scientific method, although each science has its own focus. **Social sciences** focus on human behavior. Physical sciences focus on natural phenomenon. Psychology is a social science. Chemistry is a physical science. Economics is a social science, which means that economists study human behavior confronted by scarcity through application of the scientific method. The scientific method will be explored in Chapter 2.

▶ Summary

Now putting all the pieces back together again, the definition of economics is

> *Economics is a social science that studies how society chooses*
> *to allocate its scarce resources, which have alternative uses, to*
> *provide goods and services for present and future consumption.*

You have been exposed to a general description of the meaning of economics. What have you learned so far? So far you should have in mind that economics is a social science that studies how the scarce resources (land, labor, capital, and entrepreneurship) are used. Scarcity is a situation that we cannot eliminate. We have to choose how to use those scarce resources since not all wants can be satisfied.

One concept builds on another — scarcity, choice, opportunity cost. But don't lose perspective. All that we are doing is describing the conditions imposed upon us by the real world. We are identifying and explaining the circumstances that make necessary the study of economics. Remember that this chapter is just an overview, and now you are ready to begin another chapter to explore the main tool economists use to study scarcity, models.

▶ Key Concepts

economics	entrepreneurship
goods and services	free good
resources	scarcity
land	allocate
labor	opportunity cost
capital	social science

▶ Discussion Questions

1. In your backyard you raise tomatoes to sell. What are the inputs used and how would an economist classify them as scarce resources? The scarce resources are land, labor, capital, and entrepreneurship.
2. Is money a scarce resource? Isn't our problem really not having enough money?
3. Sometimes time and technology are suggested as resources. Which resource already defined includes time? Technology?
4. How would an economist interpret the expression, "It's not worth it."
5. Disney charges one fee to enter its park and no fee for the individual rides. What is the opportunity cost of a ride at Disney? What is scarce for the average park visitor?
6. A lemon-scented dishwashing soap was distributed as a free sample. Some people mistakenly thought it was a lemonade mix and served it. Was this sample free? Is any sample really free?

7. What is the opportunity cost to the student of a college education? The parents? The society?
8. How can seed corn show the choice between present and future consumption?

▶ **Self-Review**

● Fill in the blanks

good	Anything that satisfies a want is a _____ . The factors of
land, labor	production needed to produce goods are _____, _____,
capital, entrepreneurship	_____, and _____. Because human
scarcity	wants are unlimited and resources are limited, _____
	results. Because there are not enough resources to produce
choose	all the goods that are desired, we must _____ how to
	use the resources we have.
alternative	Resources have _____ uses. The value of
opportunity	what you did not choose is the _____ cost of
social	what you did choose. Economics is a _____ science. A
	social science studies aspects of human behavior through
scientific	application of the _____ method.

● Multiple choice

1. Economics focuses on:
   a. people and how resources are used to satisfy human wants.
   b. money.
   c. banks.
   d. government control of the economy.
2. A resources is scarce if:
   a. there is not very much of it.
   b. it is not needed or wanted.
   c. the quantity people want is more than is available.
   d. there is more available than people want.
3. Select the free good.
   a. The lunch your friend buys you.
   b. Your winnings in the lottery.
   c. Hand-me-down clothes.
   d. None of the above.
4. Jill spent $15 on a new skirt. Then she saw a blouse for $15 that she liked better than the skirt. What was the opportunity cost of the skirt?
   a. $15.

    b. The blouse.
    c. Nothing since both cost $15.
    d. Cannot be determined.
5. Opportunity cost occurs because:
    a. resources are scarce.
    b. resources have alternative uses.
    c. we must choose how to use our resources.
    d. all of the above.

Answers: 1.a, 2.c, 3.d, 4.b, 5.d.

Chapter | 2 | METHODS

Key Topics

why models are used
elements of a model
model classification

Goals

recognize the necessity of models
understand the use of models in economics

Since economics is a way of thinking about the world, we should devote some time to the methods economists use in that thought process. The major tool used by economists is a model. In this chapter we will discuss why models are used and what the elements of a model are. In addition we will discuss how models may be categorized. These topics are important. You will be introduced to many economic models in this book, and they will make more sense if you understand what they are and why they are used.

Why Models Are Used

There is one fundamental reason why economists make models. They want to understand the economic aspects of the world around them. So why not study the world? The answer is that the world is too complex for a single human (or even many humans aided by computers) to understand. Thus to understand the world requires that the world be simplified. The major tool used by an economist is a model. A **model** is a simplification of reality. Examples of models are globes, toy fire trucks, the law of gravity, and the law of demand. Model worlds must be constructed, but they are not miniaturizations of the real world, they must be simplifications. This is the same technique used in any other science. As you learned in the previous chapter, economics is a social science. Economics is distinct from a natural science — a science which studies physical aspects of the world rather than human behavior. Yet all science shares the same methodology which is called the scientific method. The scientific method is a procedure that attempts to deduce the cause of some effect.

The scientific method observes events, attempts to detect patterns, hypothesizes theories, tests theories, and reaches conclusions. This process results in a theory or law that, when applied correctly, will predict an outcome. As you will learn, the law of demand predicts, all other things staying the same, that if the price of lobster dinners falls to ten cents, then more lobster dinners will be purchased. A theory predicts what will happen, not what we want to happen. The value of economics will be in the ability of its theory to correctly predict outcomes.

Scientists observe that a certain thing happens, such as the phases of the moon, and ask "Why does this happen, what causes it?" With the moon, the problem the scientist faces is that there is no place for him to stand so he can see the explanations for the phases. Standing on earth has caused the puzzle and standing on the moon may help except that then there will be "phases of the earth" to explain. Even if there were a place to stand, there is no way for the scientist to manipulate the planets and the moon to see why the phases occur. In some sense the problem is too big. How can the scientist simplify and scale the problem down to a manageable size. To simplify, the scientist will throw out all variables which are not relevant. Is the grasshopper migration from last year relevant in explaining why the moon has phases? If not, ignore it. Such simplification helps reduce the size of the problem. Once the size of the problem is reduced, we are on our way to a model and understanding.

In some cases the modeling process can be taken a step further. One convenient aspect of the natural sciences (that social sciences do not have) is that sometimes physical models can be built. In our example a physical model of the solar system will suffice. Start with a light bulb, an orange and a walnut. Then by physically moving "the planets" in the model, the scientist can see exactly why the phases of the moon occur. (It has to do with the relative position of the earth, the sun, and the moon, but that is another story.) In any case, there is now a method to predict when the phases of the moon will occur. These predictions can be tested to see if they come true. If this method does predict, it becomes an accepted scientific model.

Even when physical models cannot be built the process of simplification can lead to understanding. In economics, physical models are rarely used, yet the process of simplifying does yield models which explain economic aspects of the world. This process of simplifying and scaling down is a basic technique of science. It is sometimes called modeling or model building. This technique is used in any field that claims to be a science and since economics is a science, economists use it too. In fact this book is full of the main models that most western economists use to understand economic aspects of the world and to make predictions about economic events. Thus the idea of trying to understand the world really breaks down into two parts. First is to attempt to understand or explain a phenomenon and second is to predict what will happen next. The idea of the latter is that if a process is truly understood, the next event in the process can be predicted. Thus the purpose of a model is to explain or predict. What do these things mean in the context of economics?

Questions which we expect economics to be able to answer are questions like what will the price of potato chips be? What will the level of employment be next year? These questions are predictive questions. They cannot be answered until the following questions are answered. What determines the price of potato chips? What determines the level of employment? These are explain questions. To answer these explain questions, a model is constructed. To obtain predictions, appropriate facts are put into the model, and the model provides the prediction.

We now see that there are two kinds of questions we need to answer: explain questions and predictive questions. Further the predictive questions first required that the explain questions be answered. Let us look at these two questions and their relationship starting with the explain question — since it must come first.

Any model which explains how some economic variable is determined is an equilibrium model. The idea of equilibrium is that some forces balance each other out. Thus the models studied in this book are equilibrium models. They explain how some economic variable is determined. They also play a role in prediction. When some underlying variable in the model is changed, the forces move us to a new equilibrium. Thus by comparing the two equilibria, an economist can predict what will happen when the variable changed.

So far this discussion may seem abstract; it is. Yet the idea discussed here is central to your understanding of economics. The basic technique employed by economists using models to predict has been given and you will frequently see examples of it throughout the book. But perhaps more importantly, the fact that equilibria are needed to make a prediction should enable you to realize that equilibrium models are basic to understanding economics. So if in chapters

to come the discussion centers on why the equilibrium is where it is, you will
know two reasons why:

A. We want to explain why equilibrium occurs where it does to demonstrate
   an understanding of the process (answers the explain question).
B. It is only by generating several equilibrium positions (at least two) that
   predictions about what will occur can be made (answers the predictive
   question).

Elements of a Model

Now after all that, what is a model? Basically, as you saw above, a **model** is a
simplification of reality. The next question is, how is a model constructed? To
answer this question, what goes into a model must be determined. The basic
ingredients of a model are definitions, assumptions, and conclusions. Each of
these items is discussed next.

Definition gives a name to an idea. You are probably aware of the importance
of definitions. The importance is doubled in economics because many of the
words economists use are everyday words. So if you associate the word with
its everyday meaning you will misunderstand the economist. For example, the
common meaning of capital is money. But for an economist, capital means
tools of production. You can see the difference. So it is important for you
to learn the definition of terms. The definitions of important terms will be
clearly marked; you will want to watch for them and be sure you understand
the definition being given before reading on.

The second important element of a model is the set of assumptions being
made. Assumptions play two roles. In the first place, they tell us which
variables are important in the analysis and which things may be ignored.
Therefore **assumptions** are the simplifying device. The second important
role for assumptions is that they provide relationships between (or among)
the variables. For example, economists frequently assume that the number of
units of a good that a consumer wants has a particular relation to the price.
Thus assumptions play a major role in a model. They act to simplify reality
into a model world different from the real world, and they tell us how the
model world works. In other words, assumptions describe the world in which
the analysis will take place. How will you know when you are about to meet
an assumption? Usually, certain words will alert you. When an economist
says "If ...", you know that what follows the "if" is an assumption. Certain

other words may also indicate an assumption: "given", "suppose", "what if" and others.

Once the assumptions have been given and a model world is set up, what comes next? The main thing is that some conclusion needs to be made from the assumptions. In other words the model should then tell us what happens next. The **conclusion** that is drawn from the model is a prediction of behavior; it is a testable hypothesis. Using actual human behavior, we could see whether or not the predicted behavior actually occurred. How will you know when a conclusion is being given? A conclusion is usually signaled by the word "then".

The main elements of a model, definitions, assumptions, and conclusions have been described. You will be more able to understand the models in this book if you keep the elements of a model in mind. But there is another aspect of modeling. If for some reason you find it desirable to disagree with the conclusion of an economist, then the proper strategy is to search out the assumptions made and challenge them. Thus you need to be able to identify the assumptions the economist has made so that you can react to the analysis. In this book you will see different kinds of assumptions that economists typically make and what impact they have on the outcome of the analysis. This is one of the tools you should carry with you from this class.

Finally note that a model may be presented in several different forms. The model may be stated verbally, or mathematically. In either case, you are likely to see graphs as a part of the model. You should not be surprised if a model is presented using all three forms.

Model Classifications

Why models are used and the elements of models have been discussed so far. Now let us see how models are classified. How will this help you? The main benefit is that the classification provides clues to which model fits with the discussion you are reading or hearing. There are two fundamental ways to classify models. First is whether the model is positive or normative. Second is in terms of content, is the model primarily micro or macro? The positive/normative classification is discussed first.

A model either *describes* the way the world is or *prescribes* how it should be. Models which describe are called **positive** models and those that prescribe are called **normative**. How are they different? Positive models provide descriptions about the world. Using data from the world, these descriptions can be tested to see if they are false. Positive: your hair is six inches long. Statements reflecting what *should* or *ought* to be are normative statements. They are not capable of being proved false. Normative statements reflect personal value judgments. Normative: you should get a hair cut.

The line dividing positive and normative is thin and sometimes blurred. Some economists start with positive economic models, then, based on these positive views, will then make a normative argument. For example an economist might argue that to ease the federal deficit and provide for long term economic stability, income taxes should be raised by five percent. The five percent figure (and the increase in taxes rather than a decrease in taxes) was obtained from a positive economic argument. But whether the goal of removal of the deficit is the best goal is a matter of opinion. Thus this argument combines both normative and positive aspects. And that is usually the way it is, so you will want to be able to identify which part of the argument is positive and which part is normative.

Why is this difference important? If a model is positive, you will want to be sure that you think it has included the important aspects of the world being described. If someone were to argue that the number of twenty-year olds in school did not depend on how much college tuition was, you would probably think that this model did not describe reality very well. You realize that price has an important impact. If a model is normative, it is important for you to realize that someone is trying to convince you of the way *they* think things should be. You must decide whether or not the argument is persuasive before you agree. Whether or not the argument is persuasive may depend on whether or not the argument conflicts with your opinion of the way you think things should be. When you hear or see an economic argument being made, be sure to recognize whether the argument is basically positive or basically normative.

Models are also classified by content. There are many different ways economics can be divided up in terms of topics. Rather than focus on the fine distinctions, we will discuss two broad categories. These are macroeconomics and microeconomics. Macro is about the economy as a whole. Micro is about how the individuals in the economy make decisions. Micro involves both consumers and firms. Why is this distinction between macro and micro important? The main reason is that the basic tools used to study the two kinds of problems are different; the problems which are of interest in macro require macro tools and the micro problems need micro models. So you will need to be able to recognize which kind of problem is being discussed so that you will know which tools to apply.

How does the positive/normative classification fit in with the macro/micro content? They are independent. Thus models may fall into any one of four categories.

Model Types	Macro	Micro
Positive	×	×
Normative	×	×

▶ Summary

In this chapter we have discovered the importance of modeling in economics. It is inescapable because of the complexity of the real world. Models are a simplification of reality. Models are composed of definitions, assumptions and conclusions. The basic purpose of models is to explain or predict. There are broad categories into which economic models fall. They are positive macro, positive micro, normative macro and normative micro. The next chapter will introduce you to a model of scarcity and put into practice the concepts you have learned. You will discover more specific and clearer descriptions of topics introduced by the definition of economics.

▶ Key Concepts

model	positive
definition	normative
assumptions	micro
conclusion	macro

▶ Discussion Questions

1. Which statements are positive and which are normative?
   a. Children should be seen but not heard.
   b. The cost of a college education is increasing.
   c. Electricity is too expensive.
   d. Hospitals had more vacant beds this year than last.
   e. There are more dandelions than people on my block.
   f. It's not fair.
2. Is this book a model? Of what? Explain.
3. Explain the eclipse of the moon without using a model.

4. Which statement is positive and which is normative? The average student is registered for six classes and that is too many.

5. Which of the following is a micro positive statement? Micro normative? Macro positive? Macro normative?

   a. The unemployment level is too high

   b. The inflation rate in 2006 was 2.7%

   c. College tuition should be lowered.

   d. The price of gasoline is rising.

▶ Self-Review

• Fill in the blanks

model	A tool that simplifies reality is a _____. A model includes
definition	three elements, _____ which names a concept,
assumption, conclusion	_____ which simplifies reality, _____
	which provides a testable prediction about reality. Models
positive	that describe are _____, and models that prescribe are
normative, macro	_____. Models of the whole economy are _____
micro	models, and models of individual behavior are _____
	models.

• Multiple choice

1. Which is not an element of a model?

   a. conclusion

   b. resources

   c. definition

   d. assumption

2. Select the normative statement.

   a. This chapter is longer than the previous.

   b. This chapter is easy.

   c. This is not the last chapter.

   d. This chapter is about methods.

3. You find models used in:

   a. physics.

   b. economics.

   c. chemistry

   d. all of the above.

4. A positive statement is:

   a. always true.

b. can be tested against real world data.

c. is a matter of opinion.

d. only arises in a natural science, not a social science.

5. The conclusion of the statement "If the price of gasoline rises with nothing else changing, then people will buy less gasoline," is:

a. the price of gasoline rises.

b. people will buy less gasoline.

c. with nothing else changing.

d. not found in the statement.

Answers: 1.b., 2.b., 3.d., 4.b., 5.b.

| Chapter | 3 | **PRODUCTION POSSIBILITIES**

Key Topics
- production possibilities
- scarcity, choice, and opportunity cost
- law of increasing costs
- changing the assumptions — employment
- changing the assumptions — resources and technology

Goals
- understand production possibilities
- understand that scarcity forces choice
- understand the law of increasing costs and why it is true
- understand what happens to production possibilities when the assumptions change

In this chapter you will see one way in which an economist views the problem of scarcity, and you will review the fundamental fact that in making choices, costs are imposed. This will be accomplished using a simple model that reflects scarcity. The basic meaning of scarcity is that society cannot have as much as it wants of all goods. Goods are produced from resources, and resources are scarce. To get more of one good, some amount of another good must be given up. What determines the combinations of goods society can have? We need to know the amount of resources available and how to produce the goods we want from these resources. Knowledge of how to turn resources into output is called **technology**. So given the amount of resources and the technology, we can determine the combinations of output that society is capable of producing.

A Model of Scarcity

Recall that a model is used to simplify reality so that reality can be understood and, it is hoped, managed. The model that is about to be introduced, the production possibilities model, provides a clearer understanding of the resource allocation problem. The production possibilities model is designed to tell us as a society what combinations of output we could possibly choose. The assumptions of the production possibilities model are:

1. Two alternative goods
2. Full employment of resources
3. Fixed amount of resources and technology

Let us first review these assumptions. The model considers output of only two different goods. In fact any number of goods could be included. But limiting the model to just two goods certainly makes the model easier to use and, more important, still contributes to an understanding of reality. Full employment of resources indicates that there will be no unemployment or underemployment of land, labor, capital, or entrepreneurship. We want to know what potential combinations of output we could produce with our greatest effort. A fixed amount of resources and technology tells us that we are producing at a given, fixed point in time. A realistic assumption is that there are only so many resources and a certain level of technology available at that moment. While it may be true that over time the amount of resources and technology may change, at the actual time of production they are fixed.

The **production possibilities model** shows all possible combinations of two different outputs that the society is capable of producing. Of course the amount of each output depends in part on the amount of resources put into the production of each good. Suppose that the two goods are loaves of bread and vats of wine. If we increase the resources put into the production of bread, we must shift those resources over from the production of the alternative good, wine. Remember that all resources are already fully employed producing bread or wine and that this time period is not long enough to change the technology or the total amount of resources available. Since more resources are now used to produce bread, more bread is produced. Further, since fewer resources are now used in wine production, less wine is produced. Under the assumptions of the model, we can determine the maximum amount of bread or the maximum amount of wine that could be produced. These combinations can be written in a table.

Combination A in Table 3-1 shows the maximum amount of bread we could produce if all resources were used to produce bread. How much wine could also be produced? With all resources being used for bread, no resources are left

Table 3-1   Two Possible Combinations of Output

	Loaves of Bread	Vats of Wine
A	20,000	0
F	0	5

Combination A shows the amount of bread that can be produced if no wine is produced and combination F, the amount of wine that can be produced if no bread is produced.

Table 3-2   Production Possibilities

	Loaves of Bread	Vats of Wine
A	20,000	0
B	18,000	1
C	15,000	2
D	11,000	3
E	6,000	4
F	0	5

This table shows several combinations of bread and wine that can be produced with a fixed amount of resources and technology.

to produce wine, so wine could not be produced. This is what combination A indicates, 20,000 loaves of bread and zero vats of wine as a possible combination of output. If all resources go into the production of wine, combination F shows another production possibility, zero bread and a maximum of 5 vats of wine. The definition of economics reminds us that resources have alternative uses. Therefore, resources not used in the production of bread can be used elsewhere, and bread is actually "transformed" into wine.

What if society wants to produce both bread and wine? Is this possible? Yes, if society devotes some resources to the production of bread and enough resources remain to produce wine. This can be seen in Table 3-2. In fact there are more combinations of bread and wine than we can easily write in a table. A graph will more readily show all possible combinations of output. In the graph in Figure 3-1, wine is measured on the horizontal axis and bread on the vertical axis. We have taken the production possibilities table and plotted it. We call the resulting curve the production possibilities curve. To plot point A we measured up the vertical axis to the 20,000 loaves of bread mark. Since we are on the bread axis, this signifies zero wine. Thus, point A shows the combination of

20,000 loaves of bread and zero vats of wine. Point F shows the combination
of zero loaves and 5 vats of wine.

Another combination of output of both bread and wine is shown by point
B. To plot this point, measure up the vertical axis to the 18,000 mark and
then move to the right until directly over 1 vat. Point B represents 18,000
loaves and 1 vat of wine. Another possible combination of output is shown at
C, 15,000 loaves and 2 vats of wine, or 11,000 loaves and 3 vats of wine at
point D. Or 6,000 loaves and 4 vats of wine at point E. What we now have is
a production possibilities curve, Figure 3-1, showing *all* possible combinations
of the two different goods this society is capable of producing. This includes
the combinations of bread and wine represented by the points A and F, as well
as B, C, and E. This also includes all the other combinations of output that
have not been discussed but are indicated by the large collection of points that
together make up the production possibilities curve.

The very name of this model sends a message. What are the possibilities of
production for society? Look at the curve. The society's production alternatives
are clearly displayed. It is easy to see where the model gets its name, and the
name is a handy reminder of the significance of the model. The production
possibilities curve is a collection of points representing all the various alternative
combinations of two different goods that this society is capable of producing.

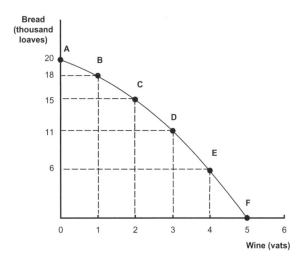

Figure 3-1   Production Possibilities Curve
This graph of Table 3-2 is the production possibilities curve. The curve shows all possible
combinations of output of bread and wine.

Scarcity, Choice, and Opportunity Cost

The existence of a production possibilities curve is a reminder of the existence of scarcity. Without scarcity, society could have all it wanted of both bread and wine. Resources would be unlimited, and if all of society's resources were devoted to the production of bread, for example, then an unlimited (infinite) amount of bread could be produced. At the same time, there would be enough resources left over to produce an unlimited amount of wine. Thus there would not be a production possibilities curve since points on the curve represent a limited, not an unlimited, output of bread and wine. Yet from the first chapter we know that resources are limited, scarcity does exist, and infinite output is simply impossible. Hence production possibilities exists, and choices must be made.

Choice is indicated on the production possibilities curve by being at one combination of output rather than another. It is an either/or situation. You choose one combination; you cannot also choose another. There are not enough resources. We cannot have the combinations of output indicated by both A and B. It is A or B. B or F. Thus production possibilities reflects scarcity. As we move from one point on the curve to another, costs are imposed. These costs occur because we must give up something to gain something. Scarcity forces choice, which results in opportunity cost.

Opportunity cost is shown by production possibilities. When you move from one point to another point on the production possibilities curve, you gain more of one good — wine, for example. The extra wine is the gain. But there is also a loss. To produce more vats of wine, resources had to be shifted from bread to wine. More resources allocated to wine, more output of wine. Less resources allocated to bread, less output of bread. To gain one additional vat of wine, some bread was sacrificed. Limited resources used elsewhere result in opportunity cost. To see this more clearly, consider the production possibilities curve shown in Figure 3-2. Suppose that we start at point B. At B, 18,000 loaves are produced together with 1 vat of wine. What does it cost to increase wine production to 2 vats? To increase wine production to 2 vats, it is necessary to move from point B to point C. Bread production therefore fell from 18,000 loaves to 15,000. So the answer is that we must give up 3,000 loaves. The opportunity cost of the second vat of wine is 3,000 loaves of bread. Moving from one point to another on the production possibilities curve always involves an opportunity cost. The opportunity cost of one good is always measured by the amount given up of the other good. So the production possibilities curve clearly identifies opportunity cost.

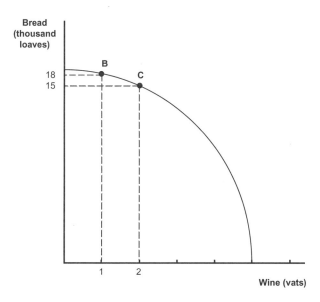

Figure 3-2   Production Possibilities and Opportunity Cost
What happens when we go from point B to point C? Wine production increases from 1 vat to 2 vats while bread production falls from 18,000 to 15,000 loaves. The opportunity cost of more wine is less bread.

Each society must face the choices imposed by scarcity. The production possibilities curve itself indicates the existence of scarcity; movement along the curve from one combination or choice to another reflects opportunity cost. Moreover, society's production possibilities curve also reflects the law of increasing costs. This law can be revealed by a closer examination of the opportunity costs and is the topic of the next section.

Increasing Costs

So far the production possibilities curve has had a distinctive "bowed-out" shape. This shape is a result of the cost required to get more of any one good. The **law of increasing costs** means that as society obtains an extra unit of one good, ever-increasing amounts of the other good must be sacrificed. This law implies that for each additional vat of wine produced, the opportunity cost, in terms of the number of loaves given up, must increase. Now let us discover why a bowed-out production possibilities curve is the result of the law of increasing costs, and why the law itself is true.

To see that the bowed-out shape is implied by the law of increasing costs, consider Figure 3-3. Start at A where no wine is produced and all resources are used to produce bread. Now move down the curve from A to B. As wine output is increased from zero vats to 1, bread production falls from 20,000 to 18,000 loaves. Two thousand loaves of bread must be given up. Next move from B to C. The output of wine increases by an additional vat. How many more loaves must be given up to get the second vat of wine? Three thousand loaves, since bread production falls from 18,000 to 15,000 loaves. Is this increasing costs? The law of increasing costs requires that for each additional unit, *more* is given up than was given up for the previous unit. In this case, we are giving up 3,000 loaves to get the second vat of wine, which is *more* than the 2,000 loaves given up to get the first vat. Thus the law is in effect. As we continue to move down the production possibilities curve, and wine production is increased by one vat, how many additional loaves must be given up? When we increase wine production from 2 vats to 3, 4,000 loaves must be given up. The law of increasing costs continues to hold. Further, if we continue to increase the wine output to 4 vats, 5,000 additional loaves are given up. These opportunity costs

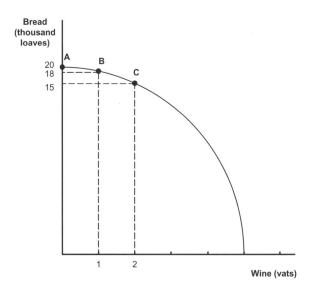

Figure 3-3   Increasing Costs and the Bowed-out Shape
The law of increasing costs causes the bowed-out shape of the production possibilities curve. The law of increasing costs says that to get one more vat of wine, there must be more bread given up than for the previous vat of wine. As we move from points A to B to C and always increase wine output by 1 vat, the bread given up is always more than for the previous vat of wine.

Table 3-3   Opportunity Cost of Wine in Terms of Bread

For Each Additional Vat of Wine	Cost in Loaves of Bread
1st	2,000
2nd	3,000
3rd	4,000
4th	5,000
5th	6,000

In this table we see the opportunity cost of each added vat of wine. As more and more wine is produced, the cost, in loaves of bread given up, increases. This illustrates the law of increasing costs.

are summarized in Table 3-3. Note that in this table the opportunity cost of each additional vat of wine, in terms of the good given up — loaves of bread — is increasing. Thus it appears that the law of increasing costs accompanies the bowed-out shape.

Increasing Costs Explored

Notice that we have moved *down* the production possibilities curve, exchanging bread for wine. Does the law of increasing costs also apply if we move *up* the curve? Consider the amount of wine we must give up to get another 1,000 loaves of bread. Start at point F, Figure 3-1, where only wine is produced and no bread. To get the first 1,000 loaves, one-sixth of a vat of wine must be given up. How do we know that? If 1 vat is given up, then 6,000 loaves of bread can be produced. So to get 1,000 loaves, only one-sixth of a vat must be given up. Next move up the curve to point E, Figure 3-1, where 4 vats and 6,000 loaves are produced. Now, to get another 1,000 loaves of bread, one-fifth of a vat of wine must be given up. This is because if 1 vat is given up, 5,000 more loaves can be produced, so 1,000 extra loaves cost one-fifth of a vat of wine. Since one-fifth is more than one-sixth, the cost of bread in terms of wine given up has increased. If we continue moving up the curve, it will be seen that the law of increasing costs holds. Check this conclusion with Table 3-4. So, it does not matter whether we are giving up bread to get wine or giving up wine to get bread. The law of increasing costs holds whether we move up or down the bowed-out production possibilities curve.

To test your understanding of the law of increasing costs, look at the curve shown in Figure 3-4. Is the law of increasing costs shown here? Start

Table 3-4   Opportunity Cost of Bread in Terms of Wine

For Each Additional 1,000 Loaves of Bread	Cost in Vats of Wine
1st	1/6
2nd	1/5
3rd	1/4
4th	1/3
5th	1/2

This table shows that the law of increasing costs is also true when we move up the production possibilities curve. Here the cost of each additional 1,000 loaves of bread, in terms of vats of wine given up, increases.

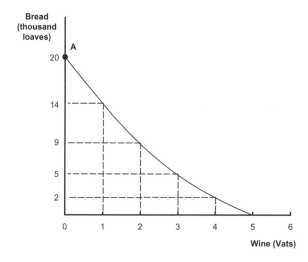

Figure 3-4   Production Possibilities without Increasing Costs
This figure shows that when the production possibilities does not bow out, the reductions in bread production will get smaller and smaller for each additional vat of wine.

at A where no wine is produced. If wine production increases to 1 vat, bread production falls from 20,000 to 14,000, or by 6,000 loaves. If wine production increases to 2 vats, 5,000 more loaves are given up. Does the law hold? The law of increasing costs requires that for each additional unit, *more* is given up than for the last previous unit. In this case, we are giving up 5,000 loaves to get the second vat of wine, which is *less* than the 6,000 loaves given up for the first vat. The curve illustrated in Figure 3-4 neither bows out nor shows increasing costs. Only when increasing costs are present will the production possibilities curve bow out.

So far we have discovered that the bowed-out shape of the production possibilities curve is due to the law of increasing costs. Why do we expect that law to be true? A basic fact that causes the law to be true is that all resources are *not* equally good substitutes in the production of all goods. To see this, start with the bowed-out production possibilities curve at the point where all resources are used to produce bread and no resources are used to produce wine. Suppose now that 1 vat of wine is to be produced. Resources are shifted from the production of bread to the production of wine. Which resources will the bread producer give up first? Those resources least useful in the production of bread. Thus for the first vat of wine, only a small part of the bread production must be given up. What if a second vat of wine is produced? The bread maker has already given up the least useful resources (from the point of view of making bread) so more useful resources have to be given up. The result is that bread production is reduced by more loaves than before. As we continue to increase wine production, the bread producer is forced to give up better and better bread-making resources. Thus the reduction in bread production must get greater and greater. So although resources have alternative uses, resources themselves are specialized and are not equally productive in one use as in another. The result is the law of increasing costs and, consequently, the bowed-out production possibilities.

Once the production possibilities curve is known, what combination of output will society choose? The production possibilities model does not tell society what choice to make. It only shows society the combinations of output from which the society can choose. Without knowing the values and goals of the society, the choice is not obvious. The decision of whether to increase the output of one good and reduce the other is resolved by a simple question — does the society value what it gains more than it values what must be given up?

Changing the Assumptions — Employment

Several assumptions have been used in drawing the production possibilities curve. Now let us start to relax some of these assumptions and see the meaning of a point inside the curve, a point outside the curve, or a shift of the entire curve. So far the basic scarcity condition has been emphasized. That condition implies that an increase in the production of one good requires a decrease in the production of the other. Is this always true? Several situations suggest otherwise.

First, what if not all resources are used? This is a situation of unemployed resources. By fully employing all resources and thereby increasing total inputs, the output of at least one good would have to increase. But now there would be no reduction of the second good. There are now enough resources to continue producing the second good at the same level. No resources would have to be shifted away. So when there are unemployed resources, the basic scarcity condition may not apply. Look at Figure 3-5. When some resources are unemployed, we are at a point inside the production possibilities curve — point Z, for example. The use of all available resources might enable us to reach point M on the curve. This represents an increase in wine without an accompanying decrease in bread. Or the use of all resources might permit us to choose N rather than Z. Point N represents an increase in bread this time, without any decrease in wine production. Or we could employ the idle resources for the production of both bread and wine and relocate on the curve at any point between M and N and enjoy increased output of both goods without any reduction in either.

There is another situation where the basic scarcity condition may not apply. This occurs when resources are underemployed and therefore not used

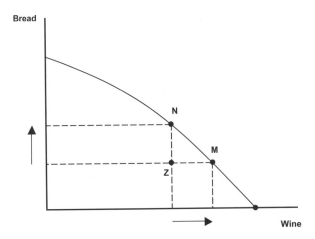

Figure 3-5   Inside the Production Possibilities

If resources are unemployed, we are inside the production possibilities. The output of either or both goods can be increased without decreasing the output of either good. If we start at Z with unemployed resources, we can use all the unemployed resources to produce more bread and reach N. Or the unemployed resources can be used to produce more wine so that we reach M. Use of the unemployed resources to produce more bread and wine will reach combinations between N and M.

efficiently. Consider what might happen if a baker and a wine maker trade jobs. The level of employment has not changed. But what about output? Probably less bread and less wine would be produced. By having these two specialists switch jobs, neither output increases and both outputs fall. The baker and the wine maker are underemployed in the sense that each is unable to contribute as much to output as previously. Such inefficient use of resources would also put us inside the production possibilities curve. Therefore, any point inside the production possibilities curve represents unemployment or underemployment of resources, both an inefficient use of resources.

What does the curve itself represent? The curve is sometimes referred to as the production possibilities frontier. Only when using all of our resources in their most efficient and productive capacity can we reach a point on the frontier. The frontier represents the limit of our physical capability to produce. Any unemployment or underemployment of resources will leave the society short of its possibilities, or graphically, inside the production possibilities curve. The full utilization of our resources, the so-called full employment assumption, is critical if we wish to reach any of the combinations of output shown on the curve.

What about combinations of output beyond the frontier? The production possibilities curve is a model that emphasizes an important fact about the world. We cannot have more of all goods from a fixed quantity of resources with fixed

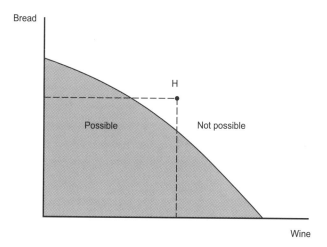

Figure 3-6   Outside the Production Possibilities
In this figure we see that some combinations of wine and bread are not available to the society. These are combinations outside the production possibilities. Only the combinations on the curve or inside the curve are possible choices for the society.

technology. Note in Figure 3-6 that society cannot obtain combinations of output beyond the frontier. The output of bread and wine represented by point H is not possible. Society is capable of producing that much bread, for example, but there are not enough resources left over to also produce the indicated volume of wine.

Changing the Assumptions — Resources and Technology

So far we have considered the production possibilities at a given point in time. But what happens over time? The relaxation of the fixed resources and technology assumption increases the production possibilities. What if there is a change in the quantity of resources available? If an added resource is useful in the production of both goods, the production frontier will shift outward to the right. The reason is that if there are more resources, more of each good can be produced.

What if there is an improvement in the technology that applies to both goods? This means that the same amount of output can be produced with fewer resources, since an improvement in technology improves the quality of resources. This also means that with the same amount of resources as before more output can be produced. Therefore, an improvement in technology has an impact similar to an increase in resources — an increase in output for at least one good. Figure 3-7 shows the outward shift of the production possibilities curve. This represents economic growth caused by an increase in resources or an improvement in technology used in the production of both goods. Once again, more wine, for example, could be obtained without a decrease in bread. This, perhaps, is what makes economic growth so desirable — the possibility of more of every good.

Or suppose that a new way to produce bread is discovered. What would happen to production possibilities? In Figure 3-8 note that even if we use all our resources to produce wine, there will be no change in the amount of wine produced. But if we use all our resources to produce bread, more bread can be produced. In fact, given the improvement in the technology for producing bread, we can now produce more bread than before with the same amount of resources. Thus the production possibilities curve swings outward as shown. You are aware that economic growth shifts the production possibilities curve to the right. If the new resource or new technology applies equally to both goods, the result will be an increase on both axes. If the new resource or technology applies to only one good, then the curve will only shift outward on that axis,

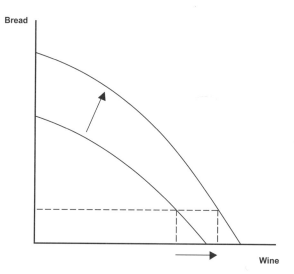

Figure 3-7   Shifts in Production Possibilities

The production possibilities shifts outward due to economic growth. This economic growth could be caused by an increase in resources or an improvement in the technology used to produce both goods. Economic growth means that compared to the old production possibilities, we can produce more of one good without giving up any of the other.

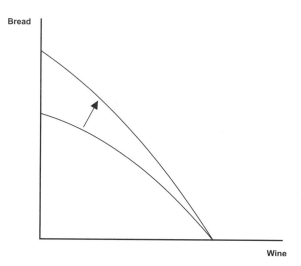

Figure 3-8   A Change Affecting One Good

This figure shows economic growth when the technology for bread only is improved. In this case we can produce more bread if we use all our resources to produce bread, but if all resources are used to produce wine, wine production does not increase. This shift in production possibilities shows that we can have more of both goods unless all we want is wine.

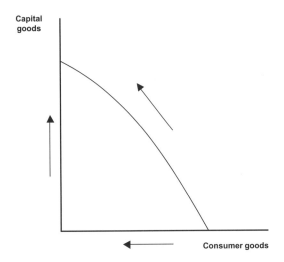

Figure 3-9   Consumption, Capital, and Growth
The point we select on the production possibilities curve today will be a factor determining our production possibilities tomorrow. The more capital produced today, the less consumption today, but the greater the economic growth and production possibilities tomorrow.

as shown here for bread. But regardless of the location of the new production possibilities curve, points outside it will always be unattainable. The production possibilities curve represents the frontier beyond which society cannot reach.

How much economic growth is desirable? The answer depends on what we have to give up to get more growth. One way to get more growth is to produce more capital. With more capital — more resources — tomorrow's production possibilities increases. However, when we produce more capital, we must reduce the production of consumer goods today. This trade-off between capital and consumer goods is shown in Figure 3-9. If we desire large rates of growth, we are postponing consumption from today to some time in the future. With economic growth and more production, we can consume more later. How much consumption are we willing to give up today, and how much will the extra consumption be tomorrow? Society must make choices between the present and the future.

▶ Summary

What have you learned in this chapter? You have already seen that resources are scarce in the sense that the wants and the needs of people are far greater than the ability of the resources to satisfy. This idea of scarcity has been explained in the context of a model called production possibilities. This model assumes that resources are used efficiently and that all resources are fully employed. Further, a fixed amount of resources and technology is assumed. The production possibilities model illustrates that once on the curve, more of all goods cannot be obtained. In fact, to produce more of any good means that the society must get less of another. Observe, too, that the curve will have a bowed-out shape, reflecting the fact that different kinds of resources are not equally good substitutes in the production of all goods. A point inside the curve occurs if resources are unemployed or underemployed. The production possibilities curve shifts outward if the technology changes or new resources are added. Points outside the curve cannot be obtained because of the limitations imposed by scarcity.

The production possibilities model illustrates the common economic problem faced by all societies — scarcity. The next chapter shows us that different societies have developed different solutions to the economic problem.

▶ Key Concepts

technology
production possibilities model
law of increasing costs

▶ Discussion Questions

1. One goal of the United States in the early 1960s was to send a man to the moon and return him safely. What were alternative uses for the scarce resources used?
2. Suppose that you have two alternative uses of your time, study and leisure. Draw a production possibilities curve that shows what happens to your grade-point average and leisure as you increase your study time. Would you expect the curve to be bowed out? Why or why not?
3. Bark College boasts that it offers the best possible education. Can this boast be true? Draw a production possibilities curve with quality of education on one axis and quantity of education on the other. How many students does Bark serve at the highest quality?
4. We normally do not expect society to be on its production possibilities curve. What does it mean to be inside the production possibilities curve? Can we be outside it?

5. What is the effect of zero population growth on a nation's production possibilities? A reduction in the water table? An increased emphasis on current consumption? The discovery of an energy-saving technology?

6. Suppose that there is a country that produces two goods, oranges and peanuts. What will happen to the production of oranges as the peanut fields are turned into orange groves 10 acres at a time? Will the output of oranges increase at an increasing rate or decreasing rate? Explain why.

▶ Self-Review

• Fill in the blanks

production possibilities	All possible combinations of two different outputs that a society is capable of producing are shown by a _____ model. The assumptions
two	of the production possibilities model are _____ alternative
resources	goods, full employment of _____, and a fixed
resources, technology	amount of _____ and _____.
more	When we move from one point to another on a production possibilities curve, we get _____ of one
less	good but _____ of the other. The amount of the
opportunity cost	good given up is the _____.
increasing costs	Production possibilities bows out due to the law of _____. As society obtains equal extra
increasing	amounts of one good, ever _____ amounts of the other good are given up. The opportunity cost for
increases	an additional unit of a good _____. The law of increasing costs is true because resources are not perfect
substitutes	_____ for one another. When resources are
inside	unemployed, we are _____ the production possibilities curve. Impossible combinations of output are those
outside	points located _____ the curve. The production possibilities curve will shift out if there are more
resources, technology	_____ or improved _____. If these changes apply to only one good, the production
axis	possibilities will shift out on only one _____. An outward shift of the production possibilities is known as
economic growth	_____.

● Multiple choice

1. Which is true of points inside the production possibilities curve?
    a. They are impossible to achieve.
    b. To obtain more of one good, we must give up some of the other.
    c. We cannot get more of any good.
    d. There are unemployed resources.
2. The production possibilities curve shows:
    a. what combinations of output can be produced.
    b. that scarcity occurs.
    c. that to get more of one good means less of another.
    d. all of the above.
3. The production possibilities curve illustrates scarcity by showing that:
    a. we cannot always produce more of both goods.
    b. limited resources yield limited amounts of goods.
    c. we cannot produce outside the production possibilities.
    d. all of the above.
4. The law of increasing costs implies that:
    a. more bread requires greater and greater sacrifices of wine.
    b. costs always increase.
    c. more bread requires less wine.
    d. more wine requires less bread.
5. When a new grape fertilizer is developed, what will happen to a wine-bread production possibilities?
    a. More wine but less bread will be produced.
    b. More bread but less wine will be produced.
    c. The production possibilities will shift out on the wine axis but not on the bread axis.
    d. The production possibilities will shift outward parallel to itself.

Answers: 1.d, 2.d, 3.d, 4.a, 5.c.

Chapter	4	ECONOMIC SYSTEMS

Key Topics
    allocation of resources
    economic goals
    economic systems
    circular flow model

Goals
    understand the economic questions
    know the economic goals
    be able to identify the economic systems
    understand the circular flow model

Our focus is on scarcity. The fundamental fact is that scarcity cannot be avoided. Thus choices must be made concerning how resources are to be used. Some people favor one use, while others favor another. As a result, scarcity generates conflicts over how resources should be used. A large part of the interest in economics comes from the fact that there is no simple way to resolve that conflict. There is no solution for resource use to which all would agree. The major part of this chapter surveys some of the alternative methods used to resolve the conflict caused by scarcity. The chapter concludes with a simple model illustrating resource use in our own economy.

Allocation of Resources

Suppose that we are about to design a process for resolving the conflict over resource use. In other words, we are not now deciding how to use the resources, but we are deciding who should make that decision and by what rules. Then once the process is chosen, what do we expect it to do for us? Any process which allocates resources must be able to answer three basic economic questions:

1. *What* goods will be produced and in what quantities?
2. *How* will resources be combined to produce the goods?
3. *For whom* are the goods produced? How much of each good will each consumer get?

The *what* question is a question of what to produce and in what amount. Recall that resources have alternative uses, meaning that land, labor, capital, and entrepreneurship in one combination can be used to produce shower curtains; in another, bubble gum; and in yet another, physical education instructors. Somehow, every society must determine which of all the many possible goods will be produced with the limited resources. All that society wants of each good cannot be produced; therefore, the society is forced into choice. Not only must the society choose what is to be produced, but the particular quantity of each good as well. Decisions have to be made whether to produce wedding rings or not, tanks or not, and if so, what quantity of wedding rings, what quantity of tanks, and what quantity of all other goods. The answers to the what question become society's shopping list.

The *how* question is basically a question of production. How is each good to be produced? Which resources are to be used up in the production of the good and which method of production, the technology, will be employed? A labor-intensive method using much labor and little capital is one alternative; a capital-intensive method is another. A farm may be cultivated with a lot of hired help, or much labor can be replaced by a tractor.

The *for whom* question is a question of allocation. Recall from Chapter 1 that allocation means distribution. Who will consume the goods created by answering the two previous questions? There are many potential ways to allocate, ranging from an equal share for everyone, to each according to his or her contribution. There is no "right" method. The allocation method that is selected will reflect the values of the society.

The combined answers to these questions is called the **allocation of resources** or **resource allocation**. A tremendous amount of effort is required to answer these questions for an entire society. A complete specification of all goods to be produced (by color, size, style, etc.) and their quantities must be given as well as assuring that the proper quantity of resources is available at each production site. Communication and transportation networks have to be established. All the final output must be somehow divided among the consumers. Note that if intermediate products exist — capital goods that are produced and then are used as an input in the production of another good (steel, for example) — the problem becomes even more complex. Surely it is not easy to design a process to answer these basic economic questions — what, how, and for whom.

Alternatives and Goals

What different processes are there to help answer the economic questions? Some alternatives are given now; you should try to think of others.

1. One person makes the decisions.
2. One person makes the decisions with the advice and consent of a council.
3. A group of experts makes the decisions.
4. All individuals in the society decide together.
5. All individuals participate by following their own self-interest.

What distinguishes these alternatives? The main difference seems to be the extent to which control of the decision making is centralized. In alternative 1, all control is given to one individual, which is in some sense a dictatorship. In alternative 5, control rests with the individuals. Which of these alternatives should be chosen? The best one, of course. But what is "best"? The best use of resources will be evaluated by how well a process achieves the goals of society.

A representative list of possible economic goals follows.

1. Economic growth
2. Efficiency
3. Economic freedom
4. Equitable distribution of income
5. Clean environment
6. Full employment
7. Price stability

By economic growth, an economist generally means growth in the value of output of an economy. Efficiency means that the amount of one product cannot be increased without decreasing the output of another good. Economic freedom can mean freedom of the consumers to get the goods they want at prices they are willing to pay. Or it can mean that the producers have the freedom to sell the goods they want at prices they want. Equitable distribution of income means that somehow those who deserve rewards, however "deserve" is defined, get them. Clean environment means that the environment is not polluted, or at least is not polluted to an undesirable extent. Full employment means that those who want to work either have jobs or can find jobs. Price stability means that inflation is not unacceptably high.

As it turns out, not all these goals can be achieved simultaneously. Opportunity cost again. We may be able to achieve full employment but only by trading off price stability. Chapter 29 further explains this trade-off. If we have efficiency, we may not have an equitable distribution of income. When goods are produced as cheaply as possible, labor may be paid starvation wages. Economic freedom may conflict with a clean environment. Is there a right to pollute? Thus even though all the goals might be desirable, they may not all be achievable at the same time. Different societies may value different goals. Societies that prefer economic freedom will choose to allocate resources by methods that stress freedom. Societies that place the highest value on economic growth will choose methods that ensure economic growth.

In fact, as we look around, we see examples of different societies each using a different process of resource allocation. The economy of the United States seems to be most like alternative 5. Although the government does play a significant role in our economy, individuals are allowed to pursue their own interests within the limits of the laws and regulations established by the government. Communist economies are more like alternative 2. In the former Soviet Union, the resource allocation question had been answered to a large extent by a central planning agency with guidance from the top political leaders.

Economic Systems

The process used by each society to answer the basic economic questions determines the **economic system** of the society. One economic system can be distinguished from another by asking who owns and controls the scarce resources within that society. The ownership of the resources will reflect the degree of centralization of control. The major economic systems are capitalism, socialism, and communism. Under **capitalism**, individuals own and control the scarce resources. Private property rights are highly valued. Under our capitalistic system in the United States, you are an owner of resources, at least the human resource of labor. If you own a business, you almost certainly employ capital, and if you are indeed fortunate, you may have an oil well or two, the resource land, tucked away. Later in this chapter you will discover why you are willing to let others use your resources.

The opposite extreme of a capitalistic system is communism. **Communism** is identified by the public — government — ownership of resources. This is a system of central planning. Under pure communism, not only would the use of land and capital be determined by the government, through a central committee, but even your labor would not be yours to allocate. You might be employed in whatever salt mine or other capacity the committee believed to be in the best interest of society, and not necessarily in the manner most satisfactory to you.

Yet in practice there is no society that has a system of pure capitalism or communism. Each society seems to employ some varying combination of private and public ownership of the scarce resources. A society that emphasizes the private ownership of resources is classified as capitalism, and a society that emphasizes public ownership of resources is classified as communism. So capitalism and communism are opposite extremes on the scale in Figure 4-1. A society that does not clearly emphasize either extreme but favors a combination of private and public ownership is identified under the economic system of **socialism**.

How does an economic system answer the economic questions? In a capitalistic system the "what to produce" question is decided by the individuals. The individuals are the owners of the resources as well as the consumers of the final output. You may have heard the expression "the consumer is king." Consumer demand for a product will determine if, and how many, resources will be allocated toward its production. Capitalism resolves the "how" question by the profit motive. The least expensive resources and the most efficient technology will be employed. Under capitalism, the allocation question, the "for whom" question, is resolved by most resources and goods being distributed by price. Those holding resources valued by society will receive an income enabling the individual to participate in the consumption of output. Under capitalism, these answers to the economic questions are determined in markets.

Figure 4-1   Economic Systems
This line shows the range of possible ways in which an economic society could be organized. Capitalism stresses private control of the resources, whereas communism depends on public control. Socialism is located between the two extremes and neither public nor private control dominates.

The United States has a market economy. **Markets** are a situation where buyers and sellers meet to negotiate price and to trade. It is left to the chapters that follow to explain the system of capitalism in more detail.

A communistic system settles the "what" question through collective government decision making by means of a central committee. In the former Soviet Union, the committee determined the output that it believed best met the goals of the society. If the committee believed that the goals of the society would be best met by the production of broccoli, that is what would be produced. Just tons and tons of broccoli. Also, a central committee would determine how the output would be produced. Resources would be allocated by the central state in the manner it believes most appropriate, including assigning your labor to the broccoli farm even though that may not be your preference. And, finally, the "for whom" question was also resolved by the state. One for all, or all for one, or any other scheme. The usual solution was that those who got in line early got the goods.

Economies vary from the strict definitions of the economic systems. The Soviet Union was a communistic society but experimented with an increase in the amount of decentralization. Therefore as economic systems become modified, so must we modify our descriptions. *Perestroika* (restructuring the system), *glasnost* (open discussion), competition, profit and private control over resources were radical new ideas in the former Soviet Union. China, too, is permitting some degree of private control over resources, particularly in the agricultural area and in some industries. The economic systems of these former communist countries are moving toward capitalism, but not capitalism as we know it; it would be their own system, not ours. How much the economic system of these countries change will be limited by their own internal political considerations. However, Cuba still maintains a communistic system.

The system of socialism uses a combination of individual and governmental decision making for the allocation of resources. Great Britain and Sweden have socialistic economic systems. In Great Britain the health care system is perhaps the most obvious socialistic feature. The national health care system provides health care to all, and the health care is paid out of taxes. In Sweden not only is health care provided by taxes, but many other goods are also available, including day care for children.

The United States is often identified as a mixed market economy. This is due to the extent of government participation in our economy, which occurs in many ways. Government provides services such as defense, schools, roads, police, and fire protection. It also regulates business. Some regulations involve safety in the workplace while other regulations may involve pricing practices or labor policies. But there remains a broad area of decision left to individual choice. Our capitalistic system is still known as a free market or private enterprise economy.

The Circular Flow Model

One model of our capitalistic system is the **circular flow** of economic activity. It illustrates the interrelationships existing between the sectors and markets in our economy. Discussion of the government sector will be postponed until later chapters. The two sectors that we will consider now are consumers, which all of us ultimately are, and business. These two sectors interact through the two markets shown in Figure 4-2, the resource market and the product market. The resources flow from their owners, the consumers, through the resource market to business. Business converts the resources into final products, which flow to the consumers through the product market.

This circular flow of resources and products is guided by a flow of money and income moving in the opposite direction. Figure 4-3 is a more complete circular flow model. You can see that business provides goods to the product

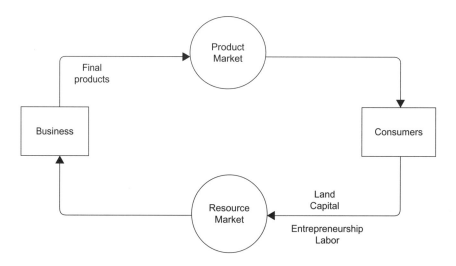

Figure 4-2   Resource and Product Flow
Resources flow from consumers to business through the resource market. Business uses these resources to produce the final products that flow through the product market to the consumers.

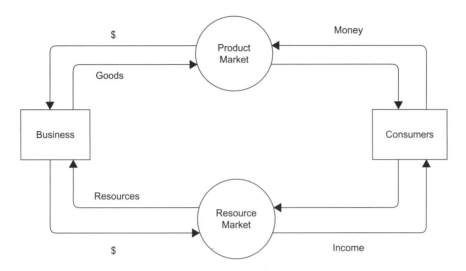

Figure 4-3   The Circular Flow Model
This figure includes the information in Figure 4-2 showing the flow of resources from consumers to business and the flow of products produced from those resources back to consumers. In addition this figure shows the opposite flow of money and income. Note that the money is paid to firms by consumers for the products that the firms produce and business pays the money in turn to the consumers for the use of resources.

market in exchange for the money received. That money is used by business to purchase resources from the resource market. The money then serves as income to the consumers who sold their resources to business and who now can purchase from the product market.

The final satisfaction obtained by consumers through consumption in the product market is what encourages us, the consumers, to sell our resources, labor being one, through the resource market. Each market is a situation where buyers and sellers meet. Business is a seller of products through the product market and a buyer of inputs through the resource market. Consumers purchase products from the product market and sell their resources through the resource market. This model helps emphasize the importance of markets in our society, and future chapters will detail the functioning of a market.

The circular flow model provides us with a bird's-eye, though simplistic, view of how the entire economy interacts. Just as in the expression "No man is an island...," so also no part of the economy is isolated or can be completely discussed without consideration of the impact on and from the other sectors.

▶ Summary

Scarcity is a condition that exists in all societies. It cannot be avoided and it requires that decisions be made. Every society must find the answer to three basic economic questions: what, how, and for whom? The point of this discussion has been to acquaint you with the meaning of the term "allocation of resources" and to suggest that there are alternative processes by which the actual allocation decision can be made. The major allocation schemes are the economic systems of capitalism, socialism, and communism. Since our economy in the United States is basically one of individual choice, or capitalism, that model will be the one emphasized in the remainder of this textbook.

The circular flow model shows the importance of markets in a capitalistic system. What makes these markets work and how the resource allocation problem is answered begins in the demand and supply chapters that are next.

This completes the first module of this text. The next module will explain the process that our society uses to allocate resources within the limitations of scarcity.

▶ Key Concepts

allocation of resources   socialism
economic system   markets
capitalism   circular flow model
communism

▶ Discussion Questions

1. In the economic system at the North Pole, how will Santa solve the economic questions of what, how, and for whom?
2. To produce cars, what are the alternative resources and technologies that can be used? Explore the how question.
3. What economic goals might you choose for your society and how might they trade off?
4. Can you identify the following economic systems?
    a. Centralized economic planning.
    b. Individual choice with private ownership.
    c. A combination of some public ownership and control and some private.
5. Need a wealthy nation like the United States be concerned about scarcity? What do all economic systems face in common? How do different economic systems deal with the problem of scarcity?

6. Allocating resources includes allocating labor. In the medieval period, sons took the occupations of their fathers. How is labor allocated under communism? Under capitalism?
7. What is the current news on the economic systems of Russia, Eastern Europe, and the People's Republic of China?
8. Reverse the consumer and business sectors in the circular flow model. Are the flows shown by the model now correct? If necessary, redraw the flows.

▶ Self-Review

• Fill in the blanks

what, how	The three economic questions are _____, _____, and
for whom	_____. An answer to the three economic questions
allocation of resources	is an _____. The goods to be
what	produced and the quantity answers the _____ question.
	The combination of resources used to produce the good
how	answers the _____ question. Who gets the goods answers the
for whom	_____ question. The method used to answer the
economic	basic economic questions is an _____ system.
	Economic systems can be distinguished by the degree of
resources	centralization of control of the _____. If resources
	are owned and controlled by the individuals in the society,
capitalism	then the system is _____. If the resources are
	owned and controlled by the government, then the system is
communism	_____. A system in which ownership of resources
	is shared by the government and the individuals is
socialism	_____. A model which shows the links between
circular flow	consumers and business is called the _____
income	model. Consumers obtain _____ by selling their
	resources to business. Businesses use the resources to
consumers	produce goods which they sell to _____. These
resource	transactions occur in the _____ market and the
product	_____ market.

• Multiple choice

1. The question that asks who will get the output is:
   a. the what question.
   b. the how question.
   c. the why question.
   d. none of the above.

2. Find the false statement.
   a. Economic goals may conflict.
   b. The economic goals pursued depend on the values of society.
   c. Economic goals are always equally desirable.
   d. The best use of resources depends upon the goals of society.

3. A society produces output through the use of robots. This society is responding to the economic question of:
   a. what to produce and how much.
   b. how to produce.
   c. for whom to produce.
   d. all of the above.

4. In this economic system, resources are allocated by a central planning committee. It is a system of:
   a. capitalism.
   b. socialism.
   c. communism.
   d. impossible to tell.

5. In the circular flow model, in which market are consumers the sellers and business the buyers?
   a. Product market.
   b. Resource market.
   c. Final market.
   d. None of the above.

Answers: 1.d, 2.c, 3.b, 4.c, 5.b.

Module | 2 | PRICE DETERMINATION

In the previous chapters we saw that scarcity is the economic problem. The solution that our society chooses places an emphasis on individual freedom of choice. How can freedom of choice solve the economic problem? If each individual is allowed to pursue his or her own self-interest, why doesn't chaos result? This module is designed to answer that question. We start with a consideration of the chaos question and then discuss the meaning of price.

Chaos and Markets

Why doesn't the pursuit of self-interest end in chaos? Millions of people are allowed to do what they want. Yet the outcome is as if there were a detailed plan. We begin here to investigate how a society functions without central planning. In our society, one person in pursuit of self-interest cannot impose choices on another. Any choice that one person wants that would affect another must be agreeable to both. Suppose that one person has apples and another has beans. If the person with the apples wants beans, he cannot just take them. The person with the beans would not agree to that. But if the person with apples wanted to trade apples for beans, the beans owner might be willing. And if both agree, it must be that both have gained. Either one could have said no. So no one has imposed his or her wishes on the other.

When trade occurs, economists say that a market has formed. The term "market" generally refers to the fact that people are getting together to trade. Through markets, the goods that people want are provided. A market is an organizing device that permits each individual to pursue his or her own self-interest, and the result is not chaotic as it might first seem. An important consideration is the rate at which goods trade. What do we have to give up (in apples or money) to get another pound of beans? This is the price of the goods to be traded. How is the price determined? Price determination will occupy our attention throughout this module. We will find that the market establishes both the quantity that is traded and the price.

Price

Since price is an important and frequently used concept, we should clarify what is meant by price. **Price** is what we have to give up to get another unit of the good. Price can be measured in several ways. Perhaps the most usual way to represent price is with money. When expressed in dollar terms, price is always measured in dollars per unit of the good. That is because the price is what you have to give up (in dollars) to get another unit of the good. We may not always say dollars per unit when referring to the price, but we always mean it.

Another measure of price is the rate at which we trade one good for another. In this case, price tells us how many units of one good will be given up to get one unit of another good. Perhaps 6 apples are given up for 1 pound of beans. Then the price of 1 pound of beans is 6 apples. A third way to measure price is in terms of satisfaction forgone because of what was given up. In other words, the consumer chose to consume a good and gave up some consumption of other goods. Therefore, price is a measure of what is given up either in terms of money, goods, or satisfaction. Price is the opportunity cost of having another unit of the good.

What role does price play in the allocation of resources? There are two roles. First, the price rations the goods. Recall that one problem to be solved is who will get the good. There is not enough of each good so that every want can be satisfied. The price system solves this problem as follows: Based on the price, each individual decides whether or not he or she wants the good and can afford it. If the individual wants the good and can afford it, then the good is purchased. As you will learn in this module, if the amount demanded of a good at the going price is more than is available, the price will adjust to higher levels. At higher levels, as you can imagine, fewer units of the good will be demanded. So the price will keep going up until the amount demanded decreases and is equal to the available amount. Thus the price will determine who gets the good and who does not.

Price in its second allocation role, discussed in the next module, directs the flow of resources. Suppose that the price of some good goes up. What will happen? Since the price went up, the sellers are now making more profits, and that attracts new sellers. More resources will be used to produce more of the good. Note that neither of these allocation roles for price requires any central planning or government interference. Each seller is trying to follow his or her own self-interest and ends up providing the goods that people want at prices that people are willing to pay, within the limitations of scarcity.

Overview

This module discusses price determination. The first three chapters show how price is determined by the interaction of supply and demand. As we have seen, prices are needed to trade goods, and there are two parties involved in a trade. For any given commodity, some want the good and others give it up. The individuals wanting the good we will call the demanders, and the persons offering the good for sale are called the suppliers. You should be aware that it is the demand in the market and the supply in the market that determine the price, not the demand of an individual or the supply of an individual. But to obtain the supply or demand in the market, we must start with the individuals. So in Chapter 5, the demand of the individual consumer will be discussed, and in Chapter 6, the supply of the individual producer will be the focus of attention. Then in Chapter 7 the market demand and the market supply will be obtained and used to determine the market price and quantity. Chapter 8 is an extension of these concepts.

Chapter | **5** | **DEMAND**

Key Topics

demand

law of demand

change in quantity demanded

change in demand

determinants of demand

Goals

know the definition of demand

understand that demand slopes downward to the right

understand when we move along demand

understand when demand shifts

In Chapter 4 you discovered that an economic system must answer three basic questions: what to produce, how to produce, and for whom. In a market economy, which goods are actually produced depends in part upon the willingness and ability of the consumer to buy (helps to answer what). The resulting scarce goods are allocated to those who are willing and able to buy them (answers for whom). To examine how markets answer the three basic economic questions, we need to find some way to represent the willingness and ability of the consumer to buy the goods. The concept called demand summarizes this willingness and ability of the consumer. The ability and willingness of producers to transform the resources into goods the society wants is summarized in the concept of supply (helps to answer what and answers how). Supply is the subject of the next chapter. In the current chapter, only decisions of the buyer will be examined. Buyers generate demand for goods and services by choosing the goods and services they will consume. Therefore this chapter will focus on demand.

Demand

Demand is a familiar concept that is much misunderstood. Many people believe that demand is what you wish for or want. If that were an accurate description of demand, then we would no doubt be riding in Ferraris while also enjoying all the other goods we might ever want. This certainly does not fit our description of scarcity and the real world. Then there are people convinced that demand is what we actually get. If there are *six* pairs of socks under the Christmas tree, that must be demand, or so they believe. They see demand as a certain amount. In fact, demand is neither what we want nor what we actually get. Since demand is a word in frequent use outside of economics, the word has taken on many different meanings. No wonder when demand is applied to economic situations, it is often misunderstood.

Demand is a list or schedule of all alternative (different) quantities of a particular good that a buyer would be willing and able to buy at alternative prices. Several observations should be made about the definition of demand. One critical observation is that because the focus of demand is on the price and the quantity, demand is studied at a point in time when all other considerations are frozen; frozen, that is, in the sense of not having enough time to change. If other considerations besides price change, we cannot tell whether the change in the quantity was due to price or to other considerations. The idea of demand is to see how the buyer reacts to a change in *price*. So those other considerations are frozen and will be discussed later. For now, the only thing changing that can affect the quantity is price.

Another observation is that demand reflects both willingness *and* ability. A consumer may have enough money but may not be willing to buy the good. Or a consumer may want the good but may not have enough money. So not only must the consumer want the good; the consumer must also have the financial ability to pay the price. The price is the opportunity cost, for convenience measured in money terms. The final observation is to consider who is the demander. When you think of demand, think buyer. Demand represents buyer choice, not seller choice. In fact it makes no difference whether there are many, few, or any sellers of that good. If the consumer is willing and able to purchase the good, then there is a demand. Demand focuses solely on the decisions of the buyer, and in this chapter, only the demand of an individual buyer is considered.

How can your demand for a good, such as bottles of hair oil per month, be determined? One simple way is to ask you. Demand is a "what if" situation.

What if the going price of hair oil were $2 a bottle — how many bottles would you be willing and able to buy? Now what if the price of hair oil increased to $4, how many bottles would you now be willing and able to buy? And so on through some possible prices of hair oil. What we find is the **quantity demanded**, the amount you are willing and able to buy at a specific price. When we have found the quantity demanded at each price, we have found your demand. You alone know your demand for hair oil until you provide the demand schedule recorded by Table 5-1. You noted the price of hair oil and then chose the quantity that you would buy at each different price of hair oil. Thus demand is obtained by the buyer making choices. The buyer determines the quantity to purchase, but not the price. You will see how price is determined in Chapter 6.

There is no requirement that any of the prices in the demand schedule actually occur. We are developing a statement describing your behavior *if* any particular price did occur. According to Table 5-1, if the price of hair oil were announced to be $8, you would purchase 1 bottle, and if the price were lower, you would buy even more. How do we know all this? You said you were willing and able to buy. You have revealed your demand. Notice that at $4 a bottle, you said you would purchase 5 bottles and spend $20 ($4 times 5 bottles). Chapter 8, Price Elasticity, will discuss the relation between the price and the amount you spend. And if the price were $8 each, you are able and willing to spend $8 for 1 bottle. So if the price were actually $8, you would purchase 1 bottle of hair oil, as you said. If you were asked to draw a circle around your demand in Table 5-1, where would the circle be? Around $8? $2? Around $4 and the quantity of 5? Recall that Table 5-1 is your demand schedule. Therefore the

Table 5-1   Demand Schedule for Hair Oil

Price ($ Per Bottle)	Quantity Demanded (Bottles)
$10	0
8	1
6	3
4	5
2	8

This table is the demand schedule for hair oil. It shows the amount of hair oil that a buyer would be willing and able to buy at each price.

entire table should be circled to capture the alternative prices and quantities represented by demand.

What happens if the price of hair oil is $5 a bottle? There is no $5 in Table 5-1. We could add more information to the table by asking you, the buyer, for more information. But to obtain the quantity demanded at all prices would require a lengthy table. Another way to summarize demand is with a graph. A graph can readily contain all the information in the table and more. In Figure 5-1 the quantity demanded (bottles) is measured across the bottom of the graph, and the price ($ per bottle) is measured going up the side of the graph. The demand curve is a plot of the demand schedule. To plot the information given in Table 5-1, we would do the following. Start with the $10 and zero bottles. Measure up the side of the graph — the price axis — until you get to $10. This is the point representing $10 and zero bottles, shown as point A in Figure 5-1. For the next point, $8 and 1 bottle, measure up the side of the graph to $8 and then over to the right until you are just above the 1. This point represents the 1 bottle demanded at the price of $8 per bottle and is labeled B. Continue this process to obtain the points plotted in Figure 5-1. When the points are connected, the downward-sloping line is demand and is labeled D. When an economist says the word "demand," he or she means the whole curve, not just a point on the curve. The demand curve permits us to read between the

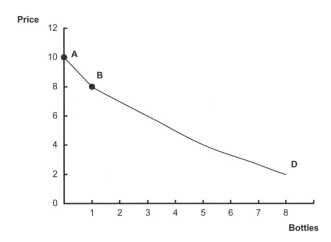

Figure 5-1   The Demand Curve for Hair Oil
This figure shows the demand curve for hair oil based on the information in Table 5-1. The demand curve shows the amount of the good a buyer is willing and able to buy at each price. Here at the price of $5 each, the quantity demanded is 4 bottles.

prices on the schedule. You can read the demand curve in Figure 5-1 to find
that the quantity demanded at the price of $5 each is 4 bottles.

The Law of Demand

Look again at the demand curve plotted in Figure 5-1. The curve is composed
of all the alternative prices of the good and the particular quantity that would
be purchased at each price. A certain relationship is established between the
price and the quantity demanded. This relationship is known as the law of
demand. The **law of demand** shows an *inverse* relationship between the price
of a good and the quantity demanded of that good. When price goes in one
direction, the quantity demanded goes in the opposite direction. Figures 5-2
and 5-3 illustrate this law clearly. As the price *decreases* from $6 to $4, the
quantity demanded *increases* from 3 to 5 (Figure 5-2). Part of the law of
demand states that as price falls, more is purchased. This is indicated by the
quantity demanded increasing.

The other part of the law of demand states that as price rises, less is
purchased. This is indicated by the quantity demanded decreasing. As the
price *increases* from $4 to $6, the quantity demanded *decreases* from 5 to
3 (Figure 5-3). Observe in Figures 5-2 and 5-3 that the downward-sloping
demand curve, from left to right, is a perfect reflection of the law of demand.

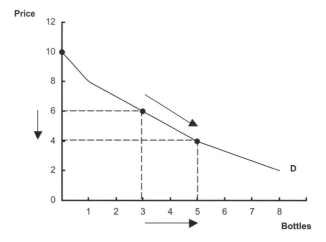

Figure 5-2   An Increase in the Quantity Demanded
Here we see that if the price decreases, the quantity demanded increases. In this case, we are
moving along the demand curve, and demand does not change, but the quantity demanded does.

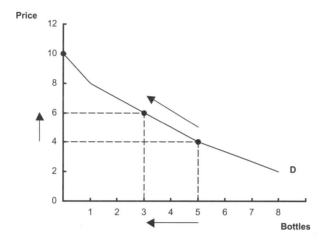

Figure 5-3   A Decrease in the Quantity Demanded
Here we see that if the price rises, the quantity demanded falls. Again realize that we are moving along the demand curve, so demand does not change, only the quantity demanded.

A movement downward along the demand curve represents a fall in price and a corresponding increase in the quantity demanded. A movement upward along the demand curve represents an increase in price and a corresponding decrease in the quantity demanded.

There is clear evidence of the law of demand at work all around us. Postage rates increase and fewer Christmas cards are mailed. The quantity demanded has fallen as the price has risen. Retail stores advertise sales. Sales serve to increase the quantity demanded by lowering the price. Buyer response to higher fuel and energy prices will lead to smaller and more fuel-efficient cars, and, in homes, cooler temperatures and sweaters. There is a lower quantity demanded of energy at the higher price. Buyers do respond to changing prices. We are sensitive to sacrifice and changing opportunity cost.

What is the reason for the law of demand and the downward-sloping demand curve? Why would we expect a consumer to buy more of a good if its price fell? Part of the explanation lies in the **substitution effect** of a change in price. As the price of hair oil goes down, hair oil becomes an attractive substitute for other goods. Thus the consumer buys more hair oil to replace those goods. For example, as the price of hair oil goes down, the consumer will buy hair oil to use as lubricant in the lawn mower. If price goes down far enough, the consumer will even buy it to burn as fuel. So one reason why the consumer buys more of a good as the price falls is that the good becomes an attractive substitute for other goods. The consumer buys more of the good and, consequently, less of other goods.

Another part of the explanation as to why the demand curve slopes downward is the **income effect** of a change in price. As the price of a good goes down, the consumer is able to buy more of the good than before the price fell. Therefore the consumer appears to have more income. Note that the amount of money that the consumer actually has remains unchanged. Yet the purchasing power of the money increases as the price falls. For $100, the consumer can buy two $100 suits on sale at one-half off. Thus as the price falls, the consumer can afford to buy more. Income *seems* to rise and the quantity purchased rises. We now have a second reason to explain why the demand curve slopes downward. And if price rises, these substitution and income effects due to a change in price work in reverse to explain why the consumer would buy less of the good. Other goods would become attractive substitutes for hair oil, and the purchasing power of money would fall; therefore, the quantity demanded of hair oil would fall as the price goes up.

People respond to a change in price. That is what the law of demand tells us. The law of demand also specifies the inverse relation of the response. But do not try to interpret more from the law of demand than there is. For example, the law does not tell us how much the price must change before we would respond. It just states that there can be a price change significant enough that we will respond. What if you are planning to get married? And what if the price of a marriage license increases? You might reply that you are going to obtain a license and get married anyway. The law of demand simply predicts that there is a price that either you may not be willing to pay or you may not be able to pay. There is some higher price at which you would rather not have the good, considering what else you would have to give up to pay that price. Or the price could go so high that it was greater than the amount of money that you have and could get; hence price is greater than your ability to pay. As a result, there must eventually be a fall in marriage licenses purchased as the price rises.

The law of demand describes how we behave; it does not tell us how to behave. All it does is predict the way we sooner or later respond to changing prices. As the price of Ferraris falls to a nickel each, the law of demand predicts that you would tend to buy more Ferraris than you did at the higher price. Now isn't this an accurate prediction?

Change in Demand

One thing and one thing only changes the quantity demanded of a good — a change in price of that good. And that is the precise focus of the law of demand — the inverse relationship between price and the amount bought. We are all aware of the impact of price on our buying decisions. But we are also aware that there are other factors besides price that determine whether or not we buy a good and in what quantity. Our willingness and ability to purchase may be affected by changing conditions that we will now call the determinants of demand.

What are these determinants of demand? If you experience a change in taste or preference for a good, a change in income, an expectation of a change in the price of a good, or a change in the price of a related good, then demand itself may change. This is because your willingness and/or ability to buy the good is affected. Now, our discussion will no longer be concerned with just one point in time but rather over some period of time. This is a length of time just long enough for the determinants of demand to change and then again be frozen. As the determinants of demand change, so will the amount that you are willing and able to buy at each price. Observe closely that this change in the amount of the good bought is not caused by a change in the price of the good.

You should clearly understand demand before considering the impact of a change in a determinant of demand. Demand is not just a quantity of 8, or just the price of $6 and the quantity demanded of 3. Demand is the whole schedule or entire curve. When price changes, there is no change in the demand schedule. Table 5-1 still shows your demand, the entire list that records your demand information for hair oil. When price changes, the only effect is that we move on the price column from one price to another and then look up the new quantity demanded. And the law of demand has already predicted that the quantity demanded would move in the opposite direction from price.

Look again at Figure 5-1, which shows your demand curve for hair oil. That entire curve, with all the possible prices combined with their quantities demanded, is your demand. When the price changes, the demand curve does *not* change. In Figure 5-1, we move down the demand curve as price falls and the quantity demanded therefore increases. We move up the demand curve as price rises, and the quantity demanded therefore decreases. The demand curve still goes through the same points and stays in the same place.

Yet it is possible for the demand curve to move. But if a change in the price of the good cannot change demand, then what can? When a determinant of demand changes, your entire demand changes. Then Figure 5-1 would no longer show your demand, and we must start the "what if" questions and find your demand all over again. Only now your demand will be different. Recall that the **determinants of demand** include a change in taste for a good, a change in income, an expectation of a change in the price of a good, and a change in the price of a related good. Each of these will be discussed in turn.

Watch a few reruns of old Elvis Presley movies and see what happens to your demand for hair oil. Suppose that you want hair oil more than before. This reflects an increase in taste or preference. Figure 5-4 shows your old (D_1) and new (D_2) demand for the good. At the price of $4 a bottle, you would now purchase 8, whereas before you would have purchased 5. You can see that at each and every price you will purchase more hair oil than before. Note that there was not an increase in the quantity demanded. That can only be brought about by a fall in price. The old quantity demanded associated with each price no longer exists, only the new. If someone were to ask you how much hair oil you would buy at $4, you would not reply "either 5 or 8 bottles." There is only one quantity that you would now buy at that price, 8 bottles as shown by the new demand curve. Recognize that the price of hair oil did not change. So there is no change at all in the quantity demanded. But of course there is a change, a change in demand. More would be bought than before at each and every price. The demand curve will shift or move to the right.

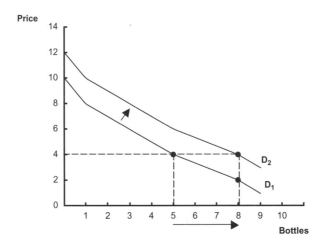

Figure 5-4   An Increase in Demand

This figure shows the demand for hair oil increasing. Here the whole demand curve shifts to the right from D_1 to D_2. More will be bought at each and every price. Now at $4 each, 8 bottles would be bought rather than 5.

An increase in demand also means that you would be willing and able to pay a higher price than before, if necessary, for each and every quantity. Refer to Figure 5-5. You want the good more than before, and if necessary, you would pay $4 rather than $2 for each of 8 bottles.

An increased taste or preference for the product shows that you are more willing to purchase the good than before, hence the increase in demand. If there is a reduction in taste, demand for the product decreases. Figure 5-6 shows a fall in demand. The demand curve shifts to the left. A decrease in demand shows that the buyer is willing and able to buy less than before at each and every price. When electronic calculators first came on the market, there was a decrease in demand for the mechanical machines. People wanted to have the modern electronic calculators, so there was a change in taste away from the mechanical calculators to the electronic calculators — and thus an increase in demand for electronic calculators.

The buyer's ability to buy is affected by a change in income. An increase in income usually indicates an increase in demand (Figure 5-5), a decrease in income, a decrease in demand (Figure 5-6). This is true of all the so-called normal goods. Almost all goods are normal. So as your income increases, we can expect that your demand for vacations or dinners at a restaurant will increase. For a **normal good**, demand increases as income increases. The exception is with products referred to as inferior goods. Inferior goods are consumed out of financial necessity, not because of preference. As your income increases, you tend to purchase less of the **inferior good**, and more of the good you prefer, the normal good. And as your income falls, you purchase more of the inferior good than before, even though its price remains unchanged. Since so many goods are normal, it is difficult to find a clear example of an inferior good. What is inferior to one person may be normal to another. One example we might use for an inferior good is "brown bread." It was once true that the poor ate brown bread because it was inexpensive. As income rose, there would be a switch to white bread, and consumption of brown bread would fall. Thus brown bread was an inferior good. Consequently, as income fell, demand for the inferior good would increase and demand for the normal good would decrease. On the other hand, with the current emphasis on health, brown bread may now be a normal good. Review the relationship between income and demand in Table 5-2.

Other determinants can also change demand. An expectation of a price increase, if acted upon, can cause demand to increase. If you hear a rumor that the price of hair oil is going up in the near future, you might rush out and buy

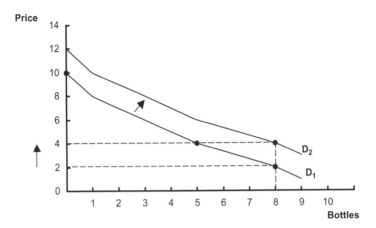

Figure 5-5   An Increase in Demand
In this figure we see that another way to think about an increase in demand is that the buyer
would pay a higher price at each quantity. Here $4 rather than $2 would be paid for each of
8 bottles if necessary.

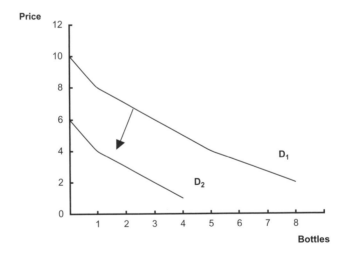

Figure 5-6   A Decrease in Demand
This figure shows a decrease in demand. The demand curve is shifting left. Less will be bought
at each and every price; a lower price would be paid for the same quantity.

Table 5-2   What Happens to Demand When Income Changes

Income	Demand for the Normal Good	Demand for the Inferior Good
rises	rises	falls
falls	falls	rises

This table shows the relationship between a change in income and the change in demand that results. If income rises and the good is normal, then demand rises. If the good is inferior, an increase in income causes demand to fall.

more hair oil now before it does become more expensive. Take note that the price has not changed, only that you expect it to. The result is an increase in demand since more is bought than before at each and every price of the good. If the expectation, however, is for a fall in price, then you may reduce your buying while waiting for the price to fall. The result is a decrease in demand.

A change in the price of some related good may in turn affect the demand for the good in question. Two goods can be related either as complements or substitutes. Goods that are not related are independent. For goods that are **complements**, if you purchase more (less) of one, you purchase more (less) of the other. There are many common examples of complements that will come to mind, such as beer and pretzels, peanut butter and jam, bread and butter, cameras and film, cars and gasoline, and tennis rackets and tennis balls. With **substitute** goods, on the other hand, if you buy more (less) of one, you buy less (more) of the other. Examples of substitutes are sugar and saccharin, butter and margarine, coffee and tea, and attendance at any other school and Harvard.

Note that whether goods are substitutes or complements is an individual matter. While tea may substitute for coffee in one household, hot chocolate may substitute in another.

Suppose that there are two goods, the first good and a related good. What happens if the price of the first good falls? The law of demand predicts an increase in the quantity demanded of the first good. More would be bought at the lower price than at the higher price. But what about the related good? If the two goods are complements, the demand (not the quantity demanded) for the related good will increase. As more is bought of the first good as its price falls, then more is bought of its complement. More of the complement is purchased at the same price. As the price of turkey falls, more turkey and more of its complement, cranberries, are bought. The quantity of turkey demanded increases, as does the demand for cranberries. But if two goods are substitutes, less will be bought of the related good as the price of the first good falls. As

Table 5-3   What Happens to Demand for a Related Good When the Price of the First Good Changes

First Good		Demand for the Related Good	
Price	Quantity Demanded	Complement	Substitute
rises	falls	falls	rises
falls	rises	rises	falls

This table shows the relationship between the price of a good and the quantity demanded of that good as well as the demand for a complement or substitute. So if the price of a good rises, the quantity demanded of the good falls, the demand for a complement falls, and the demand for a substitute rises.

the price of turkey falls, more turkey and less of its substitute, chicken, is bought. Demand for chicken falls.

And what happens if the price of the first good increases? As the price of peanut butter goes up, less of the complement good, jam, will be bought. Demand for the complement falls. And as the price of peanut butter goes up, more tuna will be substituted. Demand for the substitute increases. So with a knowledge of demand and the relation between goods, it is possible to predict how a change in price of one good can affect the amount of another you might buy. The demand curve for one good may be shifted by the price change of another good. Thus we are able to classify goods based on how the demand curve shifts when the price of the related good changes. If demand for a good increases as the price of another good goes up, the two goods are substitutes. If the demand for a good decreases as the price of another good goes up, then the goods are complements. Review this relation between goods in Table 5-3.

Demand and Quantity Demanded

The economist carefully distinguishes between demand, which is the entire curve, and the quantity demanded, a point on the demand curve. When the economist uses the phrase "change in demand," the entire demand curve has shifted. Contrast this to the phrase "change in the quantity demanded." What is the difference in meaning? A **change in the quantity demanded** means a movement along a demand curve in response to a price change. Accordingly, a change in price of a good is the only occurrence that can cause a change in the quantity demanded for that good. This is the focus of the law of demand, the response of the buyer to a change in price. A **change in demand** means that something else besides the price of the good has changed and affected the willingness and ability of the buyer. This change in a determinant of demand shifts the entire demand curve.

You should be able to see the difference between these two concepts in Figure 5-7. In Figure 5-7A, as the price of pizza goes up, you buy less pizza, a change in the quantity demanded. The demand for pizza remains unchanged. The quantity demanded decreased just as your demand curve indicated. You had already revealed that you would buy less pizza at a higher price. However,

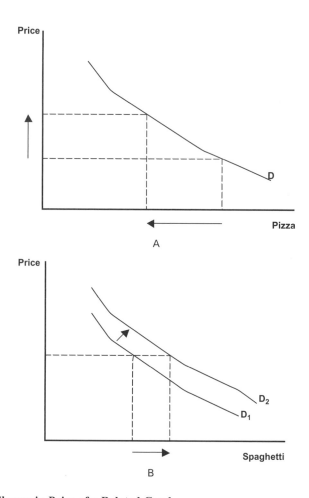

Figure 5-7   A Change in Price of a Related Good
In graph A the price of pizza rises and the quantity demanded falls. In graph B, the demand for spaghetti increases due to the rise in the price of pizza. More spaghetti is bought at the same price of spaghetti. The entire demand curve moves.

there is a change in demand for spaghetti. Demand for spaghetti increased as the price of its substitute, pizza, went up. So at each and every price of spaghetti, you buy more spaghetti than before the price of pizza increased. This is shown in Figure 5-7B as the demand for spaghetti increases from D_1 to D_2. Now for a moment, consider only your new, higher demand for spaghetti. What if the price of spaghetti fell? There would be an increase in the quantity demanded of spaghetti as you move down the existing D_2 demand curve. And now you should be able to predict a fall in demand for pizza. The demand for pizza would shift to the left, indicating that less would be bought than before at each and every price. After all, you are eating more spaghetti and less pizza. You will see the impact of both a change in price and a change in a determinant again in the next chapter.

▶ Summary

This chapter introduced the concept of demand. Demand has been summarized as the willingness and ability of the buyer to buy goods at each possible price. The law of demand highlights the inverse relationship between price and quantity demanded. The demand curve slopes downward to the right, reflecting the law of demand, explained by both the substitution and income effect of a change in price. Movements along the demand curve are called changes in the quantity demanded; shifts of the entire demand curve are called a change in demand. A change in the price of the good causes a change in the quantity demanded. A determinant of demand must change before demand changes. The determinants of demand include a change in taste, change in income, an expectation of a change in the price of a good, and a change in the price of a related good. Demand is half the story of price determination. In the next chapter, we will introduce the other equally important participant in price determination, supply.

▶ Key Concepts

demand	normal good
quantity demanded	inferior good
law of demand	complements
substitution effect	substitutes
income effect	change in quantity demanded
determinants of demand	change in demand

▶ Discussion Questions

1. Buffalo Sam's Snowshovels commissioned a marketing consultant to find the demand for its shovels. The report came with the statement that the demand was for 80,000 shovels. The bill also came. If you were Buffalo Sam, should you pay the bill? Why or why not?

2. Provide an example of an inverse relation in addition to the law of demand.

3. Suppose that you are on your way to the ice cream parlor. You have only enough money for a single scoop. When you arrive, there is a special for economics students, two scoops for the price of one. When you walk out with two scoops, you are showing that the law of demand works. Explain why the law of demand works.

4. The Too-Sweet Cereal Company is considering a new advertising campaign. What impact would Too-Sweet hope the advertising to have on the demand for its product?

5. The price of personal computers has dropped. As a result, what has happened to the demand for computers?

6. When income rises, what would you expect to happen to the demand for cultured pearls as opposed to the demand for imitation pearls?

7. Give an economic explanation for the sequence of events that start when the price of movie theater tickets rises. What impact would there be on the demand for popcorn, video cassette recorders, and video cassette tapes?

8. Which of the following illustrates a change in demand? A change in the quantity demanded?
   a. You develop a craving for *shrimp* and buy more.
   b. The price of *shrimp* falls and you buy more.
   c. The price of shrimp falls and you buy more *cocktail sauce*.
   d. The price of shrimp falls and you buy less *lobster*.

9. When the price of swim suits rises, what happens to the demand for swim suits? What happens to the demand for swim towels?

10. What is the difference between the income effect and a change in income?

11. Uncle Effron says that the law of demand is false. He says house prices rise and so does the number bought. Is Uncle Effron right about the law of demand? Explain.

▶ Self-Review

• Fill in the blanks

demand

The schedule of different prices and the amount that the buyer is willing and able to buy at each price is known as _____. When price changes the amount the buyer will

quantity demanded	buy, the _____ changes. There is an
inverse	_____ relationship between price and quantity demanded.
law of demand	The relation is know as the _____. This
	means that as the price goes up, the quantity demanded goes
down	_____. And as the price goes down, the quantity demanded
up	goes _____. The quantity demanded can be changed only by
price	a change in _____. A change in a determinant of demand
demand	will change _____ itself. The determinants of
related goods, taste	demand include the price of _____, _____,
income, price	_____, and the expectation of a change in _____. An
normal	increase in income will increase demand for a _____
	good. When demand increases, the demand curve shifts to
right	the _____. An expectation of lower prices would
decrease	cause demand to _____. A decrease in demand
left	means that the demand curve shifts to the _____.
substitutes	Goods that are related are either _____ or
complements	_____. When the price of one good rises, the
rises	demand for its substitute _____. An increase in the price of
substitute	butter increases the demand for margarine, its _____.
	When the price of one good rises, the demand for its complement
falls	_____. An increase in the price of shoes decreases demand
complement	for shoelaces, a _____. An increase in the price of
quantity demanded	shoes results in a decrease in the _____
demand	for shoes. Also there is a change in _____ for shoelaces.

- Multiple choice

1. The substitution effect:
   a. means that the quantity demanded increases as the price falls because the lower price makes the good a more attractive substitute.
   b. shows how the demand curve changes when a substitute is introduced.
   c. tells why a substitute is always worse than the real thing.
   d. is unrelated to demand.
2. When your school increases tuition, the demand for education at its rival:
   a. rises.
   b. falls.
   c. does not change.
   d. shifts to the left.
3. Which does *not* cause a change in demand?
   a. A change in the price of the good.
   b. A change in the price of a related good.

c. A change in income.

d. Expectations of a change in price.

4. Two goods are substitutes if:

a. an increase in the price of one causes the demand for the other to rise.

b. an increase in the price of one causes the demand for the other to fall.

c. they are not complements.

d. when the price of one good rises, the price of the other good falls.

5. If the demand for good A goes up as the price of good B falls, you can conclude that goods A and B are:

a. substitutes.

b. normal goods.

c. useful goods.

d. complements.

Answers: 1.a, 2.a, 3.a, 4.a, 5.d.

Chapter	6	SUPPLY

Key Topics
  supply
  law of supply
  change in supply
  change in quantity supplied
  determinants of supply

Goals
  know the definition of supply
  understand that supply slopes upward to the right
  distinguish supply and a change in supply

In this chapter we concentrate on supply. Supply is a reflection of the choices of the seller, the producer of the good. Knowledge of how the seller responds to a change in price or other change is critical, since it is the producer that uses up resources in the production process. So if our concern is the allocation of resources, decisions of the seller are important. After all, it is the willingness and the ability of the producer to transform the resources into goods the society wants that helps to answer the what to produce question and resolves the how to produce question. There is much for you to learn about supply. You should be relieved to know that your understanding of the basic elements of demand will make your understanding of the basic elements of supply much easier.

Supply

Like demand, supply is a common term that has accumulated many meanings in our language. Supply is commonly thought of as the amount of output a producer makes. But in economics, supply has just one meaning. **Supply** is the list or schedule of alternative prices and the amount of the product that the seller is willing and able to offer for sale at each price. A crucial assumption is made in the case of supply, just as it was with demand. Supply is determined at a point in time when all other considerations except the price of the good are frozen. That is because the focus of supply is the response of the seller to a change in price. Also recognize that supply is focused on the decisions of the seller only. The actions of buyers have no effect on supply whatsoever. Supply is the outcome of seller choice. The seller decides how much output to produce. Notice that the firm does not set the price, but once given the price, the firm selects a quantity.

Suppose that we wish to find the supply of a particular producer of hair oil. Our interest at this time is with only one firm and the individual supply of that firm. One way to determine the supply would be to ask the seller a series of "what if" questions. What if the going price of hair oil were $10 a bottle — how many bottles would you, the seller, be willing and able to offer for sale? And so on through the various possible prices. The answer to this "what if" question is the quantity supplied. The **quantity supplied** tells the amount a seller is willing and able to produce at a specific price. All the quantities supplied taken together with their prices yield supply.

In Table 6-1, the firm, the seller, has revealed how many bottles it would be willing and able to produce each month at various prices. This supply schedule tells us that at a price of $10 per bottle, the firm would produce 8 bottles. If the price went down to $8 per bottle, the firm would be willing and able to produce 6 bottles of hair oil. If the price goes down to $6, only 3 bottles would be produced and offered for sale. The rest of the schedule is read in the same manner. As was true in the case of demand, a table is not an efficient way to display all the information concerning the supply decisions of the firm. It

Table 6-1   The Supply Schedule for Hair Oil

Price ($ Per Bottle)	Quantity Supplied (Bottles)
$10	8
8	6
6	3
4	1

This table is the supply schedule for hair oil. It shows the amount of hair oil that a firm would be willing and able to offer for sale at each price.

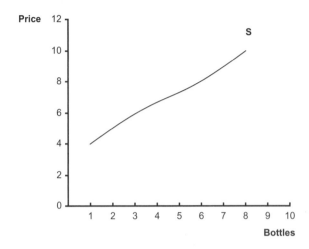

Figure 6-1   The Supply Curve for Hair Oil
This figure is the supply curve. It is based on the information given in Table 6-1. The supply curve shows the amount of hair oil that a firm would produce at each price. Note that supply has an upward slope.

would require a table of infinite length to show how the firm would respond to every possible price. A more useful way to display the supply information is in terms of a graph.

The graph in Figure 6-1 measures the quantity supplied (bottles) across the bottom of the graph. The price ($ per bottle) is measured up the side. All the information from Table 6-1 is on the graph. Start with the combination $10 and 8 bottles. To plot this point on the graph, measure up the side of the graph — the price axis — to $10 and then go directly to the right until you are just over 8 bottles. This is the point $10 and 8 bottles. For $8 and 6 bottles, measure up the side of the graph until you get to $8. Then go to the right until you are just above the 6. This point represents $8 and 6 bottles. The remainder of the table is plotted on the graph in the same manner. As the points are connected, a line or curve results. The upward-sloping line is called the supply curve, or supply, and is labeled S. This upward slope reflects the law of supply, just as the downward slope of demand reflects the law of demand.

The Law of Supply

Figure 6-1 clearly shows the law of supply. As the price of hair oil *decreases* from $10 to $8, the amount the producer is willing and able to offer for sale *decreases* from 8 to 6 bottles. As the price *rises* from $4 to $6, the amount the producer is willing and able to offer for sale *rises* from 1 bottle to 3 bottles. The law of supply states that as the price goes up, the quantity supplied goes up. And as the price goes down, so does the quantity supplied. The **law of supply** shows a *direct* relation between the price of a good and quantity supplied of that good. Producers will offer more for sale at a higher price, and less at a lower price.

If you were a seller, it is not too difficult to recognize that at least your willingness to produce depends upon the price. You would certainly be more willing to carry the Statue of Liberty on tour from city to city on your back for $50 per day than $14 per day. And even more willing at $80. But as you can see, there is more to this matter than willingness. There is also the question of ability. Ability to produce will also vary with price. If price rises, the firm has an incentive to increase production. The firm will hire more resources, and the resources eventually become less productive, which will drive up the production cost per unit. The relationship between cost and output will require more explanation, and Chapter 10, Cost, is devoted to that topic. Since the cost per unit has increased, the only way the firm can afford to produce more is if the selling price would also rise. So as the price of a good increases, so does the willingness and the ability of the producer. As a consequence, the law of supply shows a direct relation between price and quantity. Keep in mind that the law of demand specifies an inverse relation between price and quantity demanded and that the law of supply specifies a direct relation between price and quantity supplied.

Change in Supply

As on the demand curve, the only way to move on a supply curve is for the price to change. A movement along the supply curve is a **change in the quantity supplied** and occurs when the price of the good changes. That is what the supply curve illustrates, the response of the seller to a change in price. Everything else is assumed constant and unchanging. But what if something else does change, something else besides the price? This is possible over time. Over time, the determinants of supply can change. Then, just as in the case of demand, the entire curve will shift. A **change in supply** is a shift of the whole supply curve and occurs when a determinant of supply changes. Now the information represented by the old supply curve is no longer true. At each and every price, the seller is willing and able to produce a different amount

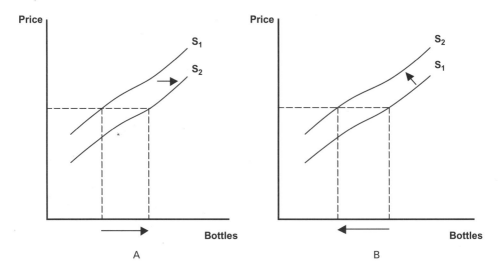

Figure 6-2   An Increase and Decrease in Supply
Graph A shows an increase in supply. The supply curve moves to the right. An increase in supply means that the firm will produce more at each price. Graph B shows a decrease in supply. Here the supply curve moves to the left. At each price, the firm will produce fewer units than before.

than before. This is shown in Figure 6-2. Figure 6-2A illustrates an increase in supply; Figure 6-2B, a decrease in supply. Recall that when demand increases, the curve shifts to the right of itself. So does supply. And when demand decreases, the demand curve shifts to the left of itself. So does supply. Right for an increase; left for a decrease. A shift in the supply curve means that at each and every price, the seller is willing to sell either more or less than before. There has been some occurrence that has affected either the willingness and/or the ability of the seller. When supply increases, the seller is willing and able to sell more than before at each price (Figure 6-2A). When supply decreases, the seller will sell less than before at each price (Figure 6-2B).

To gain additional understanding of the meaning of a shift in supply, consider the following. When supply increases, the seller is willing and able to offer the same quantity at a lower price (see Figure 6-3). And when supply decreases, the seller requires a higher price to call forth the same quantity as before. Figure 6-4 illustrates that if there were an increase in production cost, and consequently a decrease in supply, the only way the producer would and could produce the same quantity is at a higher price.

The determinants of supply are capable of shifting the entire supply curve. The **determinants of supply** include changes in nature, the cost of production,

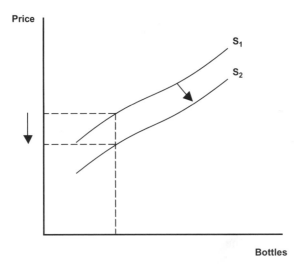

Figure 6-3   An Increase in Supply

In this figure we again show an increase in supply. An increase in supply also means that the firm would be willing to accept a lower price to produce the same quantity as before supply increased.

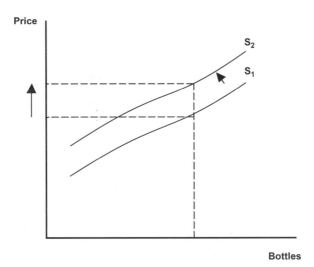

Figure 6-4   A Decrease in Supply

This figure shows that if supply falls, then at each quantity the firm requires a higher price. Thus when the supply decreases, the supply curve shifts up and to the left.

the price of other goods, and the expectation of a change in price. Each determinant of supply will be discussed in turn. Consider, first, how nature can influence supply. A drought can affect the supply of an agricultural product. During a drought an individual seller is less able to produce; hence the seller is offering less for sale at each price. This is a fall in supply illustrated by Figure 6-2B. Thus nature can have an impact on supply with floods, freezes, and so on. On the other hand, when nature cooperates and a bumper crop occurs, the seller is able to offer more for sale at each price. Figure 6-2A represents this increase in supply.

A critical determinant of supply is the cost of production. A change in the cost of production, as brought about by either a change in technology or the price of inputs, directly influences supply. Observe that the producer is not responding to any change in the price of the product, but to a change in the cost of producing the product. An improvement in the technology, or a reduction in the price of the resources, will lower the production cost. As the cost of production falls, supply will increase (not the quantity supplied). At each price, more will be offered for sale than before. As production cost rises, supply will decrease. A change in production cost affects the ability of the producer to produce.

Supply also depends on the price of other goods. Here we are *not* considering substitutes and complements; here we are concerned only with the seller and the productive capabilities of the seller. Some producers have the flexibility of readily switching from the production of one product to another. For example, farmers, at the time of planting, could plant either turnips or rutabaga. If the price of rutabaga went up, you would expect the law of supply to apply to rutabaga. As price goes up, so does the quantity supplied. You would expect farmers to respond to a higher price of rutabaga by producing more rutabaga. But what about turnips? At the same price of turnips, fewer would be produced than before. Why is this? Farmers are busy planting rutabaga instead. Therefore there has been a fall in supply of turnips, in response to an increase in the price of another product, rutabaga. These situations are shown by Figure 6-5.

How would you respond to an expected future price of tomatoes at $100 each? Like the rest of us, you would probably become a producer by plowing up the backyard and planting tomatoes, or at least crowding tomato plants along the window sills. This increase in tomato production would be true for backyard tomato growers and farmers too. So the expectation of an increase in price increases supply. What if the expected price is one cent each for tomatoes?

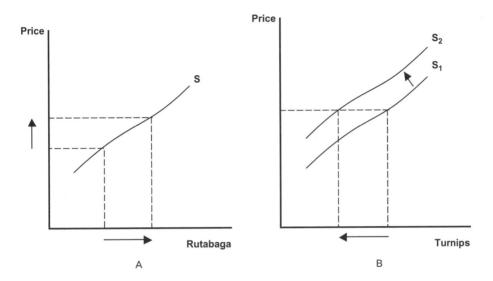

Figure 6-5   A Change in the Price of a Related Good
This figure shows that as the price of rutabaga goes up, the quantity supplied also rises, but the
supply of rutabaga does not change. Farmers respond to this increase in the price of rutabaga by
planting more rutabaga and fewer turnips. Thus the supply of turnips falls as the supply curve
for turnips shifts to the left. Fewer turnips are produced at the same price of turnips.

We might predict a decrease in the supply of tomatoes. Note that the price of
tomatoes does not change in either example. There is only an expectation of
a change in price. The quantity supplied did not change in either case; as yet,
there is no change in price. The outcome is a change in supply itself.

So it should be clear that the amount of production forthcoming from a
producer is dependent not only upon the price of the product but also upon
additional factors, the so-called determinants of supply. As a determinant of
supply changes, a producer will respond by changing supply.

▶ Summary

This chapter concentrated on supply, the law of supply, and the causes of a
change in supply. The laws of demand and supply together reflect very different
relations between price and quantity. Demand points out an inverse relation
between price and quantity demanded, and supply shows a direct relation
between price and quantity supplied. These laws will be applied in the following
chapter. We will be concerned with the difference between the impact of a

change in price and the impact of a change in anything *but* price on demand and supply. The graphic result is the difference between a movement along the curve when there is a change in price and a shift in the entire curve when something besides price, a determinant, changes.

If you have these facts well in hand, you are prepared for the next chapter. Demand and supply are tools that permit you to analyze the competitive markets of a capitalistic system and to achieve some degree of expertise in understanding the process that determines how resources are used.

▶ Key Concepts

supply	change in quantity supplied
quantity supplied	change in supply
law of supply	determinants of supply

▶ Discussion Questions

1. When interviewed on the six o'clock news, the president of Yule's Shoes said that its new plant would supply 1,000 pairs of shoes a day. Why would an economist find this statement misleading?
2. Provide examples of a direct relation besides the law of supply.
3. Which of the following illustrates a change in supply? A change in quantity supplied?
   a. The price of mopeds rises and more are produced.
   b. The price of bikes rises and fewer *mopeds* are produced.
   c. A major advancement is made in moped technology.
4. An oil refinery can produce gasoline or diesel fuel. When the price of gasoline rises, what happens to the supply of gasoline? The supply of diesel fuel?
5. A union in the widget industry successfully negotiates a new contract and raises wages. What happens to the supply of widgets?
6. When a new hybrid corn is developed that has low moisture requirements and is highly resistant to disease, what happens to the supply of corn?
7. When the price of Dr. Leedom's Fabulous Elixir goes down, will Dr. Leedom increase or decrease production? Explain.
8. Suppose that you are an economics tutor and are paid $3.00 per hour. If the wage went up to $15.00 per hour, because of your incredible ability, would you tutor more or less? Explain.
9. Uncle Effron does not believe the law of supply. He says that he's seen the price of gasoline go up, but a smaller quantity of gasoline is produced. Is Uncle Effron right about the law of supply? Explain.

▶ **Self-Review**

• Fill in the blanks

	The schedule of different prices and the amount that the seller is willing and able to offer for sale at each price is
supply	known as _____. When the price changes, the amount the
quantity supplied	seller will sell, the _____ changes. There is
direct	a _____ relation between price and the quantity supplied.
law of supply	The relation is known as the _____. This means
up	that as price goes up, the quantity supplied goes _____.
	And as the price goes down, the quantity supplied goes
down	_____. The quantity supplied can be changed only by a
price	change in _____. A change in a determinant of supply will
supply	change _____ itself. The determinants of supply
nature, production	include a change in _____, the cost of _____,
other goods	the price of _____, and the expectation of
a change in price	_____. When supply decreases, the supply
left	curve shifts _____. A shift of the supply curve to the right
increased	means that supply has _____.

• Multiple choice

1. Supply tells:
   a. how much is produced.
   b. how much is purchased.
   c. how much it costs.
   d. how much is produced at each price.
2. The quantity supplied is directly related to price because:
   a. the total cost of production rises as more is produced.
   b. more output requires more input which becomes less and less productive. Thus the extra cost per unit rises and increases the price.
   c. the cost of labor goes up as more labor is demanded.
   d. It is not. Everyone knows that as you produce more, you give quantity discounts so price and quantity supplied are inversely related.
3. The law of supply says:
   a. as price goes up, the quantity supplied goes up.
   b. as price goes down, the quantity supplied goes down.
   c. as price goes up, the quantity supplied goes down.
   d. both a and b.
4. When the price of an input falls, there will be:
   a. an increase in supply of output.

   b. a decrease in supply of output.

   c. an increase in quantity supplied of output.

   d. a decrease in quantity supplied of output.

5. If you are a farmer and expect the price of soybeans to rise, you will:

   a. increase the supply of soybeans.

   b. increase the quantity supplied of soybeans.

   c. decrease the quantity supplied of soybeans.

   d. decrease the supply of soybeans.

Answers: 1.d, 2.b, 3.d, 4.a, 5.a.

Chapter	7	MARKET EQUILIBRIUM

Key Topics
market demand and supply
surplus
shortage
equilibrium
shifts in demand or supply

Goals
understand how market equilibrium is achieved
use equilibrium to explain changes in price and quantity
utilization of the tools of supply and demand

A market has been defined as a situation where buyers and sellers meet to negotiate price and trade. This short, simple explanation does not begin to convey the immense importance of markets functioning within a capitalistic system. It is the meeting of these buyers and sellers that will determine the price of the good and, therefore, how much buyers will buy and how much sellers will produce. This in turn will determine how resources will be allocated and the success of the economic system in meeting the objectives of the society. All this occurs within the constraints imposed by scarcity. To see how this market solution is brought about, we must investigate how markets operate and the significance of market equilibrium.

Market Demand and Supply

Until now, our concern has been the demand of the individual buyer and the supply of the individual seller. How can this information be used to determine the market price? The demand of one buyer and the supply of one firm do not determine price for all. Somehow we need to represent the total demand of all buyers of the product and the total supply of all sellers. Market demand and market supply are the appropriate tools for determining the market price. So first we will find the market demand and market supply. The market demand can be obtained by adding together the demand of the various individuals in a market for a particular good.

Suppose that there are two individuals, Ann and Chris, and that each has a demand for pickles. Given the fact that both must pay the same price for pickles, we can determine how many pounds of pickles Ann and Chris would individually buy at that price. Then at that price we can determine the total pounds of pickles that Ann and Chris would buy together. Using the demand curves provided in Figure 7-1, at $6 per pound, Ann would buy 4 pounds and Chris would buy 7 pounds of pickles. According to their individual demand curves, the total quantity demanded by Ann and Chris at $6 is 4 plus 7, or 11 pounds. This is the quantity demanded in the pickle market at $6, if these two are the only buyers. Consider $3 per pound. Now Ann would purchase 5 and Chris 9 pounds of pickles. The quantity demanded in the market at $3 is what Ann and Chris together would purchase, 5 plus 9, or 14 pounds. The process is continued for each price, and the market demand for pickles results. This process of adding the individual demands to obtain the market demand is called horizontal addition.

If more buyers are added, the market demand curve will shift to the right, because each additional buyer adds to the total quantity demanded in the market at each price. The market demand will have the same general appearance as the individual demand curves. It slopes downward to the right. Everything that has been said of the individual demand curve is also true of the market demand. As price falls in the market, more will be bought. As price rises, less will be bought.

The same method of horizontal addition is used to obtain the market supply. By adding up the amount that each individual firm will supply at a given price, the quantity supplied in the market at that price will be found. To obtain the market supply, this process is repeated for all possible prices. The market supply curve slopes upward to the right. The market supply shows a direct relationship between price and quantity supplied, just as do the individual supply curves.

You have seen how the market demand and supply are constructed. The same determinants that cause the individual demand or supply curves to shift will also shift the market demand or supply. But now an additional determinant is the number of buyers (for demand) or the number of sellers (for supply). As fewer consumers seek to buy the product, market demand will fall. You can see

that if Chris leaves the market, the market demand would consist only of Ann
and her demand. At each price in the market, less will be bought than before
Chris left. And as more firms enter the market, the market supply will shift
to the right. At each price, more is offered for sale than before. So as there
is a change in the number of buyers or sellers, a change will result in market

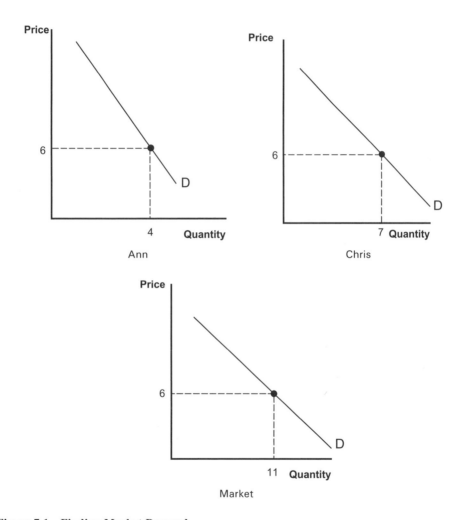

Figure 7-1   Finding Market Demand
This figure shows how the market demand is obtained from individual demand curves. The
procedure is to find the quantity demanded for each consumer at a given price, say, $6. Then
add up those amounts, 4 for Ann and 7 for Chris. That sum will be the quantity demanded in
the market at the given price. Repeat this process at each price, and you have the market demand
curve. This process is called horizontal addition.

demand or supply. You will soon see that this may have a significant impact
on the price you pay.

Surplus

A market consists of buyers who demand and sellers who supply. Buyers
always want to buy at lower prices and sellers seek to sell at higher prices.
Somehow a compromise will be worked out. Look at the market for garter
snakes represented by Figure 7-2. Suppose that the going price for the good is
$10. Then the amount that the sellers are able and willing to sell at that price
is 25 snakes. However the amount that the buyers are willing and able to buy
at that price is only 5. The quantity supplied exceeds the quantity demanded
at the going price; this is the meaning of **surplus**. Observe that the phrase
"at the going price" is a critical part of the definition. If the price is not identified,
neither the quantity demanded nor the quantity supplied is known. If neither
quantity is known, it will not be known whether or not there is a surplus. In this
market there is a surplus of 20 garter snakes at the going price of $10 each.

If the price were not permitted to change, then the surplus would be
permanent. The price is encouraging sellers to produce more than buyers

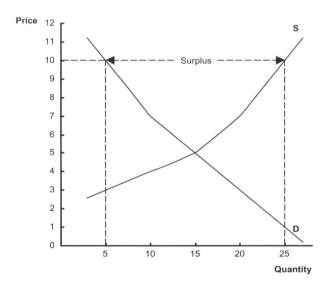

Figure 7-2   Surplus
This figure shows that at $10 each, the quantity demanded is 5 units while the quantity supplied
is 25 units. There is a surplus of 20 units.

will buy at that price. This is not an uncommon situation. On occasion, the government has set the price to benefit the seller. Certain agricultural markets provide an example of these price supports. The price is higher than it normally would be for the consumers, and they buy less. Fixing or freezing the price at a surplus level has its difficulties. Someone must purchase the remaining amount of production that buyers refuse to buy. That someone is the government through the assistance of taxpayers. Buying and storing the excess production is costly. Crop limitation programs reward the farmer for reducing production and eliminate the surplus at the support price. This results in the intended price support for the farmer without the resulting burden of the surplus.

But what if there were no government interference with price and price were permitted to reflect certain forces at work in the market? Then something remarkable begins to happen. What do sellers do with all this surplus on hand? Obvious use can be made of the law of demand. When the price falls, buyers buy more. So the sellers' solution is for price to fall. Carefully consider Figure 7-3 to see the twofold impact of the falling price. As price falls, the

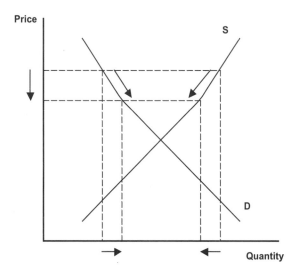

Figure 7-3 A Surplus Causes the Price to Fall
This figure shows that because of the surplus, the price in the market falls. This has two impacts. First, because of the lower price, there is an increase in the quantity demanded. Second, because of the lower price, there is a decrease in the quantity supplied. Thus the fall in the price has helped to reduce the surplus. But note that a surplus still exists so that there is still downward pressure on the price.

quantity demanded increases, so there is a downward movement along the demand curve. But as price falls, sellers produce less. This starts a movement downward along the supply curve as the quantity supplied declines with the falling price. Both the laws of supply and demand are at work. Yet the surplus, though declining with falling price, will continue to exist as long as the quantity supplied at the going price exceeds the quantity demanded. However, buyers wish to buy more and more as the price falls, and sellers wish to sell less and less. The end of the surplus is in sight.

Shortage

Consider a market with a different situation. Figure 7-4 shows an established price of $3. At that price, the quantity demanded of 20 exceeds the quantity supplied of 5. Whenever the quantity demanded is larger than the quantity supplied at the going price, a **shortage** exists. Buyers are trying to buy more than sellers have for sale at that price. Neither is this an unusual situation. Government, in an attempt to assist buyers, has on various occasions with various goods controlled price at a shortage level. One example in our society

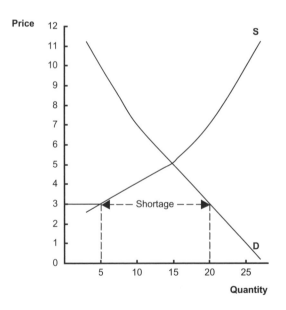

Figure 7-4   Shortage
At the price of $3 each in this market, the quantity demanded is 20 units while the quantity supplied is 5 units. There is a shortage of 15 units.

has been energy. But certainly the pricing of Super Bowl tickets and many other goods establishes the fact that shortages do exist. At the set price, the applications for tickets are greater than the number of seats available. A market is capable of making shortages disappear.

What if price were free to respond to market forces? Many buyers are competing to purchase an insufficient quantity of goods. Individual buyers will begin offering a higher price to ensure that they obtain some of the limited quantity. As the price begins to rise, two powerful market forces are set into motion. At higher prices, some buyers will find that they are unable or unwilling to obtain the good. And at higher prices there will be an increase in the amount offered for sale. The rising price is reducing the shortage. Figure 7-5 illustrates a movement upward along the demand curve and the supply curve in response to higher prices. Yet at each higher price, as long as the quantity demanded still exceeds the quantity supplied, a shortage, though reduced, still exists. In turn, the existing shortage will provide buyers with the incentive to bid up price even more. The elimination of the shortage is in sight.

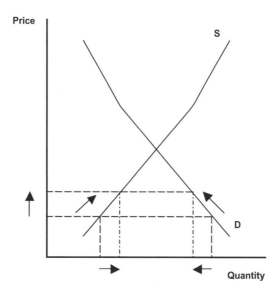

Figure 7-5   A Shortage Causes the Price to Rise
This figure shows that because of the shortage, the price in the market rises. This has two impacts. First, because of the higher price, there is a decrease in the quantity demanded. Second, because of the higher price, there is an increase in the quantity supplied. Thus the rise in the price has helped to reduce the shortage. But note that a shortage still exists so that there is still upward pressure on the price.

Equilibrium

Where will these falling and rising prices end? The answer is at equilibrium. The concept of **equilibrium** is that of a balance of forces. This condition is often encountered in a physical context. If two people sit on a teeter-totter until it is exactly balanced with neither person moving, then the teeter-totter is in equilibrium. The force pushing up is exactly offset by the force pushing down. Once equilibrium is achieved, no motion results. This need not always be the case, but for the models in this book, that is the meaning of equilibrium. In the market, there is a price that does not change, a price such that forces are exactly in balance. These forces are supply and demand. Market equilibrium occurs at the intersection of the market supply and the market demand curves. This point of intersection is called the **equilibrium point**. The equilibrium point indicates the equilibrium price and quantity, which are also known as the market price and quantity.

Equilibrium in the market represented by Figure 7-6 occurs at the price of $5. At the equilibrium price of $5, the quantity demanded of 15 exactly equals the quantity supplied of 15. Only at equilibrium are the quantities demanded

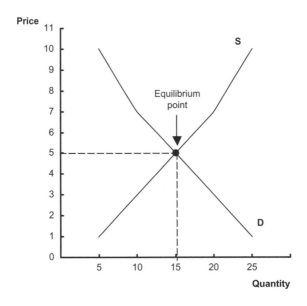

Figure 7-6   Equilibrium
The equilibrium point occurs at the intersection of supply and demand. This determines the equilibrium price at $5 and the equilibrium quantity at 15 units. Only at equilibrium will the quantity demanded and quantity supplied be equal.

and supplied equal. The market or equilibrium quantity is 15. The equilibrium price will not have any tendency to change.

Why will price tend naturally toward equilibrium? Any price above or below $5 in this market will be in motion. Consider a price above equilibrium. Any price greater than $5 will create a surplus. At any price higher than the equilibrium price, the quantity offered for sale is greater than the amount purchased. The competition among the sellers to reduce the surplus will cause price to fall. Price will continue to fall, as long as the quantity supplied is greater than the quantity demanded, until equilibrium is reached. Finally, the quantity supplied will exactly equal the quantity demanded, and the market will be cleared. Any producer selling at $5 will find a ready buyer. Sellers can sell all they are willing and able to produce at that price. The surplus is eliminated, and sellers no longer have any need to lower the price to increase sales.

And what is the situation at any price below equilibrium? The shortage provides buyers with the incentive to offer a higher price. As the price rises, the excess of the quantity demanded over the quantity supplied becomes less until at last the two are equal. There is no longer any need for buyers to bid up the price, as the market is cleared. Every buyer willing and able to purchase the good at $5 will find a ready seller. Buyers can buy all they are willing and able to buy at that price.

A price at a level other than equilibrium sets forces in motion. A price higher than equilibrium intensifies the competition between sellers and tends to drive down the price. The independent actions of both the sellers and the buyers eliminate the surplus. Both sellers and buyers are acting in their own self-interest. Sellers want to sell less as price falls, and buyers want to buy more. This activity eliminates a surplus as the price falls toward equilibrium. And, in a similar manner, a price lower than equilibrium will tend to be driven up by the increased competition among buyers. Buyers tend to buy less at the higher prices and sellers are provided the incentive to produce more. This interaction from both sides of the market, between buyers and sellers, will eliminate the shortage as the price rises. Once price has reached equilibrium, there will be no tendency for it to rise or fall any farther. If it does, it will be driven back to equilibrium by the resulting surplus or shortage. Therefore, the interaction among the buyers and the sellers of a market determines the equilibrium price and quantity. And once price reaches equilibrium, it will not change unless some event outside the market interferes with the equilibrium position.

You have seen the process by which price is determined. Once price is determined, we know the actual quantities demanded and supplied. And

knowing how much producers will produce indicates the amount of resources
that will be allocated to the production of each product.

An Increase in Market Demand

Market equilibrium results as buyers and sellers respond to changing prices,
setting in motion the laws of supply and demand. But you already know that
buyers and sellers are affected by changes other than price. These are the
determinants of demand and the determinants of supply. A change in these
determinants can cause a change in the equilibrium position in the market. Let
us explore this possibility and at the same time discover how the market forces
of supply and demand allocate resources.

What would happen to the equilibrium price and quantity of automobiles
if, for example, consumer income in the United States increased? First, we
would expect that the demand for normal goods would increase. Assume
that automobiles are normal goods and that the auto market were initially in
equilibrium; then the impact of an increase in demand in the automobile market
is illustrated by Figure 7-7. The original D_1 demand curve no longer exists as

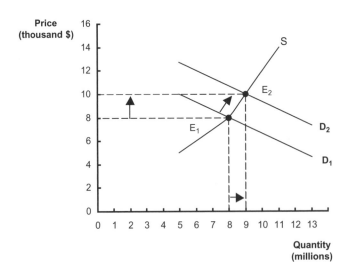

Figure 7-7   An Increase in Demand
Here we see the impact on the equilibrium price and quantity of an increase in demand from
D_1 to D_2. Before demand changes, the equilibrium at E_1 is a price of $8,000 and 8 million cars.
Once the demand shifts to D_2, the equilibrium will move to E_2. Now the market price is $10,000
and the quantity is 9 million.

it has been replaced by the D_2 curve to the right. The old equilibrium price of $8,000 and the old equilibrium quantity of 8 million autos at point E_1 are no longer relevant. The new equilibrium point (E_2) at the intersection of the demand and supply curves, D_2 and S, indicates an equilibrium price of $10,000 and an equilibrium quantity of 9 million automobiles.

At any point in time, there can be only one equilibrium in a market. As income and demand increased, so did the competition among consumers for autos. The equilibrium price was driven up, and more resources were allocated to the increased production of automobiles. The method of looking at the result of an increase in income compares only the beginning (E_1) and the ending (E_2) equilibrium in the market. We do not know how long this adjustment process will take, but until quantity supplied equals quantity demanded, the market forces will continue to move price and quantity toward equilibrium.

For a clearer understanding of the market, consider how we arrived at the new equilibrium. Look carefully at Figure 7-8. What happens when there is

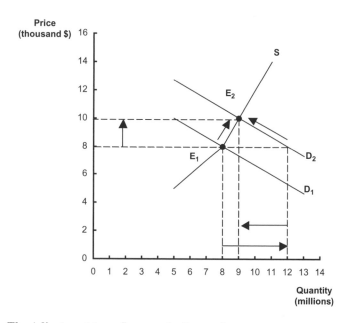

Figure 7-8 The Adjustment to an Increase in Demand
Start at equilibrium E_1. Then increase demand to D_2. How do we reach equilibrium at E_2? There would be a shortage of cars at $8,000 since 8 million cars are produced, but 12 million cars are demanded. Because of the shortage, the price will rise. As the price moves to $10,000, the quantity demanded falls from 12 to 9 million and the quantity supplied increases from 8 to 9 million. Equilibrium occurs at E_2.

an increase in income and the demand curve shifts to D_2? The immediate result is a shortage. At the going price of $8,000, consumers no longer buy 8 million autos but attempt to buy 12 million instead. The complication is that at the same price of $8,000 a car, sellers are willing and able to produce only the same amount as before, 8 million. So at the old equilibrium price, the quantity demanded now exceeds the quantity supplied, creating a shortage of automobiles.

Fortunately, the market has the ability to eliminate any shortage, so the shortage will be temporary. What will happen? The competition among buyers will cause the price to rise. At a higher price, buyers react by deciding that they will buy fewer autos than they had previously planned, and sellers decide that it will be more profitable to increase production. So as the price is driven up by the competition among buyers for the limited quantity of autos, two adjustments begin. The quantity demanded falls back along the new D_2 demand curve, and the quantity supplied increases along the S supply curve.

Review what has happened. An increase in demand created a temporary shortage. The market price rose and the buyers and sellers respond exactly as predicted. There was a change in demand but no change in supply. Sellers indicated by the supply curve that they would produce 8 million autos at $8,000 each and 9 million autos at $10,000. Sellers simply produced more at a higher price. This is an increase in the quantity supplied of autos. Therefore, when the market is cleared and again in equilibrium, it will be at the E_2 level. The market has adjusted and eliminated the temporary shortage of automobiles. But although there is no longer a shortage of autos, autos still remain a scarce good. The evidence is that there is an opportunity cost, or price, for autos. Also notice that this market model predicts that equilibrium price and quantity will both increase when demand increases.

Shifts in Market Demand and Supply

Economic predictions are made by moving from equilibrium to equilibrium. Thus, to predict or determine the impact of a change in a market:

1. Start at an initial equilibrium position.
2. Determine whether the change affects
   a. supply.
   b. demand.
   c. both supply and demand.

3. Shift (as determined in step 2)
   a. supply.
   b. demand.
   c. both supply and demand.
4. Find the new point at which equilibrium occurs, compare the new equilibrium to the initial equilibrium from step 1, and find the impact on
   a. equilibrium price
   b. equilibrium quantity.

The key to this process is step 2. What causes a shift in demand or supply? The answer, of course, is the determinants of demand and the determinants of supply. Any change in the number of consumers, taste, income, buyer expectation of a future change in price, or price of a related good will change the market equilibrium. This is also true of any change in the number of sellers, nature, cost of production, price of other goods, or seller expectation of a future price change.

Figure 7-9A represents the increase in equilibrium price and quantity for frog eggs after an announcement that frog eggs prevent cancer. Demand increased (change in taste), as did the equilibrium price and quantity. Can you predict the impact of a fall in demand? What if consumer taste for diet soft drinks decreases because thin is "out"? Figure 7-9B shows the result. The equilibrium price of the good will fall, as will the amount bought and sold. And what if supply were to increase, because of a breakthrough in technology used in the production of personal computers? The market price would be lower and the market quantity would increase as in Figure 7-9C. And if the supply of oranges is reduced as the result of a freeze in Florida? Figure 7-9D indicates an increase in the market price and a reduction in the amount bought and sold. Oranges are relatively more scarce than before. The market reflects increased scarcity through higher price.

We have seen that the market is capable of adjustments. Shifts in supply or demand will be adjusted to by the market, and the resulting scarcity of the good will be reflected by the market price. The price in turn establishes the quantity bought and sold. The willingness and ability of buyers and sellers are automatically included in the market, and an efficient scheme of resource allocation results. Price performs a rationing function of allocating resources only to those willing and able to pay the opportunity cost.

Recognize that the market responds to consumer demand. As demand increases, so does the allocation of resources into that market. Figure 7-9A

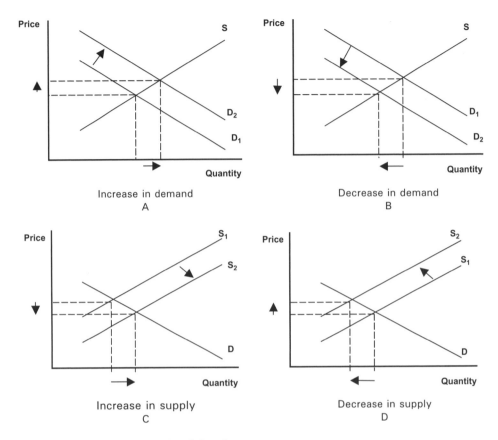

Figure 7-9   Shifts in Demand and Supply

This set of figures shows some of the possible ways that demand and supply can change, and what happens to the equilibrium price and quantity because of the shift. Panel A shows an increase in demand, so the equilibrium price and quantity both rise. Panel B shows a decrease in demand. The equilibrium price and quantity both fall. Panel C shows an increase in supply, which lowers the equilibrium price and increases the equilibrium quantity. Panel D shows a decrease in supply, which causes the equilibrium price to rise and the equilibrium quantity to fall.

represents this impact of an increase in demand. Resources flow from the production of goods that consumers value less into the market with increased demand. Figure 7-9B shows the impact of a fall in demand. Resources are reallocated from this market to other areas of production that consumers and society value more. In a capitalistic society, markets do allocate resources and respond to consumer demand.

We have seen how price is determined by supply and demand. However, not all prices are determined this way. To use supply and demand, the market must be competitive. What does it mean to say that the market must be competitive? Aren't all markets competitive? We will have much more to say about "competition" later, but, to an economist, some markets are competitive and some markets are not. The main requirement for a competitive market is that no buyer or seller can affect the price of the good. This requires the absence of coercion (force). If a firm can produce a good and offer it for sale at a price it chooses, without concern of what other firms will do, the firm can coerce the buyer to pay its price. This situation is not competitive. On the other hand, if the price a firm can get is the price that other firms receive — the price set by the market — then the firm cannot coerce the buyer into paying a higher price. To an economist, this situation more closely approaches competition. But the point is that if a firm or buyer has coercive power, then the tools of supply and demand do not apply. Some other price-determining principle is at work. These issues are more fully explained in Chapters 14 and 15. When a discussion involves supply and demand, assume a competitive market.

▶ Summary

This chapter was about market equilibrium. Equilibrium occurs at the intersection of the market supply and market demand curves. This equilibrium point establishes the market or equilibrium price and quantity. When the market is not in equilibrium, either a surplus or a shortage occurs. In the future, when economists use the term "price," you may be sure that the price they have in mind is the equilibrium price. This will be true even though the word "equilibrium" is omitted.

This chapter introduced another important concept. By starting at one equilibrium, recording some market change, and reaching a new equilibrium, we can predict the impact of the change on equilibrium price and quantity. This technique of comparing the two equilibria is the heart of economic analysis. We will use this method in a variety of models to generate an understanding of the economic forces surrounding us.

You have now been introduced to a powerful tool of economic analysis, supply and demand. Look around and see how the tool can be used. You will be amazed at the amount of behavior that can be explained by these simple concepts. Yet, there are other questions to answer. How can you buy less and spend more? This is one topic of the next chapter.

▶ Key Concepts

surplus
shortage
equilibrium
equilibrium point
shifts in market supply and demand

▶ Discussion Questions

1. The equilibrium price for gloves is $10 a pair. What happens at a price of $15 a pair? At a price of $5 a pair?
2. Have you ever cleaned a messy room, cluttered purse, or dirty car? Explain what eventually happens and how this illustrates equilibrium.
3. Explain how price reaches equilibrium.
4. The supply of coal in the United States is sufficient to last for at least 2,000 years. What is wrong with this statement?
5. The demand for large automobiles fell when the price of gasoline rose. What happened to the price of large autos? The number of large autos bought and sold? The supply of large autos? The quantity supplied? The quantity demanded?
6. When Pokemon caught on, production could not keep up with the increase in demand. Describe the situation in the market. What would you expect to happen to the equilibrium price and quantity?
7. Suppose that after a California earthquake, there was an increase in the supply of seismologists. What will happen to the wage for seismologists? What will happen to the number of seismologists hired?
8. Explain what will happen to the equilibrium price and quantity of petunias
   a. when the price of plant fertilizer goes up.
   b. when petunias are discovered to reduce the chances of catching a cold.
   c. when the cost of production is reduced by the development of new varieties with three times as many seeds.
   d. when the membership in the Petunia Lovers of America Club falls.
9. Describe what will happen in the market for broccoli if the supply increases due to a better broccoli plant. Next describe what happens in the market for Brussels sprouts, a substitute. Finally, what happens in the market for land especially suited for growing Brussels sprouts?
10. How do ticket scalpers at the Super Bowl indicate that the market is not at equilibrium?
11. If enough people expect the price of a candy bar to increase, how might that affect demand and the price of the candy bar?

▶ Self-Review

• Fill in the blanks

market	The sum of the individual demands is the _____
market	demand. The sum of the individual supplies is the _____
	supply. An additional determinant of market demand is the
buyers	number of _____. An additional determinant of market
sellers	supply is the number of _____. If at the going price the
	quantity supplied is greater than the quantity demanded, we
surplus, fall	have a _____ and the price will tend to _____. If
	at the going price the quantity demanded is greater than the
shortage	quantity supplied, we have a _____ and the price will
rise	tend to _____. Only when the quantity demanded and
equilibrium	supplied are equal will the market be in _____. An
increase	increase in demand causes the market price to _____
increase	and the quantity to _____. A decrease in demand
decrease	causes the market price to _____ and the quantity
decrease	to _____. When supply increases, the market price
decreases, increases	_____ and the quantity _____. And when
increases	supply decreases, the market price _____ and the
decreases	quantity _____.

• Multiple choice

1. A surplus means that at the going price:
   a. the quantity demanded is greater than the quantity supplied.
   b. the quantity supplied is greater than the quantity demanded.
   c. sellers want to sell more than buyers buy.
   d. both b and c.
2. At equilibrium:
   a. the quantity supplied is greater than the quantity demanded.
   b. the quantity demanded is greater than the quantity supplied.
   c. the quantity demanded is equal to the quantity supplied.
   d. both a and b.
3. If the price rises, there must have been:
   a. a decrease in demand and a decrease in quantity supplied.
   b. an increase in supply and a decrease in quantity demanded.
   c. an increase in quantity demanded and quantity supplied.
   d. an increase in demand and an increase in quantity supplied.
4. When supply decreases:
   a. the equilibrium price increases and the equilibrium quantity falls.

    b. the equilibrium price decreases and the equilibrium quantity rises.

    c. the equilibrium price increases and the equilibrium quantity rises.

    d. the equilibrium price decreases and the equilibrium quantity falls.

5. When the price of gasoline went up, the demand for large cars went down, and the demand for small cars went up. You would expect:

    a. the price of small cars to go up because of the increase in demand.

    b. the price of large cars to go up to encourage more people to buy small cars.

    c. the price of small cars to go up because of the increase in quantity demanded.

    d. the price of large cars to go down because of the increase in supply of large cars.

Answers: 1.d, 2.c, 3.d, 4.a, 5.a.

Chapter | 8 | PRICE ELASTICITY

Key Topics
price elasticity of demand
determinants of price elasticity of demand
price, elasticity, and total revenue

Goals
understand the meaning of elasticity of demand
find the determinants of price elasticity of demand
explore the relationship between price and total revenue

You are aware that buyers and sellers respond to a change in price. But by how much does the price have to change before there is a response? With some products, buyers seem to be more responsive to a change in price; with other products, less. Sometimes how much money is involved seems to matter; in other cases, the amount of money does not seem to be so important. And what about situations in which buyers seem to respond very little, if any, to a change in price? Are we looking at a breakdown of the law of demand?

Your first impression might be that there is no rule which relates responses to price changes. But economists, as social scientists, try to make sense out of the world. Economists become concerned with tracking these responses to a change in price and translating them into something meaningful and useful. Concentrating on the responses of buyers and sellers to a change in price provides more insight into the laws of supply and demand. In addition, information can be gathered to develop relationships between price and other changing factors, so that, for example, we might know the change in the amount of money you will spend on a product when its price changes. And do bananas and oil really have anything in common? We can begin to resolve these many questions by finding what is meant by the price elasticity of demand.

Price Elasticity of Demand

You have learned that as the price of a good increases, the quantity demanded by the buyer decreases. A question of obvious interest is, when the price goes up, how much will the quantity demanded fall? If price were to increase by a large amount, should we expect a large reduction in the quantity bought? Not necessarily. And if price decreases just a little, is it safe to assume that not much more would be bought? Not at all. To make the relationship between the change in price and change in quantity demanded more precise, economists have defined a concept called the price elasticity of demand. Or once it becomes clear that the subject is the buyer, then simply the term elasticity will do. **Elasticity** of demand measures the response of the buyer(s) to a change in price. If the response of the buyer (change in quantity demanded) is large compared to the price change, then demand is labeled elastic. Elastic means very responsive or stretchy, as an elastic band. If the response of the buyer is small compared to the price change, then demand is labeled inelastic. Inelastic means not so elastic, or responsive, to a change in price.

Yet calling responses large or small is not very precise. More precision can be obtained by calculating a simple ratio, the **coefficient of price elasticity**.

$$\text{coefficient of price elasticity} = \frac{\% \text{ change in quantity demanded}}{\% \text{ change in price}}$$

When referring to elasticity, the change in price or quantity is *always* expressed as a percentage. Even if we do not always say percentage change in price or quantity when discussing elasticity, we always mean it. There are only three possible results when elasticity is calculated. The coefficient will be greater than, equal to, or less than the number 1.

If the coefficient of elasticity is greater than the number 1, then demand for the good is **elastic**. This is because the percentage change in quantity demanded (QD) is larger than the percentage change in price (P). For example,

$$\frac{\% \text{ change QD}}{\% \text{ change P}} = \frac{20}{4} = 5$$

A coefficient of 5 is greater than 1 and signals that demand is elastic. Elastic demand indicates that buyers are relatively responsive to a change in price. The price change in the example was smaller, only 4 percent, but the change in the amount bought was bigger, 20 percent. Thus the percentage change in the amount bought was greater than the percentage change in price. We may interpret the results of the ratio to say that as the price of this good increases by 1 percent, the quantity demanded will fall by 5 percent. For some reason buyers are relatively sensitive to a change in the price of this particular good. That is always the case with a coefficient of more than 1. You can see this in the following ratio:

$$\frac{\%\text{ change QD}}{\%\text{ change P}} = \frac{\text{BIGGER number}}{\text{SMALLER number}} = \text{coefficient more than 1}$$

So if the response to the change in price is greater than the price change, then the coefficient is greater than 1, and demand is elastic.

A coefficient of less than 1 means that buyers are not so responsive to a change in price. Demand is inelastic. The percentage change in price is relatively large compared to the percentage change in the quantity demanded. A smaller number divided by a bigger number always results in a coefficient of less than 1. If the coefficient of elasticity is less than 1, then demand is **inelastic**.

$$\frac{\%\text{ change QD}}{\%\text{ change P}} = \frac{\text{SMALLER number}}{\text{BIGGER number}} = \text{coefficient less than 1}$$

It is possible for the percentage change in the price and in the quantity to be identical. Dividing a number by the same number always results in a coefficient of 1. In this case demand is neither elastic nor inelastic, so it is called unitary elasticity of demand. **Unitary elasticity** means that the response of a change in quantity demanded will be the same as the change in price:

$$\frac{\%\text{ change QD}}{\%\text{ change P}} = \frac{\text{SAME number}}{\text{SAME number}} = \text{coefficient equal to 1}$$

Since there is an inverse relation between price and quantity demanded, the coefficient of the price elasticity of demand will always be a negative number. If the price change is positive, the change in the amount bought is negative. The division of a negative number by a positive number results in a negative coefficient. The same is true when the price change is negative and is divided into the positive change in the amount bought. The fact that the coefficient is always negative should be understood, but the negative sign is not relevant for our purposes. Hence we will ignore the negative sign. Our focus is on the amount of response to a change in price. The size of the

Table 8-1   The Elasticity of Demand

If the Coefficient of Elasticity Is	Then Demand Is
more than 1	elastic
less than 1	inelastic
equal to 1	of unitary elasticity

This table shows the relationship between the coefficient of elasticity and the elasticity of demand. The size of the coefficient measures the response of consumers to a change in price.

coefficient of elasticity measures this response. The coefficient is compared to the number 1 to determine the elasticity of demand. This relationship is summarized in Table 8-1.

Vertical and Horizontal Demand

The elasticity is easily recognized on two special demand curves. The first case is that of vertical demand as shown in Figure 8-1. The number of units demanded remains the same regardless of the price. Since quantity demanded never changes, the percentage change in quantity is always zero. Thus the coefficient of elasticity is zero. This demand is identified as **perfectly inelastic**.

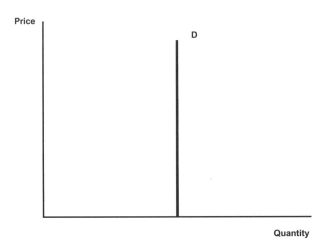

Figure 8-1   Perfectly Inelastic Demand
This figure shows the special case where demand is perfectly inelastic. No matter what the change in price, the quantity demanded does not respond. A perfectly inelastic demand curve is vertical.

No matter what the change in price, the quantity demanded does not respond. There are not many examples of goods with perfectly inelastic demand. A possible example is heroin for an addict or some good or service that is required for life, such as insulin or kidney dialysis. In these cases the consumer would be willing to pay any price (up to his or her entire income) to get the good. Yet even these goods are not examples of perfectly inelastic demand at all prices. At a price greater than the consumer's income, he or she would be forced to reduce consumption due to a lack of ability to pay. Again, the law of demand asserts itself.

In the second case of special demand, the demand curve is horizontal. Figure 8-2 shows a horizontal, or flat, demand curve. No matter how many units are bought, the price stays the same. Since the price does not change, the percentage change in price is zero. Thus the coefficient is some number divided by zero, which we will assume is infinite, surely greater than 1. Demand, in this case, is **perfectly elastic**. Examples of goods with perfectly elastic demand are rare. But this horizontal demand curve will be applied in Chapter 11. There we will discover that the perfectly competitive firm behaves as if the demand curve facing it were perfectly elastic.

The elasticity of all other demand curves lies between these two special cases. Aside from these two extremes, it is not possible to look at a demand curve and conclude its elasticity. The coefficient of elasticity is the only guide. In general, the elasticity will change as we move along the demand curve. Elasticity is therefore a characteristic of a point on the demand curve, not a

Figure 8-2   Perfectly Elastic Demand
This figure shows the special case where demand is perfectly elastic. Here the demand curve is horizontal. The price does not change as we move along the demand curve.

characteristic of the demand curve itself. In fact, elasticity is related to the amount the consumer spends on the good. Before turning to that relationship, we will investigate what factors cause demand to be elastic or inelastic.

Determinants of Price Elasticity of Demand

You might wonder what causes the demand for a good to be elastic or inelastic. Why are people so responsive to a change in price of one good and not another? The major **determinants of price elasticity** are whether the buyer views the good as a luxury or necessity, the availability of acceptable substitutes, and how large a part of the buyer's budget the purchase is. An additional and important consideration that affects the elasticity of demand is the amount of time the consumer has in which to make decisions. Table 8-2 summarizes the impact of these determinants of elasticity.

If a consumer views a good as a luxury, you would expect demand to be highly elastic. By its very nature, a luxury good is one that is nice to have but is also a good that one can do without. As the price of a luxury increases, the reduction in quantity purchased is relatively large. The same conclusion is true if the price of a luxury falls just a little. We would all enjoy more luxury, so again the quantity response is greater than the change in price. Consumers are relatively sensitive to a change in price of a luxury. Luxuries can range from diamond earrings to gourmet coffee.

In contrast, a good considered a necessity will tend to have a more inelastic demand. People are not so responsive to a change in the price of a necessity. They are reluctant to cut back as its price rises. Cigarettes and alcohol are considered necessities by some. A large percentage increase in price brings only a relatively small decrease in the amount bought. Yet people do respond to a change in price. With necessities, however, the price change must be relatively

Table 8-2   Determinants of Elasticity of Demand

Less Elastic	More Elastic
Necessity	Luxury
Few substitutes	Many substitutes
Small part of budget	Large part of budget
Less time	More time

This table summarizes the impact of the determinants of elasticity on the elasticity of demand.

large to get a response. And if the price of a necessity falls, people generally do not stampede to obtain the good. If they consider the good a necessity, they may already have enough on hand for immediate use. The savings in price would have to be considerable to persuade them to stock up. As the price of gasoline falls by even a large amount, the consumer will not fill every available container, including the swimming pool, once the gas tank is full. Thus the response to a change in the price of a necessity is less than for a luxury good.

The availability of substitutes for a good significantly affects the way in which we respond to a change in price of the good. If there are many acceptable substitutes for the good, then we are likely to be sensitive to a change in its price, because there are many alternative goods that we would willingly switch to or from. If the price of corn increases slightly, why not have beans or peas for dinner tonight instead? As long as there are other goods that we could readily use, and be willing to use, then demand for the good will be relatively elastic. And as the price of corn falls slightly at the local supermarket, there will be a greater response as some consumers pass up peas and beans and purchase corn instead.

On the other hand, if we feel that there are few acceptable substitutes, then we are not as likely to be very responsive as price changes. After all, there is not another good that we would readily switch to, or that we would want to substitute this good for. There are few ways we can escape the higher price, or enjoy the lower price. The price of telephone service illustrates this point. If the price of local phone service goes up, since there are few acceptable substitutes, the number of households with phones will not decrease significantly. There may be some grumbling and letters to the editor, but people will for the most part continue the phone service. And if the price of phone service goes down? The consumers feel fortunate and enjoy the savings, and few new households would sign up for service. So when the number of close substitutes is limited, demand may be inelastic.

What is meant by "how large a part of the budget"? Essentially, what we are asking is, is the good relatively expensive or cheap for the individual? If the good is relatively expensive, a large percentage of the consumer's budget, then you might expect demand to be more elastic. A buyer is usually more responsive to the same percentage change in the price of the more expensive of two goods. If the price of a $10 hammer increased by 10 percent, that means an additional $1. But if a $10,000 car increased in price by the same 10 percent, then that means an additional $1,000. We are much more sensitive to spending (or saving) the larger amount. We can conclude that buyers are more responsive to a change in the price of cars than hammers, since the larger the percentage of the budget, the more elastic the demand usually is. We can also conclude that a fall in the price of gum will not increase its consumption by that much more. Not many individuals will rush to the store to save only a few cents.

Some goods, such as salt, possess all three characteristics that result in a buyer being less responsive to a change in price. Salt is considered to be a necessity, has few acceptable substitutes for its primary functions, and is usually a small part of the consumer's budget. A good need not have all these characteristics, but one or more of these traits must be dominant in the mind of the buyer for demand to be inelastic. A good with elastic demand could possess one or more of the characteristics opposite to those of salt. Refer again to Table 8-2 for a summary of these determinants.

Time was also mentioned as a determinant of price elasticity of demand. There is something about the length of time that makes buyers more sensitive to a change in price. The significance is that over time the acceptability and availability of substitutes increases. We may become more willing to accept the idea of using substitutes as time passes, and our wallets feel the continuous pinch of the higher price of a good. And even more substitutes may become available over time, in response to the increase in price and growing consumer demand for alternatives. You can put this theory to a test over your lifetime given a continued increase in energy prices. If energy prices continue to rise faster than other prices, you should expect consumers to respond by increasing the use of substitutes for energy. Additional insulation is a substitute for energy consumption in a current home. Some of the substitutions may occur over longer periods of time. For example, a consumer may purchase a more energy-efficient house or one in a warmer climate.

Price, Elasticity, and Total Revenue

Once you understand the basic concept of price elasticity of demand, there is more you can do. There is a useful relationship between the price and the total revenue of the seller. Total revenue is the money the firm collects by selling the good (price times quantity sold). If demand is elastic, price and total revenue move in the opposite direction, an inverse relation. If demand is inelastic, price and total revenue move in the same direction, a direct relation. As a seller, would you expect to increase your total revenue by raising or lowering your price? It depends upon the elasticity of demand for your good.

What if demand for your product were elastic? This means that, due to the nature of the product and the attitude of the buyers, buyers will be sensitive to a change in price. If there were an increase in the price, your total revenue would fall. The reduction in quantity sold will more than offset the higher selling price on the units that you were able to sell. Total revenue will be less at the higher price. The reason becomes clear as you think about the meaning of elastic demand: the percentage change in the quantity demanded is greater than the percentage change in the price. Then, as price goes up, total revenue will be a slightly higher price times a much reduced quantity. The result is a reduction in total revenue. Contrast this to the total revenue resulting from a lowering of price with the same elastic demand. The slightly lower price will be multiplied by a greatly increased quantity. Total revenue will be greater when price is lowered if demand is elastic.

The preceding discussion established that if demand is elastic, price and total revenue are inversely related. Let us approach this relation from the point of view of the buyer. Total revenue to the seller is total spending for the buyer. They are one and the same thing seen from different sides of the counter that separates buyer and seller. Total spending is again price times quantity. So as the price of the good with elastic demand increases, the total spending on the good falls, as will the total revenue of the seller. Although the consumer is paying a higher price on each unit bought, even fewer units are purchased. When referring to price elasticity, the terms total revenue and total spending can be interchanged.

A seller faced with inelastic demand normally does not wish for the price to fall, as the result will be a fall in total revenue. Buyers would not buy that much more at the lower price, and the relatively small increase in quantity would not begin to make up for the greater reduction in price on all units that were sold. A seller faced with an inelastic demand would rather raise price and,

Table 8-3   Relation among Price, Total Revenue, and Elasticity

	Demand Is		
	Elastic	Inelastic	Unitary
If price	then total revenue		
rises	falls	rises	does not change
falls	rises	falls	does not change

This table provides a summary of the effect of a change in price on total revenue, depending on whether demand is elastic, inelastic or unitary.

consequently, total revenue. If the elasticity of demand is unitary, then there is no change in total revenue as price changes. The change in the price is exactly canceled by the change in the quantity. You will find the relationships among price, total revenue, and elasticity summarized in Table 8-3.

Bananas and Oil

At one time, the banana-producing nations of the world considered banding together. Their plan was to force through a worldwide increase in banana prices to increase their revenues. You are probably not aware of this attempt at extortion because, after some thought, it was abandoned. Why? Bananas have highly elastic demand. There are many acceptable substitutes for bananas, and they are considered a luxury, or at least something that we can do without. So if the price of bananas increases, many fewer bananas would be purchased. The total amount spent by consumers would be considerably less than before the price increase. The few extra cents that some people would pay for bananas would be more than offset by many people buying many fewer bananas, or no bananas at all. Total spending would fall and so would total revenue. If the banana-producing nations had followed through with their plan to increase revenue by raising price, they would have failed.

However, inelastic demand is an entirely different matter. The banana producers were only planning to imitate the oil-producing nations that had banded together to form OPEC (Organization of Petroleum Exporting Countries). During the 1970s, OPEC had deliberately decreased production and increased the world price of oil. The outcome for oil producers was dramatically different from the potential outcome for banana producers. OPEC made sound use of economic principles. The demand for petroleum, and its resulting products of gasoline and home heating oil, and so on, is highly inelastic. With inelastic demand, price and total revenue are directly related. Thus, as the price of petroleum increased, so did the total revenue for OPEC. Buyers consider gasoline, for example, to be a necessity, and there are not many acceptable substitutes immediately available, at least for the fuel tank. So as the price of gasoline went up, consumers did buy less — but not much less. And since the price of each gallon purchased was so much greater than before, the new total spending was higher. Consumers spent more for less gasoline than before. OPEC accomplished its objective. As it increased the price of its good, total revenue also increased.

Our discussion of OPEC has only considered the short-run impacts of an increase in price. What would you expect to happen to the elasticity of demand for gasoline over longer periods of time? Since over time demand is more elastic, you should expect that the price increase would encourage consumers to find substitutes for the now more expensive gasoline. Consumers would look for cars that would reduce fuel consumption, or they would switch to other less expensive fuels such as gasohol. They might move closer to their jobs, or they might carpool. Notice that these choices are not made right away, since people do not routinely switch cars or move to avoid higher-priced fuels. Because demand for gasoline is more elastic in the long run, as the price rose, the quantity demanded of oil products fell and the quantity supplied remained high, so that a surplus of oil hit the market. There were other economic factors that also contributed to this outcome, but in any case OPEC had to lower the price of oil.

Although we now know how total revenue and price are related, we do not have enough information to determine the amount of output (and consequently price) that the firm would prefer. Why not? The cost of production must also be known before the output level can be chosen. This discussion continues in the next module.

▶ Summary

In this chapter you have seen how an economist measures the responsiveness of the quantity demanded to a change in the price. The term the economist uses to represent this measurement is price elasticity. You have learned that the elasticity of demand for a given good depends on various determinants: whether the good is considered a luxury or necessity, the availability of acceptable substitutes, the percentage of the budget, and the length of time under consideration. The relationship between price and total revenue indicates whether demand is elastic or inelastic. If price and total revenue are inversely related, demand is elastic. If price and total revenue are directly related, demand is inelastic.

You have now completed this module, which included discussions of demand, supply, equilibrium, and price elasticity of demand. You have learned much about the workings of the basic supply and demand model. You have also been told that it is not a model that can be applied in all circumstances. To obtain a deeper understanding of the supply portion of the model, and to find how price is determined if the competitive conditions do not hold, we will now turn to the decision process of the producer.

▶ **Key Concepts**

elasticity   unitary elasticity
   (price elasticity of demand)   perfectly inelastic
coefficient of price elasticity   perfectly elastic
elastic   determinants of price elasticity
inelastic   elasticity and total revenue

▶ **Discussion Questions**

1. If the price of a good falls by 10 percent, identify the price elasticity of demand from the following responses:
   a. 20 percent more is bought.
   b. 10 percent more is bought.
   c. 5 percent more is bought.
2. Harvey has electric heat and says that he needs electricity. No matter what the price, he says he will pay it to keep warm. Harvey is denying the law of demand. Will Harvey respond to a change in price? What information is Harvey giving about the elasticity of demand? Might there a difference between Harvey's demand this winter and next winter? Explain.
3. Suppose that you are an apple grower. Would you expect the demand for your apples to be more elastic or more inelastic? Why?
4. Why is it that a bumper crop may make farmers worse off financially?
5. Many private colleges are faced with falling enrollment. However, they fear that if they lower their price to attract more students, their revenue would not be enough to cover their costs. State a case where this may not be true.
6. So So Products is concerned with falling revenues and therefore increases its price. This may be a fatal mistake. Why?
7. What if the world's diamond producers restrict output in an effort to increase total revenue? Are they likely to be successful? Explain.

▶ **Self-Review**

• Fill in the blanks

elasticity

quantity demanded

price

The response of the buyer to a change in price is measured by the concept of _____. The elasticity of demand is calculated by dividing the percentage change in the _____ by the percentage change in _____. If the buyer is relatively responsive to the change in price, the coefficient is greater than the number

1, elastic	_____ and demand is said to be _____. If the buyer is not so responsive to the change in price, the coefficient is
less, inelastic	_____ than 1 and demand is _____. And if the percentage change in the price and in the quantity are
equal to	identical, the coefficient is _____ 1, and demand
unitary elastic	is _____. A vertical demand curve is
inelastic	perfectly _____, while a horizontal demand curve is
perfectly elastic	_____. The determinants of price elasticity
necessity	are whether the buyer views the good as a _____ or a
luxury, substitutes	_____, the availability of acceptable _____, and
budget	how large a part of the _____ the good is. For a necessity,
less	demand is _____ elastic; if there are many substitutes, demand
more	is _____ elastic; if the good is a large part of the budget,
more	demand is _____ elastic. In addition, the longer the length
more	of time, the _____ elastic the demand. We know that price
elastic	and total revenue are inversely related if demand is _____.
	And if price and total revenue are directly related, demand
inelastic	is _____. This means that to increase total revenue, if
lowered	demand is elastic, price should be _____. When price
	changes and there is no change in total revenue, we know
unitary elastic	demand to be _____.

- Multiple choice

1. Elastic demand means that:
   a. the percentage change in the quantity demanded is <u>greater</u> than the percentage change in price.
   b. the percentage change in the quantity demanded is <u>less</u> than the percentage change in price.
   c. the percentage change in the quantity demanded is <u>equal</u> to the percentage change in price.
   d. none of the above.
2. If the coefficient of elasticity is less than one, then demand is:
   a. elastic.
   b. inelastic.
   c. of unitary elasticity.
   d. impossible to tell.
3. If the quantity demanded changes by 10 percent as price changes by 10 percent, then demand is:
   a. elastic.
   b. inelastic.

    c. of unitary elasticity

    d. cannot tell.

4. For which good is demand more likely to be inelastic?

    a. An inexpensive good.

    b. A good with lots of substitutes.

    c. The luxury good.

    d. Good Y over a long period of time.

5. If price increases when demand is elastic, then:

    a. total revenue increases.

    b. total revenue decreases.

    c. total revenue stays the same.

    d. supply increases.

Answers: 1.a, 2.b, 3.c, 4.a, 5.b.

Module | 3 | BEHIND THE SUPPLY CURVE

Each day of your life you interact with firms. You buy the goods they produce, and you supply the resources they use. More than once in your life you have probably wondered why some product was so expensive. Other times you may have wondered why some wages are so high and others so low. Your choice of career may depend in part on the earnings you expect to make. All of these concerns revolve around firms and the prices they charge or the wages they pay. Can there be any doubt that the decisions firms make have an impact on your life? Because of this impact, the study of the decision-making process of the firm plays a major role in this book.

Before we can start the study of the decision-making process of a firm, you should be clear about what a firm is. A firm is an organization whose main function is to produce a good or service for sale. A firm can be a bicycle producer, a doctor, a college, or a chimney sweep. An industry is a collection of firms all producing the same good. You should carefully distinguish the firm from the industry. When we are talking about the price for the industry, we will say the market or industry price. When we are talking about the price the firm charges, we will say the firm's price. Similar comments apply to the amount of output produced. Since the two, the industry and firm, are not always the same, they must be distinguished. So be aware that the distinction is there and that it is important.

The decision-making process of the firm is the common theme of the next eight chapters. The firm is the production unit in the economy, the resource user and producer of output that becomes supply. By looking at how firms behave, we are examining how the supply decision is made. For the firm, supply tells the amount to produce at each price.

You may wonder why the supply decision requires eight chapters. The supply decision is only made after the firm has carefully combined many pieces of information. Let us try to visualize the direction this module will take and the importance of the individual bits of information. You should be aware that the concepts that are to be discussed are closely related and that they will be used to build, step by step, toward the conclusions of this module. Pay close attention when concepts are being built upon concepts, or you may find that the whole structure collapses. For now, try to get a feel for the pattern that is being developed.

We start this module with a basic assumption that the firm is interested in profit. Profit is what the firm takes in (revenue or sales) minus the cost of production. So to determine profit, the firm needs to know its cost and revenue.

The two basic things that determine cost are the technology and the price of the inputs. The way in which inputs are put together to make the good is called technology. Once the technology is chosen, the amount of each input needed to produce any level of output can be determined. So one thing the firm needs in order to determine the cost of production is the technology, and the other is the price of the inputs.

Revenue is found from the price the product will sell for and the quantity to be sold. What do the price and quantity depend upon? The answer is how many other firms there are selling the good and how the other firms react to our firm's price and quantity decisions. So the revenue will be affected by the market structure in which the firm competes.

So far we have mentioned three factors affecting the firm's profit: the technology, the input prices, and the structure of the market for output. Using these factors, the firm chooses to produce that quantity of output that will yield the greatest possible profit. How are all these things put together to find supply? The economics of the firm and the firm's role in the allocation of resources is called the theory of the firm. That is what the next eight chapters are about.

By reducing the decision process of a business to its basic elements, we will see that all firms find solutions to issues such as price and output in the same manner. Thus we can evolve a set of simple statements that can describe the behavior of firms in terms of price and output, and therefore supply.

What is the impact of the firm's behavior on society? Resources will be used and output produced to provide satisfaction to consumers. But have the resources been used in a manner to create the greatest possible satisfaction for the society? That will depend upon the economic environment in which the firm operates and whether there are favorable pressures within this environment. Society must decide how it wants the environment shaped, and to do so, we as members of society should have a basic understanding of the economic forces at work.

You will have many opportunities to apply your knowledge of supply, demand, and market equilibrium in the following chapters. Do not hesitate to review Chapter 7 if you feel it necessary.

The next eight chapters involve the concepts that lead to the supply of output and the demand for inputs. In Chapter 9, diminishing returns is discussed. This is a fundamental law affecting the relationship of input and output. Cost is the topic of Chapter 10. Diminishing returns will affect cost. In Chapter 11, revenue and market structure are introduced. Chapter 12 examines profit by putting together the revenue ideas of Chapter 11 with the cost ideas of Chapter 10. The supply of the perfectly competitive firm is determined in Chapter 13, and monopoly is evaluated in Chapter 14. There we will be able to see how a different market structure affects profit. Chapter 15 looks at market structures other than perfect competition and monopoly. And, finally, Chapter 16 examines how a firm determines the amount of labor it should hire. From this evolves the demand for labor. When this demand is put together with labor supply, wages are determined. Well, start the next chapter. There you will bake cakes and grow tomatoes.

| Chapter | 9 | DIMINISHING RETURNS |

Key Topics

short run and long run
fixed and variable inputs
total and marginal product
diminishing returns

Goals

learn the concepts of total and marginal product
recognize the law of diminishing returns
understand why diminishing returns is true

Although economic concepts continually shape our lives, some concepts are not obvious and require very careful observation to detect. One of these is the law of diminishing returns. This concept, like scarcity, is a basic condition that is unavoidable, and its effects are everywhere. Diminishing returns is important because it is a basic ingredient of a firm's costs. Cost helps to determine supply, and supply and demand together determine how resources are used. So diminishing returns plays a major role in the solution of the resource allocation problem.

Suppose that you were recently hired by a bakery to bake cakes. Before you started work, you went home and practiced. You were able to bake 10 cakes a day. Would you expect to increase output at the bakery by 10 cakes? Does the number of cakes you produce at the bakery depend only upon you, or are there other determining factors? What happens to output if even more bakers are hired? When you understand diminishing returns, you will know what happens to output as an input increases. Before the law of diminishing returns is stated, some concepts used in the statement of the law will be defined and explained.

The Short Run and Variable Inputs

The first step toward understanding the law of diminishing returns is to recognize when the law applies. The major consideration is the time period. The short-run period of time is the only time period in which the law operates. You will soon realize that diminishing returns cannot be avoided in the short run. The short run must be carefully distinguished from the long run. The **short run** is a period of time in which at least one of the factors of production is fixed. The **fixed factors** of production, as the name indicates, are the inputs that cannot be increased during the short-run productive process. These inputs cannot be increased in number to produce more of a good during the short run. However, the **variable factors** of production, or variable inputs, are those inputs that can be increased during production. All inputs, both fixed and variable, are the familiar scarce resources — land, labor, capital, and entrepreneurship.

Each productive process uses variable inputs in combination with at least one fixed input in the short run. A productive process uses inputs and transforms them into output, some consumer or capital good. The mowing of the family lawn is itself a productive process, contrary to the opinion of many of those who must mow. There are inputs, both variable and fixed, and the output is a mowed lawn — a consumer good. The variable inputs — labor, mower, and gasoline — can be increased. The size of the lawn is a fixed factor. The existence of a fixed factor always identifies a short-run productive process.

Land is usually a fixed factor for a farmer. At the time the farmer plows and plants, there is a limited amount of land available. More tractors, more seed, more fertilizer can always be added, but only to a fixed amount of land. You might suggest that the farmer obtain more land by purchasing an adjoining farm. But if this addition to the farmer's land occurs, the time period has changed. If land is no longer a fixed factor, then all the inputs are variable. This fits the description of the long run. The **long run** is a period of time in which all inputs to the productive process are variable. Recognize that the critical distinction between the short and the long run is that *only* in the short run are there fixed factors.

Total and Marginal Product

The concepts of total and marginal will be used repeatedly in this text. You can simplify later chapters by giving special attention to these concepts now. This chapter concentrates on the distinction between total and marginal product. You will find this identical distinction made later between total and marginal cost, and then again with total and marginal revenue.

Product is the output that is produced. Product, output, and returns are terms that are often interchanged. **Total product (TP)** is the total output produced by the inputs of a firm. Normally one expects that as the inputs increase, so must the total product. As you will soon discover, this expected increase in total product may not happen.

Marginal means extra or additional. **Marginal product (MP)** is the change in total product as one more unit of variable input is added to the productive process. Marginal product measures the contribution to total production of another unit of input. The marginal product assists in the decision whether to employ another unit. This decision is discussed in Chapter 16.

Table 9-1 illustrates the concepts of total and marginal product with production figures from your home tomato garden. Assume that your garden fills your yard and that the only variable input is identical sacks of fertilizer. Column 1 is the units of the variable input. This column indicates the number of sacks of fertilizer used, represented by F, increasing the sacks one at a time. Always keep in mind that the only type of input that can be increased is the variable factor. The second column indicates the land, the fixed factor, which cannot be varied at this point in time due to the unwillingness of your neighbors to give up their property. Column 3 records the total product — the total output of tomatoes — after each sack of fertilizer is added. The total product is found by counting the tomatoes that would be produced if that number of sacks were applied.

Total product uses only one technology, yet there may be many possible technologies. Technology is the knowledge required to turn inputs into output. How else could you grow tomatoes in your yard? Would you need a tractor? A pair of oxen? A mule? A hoe? A different type of tomato plant? And how much labor? Fertilizer? Water? You may not need a tractor if your yard is small, but a tractor is one alternative. The point is, there is a choice of technologies available to grow tomatoes. You will get different amounts of output depending on the combination of inputs used. The total product will depend upon the technology. If technology improves, then the total product will increase.

The marginal product of a sack of fertilizer is recorded in column 4. The marginal product of the first sack of fertilizer is 50 tomatoes, which is found by subtracting the zero total product at zero sacks from the total product of 50 at 1 sack. Recall that marginal product is the change in the total product by the addition of one more unit of variable input. How much does total product change when the first sack of fertilizer is added? In other words, what is the contribution of the first sack of fertilizer to output? The answer is 50, the marginal product of the first sack. Consider the following expression (Δ means "the change in"):

$$\text{MP} = \text{marginal product} = \frac{\text{the change in total product}}{\text{the change in variable input}} = \frac{\Delta TP}{\Delta \text{input}}$$

We are adding only one sack of fertilizer at a time, so the change in input in Table 9-1 is always 1. Since we are therefore always dividing by 1, the marginal product will always be the change in the total product when one more unit of variable input is added. This is precisely the definition given for marginal product. Notice that the marginal product of the second sack is 150 tomatoes, which is the total product of the second sack, 200, minus the total product of the first sack, 50.

There are three distinct phases to marginal product. The first phase occurs when the MP is positive and increasing. This phase is called increasing returns.

Table 9-1   The Product Schedules: Tomatoes

(1) Fertilizer Sacks (F)	(2) Land	(3) Total Product (TP)	(4) Marginal Product ($\Delta TP/\Delta F$)	
0	1	0		
1	1	50	50	increasing
2	1	200	150	returns
3	1	360	160	
4	1	500	140	
5	1	620	120	decreasing
6	1	720	100	returns
7	1	770	50	
8	1	800	30	
9	1	810	10	
10	1	800	−10	negative returns

This table illustrates several concepts. In column 1, you will find the quantities of the variable input, F, fertilizer. The quantity of the fixed input is found in column 2. Note that no land is added beyond the first unit. The total product — total output — is measured in tomatoes and is found in column 3. The marginal product is the change in output due to the change in the variable input; the marginal product is found in column 4.

This phase occurs through the third sack of fertilizer. Although MP may rise at first, it eventually falls. In the second phase, the MP begins to decrease but is still positive. This phase of diminishing returns sets in when sack 4 is applied and continues through sack 9. When MP starts to fall, diminishing returns has set in and continues forever. Finally, MP decreases to the point where it is negative. In the third phase, MP, which is still decreasing, is negative. Negative returns occur from the tenth sack through any additional sacks.

How much total output can be produced? Isn't it just a matter of adding more input? No. There is a physical limit to the total product determined by the particular technology used. A different technology would generally result in a different limit to the total product. Given the technology used in Table 9-1, more variable inputs may be added beyond sack 9, but output will not be increased beyond 810 tomatoes. There the marginal product becomes negative, and the output added by each added unit of input is negative. Hence the total product falls. Now you should recognize that additional inputs may not always increase production.

The Law of Diminishing Returns

The **law of diminishing returns** states that as an increasing amount of a variable factor is added to a fixed factor, the marginal product of the variable factor will eventually fall. This short statement is deceptively simple, so carefully consider the meaning of the words.

Since variable inputs are added to a *fixed* factor, this law clearly applies to the short run but not the long run. As additional units of input are added, which in the short run can only be variable inputs, at some point the marginal, extra, output per unit of input will decline. The law does not specify which sack of fertilizer will first produce fewer tomatoes than a previous sack. The law does not identify when diminishing returns sets in; the law just states that it will. The law is very much like a fortune-teller, predicting an outcome, but vague with the exact details. As more sacks are added, the law of diminishing returns simply predicts that the extra production of tomatoes added by some extra sack of fertilizer must eventually fall.

In Table 9-1, sack 2 has an MP greater than sack 1. This is increasing returns; diminishing returns has not yet set in. Sack 3 is also in the increasing returns phase. But sack 4 contributes less extra output of tomatoes than did the previous sack. Diminishing returns has set in with the fourth sack. Sooner or later one more unit of variable input will be added to a productive process, such as sack 4, and its marginal product, the extra contribution to output of that unit, will be less than that of the previous unit. This is the point of diminishing returns.

It seems that the law can be avoided if more "fixed" as well as variable inputs were to be added to the productive process. But that puts us in the long run. The law of diminishing returns makes no prediction about the outcome when all inputs are variable. At the moment of production, certain inputs cannot be increased, such as land. Although we may add more land over time, at the point in time when we start production, we have only so much land, and a short-run condition exists. As a result, the law will set in as we add more variable inputs to the fixed amount of land. Production occurs in the short run. Diminishing returns is a short-run condition that cannot be avoided.

What is the explanation for diminishing returns? This law reflects two concepts that you have already studied: one, that some resources are fixed, and two, that resources are not perfect substitutes for one another. In the short run there are factors that cannot be increased at that point in time: the factory, the land, the number of pages in a book, the tools you have to work with, or the size of the operating room. In Chapter 3 you discovered that resources are not perfect substitutes for one another. Since it is not possible to increase the size of the garden space in our tomato example, you must substitute other inputs to increase the production of tomatoes. You are unable to increase the fixed factor, land, but the variable factor, sacks of fertilizer, can be increased to compensate. Yet more fertilizer, while productive, cannot completely substitute for the productive capabilities of land. Since fertilizer and land are not perfect substitutes, more and more fertilizer will be required to achieve each additional unit of increase in output. This means that the marginal product will fall. Consequently, we *can* increase output by increasing the variable input and substituting the variable input in place of more of the fixed factor, *but* the limitation imposed by the fixed factor dictates that the marginal product of the variable factor must eventually diminish.

Changing the factor to be varied will not avoid diminishing returns. What if the variable factor of the tomato example were labor rather than fertilizer? The first worker will plant the seed, fertilize, weed, water, and harvest. All inputs except labor are held constant. The fixed factors include a single hoe, fertilizer, seed, water, and land. If we hire another worker, the output will increase even though no more seed was planted, no more fertilizer was applied, and the same hoe was used. The marginal product of the second worker is the addition to total output when that worker is hired. If we increase labor to 3, the extra output (above what the first 2 workers produce) will be the marginal product of the third unit of labor. What eventually happens to the marginal product generated by each added unit of labor? It must fall. There are just so many seeds to plant, there is just so much fertilizer to spread, only so many weeds to hoe, and only so many plants to water and harvest. Soon each additional worker will add less to output than the previous worker. Why?

Diminishing Returns Explored

One explanation for diminishing returns is that the single hoe can be used by only one worker at a time. When the second worker is added, the hoe need not be idle while the first worker waters or fertilizes. Eventually, enough labor will be hired so that the hoe is always in use. When the next worker is hired, some labor may have to wait for the hoe to be free or substitute their hands, a less productive method. When we add more labor, the added output from an additional worker will soon decline. As more labor is substituted for the fixed factors, and since resources are not perfect substitutes, the effect will be felt in diminishing returns. If we try to increase production by increasing only labor or any other variable factor, the marginal productivity of the variable factor must eventually fall.

Can we avoid diminishing returns by changing the order in which the variable inputs are added? As we began the tomato illustration in Table 9-1, we were adding additional fertilizer. A change in the order in which we applied the identical sacks would not change any of the numbers in the marginal product column. Switching sack 2 with sack 3 would make no difference whatsoever in the marginal product of the second sack that is applied or the marginal product of the third sack that is applied. Now that the variable input is labor rather than fertilizer, it still makes no difference whether we hire the fifth person first and the first person fifth. Diminishing returns has nothing to do with the order in which the inputs are used, nor is there any assumption that one worker is more or less capable than another. Eventually, the marginal product must diminish.

Once diminishing returns sets in, the marginal product will continue to fall forever. Diminishing returns begins at the first level of input where the marginal product is not as great as for the previous unit of input. In Table 9-1 as each additional sack of fertilizer is added after this fourth sack, the marginal product continues to fall. Once diminishing returns has set in, it does not reverse itself. Once the marginal product has started to diminish, it will always diminish. There comes a point where adding more fertilizer not only decreases marginal product, but actually decreases total product. If total product falls, it is because marginal product is negative. How can fertilizer contribute negative bushels of tomatoes? Sack 10 does in Table 9-1. Too much fertilizer burns or buries the plants. This added fertilizer actually reduces output.

Labor as the variable input can also contribute negative returns. How can a worker possibly contribute negative tomatoes (without eating the tomatoes)? The negative marginal product happens because the added worker interferes with the existing workers. The worker may make a personal contribution to output but, in so doing, prevents other workers from achieving their potential contribution. The result is a negative marginal product. One explanation is that the fixed factor (such as a hoe) is being shared by an increasing number of variable inputs (workers) so that the workers no longer have sufficient fixed factor to employ and maintain their previous productivity. The added worker may appear to be adding to total production, but his or her use of the hoe reduces the contribution of the other workers so that the total produced by all workers is less. Total product falls, and the marginal product of this worker is negative. Through any fault of this worker? No. Diminishing returns.

Diminishing returns is not a law passed by the legislature. But there is every reason to believe that the law is true. It is like the law of gravity in that all of our experience seems to confirm it, and we do not know of cases where it is not true. What if increasing returns were the rule instead? What would happen? The marginal product would continue to rise as more input is added. Each unit of input would add more to output than the last unit of input. Hence total output would grow faster and faster and never stop growing. If we start with a flower pot full of dirt and add more units of a food-producing input containing a standard amount of seed, fertilizer, and water, we would get more and more extra output. Each unit of input would produce even more extra food than the unit before it. We could soon feed the entire population of the world out of that flower pot. Even more amazing, we could eventually add just one more unit of input and the food-producing capacity of that single unit alone could more than feed the world. Yet this does not happen. We cannot feed humanity using all the land that is available, let alone one flower pot. It is most unfortunate that the law of diminishing returns is true and that scarcity must be encountered.

Remember being hired as a cake baker in the beginning of the chapter? At that time we could not answer the question, "Could you increase the bakery's output by 10 cakes per day, the number you could produce at home?" Now you have the answer. Your impact on the bakery's output will depend on the mix of fixed and variable factors. If the bakery already has 100 bakers and 3 ovens, you will probably have little impact on the output. If, on the other hand, you are the third baker, you may be able to add many more than 10 cakes to the daily output. Your productivity depends not only upon you, but upon a consideration beyond your control — the law of diminishing returns.

▶ Summary

The major concept highlighted by this chapter is the law of diminishing returns. The law of diminishing returns is critical to an understanding of the basic realities around us. This law occurs during a productive process and affects the technological relation between inputs and output. Diminishing returns is a short-run condition that requires at least one fixed factor to be present. The source of the law of diminishing returns is the existence of a fixed factor together with the fact that resources are not perfect substitutes for one another.

In this chapter several other important topics were covered. Total product, a relationship reflecting technology, was introduced. Another production concept, marginal product, was obtained from total product. This concept will have a later use.

You may wonder why these production concepts are so important. They represent technology, the relationship between inputs and output. Technology is one determinant of the cost of the firm. And cost partially determines profit. Profit is the concept that will lead us to supply and the allocation of society's scarce resources. Before we can discuss profit and supply, we must first discuss cost, the subject of the next chapter.

▶ Key Concepts

short run   total product
fixed factor   marginal product
variable factor   law of diminishing returns
long run

▶ Discussion Questions

1. In which industry will the long run be longer, the steel industry or the corner lemonade stand? Explain why.
2. Explain why diminishing returns occurs.

3. "Okay, diminishing returns is a nice textbook idea, but the real world is not like that. At my dad's business, we add more machines and more labor, and output increases more and more. So I know that the law of diminishing returns is not true." What are the flaws in this statement?

4. In his 1830 essay on population, Thomas Malthus predicted that world population would increase faster than food production and that mass starvation would result. The increase in food would be limited by diminishing returns. But Malthus's prediction has not come true. World agricultural production has not yet encountered diminishing returns. Can you explain why not?

5. What is wrong with this statement? "Diminishing returns only applies to capitalistic societies. In communist societies, the government can move any factor it wants so all factors are variable."

6. Calculate the marginal product of labor from this data. Average product, column 4, can be found by dividing total product, column 2, by the quantity of the variable input (labor), column 1. For the first unit of labor, the average product is 10/1 or 10. Fill in the rest of the average products. Are the average product and marginal product the same concept? Upon the addition of which worker does diminishing returns set in?

(1) Labor (L)	(2) Total Product (TP)	(3) Marginal Product ($\Delta TP/\Delta L$)	(4) Average Product (TP/L)
0	0	–	–
1	10		10
2	22		
3	30		
4	36		
5	40		
6	42		
7	35		

7. Draw a graph of marginal product. Put labor on the horizontal axis and marginal product on the vertical axis. Use the data from question 6. Describe how marginal product changes as output increases.

8. If you had unlimited resources except for one fixed factor, could you produce unlimited output? Explain.

▶ Self-Review

- Fill in the blanks

fixed, increased	In the short run at least one of the factors of production is _____. The fixed factors cannot be _____
short run	during the _____ period of time. Those factors that can be increased during the short run are called
variable factors	_____. In the long run all factors are
variable, extra, additional	_____. Marginal means _____ or _____.
marginal	The change in the total product by the addition of one more unit of the variable input is the _____
product	_____. There are three phases of the marginal
increasing, diminishing	product: _____ returns as well as _____
negative, diminishing	returns, and _____ returns. The law of _____
increased	returns states that as an _____ amount of a
variable, fixed	_____ factor is added to a _____ factor, the
marginal, variable	_____ product of the _____ factor will
fall	eventually _____. Diminishing returns only applies in the
short	_____ run because only in this time period are there
fixed	_____ factors. Once diminishing returns sets in, the
fall	marginal product continues to _____. Diminishing returns is due to the existence of a fixed factor together with the
perfect substitutes	fact that resources are not _____ for one another.

• Multiple choice

1. In the long run:
   a. only the fixed factors are variable.
   b. only the variable factors are variable.
   c. all factors are variable.
   d. no factors are variable.
2. Which process finds the marginal product?
   a. Marginal product is the total product produced by the inputs.
   b. The marginal product is found by dividing the total product by the amount of variable input.
   c. The marginal product is the change in total product as one more unit of the variable input is added.
   d. None of the above.
3. If total product goes from 622 at the fifth unit of labor to 629 at the sixth, the marginal product of the sixth unit of labor is:
   a. 629.
   b. 7.
   c. 12.
   d. cannot be determined.

4. When diminishing returns sets in, the marginal product which was rising:
   a. falls and continues to fall.
   b. falls and then rises.
   c. continues to rise.
   d. remains constant.
5. The law of diminishing returns:
   a. is a short run occurrence.
   b. can occur in either the short or long run.
   c. occurs only in the long run.
   d. is only a textbook concept.

Answers: 1.c, 2.c, 3.b, 4.a, 5.a.

Chapter	10	COST

Key Topics
   total cost
   implicit cost
   average total cost
   marginal cost
   the average-marginal relation

Goals
   understand how costs behave and why
   understand how cost concepts are related
   relate marginal cost to marginal product and diminishing returns

Your first introduction to cost was opportunity cost in Chapter 1. Opportunity costs are always present in decision making. In the case of the firm, one opportunity cost is the cost of producing output. The cost of production is the subject of this chapter. Cost is important since it is part of the information the firm needs to decide the amount of output to supply. Supply, together with demand, determines price and how resources are allocated in a market.

When you have completed this chapter, you will have an understanding of how cost behaves when output changes. An important lesson from the study of cost is that different costs follow predictable patterns. One thing you will learn is what the patterns are and another is what causes the patterns. Different cost concepts answer different questions for the firm, so we will break cost down into three different groups. These groups are total cost, average cost, and marginal cost.

Total Cost

Your study of cost begins with the group of total cost. The total cost group is composed of three cost concepts: total fixed cost, total variable cost, and total cost. These will be discussed starting with total fixed cost. **Total fixed cost (TFC)** is the cost that does not change with the level of output. This means that the total fixed cost remains the same, or constant, whether zero or an infinite amount of output is produced. Fixed cost is not related to the level of production. Fixed cost occurs because in the short run, there is at least one factor that cannot be changed. The cost of the fixed factor is the fixed cost. The cost of this factor does not depend on the level of output produced because the amount of the factor, and therefore its cost, remains unchanged. Examples of total fixed cost are rent, insurance, and taxes. The license plate fee is a fixed cost of operating a car. The fee remains the same regardless of how many miles the vehicle is driven. If you leave your car in the garage for a year, the state still expects the same payment. The license plate fee is not related to the amount of transportation produced by the car.

A graph of total fixed cost makes the concept clear. If cost is measured on the vertical axis, and the units of output on the horizontal, total fixed cost is a horizontal line as shown in Figure 10-1. For 2 units of output, the total fixed cost is $60, as it is at 10 units and all other units of output. The fixed cost is also recorded in Table 10-1. Observe that the total fixed cost remains $60 even at zero output. If in the short run the firm shuts down, it still must pay its fixed cost. Regardless of the output level, the fixed cost remains a constant amount.

Fixed cost can change, but the change is due to changes other than in the level of production. Property taxes may change, insurance premiums may go

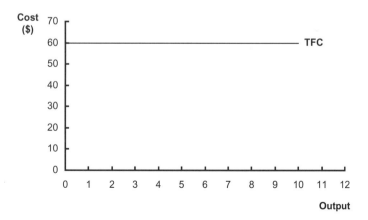

Figure 10-1 Total Fixed Cost Curve
The total fixed cost is the same at every level of output including zero output. Thus the total fixed cost is a horizontal line.

Table 10-1   Total Fixed Cost Schedule

Output (Q)	Total Fixed Cost (TFC)
1	$60
2	60
3	60
4	60
5	60
6	60
7	60
8	60
9	60
10	60
11	60

This table lists the total fixed cost at each level of output. At all output, the total fixed cost is $60. This means that no matter how much or little the firm produces, the firm must always pay $60 in fixed cost even if no output is produced.

up, or the property owner may decide to lower the rent. If the fixed cost in Table 10-1 and Figure 10-1 were to increase from $60 to $80, it would remain $80 at all levels of production, and would not change as output changes.

Not all costs are fixed. There are costs of operating an automobile that do change with the miles driven. Gasoline and oil, as well as maintenance, are examples of these costs. **Total variable cost (TVC)** are those costs that change with the level of output. If the car is not driven at all, the variable cost will be zero. The more miles the car is driven, the greater is the variable cost. Variable cost can include labor, raw materials, capital, and energy. As more inputs are purchased and output is increased, variable cost rises. Total variable cost always increases with the level of output as Table 10-2 illustrates.

The total variable cost curve is plotted in Figure 10-2. Observe that the total variable cost curve must begin at the origin, the point of zero production on the graph. When no output is produced, there is no need to pay the cost of labor, raw materials, and other inputs that will not be used. At zero output, the total variable cost is zero. But once production begins, and once production increases, so will the total variable cost. For example, at 4 units of output, the

Table 10-2   Total Variable Cost Schedule

Output (Q)	Total Variable Cost (TVC)
0	$ 0
1	45
2	60
3	72
4	80
5	90
6	102
7	116
8	136
9	162
10	200
11	242

Total variable costs are the costs that vary with the level of output produced. As the level of output goes up, more resources are needed so the variable cost of production rises.

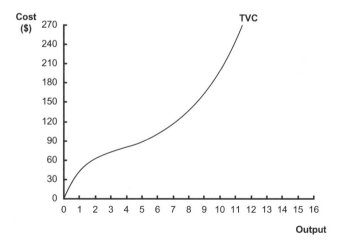

Figure 10-2   Total Variable Cost Curve
This graph of the total variable cost uses the data in Table 10-2. You can see that the TVC goes through the origin, so that at zero output, the firm has zero variable cost. The TVC rises first slowly, through unit 4, and then more quickly, but always rises.

total variable cost is $80, and $90 for 5 units of output. The total variable cost always rises with an increase in output, but total variable cost rises at different rates. Notice how the curve seems to rise very slowly at first and then how the curve seems to begin a very rapid rise around the fourth unit. Diminishing returns has a key role in determining the shape of the total variable cost curve.

Understanding total cost is now as simple as adding two numbers together. **Total cost (TC)** is the sum of the fixed cost and the variable cost at each level of output. Figure 10-3, drawn from Table 10-3, graphs the total cost group. Total cost is the highest curve since it is the total of both the fixed cost curve and the variable cost curve beneath it. This means that at each output level, 5, for example, the TC is the $150 sum of the TFC of $60 and the TVC of $90. Note carefully that at zero output, the total cost is equal to the total fixed cost. This is because the total variable cost is always zero at a zero output level; therefore, a TFC of $60 and a TVC of $0 combine to yield a TC of $60, which is the same as the TFC.

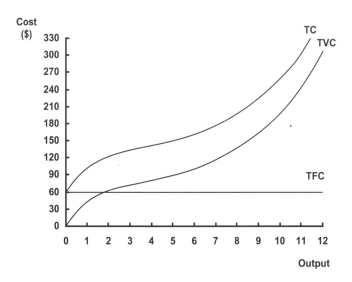

Figure 10-3   Total Cost Group
This graph shows the total cost curves on the same graph. The total fixed cost is the horizontal curve. The total variable cost is the curve that starts at the origin and rises. The total cost curve is the sum of these two. At each level of output, we add the total fixed cost and the total variable cost. Thus at zero output, the total cost is $60, the sum of the fixed cost, $60, and the zero variable cost. This process is continued at each level of output.

Table 10-3 Total Cost Group

Output (Q)	Total Fixed Cost (TFC)	+	Total Variable Cost (TVC)	=	Total Cost (TC)
0	$60		$ 0		$60
1	60		45		105
2	60		60		120
3	60		72		132
4	60		80		140
5	60		90		150
6	60		102		162
7	60		116		176
8	60		136		196
9	60		162		222
10	60		200		260
11	60		242		302

This table shows the total cost concepts. The total fixed cost and the total variable cost are shown. From those costs we obtain total cost by adding the total fixed cost and the total variable cost at each level of output.

At any level of output, the difference between TC and TVC is TFC. Look again at Table 10-3. At 3 units of output, for example, subtract the TVC of $72 from the TC of $132 and find the TFC of $60. Prove to yourself that at every level of output, the difference between the TC and the TVC is $60. Therefore, the TC curve must have the same shape and be parallel to the TVC, always $60 more. Recall that TFC is a constant, not changing with the level of output. For this reason, any change in output and TVC causes the same amount of change in the TC. When output increases from zero to 1 in Table 10-3, the total variable cost increases from $0 to $45. This $45 increase in variable cost causes the total cost to also increase $45 from $60 to $105. Whenever total variable cost increases, total cost must increase as well. It is important to note that the production of more output will always require an increase in total cost.

The Economic Concept of Cost

Economists view total cost differently from what is commonly meant by cost. Many people interpret total cost as the money spent to produce the output.

Thus they see total cost as the payments that are recorded in the accounting books. Economists call these particular costs explicit costs. **Explicit costs** are the money payments made during the production of the product. Rent, wages, and raw material cost are all easily explained opportunity costs of production and should be clearly recorded in the books. These explicit costs are the out-of-pocket costs of production.

However, these explicit costs are not total cost to the economist. An economist's concept of total cost truly means *total* cost. This economic cost includes all the opportunity costs of producing the good. The opportunity cost of all resources used in producing the good are included. The economist recognizes additional costs of production that may not be so obvious and are not found by looking at the cash outlays. These other costs are known as implicit costs. Implicit costs are the opportunity costs of production that are not explicit money payments. **Implicit costs** are the opportunity costs of owner-owned resources. Payments to workers are money costs; the cost of this labor is an explicit cost. But what about self-owned labor of the firm. A Ma and Pa grocery may not pay a salary to Ma and Pa, but their labor is a cost to the business. Ma and Pa could work instead in the neighborhood factory. If that were the best alternative for their labor, then that forgone salary is a measure of the cost of their labor in their own store. This implicit labor cost will be included by an economist in total cost. Opportunity cost may be easy to determine, such as what is given up for a bar of soap ($2), or more difficult, such as finding the value of the statement, "I like being my own boss." Yet all the opportunity costs of production are what make up total cost.

A factory owner may think that since the factory is self-owned, its cost is free. You should recognize that there are no free lunches or factories, that there is an opportunity cost to every alternative use of a resource. For example, if the owner could sell the factory, deposit the money in the bank, and collect $1 million per year interest, then the owner's use of that factory is costing the owner $1 million a year in forgone income. There is a $1 million implicit cost associated with the "free" use of this factory. Implicit costs are not as obvious as explicit costs but should not be overlooked.

An accountant considers total cost to be the sum of the explicit costs. An economist considers total cost to be the opportunity cost of the good. The opportunity cost of *all* inputs is included, owner owned or not. In this text, total cost always means the sum of all explicit *and* implicit costs associated with production. Next we rearrange the total cost into two useful cost concepts, average and marginal.

Average Cost

Once the total cost is known, you can use a simple process to find the average cost. This is the familiar process you use to find your average test score at the end of the term. First add the points per test to find the total points; then divide the total by the number of tests. This is the same process as finding a total cost and dividing by the level of output. The group of average costs is composed of average fixed cost, average variable cost, and average total cost. The first to be discussed is average fixed cost.

The **average fixed cost (AFC)** is the total fixed cost divided by the number of units produced. The result is the fixed cost per unit of output.

$$\text{AFC} = \text{average fixed cost} = \frac{\text{total fixed cost}}{\text{quantity of output}} = \frac{\text{TFC}}{\text{Q}}$$

Look at Table 10-4, which contains the data for the entire average cost group. At the third unit of output, average fixed cost is $20 per unit (TFC of $60/3) and is $10 per unit to produce 6. Figure 10-4 shows the shape of the average fixed cost curve. The downward-sloping curve clearly indicates that the average fixed

Table 10-4   Total and Average Costs

Output (Q)	Total Fixed Cost (TFC)	Average Fixed Cost (TFC/Q)	Total Variable Cost (TVC)	Average Variable Cost (TVC/Q)	Total Cost (TC)	Average Total Cost (TC/Q)
1	$60	$60	$ 45	$45	$105	$105
2	60	30	60	30	120	60
3	60	20	72	24	132	44
4	60	15	80	20	140	35
5	60	12	90	18	150	30
6	60	10	102	17	162	27
7	60	8.6	116	16.6	176	25.2
8	60	7.5	136	17	196	24.5
9	60	6.7	162	18	222	24.7
10	60	6	200	20	260	26
11	60	5.5	242	22	302	27.5

This table shows the average costs. Since the average costs are calculated from the total costs, the total costs are also shown. The average fixed cost is the total fixed cost divided by output. The average variable cost is the total variable cost divided by output. The average total cost is the total cost divided by output. You should also see that the average total cost is the sum of the average fixed and the average variable cost.

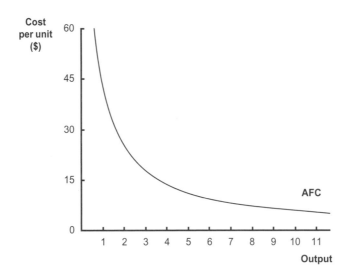

Figure 10-4   Average Fixed Cost
This graph shows the average fixed cost based on the data in Table 10-4. The average fixed cost always falls as output rises. This is because the fixed cost does not change and the number of units over which the cost is spread increases, so the fixed cost per unit will fall as output goes up.

cost *always* declines with an increase in output. This continuous decline is due to the constant fixed cost being shared by more and more units of output. The result is a smaller fixed cost per unit. This compares to what a businessperson calls "spreading the overhead." Since rent, for example, remains the same regardless of the amount of production, this fixed cost is shared equally by the output.

What if you were the only buyer of this textbook and were required to pay a price covering the total fixed cost? You would be most thankful if you were joined by another buyer and the two of you could divide the TFC between you. The TFC divided by an output of 2 would halve the TFC. When 1,000 students buy the text, the TFC is divided by 1,000, and you and many others would be sharing the TFC. The average fixed cost part of the price you pay for this textbook becomes much less as more copies of the text are produced. Notice, however, that the AFC *never* becomes zero. There is no level of output large enough to divide into the TFC to give an AFC of zero. The AFC will always remain a positive number, although ever smaller as production increases.

Average variable cost (AVC) is the total variable cost divided by the level of output. Consider the following expression for average variable cost:

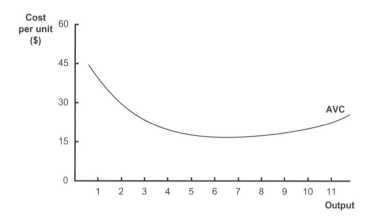

Figure 10-5   Average Variable Cost
This graph shows the average variable cost from Table 10-4. This curve is U-shaped.

$$AVC = \text{average variable cost} = \frac{\text{total variable cost}}{\text{quantity of output}} = \frac{TVC}{Q}$$

Average variable cost has the shape shown by Figure 10-5. The AVC curve is always U-shaped. This means that the AVC of production will first fall as output increases, but eventually the AVC of a unit of output will become greater, and AVC rises. You will soon learn the reason why.

The average total cost curve is also U-shaped. **Average total cost (ATC)** is total cost divided by the level of output. ATC is found by the following expression:

$$ATC = \text{average total cost} = \frac{\text{total cost}}{\text{quantity of output}} = \frac{TC}{Q}$$

Carefully note in Table 10-4 that ATC is also the sum of AVC and AFC. At the sixth unit of output, the AFC is $10 per unit and the AVC is $17 per unit. Together they give the ATC of $27 per unit. This result is identical to the expression above for ATC when the total cost of $162 is divided by the output of 6 units.

Figure 10-6 illustrates the relation of the average total cost to the two curves that compose it. The ATC is the highest curve since it is the total of the AFC and AVC. Notice, for example, that the ATC of 5 units is $30 per unit and the AVC is $18 per unit. The difference between the two is $12 per unit, the

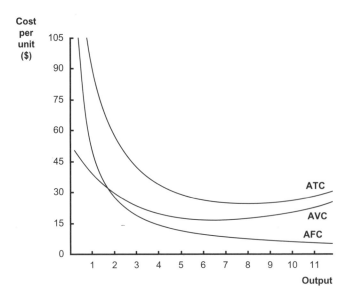

Figure 10-6   The Group of Average Costs
These three curves are the average cost group. The average fixed cost decreases for all levels of
output. The average variable cost is U-shaped. The average total cost is the sum of the average
fixed and the average variable cost curves. The average total therefore lies above the other two
curves. The average total cost is also U-shaped.

amount of the AFC at that level. This explains why the ATC and AVC curves
come closer and closer together at higher levels of output but never touch. The
difference between the two curves is the AFC, which is continuously declining.
Hence the difference between ATC and AVC becomes less and less as output
increases, but they can never touch as the AFC never becomes zero. The ATC
and AVC always remain two separate curves with the difference between them
being the AFC.

Marginal Cost

The marginal cost group consists of only one cost, marginal cost. **Marginal
cost (MC)** is the change in total cost as one more unit of output is produced.
It is the additional, extra, cost of producing one more unit. The expression for
marginal cost follows:

$$MC = \text{marginal cost} = \frac{\text{change in total cost}}{\text{change in quantity of output}} = \frac{\Delta TC}{\Delta Q}$$

Table 10-5   Marginal Cost Schedule

Output (Q)	Total Cost (TC)	Marginal Cost ($\Delta TC/\Delta Q$)
1	$105	
2	120	$15
3	132	12
4	140	8
5	150	10
6	162	12
7	176	14
8	196	20
9	222	26
10	260	38
11	302	42

Marginal cost is the change in total cost due to a change in output. As output goes from 1 to 2, there is a change in total cost of $15. The marginal cost of the second unit is $15. Can you calculate the rest of the marginal cost column?

The result of this calculation appears in Table 10-5. Each time an additional unit of output is produced, the total cost must change. Additional output requires additional input, hence an increase in total variable cost which increases total cost. You should recognize that the marginal cost of an additional unit is the change in the total cost. When production increases from 1 to 2, total cost increases from $105 to $120. This $15 change in total cost is the marginal cost of the second unit. As output changes by 1 from 2 to 3 units, the total cost increases from $120 to $132, a marginal cost of $12. The marginal cost of this third unit is $12, which is the change in total cost as output changed by one unit. The marginal cost of the fourth unit is $8, and so on. You can see why marginal cost is defined as the change in total cost as output is increased by one more unit.

Recall that as output changes, total variable cost changes, but total fixed cost remains the same. This means that a change in total cost is due to a change in total variable cost. We are suggesting that marginal cost can also be the change in total *variable* cost as output is increased by one more unit. So suppose that we try to find marginal cost by using total variable cost rather than total cost. Table 10-6 provides the data. As output changes from 1 to 2, the TVC changes

Table 10-6   Marginal Cost from Total or Total Variable Cost

Output (Q)	Total Variable Cost (TVC)	Marginal Cost (ΔTVC/ΔQ)	Total Cost (TC)	Marginal Cost (ΔTC/ΔQ)
1	$45		$105	
2	60	$15	120	$15
3	72	12	132	12
4	80	8	140	8
5	90	10	150	10
6	102	12	162	12
7	116	14	176	14
8	136	20	196	20
9	162	26	222	26
10	200	38	260	38
11	242	42	302	42

This table shows the calculation of the marginal cost based on the total variable cost and also on the total cost. The two marginal costs are the same.

from $45 to $60. Thus the change in TVC due to the change in output of one unit is $15. Hence the MC is the same $15 found by using the change in total cost from 1 to 2 units. When the TVC changes by $15, then the total cost changes by $15. If we continue finding the change in TVC, we will find the marginal cost column all over again. Marginal cost by definition measures the change in TC. Since the TFC is constant, it does not contribute to the change in TC. Only TVC changes total cost. So the change in TVC is the change in TC. The marginal cost is the same whether it is found by the change in the total cost *or* the change in the total variable cost. Now you know why there is only one marginal cost concept.

Figure 10-7 shows the marginal cost curve. This curve has a distinct hook shape that falls rapidly at first and soon begins to rise as production increases. Diminishing returns is a major cause of the hook shape of the marginal cost curve. This can be explained by the relation between marginal cost and a concept introduced in Chapter 9, marginal product. Table 10-7 illustrates this relationship. The table shows the result of hiring additional workers at $10 each in a pie factory. The total product and total cost are given, and the marginal product and marginal cost are calculated. To simplify, labor is assumed to be the only cost of production. The last column, the marginal cost, shows the result of spreading the cost of the added worker over the resulting added units of output. The second worker yields 5 extra pies and costs $10. Ten dollars spent on producing 5 pies yields a cost of $2 each. The third worker yields 10 additional pies for $10. Ten dollars spent on producing 10 pies is a cost of $1 each.

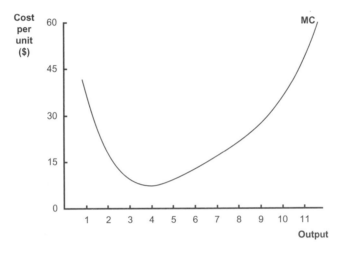

Figure 10-7 Marginal Cost
This figure shows the marginal cost curve. The marginal cost has a distinct hook shape. The shape is due to the law of diminishing returns.

Table 10-7 The Relationship of Marginal Product to Marginal Cost

(1)	(2)	(3)	(4)	(5)
Input (L = labor)	Total Product (TP = Q)	Marginal Product (ΔTP/ΔL)	Total Cost (TC)	Marginal Cost (ΔTC/ΔQ)
1	10		$10	
2	15	5	20	$2
3	25	10	30	1
4	30	5	40	2
5	32	2	50	5

This table shows the relationship between the marginal product and the marginal cost. The total product is output, Q, shown in column 2. Column 3 is the marginal product found by the change in the total product as one more unit of labor, L, is added. The total cost, column 4, is the cost of labor, $10 per unit, times the amount of labor used. The marginal cost is the change in total cost divided by the change in output, ΔQ, and is shown in column 5. The important observation is that the marginal cost goes down when the marginal product goes up, and the marginal cost goes up when the marginal product goes down. The behavior of marginal cost is determined by the behavior of the marginal product, which is determined by the law of diminishing returns. So diminishing returns determines the behavior of marginal cost.

The marginal product column shows that increasing returns holds until the addition of the fourth worker, when diminishing returns sets in. Thus the marginal product is rising to that point. But observe that as the marginal product is rising, the marginal cost is falling. Each additional worker is paid the same amount, but so far each additional worker contributes more to output than the last previous worker. Therefore the same additional cost ($10) is spread over an increasing number of pies, and the added cost per added pie falls. But notice that once diminishing returns sets in, as it eventually must, the marginal cost must rise as the marginal product now falls. This results from each additional worker contributing fewer pies, and since each worker costs the same, the added cost is spread over fewer added pies. The marginal cost therefore rises from the point of diminishing returns and continues to rise. You should now recognize that there is an inverse relation between marginal product and marginal cost.

The hook shape of the marginal cost curve is explained. As inputs are added to the productive process, increasing returns will cause the marginal product to rise, and as a result, the marginal cost to fall. But once enough input has been added to reach diminishing returns, the marginal product always falls and, as a result, the marginal cost always increases with each additional unit of output. Thus the marginal cost curve falls rapidly, bottoms out at the point of diminishing returns, and continually rises thereafter. The shape of the marginal cost curve can now be used to explain another cost behavior.

The Average-Marginal Relation

Now that you are equipped with an understanding of marginal cost, the U-shaped ATC and AVC curves can be explained by applying the average-marginal relation. The **average-marginal relation** specifies that if the marginal is greater than the average, the average will rise; and if the marginal is less than the average, the average will fall. This is a familiar relationship. If your marginal (additional) test score is higher than your average, your average score will rise. However, if the next test score is lower than your average, your average score falls. The average-marginal relationship also exists with cost. Anytime the marginal cost is greater than the average cost, the average cost must be rising. Anytime the marginal cost is below the average cost, the average cost must be falling.

Figure 10-8 shows the marginal cost curve and both the average variable and the average total cost curves. As long as the marginal cost of producing another unit of output is less than the AVC, the AVC will be falling. The AVC

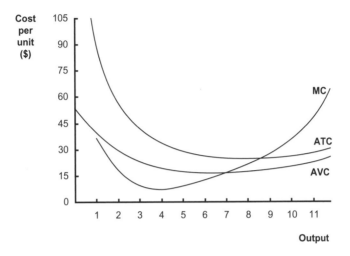

Figure 10-8 Average Total, Average Variable, and Marginal Cost
This figure shows the average total cost, the average variable cost, and the marginal cost. The marginal cost cuts each average cost at the lowest point on the average cost. This is a result of the average-marginal relation. The relation says that if the marginal is below the average, then the next unit costs less than the average and the average must fall. When the marginal is greater than the average, the next unit costs more than average and the average must rise.

is falling until the seventh unit of output. The MC is lower than the AVC to that point and is pulling the AVC down. It makes no difference that the MC begins to rise after the fourth unit; the extra cost of each unit up through the seventh unit is still less than the AVC, so the AVC must fall. The falling AVC is clearly a result of the average-marginal relation.

The point at which the marginal cost intersects the average variable cost is a significant point. This intersection marks the lowest point on the AVC. The reason is that until this level of output is reached, MC is less than the average variable cost of producing another unit and the AVC is pulled down. But at higher levels of output, in Figure 10-8 beyond the seventh unit, the marginal cost is greater than the AVC and the AVC is pulled up. The rising MC now will be higher than the AVC, and the AVC will always rise. Thus the U shape of the AVC curve. Average variable cost is pulled down when the MC is less, but AVC never falls lower than the intersection with MC because when an additional unit is produced, the MC is now always greater and will now always pull the AVC up.

All that has been said of the relation of marginal cost to the average variable cost is also true of the relation between marginal cost and the average total cost. When the marginal cost is below the ATC, the ATC is falling; when the marginal cost intersects the ATC, the ATC is at its lowest point; and when the marginal cost is above the ATC, the ATC is rising. Thus the U-shaped ATC curve.

Look again at Figure 10-8. The lowest point on the AVC is at 7 units while the ATC continues to fall to its lowest point at 8 units. These are the points where each curve intersects with the marginal cost curve. Why are these points of intersection with marginal cost at two different levels of output? This question is answered by either of two approaches. The average-marginal approach is that between the seventh and the eighth units of output, marginal cost is greater than AVC so the AVC is rising, and marginal cost is still less than the ATC so the ATC is still falling. This approach answers the question, but it may not contribute to a complete understanding.

Another approach to the question as to why the AVC reaches a minimum at a lower level of output than the ATC is the following: Since ATC = AVC + AFC, the shape of the ATC depends on the shape of the AVC and AFC. Up to the seventh unit of output, both AVC and AFC fall, so ATC also falls. Now AVC turns up but AFC continues to fall. As long as the fall in AFC is greater than the rise in AVC, ATC will fall. This must be true up to the eighth unit of output. But since the fall in AFC is getting smaller and the rise in AVC is getting greater, soon ATC will rise. Additionally, since AVC continues to rise and AFC continues to fall, ATC will continue to rise.

You should see that diminishing returns, through its effect on marginal cost, in turn affects average and therefore total cost. Diminishing returns influences the cost of production and consequently choices that we as a society will make.

▶ Summary

The purpose of this chapter is to develop an understanding of cost. These cost concepts are important since cost is information used by the firm to make supply decisions, and supply and demand together determine how resources are allocated. So an understanding of cost is essential for an understanding of the resource allocation process.

We have identified three groups of cost: total, average, and marginal. You have studied the behavior of these costs as output increases and the explanation for the behavior. The total cost group includes total fixed cost, total variable cost, and the total cost. Total fixed cost is constant and does not depend on how much is produced. Total variable cost is zero at zero output and always increases. Total cost equals total fixed cost at zero output and, like total variable cost, always increases. Total cost is the sum of total fixed cost and total variable cost. The discussion of implicit cost examined the idea that cost has an economic meaning not commonly used.

The second group of cost concepts was the average cost group, which included the average fixed cost, the average variable cost, and the average total cost. The average fixed cost curve always decreases, while the average total and average variable curves are both U-shaped. The shape of these last two curves is linked to diminishing returns through marginal cost. The third cost concept is marginal cost. Marginal cost is inversely related to the marginal product. The behavior of the marginal product is determined by diminishing returns; thus the shape of the marginal cost curve is determined by diminishing returns. The marginal cost curve is hook shaped. The intersection of marginal cost with the average variable and the average total costs identifies the lowest point on the AVC and the ATC.

The following chapter introduces revenue, the other piece of the producer's puzzle. Then in the next chapter, cost is combined with revenue, and we find profit.

▶ **Key Concepts**

total fixed cost	average fixed cost
total variable cost	average variable cost
total cost	average total cost
explicit cost	marginal cost
implicit cost	average-marginal relation

▶ **Discussion Questions**

1. Aunt Mickey owns a doughnut shop. Every month she pays bills for electricity, rent, insurance, flour, sugar, labor, and machine maintenance. Help Mickey decide which expenses are fixed and which are variable.

2. Joe the car dealer tells his television public that his prices are the lowest in town because he owns his own lot and his whole family helps out. Has Joe satisfactorily explained his low costs?

3. What is the total cost of your attending school? Have you included the implicit costs?

4. Fill in the following table.

Output	ATC	MC	TC
1		–	100
2	65		
3		20	
4	45		
5			220
6		56	
7	50		
8		90	

5. Suppose that the marginal cost of production is increasing. What information do you need to tell whether the average total cost is rising or falling?
6. Uncle Effron says that marginal cost is just a funny name for average total cost. Explain to him how they are different.

▶ Self-Review

• Fill in the blanks

fixed	Total cost is the sum of total _____ cost and total
variable	_____ cost. The cost that does not change with the level
total fixed cost	of output is _____. The cost that increases
total variable	with the level of output is _____ cost. Total
total variable cost	cost minus total fixed cost is _____.
explicit	Money payment made during production are _____
	costs. An economist's view of total cost includes the
implicit	opportunity cost of owner-owned resources, the _____
	costs. The total fixed cost divided by the number of units
average	produced is the _____ fixed cost. The average fixed
declines	cost always _____ with output but never becomes
zero	_____. The total variable cost divided by the level of
average variable cost	output is the _____. The AVC is
U	always _____ shaped. The sum of the AFC and the AVC
ATC, U	is the _____ which is also a _____ shaped curve. The
	change in total cost as one more unit of output is produced is
marginal cost, hook	known as _____. Marginal cost has a _____
diminishing returns	shape explained by the law of _____.
	The relation between marginal cost and marginal product is
inverse	_____. When the marginal cost is less than the average
falling	cost, the average is _____. When the marginal cost is

rising

lowest

greater than the average cost, the average is _____. When the marginal cost crosses the average, the average is at its _____ point.

- Multiple choice

1. An example of implicit cost is:
    a. the cost of labor.
    b. the interest cost on a loan.
    c. the cost of a machine.
    d. the opportunity cost of an owner-owned building.
2. Total cost includes:
    a. explicit costs.
    b. implicit costs.
    c. both a and b.
    d. none of the above.
3. Which cost increases with output?
    a. Total variable cost.
    b. Total fixed cost.
    c. Total cost.
    d. Both a and c.
4. Average fixed cost is:
    a. total fixed cost.
    b. total variable cost.
    c. total fixed cost per unit of output.
    d. total variable cost per unit of output.
5. The change in total cost due to a change in output is:
    a. ATC.
    b. AVC.
    c. AFC.
    d. MC.

Answers: 1.d, 2.c, 3.d, 4.c, 5.d.

$$\boxed{\text{Chapter } \boxed{11} \text{ REVENUE}}$$

Key Topics

market structure

perfect competition

total revenue and marginal revenue

monopoly

Goals

understand total revenue and marginal revenue

understand the relationship between the revenues of firms

identify perfect competition as a price taker

identify monopoly as a price searcher

Although cost is an important concern of the firm, equally important is the concept of revenue. Revenue is the money received by the firm from the sale of output. The revenue of a firm will partly depend on how many other firms are selling the good and how those firms respond to the decisions of the first firm. One firm's behavior may affect another firm's revenue. These cases of related revenue are introduced in this chapter. This chapter will also focus on the basic revenue concepts of total revenue and marginal revenue. Once these concepts are understood, we can, in the next chapter, introduce profit. The discussion of revenue will start with the ideas of market power and market structure, and then the concepts of total and marginal revenue will be considered for each of two distinct types of market structure.

Revenue and Market Structure

Firms frequently make decisions that affect the revenue of other firms. For example, when a firm changes the price of its good, not only will it affect its own revenue, but it may affect the revenue of other firms as well. This ability to control price is called **market power**. We will see how market power relates the price of one firm to the revenue of another firm.

If firm A sets its price lower than firm B, then firm A will have an advantage in the market and a larger share of the market will go to A. Thus B's revenue will decrease and A's revenue will rise, so firm B's revenue is related to firm A's revenue, as is A's to B's. The price difference between firms acts to draw consumers to the low-price firm and increase its revenue. Provided that there is more than one firm, our conclusion is that the more market power firms have, the more related are their revenues.

Market power relates the revenue of one firm to another. But where does the market power of a firm come from? The extent to which firms possess market power varies and depends on the market structure of the industry. **Market structure** refers to the elements of market organization that affect the behavior of the firms. Three elements identify the market structure: the number of firms in the market, freedom of entry, and the degree to which the product is standardized. Now we will see how each of the three elements of market structure contributes to market power. First, what effect will the number of firms in the market have on market power? As the number of firms in a market increases, the control any one firm is likely to have over price decreases. Suppose that there is only one firm in the market. Then the firm can choose a price and sell the quantity demanded by the market. In that sense the firm is the market. As soon as there is more than a single firm, each firm suddenly comes under pressure in its choice of price. If one firm sets price above the other firm, the low-price firm has an advantage. Each firm faces pressure to not raise price above the price the other firm charges. We would expect each firm to have less control over price than when there is only one firm in the market. The more firms there are, the greater the pressure to conform on price and the less control any one firm has over price. Thus the price any one firm might charge depends on the number of firms in the market.

The freedom of entry, or the ease with which a firm is able to enter the market, determines the number of firms in the market. Easy entry means that a firm can obtain the necessary technology and resources to become a seller in the industry. If folded paper airplanes were to sell for $100 apiece, perhaps many of us would soon become producers and enter the market. But in a market with significant barriers to entry, making it difficult for new firms to enter, the existing firms may each acquire some power over price. For example, it is not very likely that any of us will become automobile producers. It is very expensive to enter this market. How could we raise enough funds to purchase the capital needed to compete with General Motors? Thus, **easy entry** is the absence of entry barriers. Easy entry in a market results in more firms and less control over price; more barriers to entry result in fewer firms and more control over price.

Another element that determines market structure is how standardized the product is. A product is **standardized** if the consumer cannot distinguish the output of one firm from the output of another. The products seem identical. Two farmers growing the same grade of wheat produce a standardized product. The products are so similar that one is a perfect substitute for the other. On the other hand, cars produced by one firm are readily distinguishable from cars produced by another firm. Cars are a **differentiated**, not a standardized, good.

How does this degree of standardization influence market power? If a good is standardized, the buyer cannot distinguish your good from mine, and you know the buyer will not pay a higher price for your good. Since the goods are exactly the same, the price you get and the price I get will be the same. The more standardized the good, the harder it will be for any producer to control the price. If your good is differentiated, you are able to control price. Because your good is different, you know that some consumers will pay a higher price. If the products are differentiated, the firm has some power over price.

We have discussed three elements of market structure that affect market power, the ability of a firm to control the price it charges for a product. The first is the number of firms in the market; second, the degree of ease with which a firm can enter the market; and third, the degree of standardization of the product. These elements affect any one firm's power over price, and consequently the extent to which one firm's revenue is related to another firm's revenue.

We have seen that the market structure can influence the revenue of the firm. The complication with revenue is that, for some market structures, the revenue of one firm may be related to the revenue of other firms. Of four market structures, there are two where the revenue of firms are related. They are oligopoly and monopolistic competition. Chapter 15 will investigate the case of firms with related revenues. The remainder of this chapter concentrates on firms with unrelated revenues.

Unrelated revenues occur in either of two conditions. First is a perfectly competitive market, one in which no one firm has any control over the market price. A market is perfectly competitive when no firm has any market power. The second is the case of monopoly. Monopoly occurs when there is only one firm in the market. The lack of competition in the monopoly market gives the firm some control over price and, consequently, market power. We will now examine revenue for these two market structures, perfect competition and monopoly.

Perfect Competition

A **perfectly competitive market** is characterized by many firms, a standardized product, and easy entry. When a market is perfectly competitive, no firm has control over price. What, then, determines the price that the perfectly competitive firm charges? The price is established by the market. This equilibrium price is determined by supply and demand through the free interaction of all buyers and all sellers of the product in the industry. This price is dictated by the market to the individual firm. Every firm in a perfectly competitive market charges the same market price, and no one firm can change the price. The firm is just one of the many sellers of this standardized product.

Consider a farmer selling wheat. The output of one farmer is a mere "drop in the bucket" to the total output of all farmers in the wheat industry. What if this particular firm were to stop production? The fall in the market supply would be so slight there would not be a penny increase in the market price. If this firm chose to double or triple output, the slight increase in market supply would not cause a penny fall in market price. All of the extra output could be sold at the market price. If you feel that you could use a refresher at this point on supply, demand, and equilibrium, refer to Chapter 7.

What can one wheat farmer do? No buyer would purchase from this firm at a higher price when there are many other firms selling the identical product at a lower price. And the usual reason to lower price is to increase sales. But this firm can sell all it produces at the higher market price, so what incentive does it have to lower price? Since the quantity sold is the same, the farmer only loses by selling at a lower price. The firm can't raise price; the firm won't lower price. The price established in the perfectly competitive market becomes the price charged by the individual firm in perfect competition. The perfect competitor is a "price taker" since the firm has no control over price.

Suppose that all the firms in the perfectly competitive market get together and agree to sell at a price higher than the established market price. Could this cooperation among firms raise price? This approach will fail largely because new firms are free to enter the perfectly competitive market. If the higher price makes the industry attractive, the free entry of more firms will reduce the power of the combined firms to raise price.

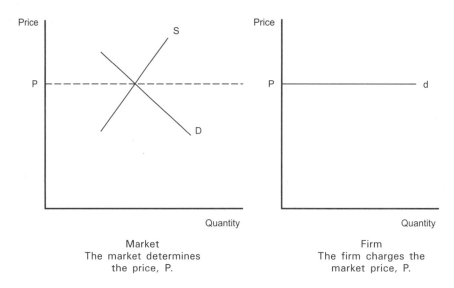

Figure 11-1 The Relationship between the Market and Firm in Perfect Competition
This figure shows that the forces of supply and demand in the perfectly competitive market establish the demand and price for the individual firm. The picture for the market is on the left and the picture for one of many identical firms is on the right. Do not confuse the downward-sloping demand curve of the market with the horizontal demand of the perfectly competitive firm.

Each individual firm in perfect competition takes the horizontal line at the market price as its demand curve. Figure 11-1 shows this relation between the perfectly competitive firm and the market. A demand curve shows the highest price that buyers are willing and able to pay for each quantity. For the firm in perfect competition, the highest price is always the same price at all levels of output and is the established market price. For each firm, price *and* the demand curve are the horizontal line established at the market price. This means that the perfectly competitive firm can sell all it can produce at the going market price. Since the firm's demand curve is horizontal, the demand is perfectly elastic, a concept introduced in Chapter 8. If the market price changes, so will the price and demand curve of all the individual firms. Figure 11-2 shows the result of an increase in market demand, D, for the product. The market price increases and so does the demand, d, as seen by the individual firm.

Total and Marginal Revenue

Now that the relation between the perfectly competitive firm and its market is

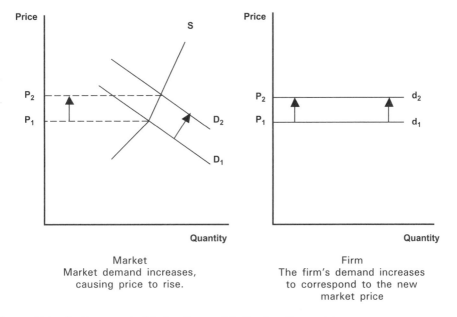

Figure 11-2   An Increase in Market Demand in Perfect Competition
This figure shows what happens to the price the firm receives when there is an increase in market demand. The market demand shifts to the right, which causes the market price to rise from P_1 to P_2. The price at which the firm can sell rises from P_1 to P_2. This means that the firm's demand has increased.

established, two revenue concepts relevant to the firm can be introduced. We start with a definition of total revenue. **Total revenue (TR)** is the total receipts of the firm from the sale of its product. To calculate total revenue, the firm multiplies the selling price by the total number of units sold.

$$TR = \text{total revenue} = \text{price} \times \text{quantity} = P \times Q$$

The total revenue depends on the market structure. In the case of perfect competition, the firm has no control over price. The price is a constant for the firm. Hence total revenue is found by multiplying the constant price by the number of units sold. Suppose that the price established in the market is \$38 per unit. Then the total revenue of a firm is given in Table 11-1. Although total revenue is an important concept, the most useful approach to revenue for an economist is marginal revenue.

Marginal revenue (MR) is the change in total revenue as one more unit is produced and sold. Marginal revenue answers the question, What is the

Table 11-1   Total Revenue for a Perfectly Competitive Firm

Output (Q)	Total Revenue (TR)
0	$ 0
1	38
2	76
3	114
4	152
5	190
6	228
7	266
8	304
9	342
10	380
11	418

This table shows the total revenue calculation for a perfectly competitive firm when the market price is $38. To find total revenue, we multiply the price times the quantity.

extra revenue from the sale of one more unit of output? The following is the expression for marginal revenue:

$$MR = \text{marginal revenue} = \frac{\text{change in total revenue}}{\text{change in output}} = \frac{\Delta TR}{\Delta Q}$$

Marginal revenue is easy to calculate in perfect competition. Start with the total revenue in Table 11-2. To find the marginal revenue, take the change in total revenue as output goes from 1 to 2 and divide by the change in output, 1 in this case. For the second unit, MR is $38. Total revenue changes by $38 ($76 – $38) while output changes by 1. Carry out this process for all levels of output to complete the marginal revenue column. Notice that in perfect competition the marginal revenue is a constant, here, $38. If the firm sells one more unit for $38, there is a $38 change in total revenue, and this $38 change is marginal revenue. Since the perfectly competitive firm cannot change the price to sell another unit, the marginal revenue of another unit always equals the price.

In perfect competition, the marginal revenue is the horizontal line shown in Figure 11-3. Not only is the horizontal line the demand curve for the individual producer in perfect competition, it is also the marginal revenue

Table 11-2   **Marginal Revenue for the Perfectly Competitive Firm**

Output (Q)	Total Revenue (TR)	Marginal Revenue (ΔTR/ΔQ)
1	$ 38	$38
2	76	38
3	114	38
4	152	38
5	190	38
6	228	38
7	266	38
8	304	38
9	342	38
10	380	38
11	418	38

This table illustrates the calculation of the marginal revenue for the perfectly competitive firm. The marginal revenue is the change in total revenue when one more unit is sold. In this case the marginal revenue is a constant $38 equal to the price of the good. The reason is that when one more unit is sold, the change in total revenue is the price of the good.

curve as well as the price. Therefore, *demand*, *price*, and *marginal revenue* for the firm in perfect competition is always the horizontal line at the market price. This combination is unique to perfect competition. There are two conditions in Figure 11-3 that identify a perfect competitor. First, the marginal revenue curve is a horizontal line. Second, only in perfect competition are the price and marginal revenue equal.

Monopoly

When **monopoly** is the market structure, there is a single seller and no acceptable substitutes for the product, and entry is restricted. The firm faces the same downward-sloping demand as the market because the one firm is the industry. The downward-sloping demand curve of the monopolist shows that the firm has market power. Unlike the perfect competitor, the monopoly firm can raise its price without losing all its sales. As a result, the monopolist does not have to take the market price as given, as does a perfectly competitive firm. Since the monopolist can establish its own most favorable price on its demand curve, and must find that price, a monopolist is called a "price searcher." Utilities

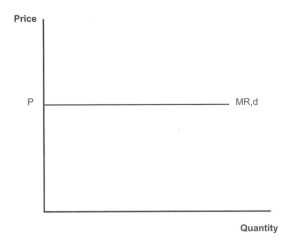

Figure 11-3   Marginal Revenue in Perfect Competition
This figure shows that for a perfectly competitive firm, price, marginal revenue, and demand are
the same curve at the market price.

are local examples of monopoly. Each town has only one electric distributor,
one distributor for natural gas, one firm offering local telephone service. You
cannot buy these goods from other firms at lower prices since each utility is a
monopoly industry.

Now we will apply the total revenue and marginal revenue concepts to the
monopolist. To calculate total revenue for a monopoly firm, we must know the
demand. The demand is necessary because it tells the quantity that can be sold
at each price, and total revenue is price times quantity sold. You can find the
total revenue for a monopolist from the demand schedule in Table 11-3. Notice
that the firm has to lower price to sell more units. Multiply the price in the first
column times the quantity in the second column. At three units of output, the
total revenue is $78 per unit for each of 3 units, or $234. Follow this procedure
at each price and quantity combination to complete the total revenue column.

Although marginal revenue for the monopolist is calculated exactly as in
perfect competition, marginal revenue is no longer a constant. This point can
be illustrated with the data in Table 11-3. To obtain marginal revenue, find the
change in total revenue as output goes from 1 to 2. In this case, total revenue
changes by $76 ($172 − $96), while output changes by 1. Marginal revenue is
the change in total revenue divided by the change in output, or $76. If this
process is continued, the marginal revenue column is completed. Observe that
marginal revenue falls.

Table 11-3 Monopoly Total Revenue and Marginal Revenue

DEMAND		Total Revenue	Marginal Revenue
Quantity (Q)	Price (P)	(TR = P × Q)	(ΔTR/ΔQ)
1	$96	$96	
2	86	172	$76
3	78	234	62
4	71	284	50
5	65	325	41
6	59	354	29
7	53	371	17
8	47	376	5
9	42	378	2
10	37	370	−8
11	32	352	−18

This table illustrates how the total revenue is obtained from demand when the firm is a monopoly. Total revenue is the price times the quantity sold. In the case of monopoly, the price falls as more units are sold, reflecting the downward-sloping monopoly demand. To obtain marginal revenue, we calculate the change in total revenue when one more unit is sold. In the monopoly case the marginal revenue falls as output increases. Further, the marginal revenue of each unit is less than the price.

To see why the marginal revenue of the monopolist falls, we first need to establish that its marginal revenue is less than price. When demand slopes downward, the marginal revenue is always less than price. To understand why, another approach to calculating marginal revenue will be helpful. Let us recalculate marginal revenue using the data of Table 11-3. If the monopolist wishes to sell another unit, it can only do so if it lowers its price. If one more unit is sold, the firm's revenue from that unit is the new, lower, selling price of that unit. But the downward-sloping demand means that the price must be lowered on all units sold. So the firm gives up the difference between the previous price and the new price on all units that could have been sold previously. See if this approach works. When the price falls from $96 per unit to $86 per unit, sales increase from 1 unit to 2. So the firm gains the selling price of $86 from the second unit but gives up $10 ($96 − $86) on the first unit, which is now sold at the lower price. Thus the marginal revenue should be $86 − $10 = $76, which agrees with our original calculation.

The importance of this approach is that we recognize that marginal revenue for the monopolist is less than the price. This is because the marginal revenue of the next unit is the price of the next unit minus the lost revenue

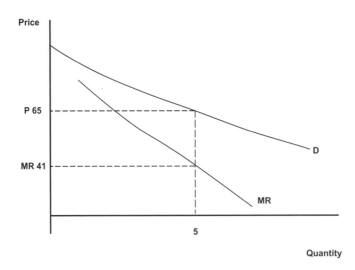

Figure 11-4   Demand and Marginal Revenue in Monopoly
This figure shows that because the marginal revenue is less than the price for a monopoly, the marginal revenue lies below the demand curve. At 5 units of output, for example, the price is $65 and the marginal revenue is only $41.

(due to lower price) on the previous units. Now we can conclude that since price falls as quantity rises, and marginal revenue is less than price, the marginal revenue must also fall.

Since price is found on the demand curve, we know that for monopoly, marginal revenue lies *below* demand. What this means is that the marginal revenue must always be less than price for a firm faced with a downward-sloping demand curve. This relation between monopoly demand and monopoly marginal revenue is shown in Figure 11-4. Select any level of output and compare the price to the marginal revenue. You will find that marginal revenue is less than price. For example, at the fifth unit of output, the price is $65 while the marginal revenue is only $41.

The monopoly firm is contrasted with the perfectly competitive firm in Figure 11-5. A graph can reveal whether or not the market structure is perfectly competitive. Recall that for the perfectly competitive firm, the marginal revenue is a horizontal line. And only in perfect competition are the price and marginal revenue identical. In monopoly, the demand curve slopes downward and the marginal revenue lies under the demand. This simple thing, the location of the marginal revenue curve, has significant consequences for society.

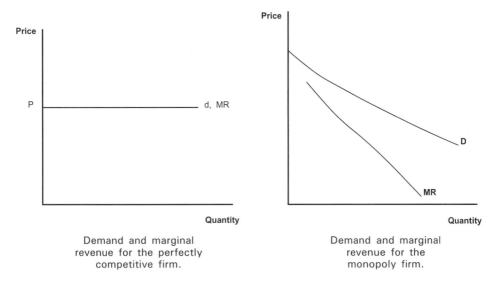

Figure 11-5   A Perfectly Competitive Firm Compared to a Monopoly Firm
This figure shows the difference between the graph of the perfectly competitive firm and the graph of the monopoly firm. In the case of perfect competition, the marginal revenue, price, and the firm's demand are the same curve. For the monopoly, the marginal revenue lies below the demand.

▶ Summary

The revenue concepts needed to help determine a firm's profit have been developed in this chapter. The effect of market structure on the firm's revenue was discussed first. Except for monopoly, the more market power a firm has, the more the revenues of different firms are related. The market power of a firm depends on the structure of the market. The market structure involves the number of firms in the market, the freedom of entry, and the degree to which the good is standardized. In this chapter, we emphasized revenue for two market structures, perfect competition and monopoly. These are market types in which the revenue of one firm is not related to that of another firm. Two other market structures where the revenues of firms are related will be discussed in Chapter 15.

Regardless of the market structure, two important revenue concepts are total revenue and marginal revenue. When the firm is perfectly competitive, the price at which the firm can sell output is constant and is determined by market supply and market demand. Total revenue in this case is a constant price times the amount of output sold. Marginal revenue is the change in revenue when one more unit is sold. In perfect competition, the marginal revenue is also the price. For a monopoly firm, the amount the firm can sell depends on the price. So to sell more units, the price must fall. This means that total revenue is no longer a constant price times output. Also marginal revenue will no longer be constant, but lies below the demand.

Now that these revenue concepts have been discussed, we are ready to move on to the firm's decision process and the origin of supply. The firm's decision process will require putting together the cost and revenue for each firm. The costs will be calculated in the same way, and the cost curves will have the same shape, regardless of whether the firm is a perfect competitor or a monopolist. Only the revenue is affected by the market structure. Our cost and revenue concepts can now be combined to understand profit-seeking behavior. The next chapter will explore the role of profit in both the perfectly competitive firm and monopoly. We are going to see what profit is and how to make the most of it.

▶ Key Concepts

market power   perfectly competitive market
market structure   total revenue
easy entry   marginal revenue
standardized product   monopoly
differentiated product

▶ Discussion Questions

1. What are the elements of market structure that generate market power? Can a perfectly competitive firm have market power? Explain.
2. Uncle Effron does not believe that one firm's revenue depends on another firm's revenue. Explain to Uncle Effron how the revenue of one firm can be related to the price of another firm.
3. Dustbowl Films considers itself a competitive firm. When Dustbowl calculates its marginal revenue, marginal revenue decreases with output. Would you say Dustbowl is perfectly competitive? Why or why not?
4. Do you agree or disagree with the following statement: Automobile producers are in perfect competition? Explain.
5. How is the price determined in a perfectly competitive market? What role does this price play for the individual firm?
6. What does marginal revenue measure?

7. The market demand curve slopes downward, the monopolist's demand curve slopes downward, and the demand curve of a perfectly competitive firm is horizontal. Explain why.

8. Explain why marginal revenue falls for a monopoly firm but not for a perfectly competitive firm.

▶ Self-Review

• Fill in the blanks

market power	The ability of a firm to control price is called _____. As the market power of firms
more	increases, the revenues of the firms become _____ related. The amount of market power depends upon
structure	the market _____. The elements of market
firms	structure include the number of _____, the freedom
entry	of _____, and the degree to which the product
standardized	is _____. Two market structures of
perfect competition	unrelated revenues are _____
monopoly	and _____. A perfectly competitive market is
many, standardized	characterized by _____ firms, a _____
easy entry	product, and _____. The perfectly competitive
price taker	firm is known as a _____ because the price
market	is determined by the _____. Its demand curve
horizontal	is a _____ line established at the market
price	_____. To find the total revenue of a firm, multiply
price, quantity	the _____ times the _____ sold. The change
	in total revenue as one more unit is produced and sold
marginal revenue	is the _____. In perfect competition
horizontal	marginal revenue is a _____ line and is
demand, price	the same as the firm's _____ curve and _____.
single	Monopoly is characterized by a _____ seller, no
substitutes, entry	acceptable _____, and barriers to _____.
price searcher	A monopolist is also called a _____.
	The demand curve for a monopolist is
downward, lower	_____ sloping. The monopolist must _____
	price to sell more. For the monopolist, marginal
below	revenue always lies _____ demand, meaning that
price	marginal revenue will be less than _____.

● Multiple choice

1. Total revenue is:
   a. the amount of profit the firm makes.
   b. price times the quantity sold.
   c. the total amount of money the firm spends.
   d. none of the above.
2. If there are many firms in a market, then it is likely that:
   a. all firms have market power.
   b. no one firm can control price
   c. the product is an essential one.
   d. there are barriers to entry.
3. Which product is standardized?
   a. Grade A eggs.
   b. Subcompact cars.
   c. Size medium shirts.
   d. Left-handed baseball gloves.   ˙
4. Marginal revenue for the perfectly competitive firm:
   a. increases.
   b. declines.
   c. is constant.
   d. cannot be predicted.
5. A monopoly firm sold its 3rd unit of output for $24. The price of the 4th unit
   is most likely to be:
   a. $48.
   b. $36.
   c. $24.
   d. $22.

Answers: 1.b, 2.b, 3.a, 4.c, 5.d.

Chapter | 12 | PROFIT

The objective of every firm is to maximize profit. Profit is the difference between total revenue and total cost. Cost behaves the same for all firms, regardless of the market structure in which they produce. Each firm competes in the resource market for inputs. The set of costs studied in Chapter 10 apply to every form of market structure. We also know from Chapter 11 that revenue varies with the market structure.

The profit objective is the motivating force for the firm. In this chapter we will see how a firm uses the profit motive to determine how much output to produce and what price to charge.

We first must understand the economic meaning of profit; then we will study the profit-seeking behavior of both a firm in perfect competition and a firm in monopoly.

The Economic Meaning of Profit

Profit is total revenue minus total cost. The economic meaning of total revenue is standard with economists and noneconomists alike — price times quantity. But for economists, total cost includes not only the explicit cost but the implicit cost as well. When total cost is subtracted from total revenue, there are three possible outcomes: economic profit, normal profit, and economic loss.

Economic profit means that total revenue is greater than total cost. The revenue of the firm more than covers the opportunity cost of all resources used. After paying the explicit cost and accounting for the implicit cost (both costs were discussed in Chapter 10), the firm has revenue left over. This remaining revenue is economic profit, sometimes called pure profit. However, a firm making a normal profit has no remaining revenue. When total revenue equals total cost, the firm makes a **normal profit**. A normal profit is also called a zero economic profit. This means that the firm exactly covers its opportunity cost, no more, no less.

A puzzling point is how a firm survives if making zero economic profit. This means, after all, that the firm is producing the good for $5 and is selling it for $5. The key to understanding a normal profit is implicit cost. What if the owner, after a careful evaluation of the alternatives, insists that she will reallocate the resources unless she makes a million dollars of "profit"? Then, in the economic sense, a million dollars is an opportunity cost of keeping the owner's resources employed in their current production. This implicit cost is included as a part of the total cost of the good. If the firm makes a normal profit, it means that the owner has made the necessary million-dollar "profit." So some of the $5 cost of the good is its share of the million-dollar "profit." What appears to be a "profit" is actually a cost. Thus the accounting books of the firm will show a $1 million profit even though the economic profit is zero, and the firm makes a normal profit.

If the consumer pays $6 for this good, the firm will make a $1 economic profit on each unit. If the consumer pays $4, the firm may eventually go out of business. At $4 a unit, not all the opportunity costs are covered. When the price the firm receives does not cover the total cost of production, including implicit costs, the firm makes an economic loss. An **economic loss** means that the total cost is greater than total revenue.

Profit Maximization

What is the goal of the firm? The most common assumption in capitalistic societies is that the firm attempts to make as much profit as possible. This assumption is known as profit maximization. **Profit maximization** means making the greatest possible amount of profit. To reach profit maximization, each firm must find its own answer to a set of critical questions: how much to produce and what price to charge. Failure to answer these questions properly can lead to the failure of the firm. This section will focus on the process that resolves these questions.

First we will use a commonsense approach to profit maximization. Suppose that we ask whether or not it makes sense to produce another unit. What would you do if the extra revenue from selling another unit of output is $10, but the extra cost of producing the unit is only $7? Would you produce and sell that particular unit? We think that you would. You would collect $10 from the sale of the good and the cost of producing it was only $7, including implicit cost. You would be ahead by $3. This $3 is extra or marginal profit, or what the sale of this last unit contributes to profit so far. **Marginal profit** is the change in profit when one more unit is produced and sold. Since your objective is to maximize profit, you would choose to expand output by this unit, since it increases profit by $3 and brings you closer to profit maximization. Your production decision should also be clear when the extra cost of producing another unit is $15 but the extra revenue from its sale is less. Why produce this extra output if it costs more to produce than it can be sold for?

We can now develop a general rule. If the marginal revenue is greater than the marginal cost, expand output; if the marginal cost is greater than marginal revenue, reduce output. When would you not be either expanding or reducing output? Only when the marginal revenue and the marginal cost are equal. When MC = MR, the firm will be in equilibrium, not increasing or decreasing production. This is the rule for profit maximization. The objective of every firm is assumed to be profit maximization, and the MC = MR rule will help the firm to achieve it.

You can see how our commonsense approach can be explained in terms of marginal concepts. Your firm would not stop production when the marginal revenue of an additional unit is $10 and the marginal cost is $8. There are two extra dollars of profit to be made by producing and selling the additional unit. The profit maximizing firm will not stop short of obtaining all the profit possible, so we predict that the firm will expand output by the additional unit and increase profit by an additional $2. When there is no more extra profit to be made by expanding output, then the firm has maximized profit and profit is at its highest level.

Sometimes the best efforts of the firm will result in an economic loss. If so, the firm will want to minimize the loss. The MC = MR rule for profit maximization is also the rule to minimize loss. To minimize loss is the same objective as to maximize profit. What if the firm produced and sold another unit and gained $1 on that individual unit? That action would make the profit go up. But what if the firm were already making a loss? It would make the loss smaller by $1. Making profit bigger is the same as making loss smaller. It does not matter whether the best the firm can do is make a profit or the best it can do is make a loss. Once the firm has decided to produce output, the profit maximization rule will leave the firm as well off as possible. No other rule can do as much for the firm.

Profit Maximization in Perfect Competition

The profit maximization rule can be seen in Figure 12-1. Here the horizontal marginal revenue curve of a perfectly competitive firm is combined with the hook-shaped marginal cost curve. The point of intersection of the marginal cost with the marginal revenue is the **profit maximization point**. The level of output that this point represents is the profit maximizing quantity. The shaded area to the left of the profit maximization point represents the *positive* marginal profit gained if the firm expands production to the profit maximization level.

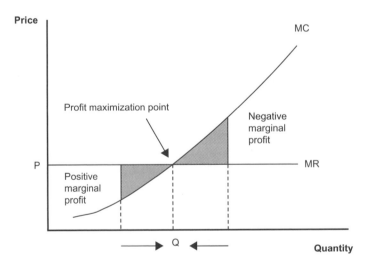

Figure 12-1   Profit Maximization for a Perfectly Competitive Firm
The profit maximization point is where MC = MR. If the firm produces a level of output where MR is greater than MC, to the left of Q, profit can be increased by the amount of positive marginal profit by increasing output. If the firm produces a level of output where MR is less than MC, to the right of Q, profit can be increased by the amount of negative marginal profit by reducing output.

Profit will be greater by this amount of marginal profit if output is expanded. We are simply following the profit maximization rule: if MR is greater than MC, expand output. You can see that to the left of the profit maximization point, MR is *always* greater than MC.

The shaded area to the right of the profit maximization point is the *negative* marginal profit that results by expanding production beyond the profit maximization level. The additional cost to produce each of these units is more than it can be sold for, resulting in a loss on each additional unit. Of course this negative extra profit reduces profit so that profit falls and is not maximized. To apply the profit maximization rule, recall that when marginal cost is greater than marginal revenue, we cut back production. Then the negative marginal profit, the loss on each unit, will be *subtracted* from profit, and profit will become greater. So profit is only maximized at the MC = MR point. If production is less than where MC = MR, there is more to add to profit by expanding output, since MR exceeds MC. If production is at an output where MC exceeds MR, greater than the profit maximization point, the loss on each of those additional units will be avoided, and the profit will be increased by reducing output to the profit maximization point. So the marginal approach is just a commonsense method of reaching profit maximization.

The decision-making process of the firm includes finding not only the profit maximizing quantity but also the appropriate price. For a perfectly competitive firm, the price is determined by the market. The perfect competitor has no choice over price and can only select the output level. But to make our decision process complete, once the level of production is determined, and here the firm can do no better than produce the MC = MR output, then the firm's demand curve determines the highest price that consumers are willing and able to pay for this level of output. Figure 12-2 shows this price which, for the perfect competitor, is the market price. Recall that the market price is the result of demand and supply interacting in the market.

We have seen how a perfectly competitive firm maximizes profit. What about a monopoly?

Profit Maximization in Monopoly

The defining characteristic of a monopoly firm is that there is only one firm in the market. A monopoly is a type of market structure with a single seller of the product and restricted entry to the industry. This means that the firm's demand curve is the market demand curve. We have established in Chapter 11

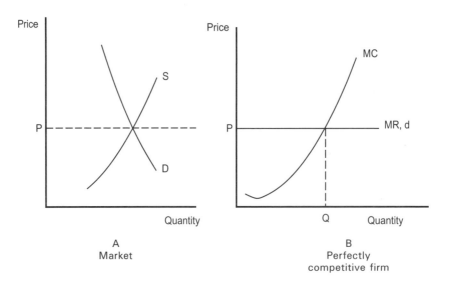

Figure 12-2   The Market Determines Price for the Perfectly Competitive Firm
The perfectly competitive market in panel A determines price by supply and demand. That price
is the price charged by the perfectly competitive firm in panel B. Find the profit maximization
point at MC = MR and drop straight down to find the profit maximizing quantity. From
that quantity, go straight up until the *demand* curve is reached. And then read off the profit
maximizing price, in this case P.

that the marginal revenue curve lies below the downward-sloping demand of
the monopolist.

A monopolist is just like any other firm in that it seeks to maximize profit.
But the monopolist, unlike the perfect competitor, must determine the price
as well as the output level. We have called the monopolist a price searcher. A
downward-sloping demand curve dictates a trade-off between price and quantity.
So a profit maximizing monopolist faces a dilemma. If the firm attempts to
charge a higher price, it knows that there will be a fall in the quantity sold.
On the other hand, if the firm seeks to increase quantity, it finds that it must
lower its price. Not only will changing price (and consequently quantity) affect
total revenue, it will also affect total cost and therefore profit. To maximize
profit successfully, the monopolist must find the right combination of price
and quantity.

The profit maximizing combination of price and quantity is shown in
Figure 12-3. First note that the marginal revenue lies below the demand and
that the MC = MR rule is used to determine both the price and the output

level. The output level is found by the profit maximization point, and once
the output level is determined, the firm will charge the highest price that
buyers are willing and able to pay for that level of output. This price is
found on the demand curve. Thus the dilemma of the monopolist is resolved
when the profit maximizing combination of output and related price is found.

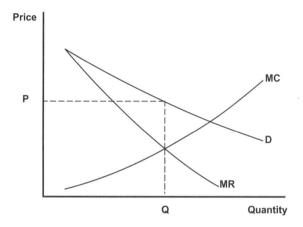

Figure 12-3   Profit Maximization for a Monopoly; Price and Output
Profit maximizing output, Q, for the monopoly occurs where MC = MR. The profit maximizing
price, P, is obtained from the demand curve.

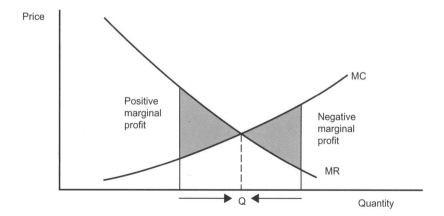

Figure 12-4   Profit Maximization for a Monopoly; MC = MR
To the left of the profit maximizing output, marginal profit is positive. Profit will be increased by
increasing output. To the right, marginal profit is negative. Profit will be increased by decreasing
output.

To prove that this is the most profitable combination of price and output for the monopolist, consult Figure 12-4. The shaded area to the left of the profit maximization point is the positive marginal profit that can be gained by expanding output to the profit maximizing level. At any level of output less than the profit maximization point, it is always true that MR is greater than MC and there is additional profit to be gained by the production of additional units. The shaded area to the right of the profit maximization point is the negative marginal profit, the reduction in profit that will result as output is expanded beyond the profit maximization point. It is always true that beyond the profit maximization point, the MC is greater than the MR and the firm makes a marginal loss on each of the additional units that is produced and sold. If output is reduced, this marginal loss will be avoided and profit will be larger. Therefore, only one level of output will maximize profit and only one price will cause that quantity to be sold.

The profit maximization rule works for every type of market structure. The only difference for the monopolist is that the demand curve slopes downward and consequently the marginal revenue lies below it. But the concept remains the same — always produce a unit on which profit goes up, never produce a unit on which profit goes down.

Perfect Competition in the Short Run

Although the MC = MR rule leaves your firm as well off as possible, you might be curious as to whether this leaves the firm with a profit or loss. Exactly how much is the profit, or how much is the loss? Is the profit an economic or a normal profit? To answer these questions we must look at the short-run outcome. In the short run there is at least one factor of production that is fixed and, as a result, firms cannot enter or leave the industry. There are three possibilities for the perfectly competitive firm in the short run: economic profit, normal profit, or economic loss.

A perfectly competitive firm with economic profit potential appears in Figure 12-5. This figure shows the price (marginal revenue and demand) and the average total cost curve. The points of intersection between demand and the average total cost are called **break-even points**. Would the firm choose to produce at a break-even point and make a normal profit? Not if it could make a greater profit. Any production level between the two break-even points on the graph yields an economic profit. This is because the price received by the perfectly competitive firm on each unit sold is greater than the average total

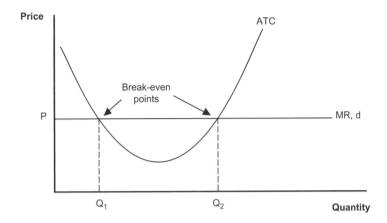

Figure 12-5   Perfect Competition; Economic Profit Potential
Economic profit potential for a perfectly competitive firm occurs at any level of production between the two break-even quantities, Q_1 and Q_2, obtained from the break-even points. The reason is that price is greater than the average total cost.

cost of producing those units. The price is greater than the opportunity cost of producing the good, the average total cost, so the firm makes an economic profit on each and every unit.

So Figure 12-5 illustrates economic profit. But how much output will the firm produce and exactly how much profit will it make? The firm can make an economic profit at any output level between the break-even points but only one output level will maximize profits. Insert the MC curve into the picture (now Figure 12-6), and the profit maximization point pinpoints the profit maximizing level of output at 10 units and the profit maximizing price at $8. Notice that the firm *could* produce and sell at its average total cost of $6 for this level of output. If so, it would just cover its opportunity cost and make a normal profit. But since the demand is high enough that the firm can charge $8, it will. There is $2 of economic profit for each of 10 units, or a total of $20 profit.

The normal profit picture for a perfectly competitive firm is Figure 12-7. You can see that there is only one output level where the price covers the cost of production, the ATC. In Figure 12-8, when the MC is drawn in, you can see that this break-even point is also the profit maximization level. A perfectly competitive firm making a normal profit is the only case where the MR, the MC, and the ATC all intersect at the same level of output. In the next chapter, we will see the importance of this intersection.

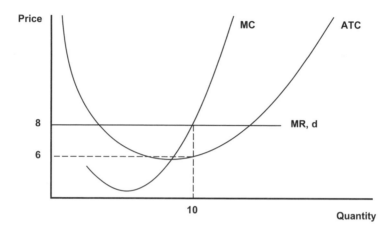

Figure 12-6   Perfect Competition; Profit Maximization; Economic Profit Case
Maximum economic profit for a perfectly competitive firm occurs at MC = MR. This firm would produce and sell 10 units for $8 each to maximize profit. The ATC at 10 units is $6. Economic profit of $2 per unit is made.

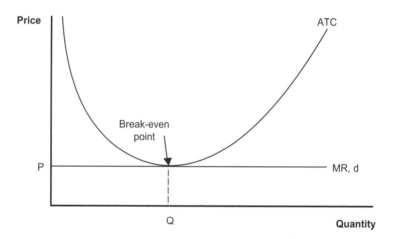

Figure 12-7   Perfect Competition; Normal Profit Potential
Here there is only one break-even point where the price covers the ATC. This shows normal profit potential for a perfectly competitive firm.

A firm suffers an economic loss when its demand is too low, its cost is too high, or a combination of both. Figure 12-9 represents the economic loss condition. The average total cost is always above the marginal revenue, the price received by the perfectly competitive firm. There is no level of output where

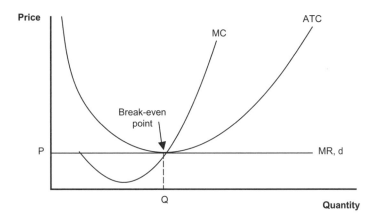

Figure 12-8 Perfect Competition; Profit Maximization; Normal Profit Case
Profit maximization occurs where MC = MR. At this output, the ATC is just equal to price. Economic profit is zero.

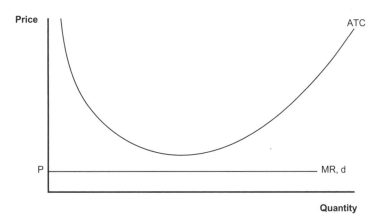

Figure 12-9 Perfect Competition; Economic Loss Potential
Since the cost of producing the good is above the selling price at every level of output, the firm will make an economic loss.

the firm can produce and receive a price that will cover its cost. There are no break-even points. At every level of output, the cost of producing a unit is greater than the selling price. The firm making an economic loss will produce at the MC = MR level *only* after another condition, discussed in Chapter 13, has been satisfied. If the firm does produce, it will be at the level where MC equals MR, the level that will minimize loss. This is indicated in Figure 12-10.

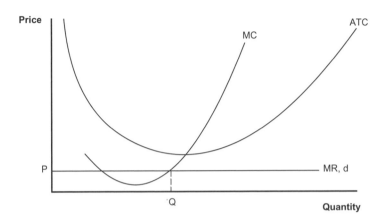

Figure 12-10   Perfect Competition; Profit Maximization; Economic Loss Case
At the profit maximizing output, the ATC is above the price. If the firm does produce, it will make an economic loss.

▶ Summary

The profit seeking behavior of both the perfectly competitive firm and the monopoly firm has been the focus of this chapter. Based on the profit maximization assumption, the profit maximizing rule was established. If marginal revenue is greater than marginal cost, expand output; if marginal cost is greater than marginal revenue, cut back output. The rule is to produce at the point where marginal revenue equals marginal cost. When a firm is producing at the profit maximizing level and charging the profit maximizing price, we know that the firm is as well off as its costs and the demand for its product can leave it.

The combination of the concepts of cost, revenue, profit, and profit maximizing behavior has determined the price and output level of the firm. In the following chapters the outcome of, first, the perfectly competitive firm and, then, the monopoly firm can be evaluated and compared.

In Chapter 6, you were introduced to the law of supply. The next chapter will provide a more complete understanding of why that law is true.

▶ Key Concepts

profit	profit maximization
economic profit	marginal profit
normal profit	profit maximization point
economic loss	break-even points

▶ Discussion Questions

1. Your accountant has managed to balance your books, and the books show that your firm has made $10.00 profit this year. Should you be happy or sad?
2. Normal profit is zero economic profit. Uncle Effron says that it is not economic to make zero profit and it is not normal. Explain the meaning of normal profit to Uncle Effron.
3. At the output where profit is maximized, the marginal revenue equals the marginal cost. Why?
4. Is the basic decision process of business any different from your own decision process?
5. How can it be true that profit is maximized when marginal profit is zero?
6. If you are a perfect competitor, what is the effect on your output level of
   a. an increase in market price? Why?
   b. a decrease in market price? Why?
7. Would a perfectly competitive firm ever advertise?
8. Uncle Effron says that a monopoly can charge any price it wants. Would you agree with Uncle Effron? Why or why not?
9. In a monopoly, when profit is maximized, then MC = MR. Is this different from the case of perfect competition? Explain.
10. Uncle Effron says MC cuts MR in two places and one can maximize profit at either output. Is he right? Suppose we start at X output and increase output. Compare MC to MR to determine what happens to profit. Can X be a profit maximum?

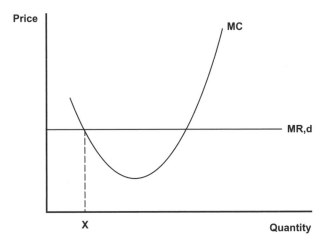

▶ Self-Review

• Fill in the blanks

profit
economic

normal
economic loss
profit maximization

expand
reduce

expand, reduce
maximized
MC, MR

output
demand

economic profit
normal profit, economic loss

The difference between total revenue and total cost is called _____. When total revenue is greater than total cost, the firm makes an _____ profit. When total revenue and total cost are equal, the firm makes a _____ profit. When total cost is greater than total revenue, the firm makes an _____. The objective of the firm is _____.
If marginal revenue is greater than marginal cost the firm will _____ output. If marginal cost is greater than marginal revenue the firm will _____ output. When marginal revenue equals marginal cost, the firm will neither _____ nor _____ output since profits are being _____. The profit maximization rule for the monopolist is ___ = ___. The profit maximization point determines the profit maximizing level of _____ for the monopolist, while the price is determined on the _____ curve at that output level. The perfect competitor faces three short run outcomes — _____, _____, or _____.

- Multiple choice

1. When a firm makes more than enough to stay in business, the firm is making:
   a. economic loss.
   b. normal profit.
   c. economic profit.
   d. cannot be determined.
2. If the marginal cost is greater than the marginal revenue:
   a. expand output.
   b. reduce output.
   c. neither expand nor reduce output.
   d. decrease price.
3. Profit maximization occurs at the output where marginal cost equals marginal revenue because:
   a. if output increases, marginal revenue less than marginal cost means that total cost goes up faster than total revenue so profit falls.
   b. if output decreases, marginal revenue greater than marginal cost means that total revenue falls faster than total cost so profit falls.
   c. profit is zero at that point.
   d. both a. and b.

4. The MC = MR rules find profit maximization for:
   a. a perfect competitor.
   b. a monopolist.
   c. both a and b.
   d. none of the above.
5. Which rule maximizes profit?
   a. maximize total revenue.
   b. minimize total cost.
   c. produce the greatest possible output.
   d. equate marginal cost and marginal revenue.

180

Chapter | 13 | PERFECTLY COMPETITIVE SUPPLY

Key Topics
shutdown decision
supply
the long-run equilibrium
evaluating perfect competition

Goals
use profit maximization to obtain the firm's supply
examine the perfectly competitive firm in the long run
discover why competition is desirable

The profit objective is the motivating force for the firm and, as we will see, helps to ensure that the perfectly competitive firm eventually acts in the best interest of society. Here we can extend our understanding of the short and long run behavior of this market structure and evaluate the perfectly competitive model for efficiency.

Once you have completed this chapter, you will have a better understanding of the important concept of supply. The outcome of the profit seeking behavior of the perfectly competitive firm will be the supply of the individual firm as well as the supply of the perfectly competitive industry. Remember that supply is one-half of the process that determines the market price and allocates resources.

From the previous chapter we know that the MC = MR rule determines the price and output level for maximum profit. Why would the firm ever choose zero output? To answer this question, we will consider the shutdown decision of the firm faced with an economic loss.

The Shutdown Decision

There are three short run possibilities for a perfectly competitive firm —

economic profit, normal profit, and economic loss. Only a firm threatened with economic loss must decide whether to continue production at the profit maximizing level of output or shut down and produce zero output. Notice that the firm is not choosing to go out of business and exit the industry; this is only possible in the long run. Fixed factors cannot be changed in the short run. The firm cannot cancel the rent on its warehouse or sell its factory; there is not enough time. In the short run the firm must continue to pay the cost of its fixed inputs but can stop the use of variable inputs. Recall that total cost is made up of both fixed and variable cost. A firm with an economic loss may be able to reduce total cost and the loss if it does not hire any variable inputs. Without variable inputs, the firm cannot produce and shuts down production.

The **shutdown decision** tells the firm to stop production if its revenue does not cover its variable cost. What rule will the firm use for this shutdown decision? A firm will continue to produce output as long as the price is greater than the average variable cost of production. A firm must make enough to cover the cost of its *variable* inputs or it is better off not producing at all. If the price a firm receives does not cover its variable cost, then it is not receiving enough to cover its costs of labor, raw materials, and so on. Why hire workers when the revenue from selling the product your workers produce does not even cover their salaries? Not only are you losing money on the workers, a variable cost, but you also do not have any revenue left to pay your rent, a fixed cost. You are making a loss on variable as well as on fixed costs. If you choose to shut down and produce nothing, you would not receive any revenue, but you would not be hiring workers on which you lose money. You would make no loss on your variable cost; your only loss is your fixed cost. Your loss would be minimized. If your cost is too high or your demand is too low, you will make an economic loss. But to minimize the loss, shut down if the price does not cover the variable cost.

Notice that the shutdown rule is *not* suggesting that you pay your variable costs first. You can pay any bills you choose, labor, rent, or whatever is most pressing. But recognize that your situation is economic loss — you do not make enough to cover *all* your costs. Our concern is not which costs you do pay; the concern is whether you produce zero or the MC = MR output. The shutdown decision provides the answer.

The **shutdown point** or shutdown price is at the lowest point on the average variable cost curve shown in Figure 13-1. That is the lowest price that just covers the variable cost. From Chapter 10 we know that the lowest point on the AVC is the intersection with the MC curve. At any price higher than the

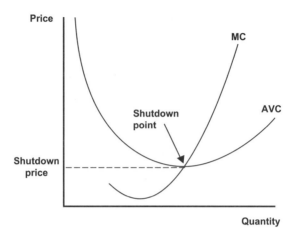

Figure 13-1   Shutdown Point for the Perfectly Competitive Firm
The lowest point on the average variable cost is the shutdown point. That occurs at the intersection of the AVC and the marginal cost. The resulting shutdown price is the lowest price that just covers the variable cost.

shutdown price, the firm will produce; at any price lower, the firm will shut down.

Supply

From our knowledge of the perfectly competitive firm, we can find its supply curve. The process of finding this curve will support your understanding of the law of supply from Chapter 6. We want to know how much output the firm will produce at each alternative price. The marginal cost curve above the shutdown point is the short-run supply curve. Look at Figure 13-2. If the price is lower than the shutdown price, P_1, the firm will not produce. As the price reaches the shutdown price or above, the level of output is determined by the profit maximization point. As price increases, this MC = MR intersection occurs at higher and higher levels of output because the marginal cost rises as output rises. The result is that the MC curve above the shutdown point is the short-run supply curve for the firm in perfect competition. That is why we have always drawn the supply curve beginning in midair, not touching either axis. The lowest point on the supply curve is the shutdown point, the intersection of the average variable cost and the marginal cost curve. At a lower price, the firm will not produce. At a higher price, every point on the supply curve

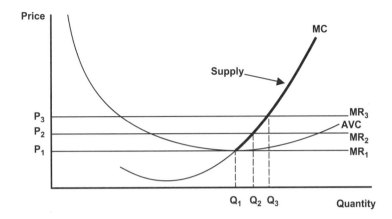

Figure 13-2   Perfectly Competitive Supply
At each price, the profit maximizing quantity of output is produced. At prices below the shutdown price, P_1, the firm will produce no output. Thus the combinations of price and quantity on the marginal cost curve above the shutdown point are the supply curve.

is a point where profit is maximized. It should be clear how important the profit maximization concept is in the calculation of supply: without the profit maximization assumption, we could not obtain the supply curve.

Recall that marginal cost is hook-shaped because of the law of diminishing returns. The part of the marginal cost above average variable cost is rising, and therefore the quantity supplied by the individual firm rises as output rises. When the price increases above the shutdown price, so does the output of the firm. We have found the source of the law of supply, which is a direct relationship between the price and the quantity supplied. If we add the marginal cost curve above the shutdown point for all the firms in the perfectly competitive industry, we will have found the *market* supply curve. Since all individual supply curves are upward sloping, so is the market supply curve, again due to diminishing returns. If we combine the short-run market supply curve with the market demand curve, we have found the market price.

What makes the market supply shift? The market supply is the sum of the supply curves of the individual firms, each of which is a firm's marginal cost curve above the shutdown point. So whatever makes the MC shift will cause the market supply to shift. Two factors causing the firm's MC to shift, and hence market supply, are technology and input prices. Since the MC is related to the marginal product, any change in technology will cause the MC to shift. The other factor shifting the MC will be the price of inputs. If inputs become more expensive, it will cost more to produce another unit than before the input price went up, so MC shifts. So far our focus has been the short run. Our next task is to understand the difference made by the long run.

Long-Run Equilibrium

The essential difference between the short run and the long run is that in the long run all factors are variable. This means that the firm must choose the amount of each input to use in the long run, including the factor that was fixed in the short run. For the tomato farmer, the short-run decisions involve the amount of labor and fertilizer, but not the amount of land to be farmed. In the long run the amount of land must also be determined. One long-run choice is to use no factors and go out of business. Only in the long run can firms leave the market. Of course, in the long run new firms can enter the industry too, bringing with them resources that were once fixed in some other use. These choices were not possible in the short run. Thus a firm has additional decisions to make in the long run.

If any firm in the perfectly competitive industry is making an economic profit, then in the long run additional firms will be attracted to the industry. Firms are attracted when the price received is greater than the opportunity cost of the resources. Figure 13-3 shows the following series of events. As firms enter the industry, the market supply is increased. See panel 13-3A. This drives down the market price and consequently the demand for each individual firm. In panel 13-3B, the firm's MR curve drops and the economic profit becomes smaller. Firms will continue to enter the industry as long as any economic profit remains. Eventually, the MR curve will be driven down until it intersects the MC at the minimum of the ATC. This becomes the picture of normal profit shown by Figure 13-4.

If firms in the industry are making economic loss, the short-run period of time is not long enough for fixed factors to be changed and for these firms to exit. Economic loss may be made in the short run, but it can be avoided in the long run by going out of business. So as firms make economic loss, in the long run the weakest begin to leave the industry. As a result, the market supply decreases, Figure 13-5A, and the market price is driven up. The reduction in supply raises price for the remaining firms. Individual firms see their demand rise, Figure 13-5B, eliminating the economic loss until eventually all surviving firms are those now making a normal profit. This result is again the normal profit picture shown in Figure 13-4.

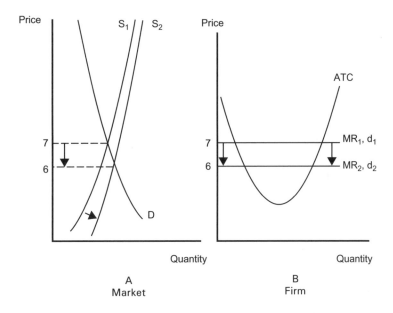

Figure 13-3 Long-run Adjustment for the Perfectly Competitive Firm
Economic profit for a perfectly competitive firm encourages firms to enter the market, market
supply to increase, and consequently, price for the firm to fall.

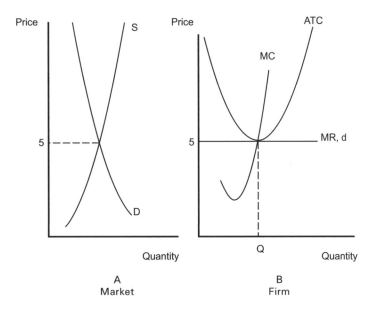

Figure 13-4 Long-run Equilibrium for the Perfectly Competitive Firm
A perfectly competitive firm experiences normal profits in long-run equilibrium.

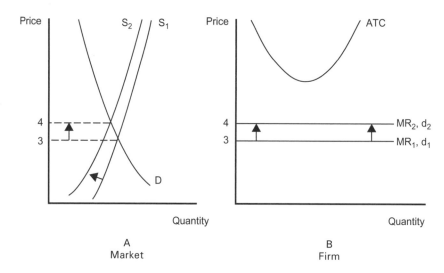

Figure 13-5   Long-run Adjustment for the Perfectly Competitive Firm
Economic loss for a perfectly competitive firm encourages firms to leave, the market supply to
fall, and consequently, the price for the firm to rise.

There is but one long-run outcome in a perfectly competitive market —
a normal profit. Economic profit attracts firms, which lowers the price and
eliminates the profit; economic loss drives firms out, which raises the price
and eliminates the loss. The survivors receive a normal profit. In the long run,
competition eliminates both economic profit and loss. Normal profit is the long-
run equilibrium in a perfectly competitive market.

An Evaluation of Perfect Competition

A major concern is whether the perfectly competitive market solves the resource
allocation question efficiently. An **efficient allocation of resources** occurs
when a good is produced at the lowest possible opportunity cost. This means
as few of society's scarce resources as possible are used up, leaving resources
free to be used in the production of other goods. Since the average total cost
of a firm measures the opportunity cost of the good at each production level,
an efficient use of resources means producing at the lowest possible average
total cost. A firm producing at a higher level of cost is not getting as much
output as possible from the resources; the evidence is the higher per unit cost.
If a firm does not produce at the most efficient level of production, there is a

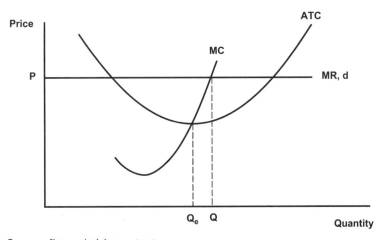

Q = profit maximizing output
Q$_e$ = efficient level of output

Figure 13-6 Economic Profit Means Misallocated Resources
This figure shows that the profit maximizing output and the efficient level of output are not the
same if the firm is perfectly competitive and makes an economic profit.

misallocation of resources. We will see that resources are misallocated if a
firm makes either economic profit or economic loss.

An economic profit signals a misallocation of resources. Figure 13-6 is the
economic profit picture. The most efficient level of production is at the lowest
point on the average total cost curve. And we know that the lowest point on
the ATC curve is the intersection with the marginal cost curve. Yet the most
efficient level is not where the firm chooses to produce; it follows the profit
maximization rule instead. The firm will choose to increase output beyond the
most efficient level of production as long as MR is greater than MC and there
is additional profit to be made. Thus the firm produces at a level higher than
the most efficient on the ATC, and society's resources are misallocated.

What if a firm makes an economic loss? Resources are also misallocated.
Figure 13-7 is the economic loss picture. In this case the firm, to minimize its
loss, produces less than the most efficient level of output. The firm will not
choose to expand output to the lowest average total cost. Why not? Marginal
cost exceeds marginal revenue and the loss increases. Thus when economic loss
is made, there is not an efficient use of resources. And what if the firm makes
a normal profit? Figure 13-8 shows the only situation when the intersection
of the ATC, the MR, and the MC all occur together. The most efficient level

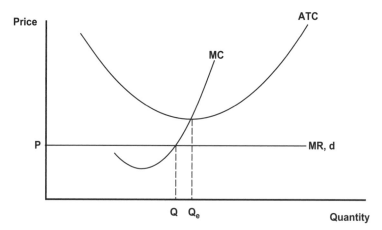

Q = profit maximizing output
Q_e = efficient level of output

Figure 13-7   Economic Loss Means Misallocated Resources
The efficient level of output and the profit maximizing level are not the same for the perfectly competitive firm making an economic loss.

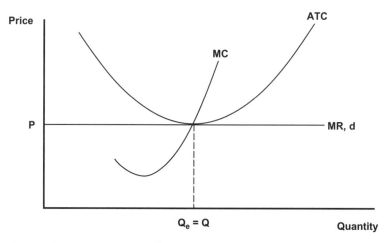

Q = profit maximizing output
Q_e = efficient level of output

Figure 13-8   Normal Profit Means No Misallocated Resources
The perfectly competitive firm making a normal profit will produce so that the efficient level of output and the profit maximizing level of output are the same.

of production in this case is also the profit maximizing one for the firm, a fortunate coincidence for society. The firm, in following its own self-interest, also acts in the best interest of society. Society's resources are allocated in the most efficient manner by the firm. Keep in mind that a normal profit signifies that all opportunity costs are covered and that the firm has no incentive to alter its behavior. This means that the price the consumer pays is the lowest possible price to persuade the firm to continue production in the long run. Society, the firm, and the consumer all benefit from a normal profit.

Consider again what happens when economic profit is the outcome. The price that the consumers pay for the good is more than enough to persuade the firm to provide the good. All a firm requires is a price high enough to cover the full opportunity cost of producing the good. When a firm receives total revenue greater than the total cost, it is receiving an unnecessary profit. The firm is receiving payment for its monetary expenditures and is being compensated for its owner-owned resources and more. Neither the consumer nor society receives any economic value for this extra payment. An economist sees this side of economic profit as undesirable.

A perfectly competitive firm making economic profit is a signal that society wants more resources allocated to this market. The fact that consumers are willing to pay more than the opportunity cost of the good shows the preference for a reallocation of resources. In the long run more firms will enter, bringing more resources. Economic loss occurs when society is not willing to pay the opportunity cost of the good and prefers to see the resources allocated to some other use. The reallocation occurs as firms leave the industry in the long run. So perfectly competitive markets respond to consumer demand, eventually increasing or decreasing the use of resources according to consumer preference.

The forces of competition tend to work in the best interest of society. If a perfectly competitive industry is in long-run equilibrium, this means that each firm is receiving a normal profit. A perfect competitor cannot change its demand, but it can find ways to change its cost. Each firm prefers an economic profit, so each firm always has incentives to find new ways to lower production cost and increase profit. If one firm lowers cost, that firm makes economic profit. You know that economic profit attracts new firms, market supply increases, and demand for the individual firm falls. The firms previously making normal profit now make economic loss and will only survive the long run by also employing a new technology to lower cost. The new long-run equilibrium will be a normal profit for each surviving firm but now at a *lower* cost of production than was possible before. Thus the good can now be produced with even fewer resources, and society has more resources left to satisfy other wants.

With a normal profit, the consumer is paying the lowest possible opportunity cost of the good. The firm will continue to produce, and the outcome could not be improved upon for the consumer or society. In the short run a perfectly competitive firm is in one of three positions: economic profit, normal profit, or economic loss. Only one of those conditions provides the efficiency preferred by society. But in long-run equilibrium, the firm in perfect competition always produces at the most efficient level of output.

But there is no "perfect" market structure. Even perfect competition may fail. First we will compare perfect competition to other market structures and then consider examples of market failure.

▶ Summary

We have seen that the firm may want to shut down production in the short run to minimize loss. The shutdown decision requires the firm to compare the price with the lowest average variable cost. If price is above the average variable cost, the firm should produce at the profit maximizing level, MC = MR. If price is below the average variable cost, the firm should shut down.

Based on the profit maximization rule and the shutdown decision, the short-run supply curve for the perfectly competitive firm was determined. You should be aware that the ideas we have developed starting with Chapter 9 have been used to obtain the supply curve. Chapter 9 discussed production and provided an explanation for the shape of the marginal cost curve, the law of diminishing returns. Chapter 10 developed the cost concepts. Clearly marginal cost and average variable cost play a key role in supply. Chapter 11 discussed the idea of revenue, particularly marginal revenue, which, together with marginal cost, are needed to establish profit maximization. The supply curve is the marginal cost curve above the average variable cost. Because of diminishing returns, this supply curve will be upward sloping. Given the supply curves for all the firms in an industry, the market supply curve can also be determined.

In the long run each firm in a perfectly competitive market will produce where price just equals the smallest average total cost; each firm will earn a normal profit. If economic profit is made, the profit will attract new firms into the market, which will cause price and profit to fall. If economic loss is made, the loss will cause firms to leave, and price and profit will rise. The long-run equilibrium results in an efficient use of resources. Thus the significant advantage of a perfectly competitive market to society is that resources will be allocated efficiently.

You should now have a better understanding of the importance of profit in determining supply and the forces that cause long-run equilibrium in perfectly competitive markets. This information is important because supply is a critical part of the price determination process. In the next chapter we leave the world of perfect competition and return to the world of monopoly.

▶ Key Concepts

shutdown decision
shutdown point
efficient allocation of resources
misallocation of resources

▶ Discussion Questions

1. Explain the shutdown decision.
2. Although the variable costs are being covered, the production manager is concerned that the fixed costs are not completely covered. He is considering shutting down production and hoping that the product price rises. What would you advise and why?
3. McDermott's Marshmallows figures its marginal revenue to be $1.37 per bag and its marginal cost to be $1.25. To maximize profit, would you suggest that it increase or decrease production? Explain why. What if marginal revenue were $1.18? Or $1.25? Would your answers change if you knew that the lowest average variable cost were $1.42? Explain.
4. Why is the marginal cost curve above the average variable cost curve also the supply for the perfectly competitive firm?
5. What causes a perfectly competitive firm's supply curve to slope upward?
6. What impact will a fall in market demand have on the price?
7. What do you predict will happen in the long run to the number of producers in a perfectly competitive industry when firms are making
   a. economic profit?
   b. economic loss?
   c. normal profit?
8. A perfectly competitive firm is efficient in the long run. What does "efficient" mean? Why is efficiency desirable?

9. Uncle Effron says when a firm is producing on its ATC curve other than where the MC crosses, the firm is intentionally wasting resources. Is he right? Why or why not? Explain.

▶ Self-Review

• Fill in the blanks

economic profit, normal profit	The perfect competitor faces three short-run outcomes — _____, _____,
economic loss	or _____. A firm faced with economic
shutdown	loss must make the _____ decision. A firm
	will continue to produce as long as price covers the
average variable	_____ cost. The shutdown point
AVC	is the lowest point on the _____ curve, which is
marginal cost	also the intersection with the _____
	curve. The short-run supply curve for the perfectly
marginal cost	competitive firm is the _____ curve
shutdown	above the _____ point. The only possible
	long-run outcome in perfect competition is
normal	_____ profit. If firms were making an economic
enter	profit, firms would _____ the market and drive
down	price _____. And if firms were making economic
leave	loss, firms would _____ the market and drive
up	price _____. When a perfectly competitive firm
	makes a normal profit, price just equals the lowest
average total	_____ cost of production and resources
efficiently	are allocated _____.

• Multiple choice

1. The shutdown point is:
   a. the lowest point on the average variable cost.
   b. the point covering fixed cost.
   c. the point where the marginal cost crosses the average variable cost.
   d. both a and c.

2. Perfectly competitive firms are making economic profit. What is the long run outcome?
   a. Firms enter, market supply increases, and price falls.
   b. Firms enter, market demand increases, and price rises.
   c. Firms leave, market supply falls, and price rises.
   d. Firms leave, market demand rises, and price rises.

3. The most efficient level of output is the:
   a. lowest AVC.
   b. lowest ATC.
   c. lowest MC.
   d. lowest MR.
4. The firm is producing 100 units of output and making an economic profit. The efficient level of output is:
   a. 100 units.
   b. more than 100 units.
   c. less than 100 units.
   d. cannot tell.
5. Which is the long-run outcome in perfect competition?
   a. economic profit.
   b. economic loss.
   c. normal profit.
   d. all of the above.

Answers: 1.d, 2.a, 3.b, 4.c, 5.c.

| Chapter | 14 | MONOPOLY

Key Topics
  barriers to entry
  long-run monopoly
  evaluating monopoly

Goals
  understand the economic impact of monopoly
  recognize that monopoly misallocates resources

Everyone seems to know about monopolies — how large they are, how they charge the highest price that they can get, how they make huge profits and are so successful at exploiting the consumer. There is little doubt that most of us believe that competition is good, and monopoly is bad. We now have the tools to evaluate factually the market structure called monopoly. In the last chapter we focused on the perfectly competitive firm. The monopoly firm is the center of attention now. As in the last chapter with perfect competition, we will examine the monopolist in both the short and the long run and evaluate the outcome from the viewpoint of society. But first we will find how a firm becomes a monopolist before we consider what it means to be one.

Barriers to Entry

One element of market structure is the degree of freedom of entry into the market. There are no obstacles or barriers to entry in perfect competition, but the same is not true under monopoly. The barriers to entry assure that there will only be one firm in the monopoly industry. **Barriers to entry** are factors that keep firms from entering the market when there are incentives for them to enter. Economic profit, for example, provides an incentive for a firm to enter a market. Barriers to entry include natural monopoly, high fixed cost, advertising, and exclusively owned resources. Government too, intentionally or unintentionally, erects barriers to entry.

Many monopolies are natural monopolies. They may be seen in small towns that have a single movie theater, bank, or Ma and Pa store. They can maintain their monopoly position as long as the town is small and far from other towns. On the other hand, natural monopolies may be as large as a utility company in a major city. A **natural monopoly** occurs when the market is large enough to support only one firm of an efficient size. One firm can charge a price that covers its average total cost. But if two firms divide the market, each would be smaller and less efficient, so that the average total cost of each rises, and neither firm could cover cost. A natural monopoly can be a small firm in a small market or a large firm in a large market. So as you can see, not all monopolies will be large.

One basis for natural monopoly is economies of scale, efficiencies of large productive capacity. **Economies of scale** cause the average total cost to decline in the long run as the productive capacity of the firm increases. When there are economies of scale, the larger the firm, the smaller the average total cost. Thus, the efficiently sized firm may be larger than the size of the market. In such a case, one firm at most can produce efficiently, and monopoly occurs. Economies of scale explain why there is only one electric distributor in town.

There are other barriers that contribute to market power for the monopolist and for other forms of market structure introduced in the next chapter. High fixed cost is one obvious source of market power. A potential railroad or chemical company may be discouraged from entry by the high fixed cost of accumulating capital resources. If entry into the industry requires large amounts of resources to start production, it will be difficult for new firms to enter. The high fixed cost is a barrier, and high fixed cost may also mean that a great deal of time is required to construct the production facility. Thus not only must the entrepreneurs raise a lot of money, they must also be patient since their rewards may not come for many years.

Advertising, like high fixed cost, increases the expense and the risk associated with entering a market. If the new firm were to fail, some of the money put into the firm would be recoverable when the buildings and other assets are sold off. But the many dollars spent on advertising to enter a national market cannot be recovered. Many firms will think twice before entering a market requiring high advertising expenditures.

Exclusively owned resources are another barrier to entry. OPEC (Organization of Petroleum Exporting Countries) controls a large enough percentage of the world's known oil reserves that it has at times wielded a considerable influence over the price of petroleum. It would be no use for firms to enter the market without their own source of petroleum. Prior to World War II, ALCOA, the Aluminum Company of America, was *the* aluminum company of America. ALCOA controlled much of the existing bauxite reserves, and without access to this crucial input it was impossible for competitors to enter the aluminum market. The source of market power for the De Beers organization is the control of the diamond supply. Clearly, the exclusive ownership of the product or the unique inputs to production is an effective barrier to keep out would-be competitors.

Barriers to entry are also erected by the government by granting monopoly power to a firm, imposing tariffs or import quotas, issuing patents, and requiring licenses to go into business. Sometimes the government gives monopoly power to a firm. Government regulation makes it illegal for you to compete with your local gas company in the distribution of natural gas. Of course, monopoly rights can also be taken away by government. Now Federal Express competes with the U.S. Post Office. AT&T, which once had exclusive rights to long-distance phone service, has been required to share the market. Some consumers may choose their electric or gas producers.

Tariffs and import quotas serve to protect whole groups of domestic producers from foreign competition and give U.S. producers market power they would not have if foreign firms were free to enter. Government patents to some extent prevent other firms from producing a particular good. Not all of the barriers to entry erected by the government are intentional. The government requires a license for many occupations, from barber to mortician. You must obtain a license from the state to be allowed to compete in these markets, in effect reducing the number of competitors and increasing the potential market power.

While barriers to entry may generate market power, there are times when firms will not take full advantage of the market power that the barrier provides. If a firm obtains market power because the government has authorized it, the firm may be reluctant to use the full extent of the market power. If it did, the government might decide to withdraw its support, and the firm would lose its monopoly position. In other cases where entry into the market is possible, though not easy, the firm may charge a price providing less than the maximum profit for fear of attracting competition.

Barriers to entry apply to all market structures except perfect competition. What are the results of barriers to entry and what are the implications for society?

In this chapter we will see the results in monopoly and in the following chapter the impact with the remaining market structures, monopolistic competition and oligopoly.

Short- and Long-Run Monopoly

The question now is what is the short-run outcome for the monopolist and what are the long-run consequences? Like the perfect competitor, there are three possible outcomes for the monopolist in the short run: economic profit, normal profit, and economic loss. Figure 14-1 represents these outcomes for the monopoly firm. In the case of economic profit, Figure 14-1A, the average total cost intersects the demand at two break-even points. Any level of output between the break-even points results in economic profit since the price the firm receives on the demand curve is greater than the average total cost of production. The second situation, Figure 14-1B, is that of normal profit. There is only one level of output where the price covers the cost of production, explicit and implicit. The third graph, Figure 14-1C, guarantees economic loss as there is no level of output where the price can cover the cost.

In the long run, a monopolist makes either an economic profit or a normal profit. No firm can survive into the long run with an economic loss. The reason the monopolist can continue to maintain economic profit from the short run into the long run is that barriers to entry prevent competing firms from entering and taking a share of the market. This lack of competition permits long-run economic profit for the monopolist. The existence of long-run economic profit is a certain sign that a firm has market power. Although it is the monopolist, unlike the perfect competitor, who can continue to earn economic profit into the long run, it is not every monopolist who will be in this enviable position. Whether the monopolist makes long-run economic or long-run normal profit depends upon the level of demand and cost for the firm. The next sections will compare the outcome in monopoly to that of perfect competition.

Higher Price and Lower Output

Would the price of a good be different if it were produced under monopoly conditions rather than under perfectly competitive conditions? Would the quantity produced be different? What other differences would there be? We start with price and quantity.

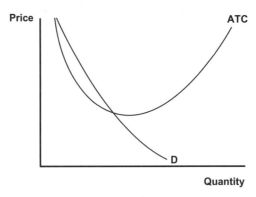

A
Economic profit potential

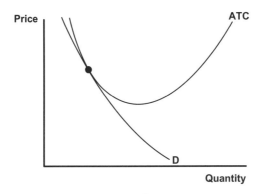

B
Normal profit potential

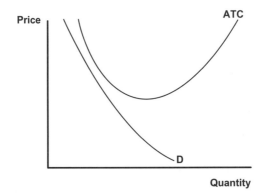

C
Economic loss potential

Figure 14-1   Short-run Potentials for Monopoly

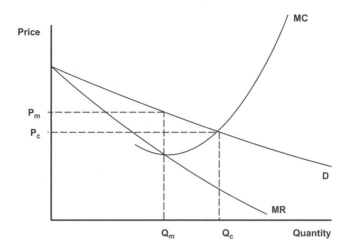

Figure 14-2 A Comparison of Monopoly and Perfect Competition
The price and output a monopoly would choose is P_m and Q_m. The price and quantity under perfect competition would be P_c and Q_c.

Assume that the cost of production is the same whether the firm is a monopoly or a perfect competitor. The monopoly would behave as shown in Figure 14-2. At profit maximum the monopoly produces Q_m units of output and charges a price of P_m. If the same firm now behaved as if it were perfectly competitive, then price would be determined by supply and demand. Notice that the demand curve for the monopolist is the market demand, which is also the demand for the perfectly competitive market. Recall from Chapter 13 that the marginal cost curve (above the shutdown point) is the supply curve for the perfectly competitive firm. Thus the perfectly competitive supply is the MC shown. In the perfectly competitive situation, Q_c would be produced and the price would be P_c. You can see that the monopoly will charge a higher price and produce a smaller quantity than in a perfectly competitive situation. This is a significant difference between the monopoly market and the perfectly competitive market.

The downward-sloping demand curve at first appeared to be a disadvantage for the monopolist. It was necessary to lower price to increase the quantity sold. But what appears to be a disadvantage is actually an advantage and a source of market power. Note that a monopolist cannot successfully charge any price it chooses. The choice over price is limited by the demand for its product. But within the limitation imposed by the demand, the monopolist is able to reduce the quantity and therefore increase the price in a manner that increases profit.

Thus the monopolist will earn economic profit under conditions that would result in a normal profit for a perfect competitor.

Misallocation of Resources

There is also a claim that a monopolist misallocates resources. A misallocation of resources means that more output could be obtained from the resources by using them in a different way. One sign of misallocated resources is if the price of the good is greater than the value of the resources going into the good. The value that society places on the resources is the opportunity cost of the resources. If the society values the resources at $5, then the price of the product should not be greater than $5. If the good could more efficiently be produced at $4, then the price should not be greater than $4. We have considered this point in the case of perfect competition and found that in the long run, the price will equal the lowest possible opportunity cost, the lowest average total cost. Now the monopoly firm will be evaluated for efficient use of resources.

Figure 14-3 shows the three short-run outcomes for the monopolist and includes the MC and the MR curves so that the profit maximization point (MC = MR) can be found and the price and output determined. The monopolist *always* produces less than the efficient level of production. Economic profit, Figure 14-3A, provides the incentive for the firm to produce at a level other than Q_e, the lowest level on the ATC where the MC crosses. Most surprising, when the monopolist makes a normal profit, Figure 14-3B, the firm still produces at a level of output that is less than the lowest point on the ATC. A monopoly making a *normal* profit is misallocating resources. Economic loss, Figure 14-3C, also results in a misallocation of resources, a fact revealed by the third graph. So unlike the perfectly competitive firm that is producing efficiently when it receives a normal profit, the monopolist always misallocates resources in the short run.

The long-run outcome is no better. Unlike the perfect competitor whose only long-run outcome is a normal profit, the monopolist will receive either economic profit or normal profit. But in both cases, the monopolist produces less than the efficient level of output. The conclusion is that the monopolist will misallocate resources in the short run and can continue misallocating resources indefinitely into the long run. The outcome for society with a monopoly firm is far different from the outcome for society with a perfectly competitive firm. While the perfectly competitive firm earning economic profit did misallocate

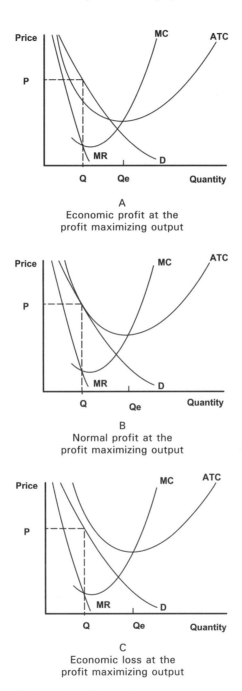

Figure 14-3   Short-run Outcomes for Monopoly
The profit maximizing output is Q, and the efficient level of output is Q_e. In no case does the monopoly choose to produce so that the average total cost is at a minimum. In all cases the monopoly misallocates resources.

resources in the short run, in the long run competitive pressure from other firms entering the market forces production to the most efficient level. Barriers to entry prevent this from happening in monopoly.

The price paid by the consumer to the monopolist will always be greater than the lowest opportunity cost of producing the good. Even if the monopoly makes only a normal profit and is not receiving any unnecessary return from the consumer, the price will still be greater than the smallest opportunity cost, the minimum of the average total cost. In this sense the consumer overpays. A perfectly competitive firm in long-run equilibrium provides the good at a price equal to the lowest cost of production.

We have identified two significant differences between monopoly and the perfectly competitive firm. One difference is that the monopoly will charge a higher price and produce a smaller quantity than will the perfectly competitive firm. The second difference is that the monopoly firm misallocates resources since the price the monopoly charges is greater than the opportunity cost of the resources. This long-run misallocation cannot occur in perfect competition.

Observe that every unregulated profit maximizing monopoly will behave this way. We cannot expect a monopoly to correct itself. If we want the monopoly to behave as a perfectly competitive firm behaves, the firm will have to be regulated by government. One reason is based on the belief that the unregulated monopoly would overcharge the consumer. A second reason is that without regulation, the monopoly would not provide a satisfactory allocation of resources.

▶ Summary

Monopolies exist for various reasons. Barriers to entry are the most common explanation and occur in many forms: a huge investment to build a plant that is both large and highly mechanized; one firm which has control over an essential resource; monopoly status having been granted by the government; or the existence of a natural monopoly.

The existence of natural monopolies means that not all monopolies are large industrial giants. It should be clear that the monopolist does not charge the highest price possible. If a firm charged the highest price possible, it may only be able to sell a single unit of the output. Perhaps the revenue from this sale would not even cover the variable cost, not to mention the fixed cost, and the firm would be left with an economic loss. The price and output the monopoly chooses depend on marginal revenue and marginal cost. As long as MR is greater than MC, the firm will continue to expand output and is not concerned with having to reduce price to increase the quantity sold. Since MR is greater than MC, profit is still rising. The objective is strictly profit maximization, not charging the highest price.

It should also be obvious that the monopolist is not guaranteed to make large profits. The cost conditions and the demand facing the monopolist will determine the possibilities for the firm. Even a monopolist can make an economic loss and in the long run be forced out of business and the resources reallocated.

Yet the downward sloping-demand curve is the source of monopoly market power. The consumer and society will not benefit because the monopoly firm will in the long run produce less than the efficient output level. This is because as the quantity is reduced, the firm has the opportunity to increase price above the average total cost of the good and the opportunity to reap economic profit. In contrast, competition will force the perfect competitor to produce and sell at the most efficient level, eliminating economic profit.

We have seen the decision-making process in both perfect competition and monopoly. The same process will be more complex for monopolistic competitors and oligopolists, for these are the firms with related revenues. We will explore this theme in the next chapter.

▶ Key Concepts

barriers to entry
natural monopoly
economies of scale
misallocation of resources

▶ Discussion Questions

1. If only one airline serves a town, does a monopoly exist? What about competition from trains, buses, and autos?
2. Assume that you own a poultry farm. Your major output is eggs. In what kind of market structure do you find yourself? You are an imaginative entrepreneur; how could you differentiate your product? What possible barriers to entry could you erect?
3. Cousin Sybil is the only palm reader within 100 miles. She has a natural monopoly. Cousin Sybil figures that her average total cost falls as more palms are read. If a new palm reader comes to town, what will happen to Cousin Sybil's profits? If Cousin Sybil were making a normal profit to begin with, what

might happen to Cousin Sybil? Can the market support more than one palm reader?

4. Does diminishing returns determine marginal cost in monopoly? If so, explain how. (Hint: Look at Chapter 10.)

5. How does the monopolist's price and quantity compare to that of a perfect competitor?

6. Explain why a misallocation of resources occurs in the long run under monopoly but not under perfect competition.

▶ Self-Review

• Fill in the blanks

barriers to entry

natural monopoly

economies of scale
fixed
resources
monopoly
tariffs
quotas, licenses

MC, MR

output
demand

economic profit
normal profit, economic loss

economic profit, normal profit

misallocates
lowest, ATC

higher
lower

Firms are prevented from entering markets by _____. When the market can support only one efficiently sized producer, the firm is a _____. If the average cost continues to decline at a large volume of production, the firm has _____. Other barriers to entry include high _____ cost and exclusively owned _____. Government barriers include grants of _____ power, protection from foreign competition by _____ or import _____, and occupational _____. The profit maximization rule for the monopolist is _____ = _____. The profit maximization point determines the profit maximizing level of _____ for the monopolist, while the price is determined on the _____ curve at that output level. In the short run, the possible outcomes for the monopolist are _____, _____, and _____. The long run outcomes for the monopolist are _____ and _____. Yet in each outcome, the monopolist _____ resources by producing at a point other than the _____ on the _____ curve. When the price and output level of the monopolist and perfect competitor are compared, we find that the monopoly price is _____ and the output is _____.

● Multiple choice

1. Which of the following is a barrier to entry?
   a. Standardized product.
   b. Low fixed cost.
   c. Natural Monopoly.
   d. Easily obtained resources.
2. High fixed cost is a barrier to entry because it:
   a. requires a firm to generate a large amount of starting money before production can begin.
   b. will usually mean a long construction period before the rewards start.
   c. requires the entrepreneur to wait a long time before the rewards start.
   d. all of the above.
3. A monopolist is guaranteed to make:
   a. economic profit.
   b. economic loss.
   c. normal profit.
   d. none of the above.
4. If a firm in perfect competition were to become a monopolist, price would:
   a. rise.
   b. fall.
   c. stay the same.
   d. not enough information to tell.
5. The price charged by the monopolist is _____ the lowest opportunity cost of producing the good.
   a. greater than
   b. equal to
   c. less than
   d. double

Answers: 1.c, 2.d, 3.d, 4.a, 5.a.

Chapter 15 | IMPERFECT COMPETITION

Key Topics

monopolistic competition

oligopoly

antitrust

market failures

Goals

recognize the complexities that occur when the revenues of firms are interrelated

understand that because of misallocation of resources, there are policies that attempt to change the way firms behave

recognize that perfect competition will not always allocate resources desirably, even in the long run

The firm that employs you is likely to be engaged in imperfect competition. Most of the firms you see around you are neither perfectly competitive nor monopoly. These opposite extremes serve as standards with which to evaluate the real world in between, that of imperfect competition. If you have an understanding of the consequences of following one extreme or the other, as explained in Chapters 13 and 14, then you can begin to evaluate real-world problems. We will examine two more market structures — monopolistic competition and oligopoly. We will see certain similarities between these imperfect competitors, and perfect competition and monopoly, but there are unique differences also. The circumstances that cause perfectly competitive markets to fail are also included in this chapter.

Monopolistic Competition

A **monopolistic competitor** competes in a market that has many sellers, a differentiated product, and easy entry. The existence of many firms and easy entry makes the market appear competitive. What distinguishes this firm from a perfect competitor is the ability to make the product unique. This differentiation of the product gives rise to market power. The name of this market structure, monopolistic competition, refers to monopoly-like competition. Each of the many firms attempts, by differentiating its product, to create its own individual monopoly. If it could only make its product different enough, it would be the only seller and have the market power of a monopolist. But before this can happen, new firms will enter the market and reduce its market power. So it is the lack of barriers to entry in monopolistic competition that limits the market power of the individual firm.

The key to monopolistic competition is product differentiation. How can the firm differentiate its product from those of all the other competitors? The usual way is to develop a distinction, real or perceived, in the product and reinforce it through the power of advertising. You may be hungry for a hamburger, but no one sells a "hamburger." There are Big Macs, Big Boys, Whoppers, Big Bufords, and the creation of each local establishment. The product that each firm produces appears unique, even if in nothing more than the convenience of the location and the friendliness of the employees. Each firm seeks to convince the public of the superiority of broiling over frying, a lower fat content, made to order, or whatever other feature may be profitable to promote. There may be only one firm that offers you the hamburger of your choice — or so the firm hopes — and it will do what it can to differentiate its product favorably.

A variety of firms are found in monopolistic competition, including restaurants, department and discount stores, gas stations, grocery stores, doctors, and lawyers. These firms are not trying to attract your business strictly on the basis of price. Rather they are competing on the basis of factors other than price. This is called nonprice competition. The share of the market that each firm attracts depends on the firm's ability to make its good or service different and more desirable than those of its competitors. Each firm is faced with a downward-sloping demand curve representing its current share of the total market. Each product has close substitutes but no perfect substitute. Whenever the demand curve slopes downward, the marginal revenue is less than the price. What is the economic outcome of monopolistic competition?

The monopolistic competitor is a profit maximizer and follows the MC = MR rule. One short-run outcome for this firm is shown in Figure 15-1. The firm produces at a level of output other than the minimum average total cost. This means that the consumer pays a higher than necessary price and

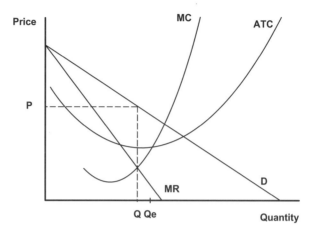

Figure 15-1   Monopolistic Competition in the Short Run
This monopolistic competitor is making economic profit in the short run. The consumer pays a higher than necessary price and the firm fails to produce at the most efficient level, Q_e, the lowest average total cost.

that the firm misallocates resources. This particular firm is making economic profit. The more the firm is able to differentiate its product, the more inelastic (Chapter 8) and more monopoly-like will be its demand. This means the greater the advantage the firm will have from reducing output and increasing price. But remember that there are other firms in this industry and that additional firms are also free to enter and compete. The control of the monopolistic competitor over its share of the market demand is always in jeopardy.

Because of easy entry, the long-run profits are forced to zero, and each monopolistic competitor earns a normal profit. The long-run equilibrium for the monopolistic competitor is shown by Figure 15-2. Notice that although the firm makes a normal profit, the firm is not producing at the output where the average total cost is minimum. The misallocation is due to the market power shown by the downward-sloping demand curve. The monopolistic competitor is not forced to the efficient level of production and the lowest possible price, as is a perfect competitor. On the other hand, the existing and potential competition prevents the long-run economic profit potential of monopoly.

Although monopolistic competition misallocates resources, there is a positive side; namely, the differentiated products that satisfy a variety of different consumer tastes. This diversity of product would not be available under perfect competition. How monopolistic competition is viewed by society depends on how the trade-off, that of lost efficiency for broader consumer choice, is valued.

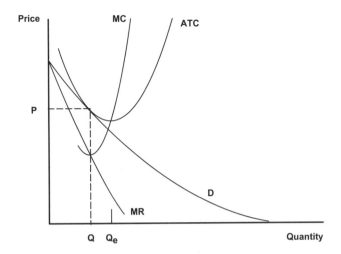

Figure 15-2   Monopolistic Competition in Long-run Equilibrium
A normal profit is the long-run result in monopolistic competition. Notice, however, that the firm
still does not produce at Q_e, the most efficient level.

Oligopoly

Oligopoly is one of the most interesting and complex forms of market structure.
Oligopoly is a market of just a few sellers, usually protected by barriers to
entry, for a product that is either standardized or differentiated. Oligopolists
that sell capital goods to other firms frequently produce a standardized product.
Carbon tetrachloride, for example, must have the same chemical composition
regardless of the producer. One quantity of the chemical is identical to another
equal quantity. There are only a few firms, all oligopolists, producing this good.
Other examples of oligopolists selling a standardized product are the steel and
aluminum industries.

Generally, an oligopolist that sells a consumer good produces a differentiated
product. An abundance of advertising encourages the buyer to believe that there
are significant differences among cars, or beers, shampoos, aspirin, cigarettes,
and numerous other products. Our focus will be on these oligopolists that
produce differentiated products and sell directly to consumers.

An important element of oligopoly is that there are few sellers. Before we
look for an industry with few sellers, we need to know which firms to count.
How do we find how many firms there are in the industry? It seems easy; all
we have to do is count them. But how many firms there are depends on what
we mean by the "industry." If the industry is defined in terms of a specific

good — steel, for instance — then we count the number of firms that produce steel. But consider the market from the viewpoint of the buyer of steel. If the price of steel goes up, buyers will find other products to use in place of steel. In many applications, aluminum has replaced steel. Other substitutes include plastics and fiberglass. If the market is construction materials, we must also count brick, cement, and glass. You can see that how the market is defined can affect the number of firms in the industry. Now we can ask how many firms are in an oligopoly.

Oligopoly involves only a few sellers of closely related goods. The number of firms is limited by the existence of substantial barriers to entry. A few sellers could be any number, but means few enough so that each seller has some control over price. Each firm has some degree of market power. An oligopolistic industry can usually be identified by the existence of the "Big Three" or "Big Four" firms that tend to dominate the industry and account for the major part of its sales. There may be more than three or four firms in the industry but not so many that an individual firm acts without considering the response of its rivals. Some examples of oligopolistic industries are the steel, personal computer, auto, chemical, oil refining, cereal breakfast food, glass container, chewing gum, and aircraft industries.

The small number of firms gives rise to a distinguishing characteristic of oligopoly — interdependence. This interdependence among firms creates a state of anxiety within the industry and, as we shall see, provides incentive for the firms to conspire for their own self-interest and against that of the public. The source of this interdependence lies in the fact that firm A cannot make a pricing or differentiation decision without considering the actions of its competitors, and these actions will in turn determine the outcome for firm A. There are different ways that firms in oligopoly may react when one firm lowers price. Other firms could lower price, increase advertising, or develop and bring out a new product line, to name a few. Not only must the firm in oligopoly be concerned about the reactions of its buyers to a change in its price or strategy, it must be concerned about the response of its competitors as well. This process of related revenues was introduced in Chapter 11.

Even though oligopolists are sensitive to the price that other firms charge for their good, there is no requirement that all firms charge the same price, especially when the product is differentiated. You are well aware that not all makes of cars are the same price. There is a variety of prices in the market for televisions, detergents, gasoline, and shampoos. When firms in an industry do not charge the same price, they are not price takers.

Oligopoly — Kinked Demand

There are a number of oligopoly models. A model of one firm must include how all the firms interact. Several different models will be considered. The first is called the **kinked demand** model. What if one firm in an oligopoly industry was considering an increase in the price of its product? The outcome for this firm depends upon how its rivals react. What if all the other firms maintained their prices at the current level? Then the first firm would find itself losing customers to competitors with relatively less expensive products and would end up with a smaller share of the market and smaller profits. Note that the firm would not lose all its customers. There are those convinced that a substitute, even though now made relatively less expensive, would not be an acceptable replacement. But there will be less loyal buyers who are not so impressed by the differentiation among products who would turn to a competitor to avoid a price hike. The competitors would find this outcome profitable and therefore would not choose to increase price if their rival did. Thus no one firm has any incentive to increase price since it will be left worse off than before.

What if one firm lowered price to attract more buyers and gain a larger share of the market? How will the other firms react? All firms will be forced to reduce their prices as well; otherwise they will lose customers to the lower-priced firm. Thus when one firm lowers price, all firms must. And the result? All firms will be worse off than before. Since all firms lowered price, no one firm is able to change its market share significantly. But now each firm is selling at a reduced price, lowering total revenue and reducing profits. Thus no firm would normally choose to lower price.

The result of interdependence is that the outcome for one firm is dependent not only on its actions, but also on the reactions of other firms. Thus any one firm will be worse off if it raises price, because no other firm will, and worse off if it lowers price, because all other firms will. This outcome is unique to oligopoly and results in rigid, or sticky, prices. Figure 15-3 illustrates the distinct demand of the oligopolist. This demand curve has two sections. On the upper section, where the firm raises its price, and since no other firm follows, the quantity demanded falls quickly as customers find new sellers. On the lower section, a decrease in price causes all the other firms to reduce price, so the quantity sold does not increase very quickly. The firm cannot successfully lure customers from other firms by lowering price.

This is the kinked demand curve of the oligopolist. The kink is the bend or point of inflection in the curve. Above the kink, demand is elastic, and the firm

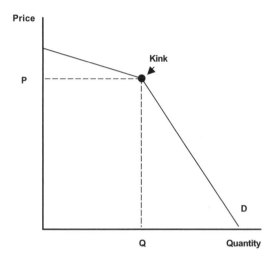

Figure 15-3   Kinked Demand; Oligopoly
Demand is elastic above the kink and less elastic below it. Due to the reaction of its competitors,
the firm has no incentive to raise or lower price. Price and quantity will tend to occur at the kink.

is worse off if it raises price, due to the inaction of its competitors. Demand is
less elastic below the kink, and the firm would lose revenue if it were to lower
price, due to the reaction of its competitors. Since the firm will not charge
a price above or below the kink, the price will tend to occur at the kink.
The kinked demand curve is an explanation for the price rigidity that occurs
in oligopoly. Since the firm finds that it cannot use price as a competitive
tool, it must instead compete through its product. So rigid prices and product
differentiation will normally characterize the behavior of oligopolists with a
kinked demand.

Apply this model to the auto industry. Car prices typically change only
to reflect cost and demand conditions. The products are clearly differentiated,
even for an individual who only distinguishes the "big" from the "little" cars.
Any one producer knows that to lower price substantially would trigger serious
reactions from other firms. Price wars are uncommon in oligopoly. However,
when there is a downturn in auto sales, one U.S. auto manufacture may lower
price in an effort to increase profit. As could be predicted, the other firms
essentially match the plan of the first so that the temporary price decreases
are similar for all firms. These price reductions exist in various forms such
as rebates, lower interest rates, or "free" options. But under usual conditions,
prices are rigid in the auto industry.

Although kinked demand explains rigid prices, the kinked demand model fails to provide a satisfactory explanation of how the oligopolist initially establishes the price. We know the kink in the demand curve occurs at the price the firm charges. But to put the kink in the curve, we first have to know the price. The strength of this model is that it focuses on the interdependence of the firms. We can see how the price decision of one firm affects the decisions other firms make, and how a firm can be harmed by any change in price it might consider. The idea of "going it alone" causes problems for the firm in oligopoly. So the kinked demand model treats firms as rivals that are plagued by their interdependence. Yet there is a way for the firms to avoid these problems. The undesirable effects that fall on one firm that tries to improve its profit will not happen if all firms cooperate to improve the profits of all. Cartels and price leadership are two models that reflect cooperative behavior. What are the incentives for cooperative behavior?

Oligopoly — Cooperative Behavior

The interdependence among oligopolies does not mean that the firms will never raise price. If all firms were to act as one and raise price together, each would maintain its share of the market, and the higher price would increase profit for all firms. You can see the temptation for the oligopolies to act together as one firm in the determination of price.

A **cartel** is a group of firms acting as one — in effect, a monopoly — to determine the profit maximizing level of output and price. Recall that in monopoly the firm was the industry and found the profit maximizing combination of output and price. The cartel does the same for its industry. Firms agree among themselves as to how the market should be divided up among the firms. A cartel agreement both divides up the market and establishes a price policy. Either the cartel sets a uniform price or the cartel allows each firm to set price for its own share of the market as the firm sees fit. In this way, the individual firm can ignore how other firms will respond to changes in price. Thus the revenue calculation of the firm is separated from other firms. OPEC is the best-known cartel. This organization of member nations (firms) attempts to charge the profit maximizing price and divides up the profit maximizing level of output among the nations. Each nation has a limit to the amount of petroleum it produces and sells, to the benefit of all.

However, cartels tend to be unstable. The monopoly power enjoyed by the cartel originates from the restriction of output and the resulting increase in price. Yet the higher price provides the incentive for each firm to produce more, not less. Of course if enough firms do produce more, the monopoly power and the cartel are destroyed. There is a natural tendency for cartels to come apart. If one firm lowers price to capture more of the market, all other firms must respond and rivalry replaces cooperation. In the case of OPEC, if one member nation lowers price, what can the other member nations do to enforce the cartel agreement? There is no international court that could impose penalties on the offending nation. The cause of the instability of cartels is that the agreement is hard to enforce. This is especially true in the United States where cartels are illegal.

Price leadership is another model of cooperative behavior in oligopoly. **Price leadership** is the practice of all oligopoly firms uniformly increasing price after an increase in price by the industry leader. The price leader may be the most powerful firm or simply one taking the position by custom. The leadership may also shift from one firm to another. This makes it appear that no one firm is the leader. Examples of industries where price leadership occurs are steel, cigarettes, autos, tires, and breakfast cereals.

These forms of collusion, or cooperation among the firms, make the market more like a monopoly. Collusion is undesirable if we want firms to set price as a perfectly competitive market would, so there is reason to try to keep this kind of behavior from happening. In the next section, the role of the government in preventing collusion is discussed.

Antitrust

Congress has passed several **antitrust** laws that attempt to keep collusive behavior from occurring. The two most notable are the Sherman and the Clayton antitrust acts. The Sherman Act was passed in 1890, and the Clayton Act in 1914. Both acts are essentially aimed at monopoly, attempts to monopolize, and actions that restrain trade. Precisely what the meaning of "attempts to monopolize" and "restraint of trade" is has been left to the courts to decide. Antitrust law applies not just to monopoly, but to large firms or groups of firms capable of monopolizing trade. The law is aimed at stopping the kind of collusive behavior described in the previous section.

Have antitrust laws been successful in preventing collusive behavior? It is hard to tell. The antitrust laws make collusive behavior illegal. But just because an action is illegal does not mean that the action will not occur. Firms that might be tempted to collude recognize that they cannot do so legally and must find ways to avoid detection. Perhaps the most publicized prosecution occurred in 1961 in the heavy electrical equipment industry. In that case the government collected evidence of collusive price setting and market division that led to conviction. The industry technique to avoid detection was to use the phases of the moon. Each firm would bid excessively high on government contracts when the moon was not in the phase assigned to the firm. The firm with the proper phase would submit the winning low bid that could be nicely padded due to the lack of competitive pressure. Several firms as notable as General Electric, Westinghouse, and Allis Chalmers paid fines, and some management spent time in jail.

Even if there are laws on the books making some economic behavior illegal, government action is required for firms to be prosecuted. Some administrations are more vigorous in enforcing antitrust laws than other administrations. In short, the effectiveness of the law in promoting a more competitive environment is not easy to assess. But the government undertakes prosecution of many firms each year. Various firms have been accused of monopolizing their respective industries. IBM was in court from 1969 to 1982 before the government dropped the case. AT&T agreed to give up its local companies in return for expanded opportunities in the communications industry. Xerox had to release some patented information to its competitors. Microsoft was ordered to split up. These antitrust cases are complex, and the volume of data to be examined is monumental. It is not unusual for cases to continue for years. Frequently the judgments, when finally reached, are appealed. So even if antitrust laws are aggressively applied, it is not clear that an immediate change in the structure of the market would occur.

Market Failures

We have looked at market structures other than perfect competition and have seen that they can lead to a misallocation of resources. Why then shouldn't every good be produced in a perfectly competitive market? Sometimes the perfectly competitive market will fail to allocate goods properly from society's point of view. There are several reasons why these market failures occur. These include natural monopoly, externalities, and public goods.

We have already discussed natural monopolies. This is a situation in which the market is not large enough to support more than one efficiently sized firm. If there can be only one firm in the industry, that firm has market power and is not perfectly competitive. So if there is a natural monopoly, the good cannot be produced under perfectly competitive conditions.

An **externality** occurs when the cost to society of production differs from the cost to the producer. For example, when a power plant produces electricity from coal, it also produces smoke. One of the goods is sold in the market; the other the plant gives away. The cost to the firm of producing electricity is the opportunity cost of the resources purchased for production. The cost to society is the same as that to the firm *plus* the cost imposed by the smoke. The cost to the firm *should* include the full opportunity cost of production including the harm caused by the smoke. The cost to the firm plus the cost of the externality is the full cost of allocating resources to the production of electricity. Why doesn't the market include the cost of the smoke in the firm's cost? If the firm can claim ownership of the air, it does not have to pay to use the air as a waste disposal, and the cost of pollution falls instead on the person who develops lung cancer. Thus, unless some nonmarket force makes the firm pay the cost of the pollution, the firm will ignore the cost. One solution is for the government to either set pollution limits or impose costs directly on the firms that pollute. With externalities, some nonmarket force is required to allocate resources efficiently.

The third case of market failure involves public goods. A **public good** is a good that we consume collectively and for which an increase in your consumption does not require me to decrease mine. Police protection, fire protection, national defense, and TV signals are all examples. With TV signals, it is true that if one more person turns on a TV set, no one has to turn one off.

Why can't public goods be provided by a market? Some are. Some people buy extra police protection by hiring a security patrol or installing an alarm system. So public goods can in part be provided by a market. But consider national defense. What if private firms produced defense? How much is national defense worth to you, and how much would you buy? Given that your neighbors buy protection, why should you? How will an enemy know that your house is the only one not protected? And if by chance your house is bombed or attacked, won't your neighbors be bombed or attacked too? So even if you buy none, the fact that your neighbors have purchased national defense protects you too. You have an incentive to buy less protection than you want. Worse yet, every buyer has the same incentive. So if national defense were provided by a market, less would be produced than society really wants, and another market failure would result. This market failure is a basis for government action. The government decides for you how much you spend on public goods. National defense and other public goods are purchased from your taxes.

Thus there are times when a perfectly competitive market will not allocate resources efficiently. These include natural monopoly, externalities, and public goods. Under most other conditions, however, the perfectly competitive market structure is capable of providing an efficient allocation of resources. Only as an exception will we find nonmarket solutions more efficient.

▶ Summary

The market structures of firms engaged in imperfect competition with related revenues have been examined. The first, monopolistic competition, is a situation with many firms, easy entry, and a differentiated product. The easy entry and many firms make the market seem competitive, but the ability to differentiate the product provides some market power to the firm. Monopolistic competitors make normal profit in the long run, but they misallocate resources.

Oligopoly is an interesting structure where a variety of models are possible. The three we discussed were the kinked demand, cartel, and price leadership. The basic difficulty in oligopoly is that the firms are interdependent and what one firm does will be affected by what other firms do. The kinked demand model accounts for price stability in oligopoly. The cartel model is more general in that it does not restrict how firms may interact; they may change price, advertising, or product line. In the price leadership model, the price leader has some advantage due to cost, size, or marketing ability.

Now that we have examined the market structures of perfect competition, monopoly, monopolistic competition, and oligopoly, one of the essential questions that every economic system must answer can be addressed — what to produce and in what quantity. You will recall this question from Chapter 4. In capitalistic systems, the goods that are produced are those that are profitable, and the quantity that is produced is dictated by profit maximization. There are cases where the market system fails to allocate efficiently. For those exceptions, government action may provide a more efficient allocation of resources.

We have seen how firms determine the amount of output to produce. But firms also buy inputs. How is that decision made? The next chapter will provide a discussion of how the firm decides the amount of a variable input to hire. The considerations that determine whether firms will hire and what they will pay should be of interest to those who enter the labor market.

▶ Key Concepts

monopolistic competition   price leadership
oligopoly   antitrust
kinked demand   externality
cartel   public good

▶ Discussion Questions

1. There is no doubt that the automobile business is competitive. Why do economists refer to this market as an oligopoly rather than a perfectly competitive one?
2. Why does marginal revenue lie below demand for a firm in monopolistic competition?
3. Why are firms in oligopoly reluctant to engage in price cutting?
4. How is the market structure of monopolistic competition different from oligopoly? Perfect competition? Monopoly? How does oligopoly differ from monopoly? Perfect competition?
5. The island country of Fincincy has a rocky coast and is considering erecting lighthouses to prevent shipwrecks. How can Fincincy collect money to build, maintain, and operate the lighthouses from the ships that use them?
6. What if the government decides to limit pollution? How much pollution should be allowed?
7. Uncle Effron says that perfect competition is the best market structure. Are there ever times when the perfectly competitive market system will fail to allocate resources properly? Explain.

▶ Self-Review

• Fill in the blanks

many

differentiated, easy

differentiate

normal profits

misallocate

few, barriers

standardized, differentiated

In monopolistic competition, there are _____ sellers, a _____ product, and _____ entry. This market structure differs from perfect competition in the ability to _____ the product. In the long run, monopolistic competitors make only _____, but they also _____ resources. Oligopoly is a market of _____ sellers, protected by _____ to entry, and producing a product that may be either _____ or _____. A characteristic of oligopoly is the degree of interdependence

_____ among firms. A model of oligopoly that shows the interaction among the firms

kinked

is the _____ demand model. When one firm

lower

lowers price, competitors _____ price. When one

maintain

firm raises price, competitors _____ price. Models of cooperative behavior among oligopolists

cartels, price leadership

include _____ and _____.

Laws that make behavior in restraint of trade

antitrust laws

illegal are called _____. Causes of

natural monopoly

market failure include _____,

externalities, public goods

_____, and _____. When the cost of production differs from the cost to society,

externality

we have an _____. If public goods were

less

provided by markets, _____ would be produced than society wants.

• Multiple choice

1. The distinction between monopolistic competition and perfect competiton is:
    a. whether or not the product is standardized.
    b. the freedom of entry in the market.
    c. the number of sellers.
    d. the number of buyers.
2. A distinguishing feature of oligopoly is:
    a. product differentiation.
    b. many sellers.
    c. interdependence.
    d. unrelated revenues.
3. When an oligopolist with a kinked demand curve lowers price, other firms will:
    a. also lower price.
    b. raise price.
    c. not change price.
    d. not change output.
4. Examples of cooperative behavior among oligopolists include:
    a. kinked demand.
    b. price leadership.
    c. cartel.
    d. both b and c.
5. Which is most likely to involve externalities?
    a. A jar of peanut butter.

b. A head of lettuce.
c. A cucumber.
d. a carton of cigarettes.

Answers: 1.a, 2.c, 3.a, 4.d, 5.d.

Chapter | 16 | DEMAND FOR INPUTS

Key Topics

marginal revenue product
marginal input cost
profit maximization
input demand
wage determination in markets

Goals

realize that the firm is a demander as well as a supplier
understand how the firm decides how much labor to use
be able to obtain the demand for labor
understand the process of wage determination

We have examined the firm's output decision; we will now shift to its input decision. The input decision deals with how much land, labor, capital, and entrepreneurship to use to produce a given amount of output. In the last seven chapters, we have viewed the firm as a seller of goods and services. The technology used and the price of inputs determined the firm's cost, and then cost and revenue determined profit. Profit maximization led to supply. The output of the firm is sold to buyers through the product market. The product and resource markets of the circular flow model were introduced in Chapter 4. Now we will reverse the role of the firm from a seller of output to a buyer of input through the resource market. We will focus on labor, but you should recognize that the conclusions made concerning labor will also apply to land, capital, and entrepreneurship.

We accomplish two things in this chapter. First you will see another side of the profit maximization decision, this time with the emphasis on the input decision rather than on the output decision. This will reveal how the firm determines the quantity of a variable input to purchase and how the firm's demand for input is obtained. Second, you will see how market forces determine the price of resources. These market solutions reflect society's values and ultimately determine an efficient allocation of resources.

Marginal Revenue Product and Marginal Input Cost

Each firm is involved in two markets. First is the product market where the firm sells output, and second is the resource market where the firm buys inputs. Until now, the discussion of the profit maximization decision emphasized the level of output to produce, where marginal revenue equals marginal cost. But output and input are two sides of the same coin. Clearly, the amount of input employed and the amount of output produced are connected. Every change in output produced requires a change in input hired, and every change in input hired results in a change in output produced. Our continued discussion of profit maximization will now emphasize the level of input that the firm should employ. Notice that the same firm is not solving two different problems. There is only one profit maximization problem. The firm chooses the amount of output to produce by profit maximization, and the firm also chooses the amount of input to employ by profit maximization.

Profit maximization is but one decision facing the firm, and both the output and the input approach use the same elements of technology, cost of the inputs, and revenue. The technology applied to the inputs produces the output that, when sold, generates revenue. In deciding whether or not to hire the unit of input, the cost of the extra input is weighed against the revenue the extra output produces. The first step in obtaining profit maximization in terms of inputs is to combine revenue and technology. This combination is summarized in marginal revenue product. **Marginal revenue product (MRP)** is the change in total revenue due to the use of another unit of the variable input.

Let us trace through the steps to calculate marginal revenue product. If another unit of a variable input is hired, there is an increase in output equal to the productivity of that unit. We know this change in output as the marginal product. Marginal product, which tells how output will change as the input varies, represents the technology. Marginal revenue is the change in total revenue from the sale of each additional unit of output. So for the firm to know how much total revenue changes with the hiring of another unit of input, it must multiply marginal revenue times the extra output the last unit of input produces, or $MRP = MR \times MP$. If the firm adds a worker who contributes

10 more units of output per day and each of those units sells for $5, then the MRP = $5 × 10 = $50.

The marginal revenue product curve must slope downward. You will recall that the MP decreases because of the law of diminishing returns. The marginal productivity of an input diminishes as more units of an input are added. When the MR is constant (which occurs in perfect competition), the shape of the MRP is the same as the shape of the MP, since MRP equals a constant times MP.

Marginal revenue product plays the same role in profit maximization that marginal revenue plays in the output approach. The role of marginal cost is played by the added cost of an added unit of the variable input. The **marginal input cost (MIC)** is the change in total cost due to the hiring of another unit of a variable input. Marginal input cost is the cost the firm pays for another unit of input. The marginal input cost of our worker is, let us say, $35 per day.

The marginal input cost is affected by the market structure of the input market, the resource market. When the firm is perfectly competitive in the purchase of input, the firm cannot change the price of the input. As a consequence, the amount of labor the firm purchases has no effect on the market price of labor. The firm pays the price of labor dictated by the market. Thus the MIC, the cost of another unit of the input, is constant and equal to the wage when labor is the variable input.

We are now ready to combine the revenue (MRP) and cost (MIC) concepts just defined to determine profit maximization. In the next section we will discuss how the profit maximizing firm with one variable input decides how many units of the input to purchase.

Profit Maximization

We have previously discussed the profit maximizing choice of output. Now you will see how the same profit maximization principle determines how much variable input the firm should employ. The case where the firm sells output in a perfectly competitive output market and buys labor in a perfectly competitive input market is discussed.

With the marginal revenue product and marginal input cost pictured in Figure 16-1, we can determine the profit maximization point. The MRP slopes downward, and in the case of the perfectly competitive input market, the MIC is a constant wage. If MRP is greater than the wage, then the firm will increase

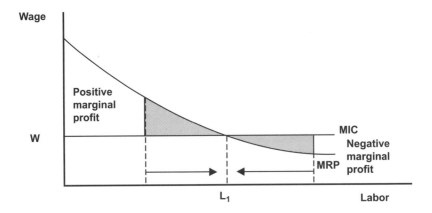

Figure 16-1   Profit Maximization: The Input Approach; MRP = MIC
The profit maximizing choice of labor is L_1 where MRP = MIC. To the left of L_1, marginal profits are positive and an increase in labor will make profit rise. To the right of L_1, marginal profits are negative and a decrease in labor will make profit rise.

profit by hiring that unit. Marginal profit, the difference between the MRP and the wage, is positive, so profit will rise. By hiring that worker, the firm moves toward profit maximization. When the marginal revenue product is greater than the wage, the firm should increase the use of the variable input.

If the marginal revenue product is less than the wage, then the firm should reduce labor to make profit rise. When the added cost of the labor is greater than the added revenue that the extra labor brings in, the marginal profit is negative. If that worker is hired, profit will fall, not rise. So by decreasing the use of labor, profit will increase since we are removing negative marginal profit.

Suppose that if you hire another worker, the worker will produce 10 units of output that sell for $5 each. But the wage, the MIC, is $35. Would you hire this unit of labor? The answer is "yes" since you would be $15 ahead; the MRP ($5 × 10) exceeds the MIC. And if the wage were $55, you would not hire the unit since your profit falls by $5; the MIC exceeds the MRP.

The preceding process results in an equilibrium position where the MRP equals the wage. **Profit maximization** from the input approach requires that MRP = MIC. This must be true since if marginal revenue product is greater than marginal input cost, the firm will increase its use of the variable input to capture the increase in profit. If MRP is less than the MIC, the firm will decrease its use of the variable input to avoid the reduction in profit.

This marginal analysis should seem familiar to you. The logic is that a firm will continue to purchase inputs as long as they add more to revenue than to cost. The weighing of the marginal benefits with the marginal cost is a common technique of economics. The profit maximization assumption leads us to the comparison of the marginal revenue (marginal revenue product) and the marginal cost (marginal input cost) added by another unit of input. Next we see how the firm determines its demand for labor or other input.

Input Demand

When the firm is perfectly competitive in both the input and output markets, we can obtain the firm's demand for labor. This will be done by varying the wage and asking how much labor the firm would hire at each wage. We have seen, by profit maximization, that the firm will choose the amount of labor so that MRP = MIC. These points all lie on the MRP curve as shown in Figure 16-2. Thus the downward-sloping MRP is the firm's demand for labor. This is a very special result that holds only if there is one variable input under perfectly competitive conditions.

Because of diminishing returns, the marginal productivity of a factor diminishes as more units are added to a process. Consequently, the value of

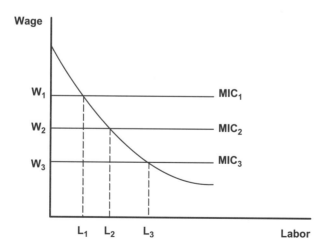

Figure 16-2 MRP Becomes Demand for Labor
At each wage, the profit maximizing quantity of labor is hired. These combinations of quantity of labor and wage are the demand. Thus demand is the marginal revenue product curve under perfectly competitive conditions.

additional units of a factor to a firm will be less since the productivity of the factor is diminished. This logically leads to a downward-sloping demand for the factor, because a firm would hire more of a factor of reduced value to the firm only if the price of the factor were reduced. The *market* demand for labor is found by adding the marginal revenue product curves of the individual firms. Since every individual MRP has a downward slope, the market demand curve will also have a downward slope. Fewer workers will be hired in the market at a higher wage.

What makes the demand for labor or another variable input in the resource market shift? Recall that the demand for input, MRP, reflects two elements — the revenue of the firm and the technology. If either of these changes, so will the demand for input. First we will discuss the impact of revenue on factor demand. The demand for any factor depends on the ability of the firm to sell its output. If the firm cannot obtain enough revenue to pay for the inputs that produce the output, the firm cannot continue producing that level of output. If the firm generates enough revenue to pay for all inputs, the firm can continue and may be able to increase production. So the demand for input depends on profitability. The more profitable the product the input produces, the more desirable the input and the greater the input demand.

The less the marginal revenue that the resources produce, the less desirable are the resources and the lower the resource demand. What if demand for a product, shoestrings, falls as more people prefer Velcro fasteners? Assuming a perfectly competitive market in Figure 16-3A, the price of shoestrings would fall. Since product demand and price (MR) for the perfectly competitive firm, Figure 16-3B, has been reduced, the profit maximization point occurs at a lower level of output. Less output and fewer resources will be needed. The demand for labor will fall, so the MRP shifts in Figure 16-4 to the left. Since the MR of shoestrings is lower, then MR × MP, which is the MRP for workers, must be lower. Fewer workers are hired than before at the same wage. A decrease in the demand for a good causes the marginal revenue of the good to fall, and consequently the demand for shoestring labor falls.

The location of the market demand curve for input depends not only upon the marginal revenue of the factors but upon the marginal productivity as well. What if the firm develops an improved technology? Worker productivity increases because of the change in production methods, and therefore each worker is more valuable to the firm. If the shoestring manufacturer replaces a worker's tape measure and scissors with a machine that automatically measures and cuts shoestrings, the worker's productivity is greater. The marginal revenue

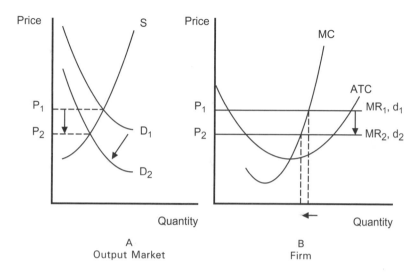

Figure 16-3 Impact of a Decrease in Output Demand

When output demand decreases, price falls in the market, and the profit maximizing output falls for the firm. Thus resource use also decreases.

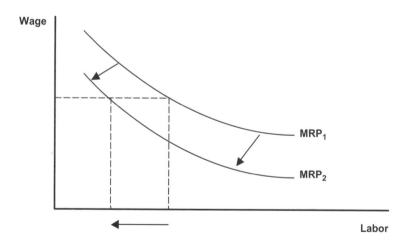

Figure 16-4 Fall in Labor Demand

The demand for labor shifts if output demand shifts. This figure continues the impact of a decrease in output demand begun in Figure 16-3. Since output price is lower in the perfectly competitive output market, and price equals marginal revenue, marginal revenue product must also be lower at each level of labor. Thus the MRP, demand for labor, decreases. Fewer workers will be hired at each wage.

product of shoestring labor has increased and so has the demand for labor. With a greater MP, MR × MP results in a higher MRP, or demand for labor. Thus if either the marginal productivity of labor (technology) or the price of the product (revenue) changes, so will the demand for labor. In the perfectly competitive market for labor, the interaction of the demand for labor with the supply of labor, as you will see, determines the going wage for labor.

How Wages Are Determined

When the firm hires inputs in a perfectly competitive market, the firm has no effect on the wage. The market determines what the wage will be and consequently how much income each individual will earn. The wage is determined by demand and supply. You are familiar with the demand for inputs and recognize that the value society places on the product will have a major influence on the wages. The value society places on a good is reflected in its price. The greater the price, the greater the MR and the higher the MRP or demand for labor. Many people who would not bother to go across the street to watch a batch of potatoes being fried would be willing to pay to watch a sizzling game of tennis played at center court. This helps to explain why the demand is greater for tennis professionals than for potato fryers.

The supply side is equally important in the determination of wage. With minimal instruction, most of us would be capable of frying some fries, but there are not many of us capable of hitting a tennis ball with the intensity, accuracy, and endurance required on the professional level of play. The lower demand and higher supply of french fry labor determines a low wage; the high demand and extremely limited supply of top caliber tennis players results in a high wage. These wages reflect society's values.

Most people do not understand the perfectly competitive market forces that determine wages and rely on their own values of what the wages should be. Tennis pros earn "too much" playing at a sport and fast-food employees work "too hard" for a minimum wage. In a perfectly competitive market, the wages that we earn are determined by supply and demand, which in turn reflect the values of society. Thus if we think that the wages are "too much," we are expressing a value different from that of the rest of society.

Of course, all of this wage determination process assumes that the market is perfectly competitive. If it is not, and firms have market power or workers have monopoly power, as in unions, then we may have reason to complain about wages being too low (due to market power) or too high (due to monopoly).

You will no doubt recognize that there is some amount of luck associated with who gets the rewards paid by the market. Most of us do not have the skill of a Roger Federer or a Venus Williams. We can only hope the market will value highly the areas in which we are skilled. If we are lucky, we are born with either a well-paying talent or wealthy parents. If not, our paths are that of hard work, at least until we win the lottery.

▶ Summary

You should now recognize that the demand for inputs is related to the supply of output. The decision that determines the amount to produce also determines the amount of variable input to hire. The firm weighs the marginal revenue product against the marginal input cost. At the profit maximum, MRP = MIC. This rule can be used to determine the firm's demand for labor. Since at each wage the firm hires the quantity of labor dictated by the MRP, the MRP is the demand for labor. It slopes downward largely because of diminishing returns.

In perfectly competitive markets, wages are determined by the interaction of supply and demand. The demand for labor reflects both the preferences of society and the productivity of labor. Once we have determined demand, its combination with supply provides the information needed to determine wages. Although this chapter has focused on the labor input, its conclusions are equally true for all other inputs flowing through the resource market.

This chapter completes our study of microeconomics, the individual parts of the economy. We have seen the economic problem of scarcity and how a capitalistic system uses market forces that answer what, how and for whom to allocate its limited resources. The remainder of the text is about how the economy works as a whole. You will discover that an entirely different set of questions will be asked.

▶ Key Concepts

marginal revenue product
marginal input cost
profit maximization

▶ Discussion Questions

1. The Internal Revenue Service (IRS), the tax collection agency of the federal government, was ordered to fire auditors to save money. The IRS responded by

saying that for each extra $100 the auditors brought in, its costs were $0.50. If the government were interested in maximizing profit, would it want to decrease or increase the number of auditors? Explain.

2. Why is labor demand the same as the marginal revenue product in the case of perfect competition?

3. Uncle Effron worked in a factory. He says that the amount of labor hired depended on the amount of work there was to do, not on the marginal revenue product. Explain to Uncle Effron that if the firm maximized profit, it hired labor to the point where the MRP equals the wage.

4. Explain how the law of diminishing returns affects the shape of the demand curve for labor in a perfectly competitive firm.

5. Aunt Ettie is trying to decide whether to hire another elderberry picker. Another picker could pick 400 quarts a week, and Aunt Ettie could sell them for $1 per quart. The new worker would cost $350 per week. Should Aunt Ettie hire the worker? What if the cost of the worker were $450 per week? Explain.

▶ Self-Review

• Fill in the blanks

marginal revenue product

marginal input cost

MRP, MIC

greater
reduce

MRP, downward
diminishing
supply, demand

The change in total revenue by the use of another unit of variable input is the _____.
The change in total cost from the hiring of a unit of variable input is the _____. Profit is maximized from the input side by hiring inputs to the point where _____ is equal to _____. A perfectly competitive firm will hire more labor if the MRP is _____ than the wage, the MIC. If the MRP is less than the wage, the firm will _____ the amount of its labor. The perfectly competitive firm's demand for labor is the _____ curve. The MRP curve is _____ sloping due to _____ returns. Wages are determined in a perfectly competitive market by the interaction of labor _____ and labor _____.

• Multiple choice

1. Marginal revenue product is the change in total revenue due to:
   a. the production of an additional unit of the product.
   b. the use of another unit of the variable input.
   c. the sale of one more unit.
   d. none of the above.

2. When the marginal revenue product is less than the marginal input cost of labor, the profit maximizing firm will:
   a. hire more.
   b. hire less.
   c. maintain the same employment.
   d. increase output.
3. Profit maximization occurs when:
   a. marginal revenue equal marginal cost.
   b. marginal revenue product equals marginal input cost.
   c. either a or b but not both.
   d. both a and b.
4. The marginal revenue product is $30. The last worker to be hired by a profit maximizing firm is paid:
   a. $25.
   b. $29.
   c. $30.
   d. $31.
5. In a perfectly competitive market, wages are determined:
   a. by supply and demand.
   b. by the sellers.
   c. by the buyers.
   d. by the workers.

Answers: 1.b, 2.b, 3.d, 4.c, 5.a.

Module | 4 | MEASURING THE ECONOMY

This module marks a significant shift in our study of economics. To this point we have focused on microeconomics; the rest of our study will focus on macroeconomics. Macroeconomics differs from microeconomics in its point of view. Both macro and micro observe the same economic forces at work. But micro looks at how the individuals behave in response to the forces, and macro observes the outcome of the forces on the entire economy. In macro our concern is not with how an individual behaves but rather with how the whole economy behaves. For example, the word income, which you may think of as your paycheck, is not what the economist thinks of when income is discussed in macro. The economist is thinking of the income of the society, not one person. You should resist thinking of how you as an individual would behave when macro relations are discussed. If the question is what happens to consumer spending when the nation's income rises, you should focus on what the society will do, not on what you would do if your income rose. The two reactions may be different.

To begin the study of macroeconomics, we will need to understand how some macroeconomic variables are measured. Once the measurement issues are settled, we can move on to understanding how these variables are determined. The first chapter in this module, Chapter 17, starts with a discussion of the two big macroeconomic problems, unemployment and inflation. The definition of macroeconomics and measurements of the level of income are discussed in Chapter 18. Chapter 19 returns to the measurement problem, and an adjustment to the measurement of income is made by means of a price index. The fundamental problem of the macro economy, the business cycle, will be the subject of Chapter 20. Approaches to the business cycle are introduced there. Once we are done with these introductory issues, we can begin to build a macro model; this activity will be the content of the two modules that follow.

Chapter 17 | UNEMPLOYMENT AND INFLATION

Key Topics
    unemployment
    causes of unemployment
    full employment
    inflation
    causes of inflation

Goals
    know what unemployment is and why it is a problem
    understand the causes of unemployment
    recognize the problem of defining full employment
    know what inflation is and why it is a problem
    understand the causes of inflation

Two of the most widely known and discussed economic problems of our society are unemployment and inflation. We introduce these topics here to show the need for remedies. This chapter is the first in a sequence of chapters designed to help you understand the forces that contribute to unemployment and inflation. An understanding of the forces is necessary to the development of remedies for these problems.

Unemployment and inflation are introduced in this chapter and their effects on society are shown. We first define unemployment, and look at the unemployment record of the United States, and determine the causes. We will also discuss the concept of full employment. Inflation is discussed next. We will define inflation and look at our inflation record and probable causes. A well-known comic claims that he "don't get no respect." We should be careful to show proper respect for the undesirable effects of unemployment and inflation and to find what we can do respectfully to rid ourselves of these plagues.

Unemployment

As one saying goes, if your neighbor is unemployed, that's a recession; if you are unemployed, that's a depression. At first, it may appear that unemployment is a personal thing, only affecting the particular individual and those around him or her. Yet a basic understanding of economics tells us that unemployment is a problem of the entire society. Chapter 3 explained that unemployment places a society inside its production possibilities curve. This is a clear indication that the society as a whole is foregoing the output that the unemployed could produce but are not. This lost output is the opportunity cost of unemployment and is what makes unemployment a major concern for society. To the rest of us, it is as disastrous for your neighbor to be unemployed as it is for you, and twice as disastrous if you are both unemployed.

When we talk about **unemployment**, what do we mean? To define unemployment, we start with the idea of the labor force. The population is divided into two parts, those in and those out of the labor force. Those out of the labor force are categorized as unable to be employed, in school, housekeeping, or "other." Everyone else between ages 16 and 65 is in the labor force. The **labor force** itself is divided into two groups, those employed and those unemployed but looking for work. The latter group, those unemployed but looking for work, is what we call unemployed.

The statistical **unemployment rate** for the United States measures the percentage of the labor force who are not able to find employment. Given a current labor force of around 140 million, a 5 percent unemployment rate, for example, means that approximately 7 million people are unemployed. The unemployment rate since 1930 is recorded in Table 17-1. You can see that in 1933 almost one-fourth of the labor force was unemployed. The highest rate in recent years was 9.7 percent in 1982. Yet this one figure tells us only the average rate of unemployment. There are additional measures of unemployment besides the national figure. Unemployment figures may also be obtained by state, age, sex, race, and many other classifications. Unemployment is not borne equally by all segments of society.

The unemployment rate may understate the true amount of unemployment. What about those individuals who are not working and are not actively seeking employment and therefore fail to count as unemployed? Certain individuals may wish to work, but consider their job opportunities as hopeless and as a result do not actively seek a job. Others may have looked for a job to the point of despair and then given up; they no longer count as unemployed. The unemployment

Table 17-1 The Rate of Unemployment, 1930–2005

Year	Rate of Unemployment	Year	Rate of Unemployment
1930	8.7%	1968	3.6
1931	15.9	1969	3.5
1932	23.6	1970	4.9
1933	24.9	1971	5.9
1934	21.7	1972	5.6
1935	20.1	1973	4.9
1936	16.9	1974	5.6
1937	14.3	1975	8.5
1938	19.0	1976	7.7
1939	17.2	1977	7.1
1940	14.6	1978	6.1
1941	9.9	1979	5.8
1942	4.7	1980	7.1
1943	1.9	1981	7.6
1944	1.2	1982	9.7
1945	1.9	1983	9.6
1946	3.9	1984	7.5
1947	3.9	1985	7.2
1948	3.8	1986	7.0
1949	5.9	1986	6.2
1950	5.3	1988	5.5
1951	3.3	1989	5.3
1952	3.0	1990	5.6
1953	2.9	1991	6.8
1954	5.5	1992	7.5
1955	4.4	1993	6.9
1956	4.1	1994	6.1
1957	4.3	1995	5.6
1958	6.8	1996	5.4
1959	5.5	1997	4.9
1960	5.5	1998	4.5
1961	6.7	1999	4.2
1962	5.5	2000	4.0
1963	5.7	2001	4.7
1964	5.2	2002	5.8
1965	4.5	2003	6.0
1966	3.8	2004	5.5
1967	3.8%	2005	5.1

This table shows the rate of unemployment as a percentage of the labor force since 1930.

Sources: 1960–2005, *The Economic Report of the President, 2006;* found on the web at http://www.gpoaccess.gov/eop/; 1950–1959: *The Economic Report of the President, 2000*; 1930–1949: *Historical Statistics, Part I, 1970.*

All series are for all civilian workers. Used by permission.

figures are consequently too low since there are people unemployed who are not counted because they are not in the labor force.

Unemployment may also be understated by underemployment. **Underemployment** occurs when workers can find only part-time employment or jobs not utilizing their skills, such as when physicists bag groceries. These individuals are in the labor force and are counted as employed. This underemployment may be significant in terms of numbers and suggests that society reevaluate the process of providing gainful employment to its members. We should recognize when looking at unemployment figures that they are only a general indicator of the level of unemployment.

Causes of Unemployment

What are the causes of unemployment? The major types of unemployment are frictional, seasonal, cyclical, and structural. **Frictional unemployment** includes those people in the process of relocating from one job to another. They might be moving across country, or taking a vacation between jobs, or finding their first job. At any point in time, about 4 percent of the labor force is frictionally unemployed. They are counted as unemployed, but they are not a source of concern. As long as workers are allowed to switch jobs and obtain upward mobility, there will always be some in this situation. It is essential in a market economy that resources, including labor, be able to respond to changing demand. These people are only out of a job for a short time, and they are voluntarily unemployed. Even during the peak demand on the labor force during World War II, there was still unemployment, essentially frictional, of about 1.2 percent.

Seasonal unemployment is also expected. Workers are laid off during the off season. Lifeguards on the lake shore in Chicago are employed in the summer and not the winter, ski instructors on the bunny slope in Vermont find the opposite true. There may be fewer construction jobs during the winter months. Since these individuals are out of work for a major portion of a year, their lack of employment is of greater concern than is that for individuals who are frictionally unemployed.

Cyclical unemployment is not expected and is a serious concern for society. **Cyclical unemployment** occurs when the economy slows down, and there are more unemployed people than there are available jobs. Then we have people who desire to work on one hand, and a desire for the products that these people could produce on the other, but the economic system cannot seem to make the two meet. People who are unemployed for cyclical reasons are wasted resources. In this case we must look to economic policy tools to stimulate the economy and therefore employment opportunities. We will explore our choices of policy tools in future chapters.

Structural unemployment concerns the attempt to put square pegs into round holes. Translated into human terms, **structural unemployment** occurs when there are many people unemployed while there are many jobs available, but the unemployed lack the necessary qualifications for the jobs. Check the unemployment statistics against the help-wanted ads in your newspaper. Typically, there are many job offerings but usually at specified levels of accountants, programmers, managers, and engineers — all requiring experience, of course. These are not the skills possessed by the majority of the unemployed. Structural unemployment is becoming an increasing problem in our rapidly changing industrial society. New skills become more rapidly obsolete as society and its technology and demands change. Structural unemployment may be one of the most pressing unemployment problems that we face. Policy tools that stabilize the economy will not be helpful. Efficient methods of matching people to jobs are needed, possibly requiring job training and relocation.

Full Employment

One important goal for our economy is to reach full employment. However, not all economists agree on a definition of full employment. Some would accept the definition that says full employment occurs when all those wanting to work at the going wage are employed. But most economists define **full employment** in terms of the percentage of the labor force not employed. In the 1960s, it was said that a 4 percent unemployment rate would signal full employment. But why isn't 0 percent unemployment full employment? Why would there be *any* unemployment at "full employment"? The answer lies with frictional unemployment. If frictional unemployment runs around 4 percent, we could accept an unemployment rate of 4 percent as a reasonable measure of full employment. If they were the only people unemployed, we would consider our economy to be fully using its available labor.

How does seasonal unemployment affect our idea of full employment? Individual economists will differ in their views of whether those seasonally unemployed should be counted in the definition of full employment or not. For example, if 2 percent of the labor force were unemployed for seasonal reasons, and the unemployment rate were 6 percent reflecting both frictional and seasonal unemployment, would we be at full employment? Some economists would say that the seasonally unemployed are truly unemployed and a source of concern. They would say that 4 percent unemployment is full employment. Others would not be so concerned about the seasonally unemployed since they will be working in season and would say that we are at full employment at 6 percent unemployment. Most economists do agree, however, that when defining full employment, we would expect zero unemployment for cyclical reasons. Some economists define the **natural rate of unemployment** as frictional plus structural unemployment. These economists would say we have unemployment only if the unemployment rate rises above the natural rate.

Recently, there has been some suggestion that the natural rate of unemployment should be around 5 or 6 percent. Changes in the labor force have resulted in more frictional unemployment. For example, in the 1970s the baby boom generation entered the job market. Also, females left the homemaker role in favor of a job with pay. Young workers and new workers in the labor force tend to switch jobs several times before finding long-term employment. Hence we would expect more frictional unemployment than before. In addition, the amount of frictional unemployment is affected by such programs as unemployment compensation. One of the purposes of unemployment compensation is to allow the laid-off worker time to look around and find the best alternative job. Thus unemployment compensation encourages people to take more time between jobs, which increases frictional unemployment.

For these and other reasons, full employment may rise from 4 percent to 5 or 6 percent unemployed. Remember that though 1 percent seems like a small difference, the labor force is roughly 140 million people. The difference between 5 percent and 6 percent unemployed is about 1.5 million people. So it does make a considerable difference whether we say full employment is 5 percent or 6 percent of the labor force unemployed.

We are not always at full employment as Table 17-1 has shown. Why not? There are at least two ways to look at the problem. First is to realize that labor is a resource that goes through a market. Markets may not work exactly the way we draw them on the chalkboard. Second is that the cause is cyclical or structural unemployment.

Why doesn't the labor market adjust as it should? When there is a decrease in demand for labor, the wage does not fall as quickly as needed to regain equilibrium. Because labor and unions resist a falling wage, the wage does not readily fall to adjust the market. A surplus of labor remains. People may be laid off and cannot find work at the going wage. Unemployment results. This view of unemployment suggests that the solution is to make the labor market more competitive so that the wage will adjust more readily.

So far we have discussed the problem of unemployment by defining what it is and then seeing what might cause it. To the extent that the cause of unemployment is cyclical, we know what to do. We should apply economic policy so that the unemployment disappears. If the unemployment is caused by structural unemployment, then economic policy designed for cyclical purposes will not do. New policy tools will have to be developed to end the unemployment. We recognize that unemployment is a serious problem for society. Not only is there the lost output but there is the human cost as well. But unemployment is not the only problem that we face as a nation. Another problem is inflation.

Inflation

As consumers, we have all become acquainted with inflation, and few of us can recall a period of time without inflation. **Inflation** is defined as a continued rise in the average level of prices. We will develop a method of measuring inflation in Chapter 19. Now we will concentrate first on the effects and then the causes of inflation.

Inflation causes a redistribution of income within a society. When you spend an extra dollar for an item, we recognize that the income of someone else increases by a dollar. So why is inflation a concern? The problem is that some people gain because of the inflation and others lose. Inflation redistributes income in ways that we may not like. Individuals whose income fails to increase with the rate of inflation will find that their income will no longer maintain their standard of living. These individuals with an unchanging level of income are said to have a fixed income. Those on fixed income are one group that are adversely affected by inflation. So are creditors who lend money and are paid back with money cheapened by inflation. And of course the poor have no need to see their limited income made even more limited by inflation. Inflation has been called a cruel tax, first because inflation is a tax in the sense that purchasing power is reduced, and second, it takes purchasing power away from those who can least afford it.

But even for those whose income rises as fast as inflation, there may be costs. If the price of medical care is rising faster than the rate of inflation, families requiring a lot of medical care will be hurt even if their income goes up as fast as inflation. If inflation is largely due to rising energy prices, people who spend a large part of their budget on energy will be hurt compared to those who do not. People whose income goes up as fast as inflation but who buy goods whose prices are rising slower than inflation benefit. You can see, then, that the main complaint against inflation is that some individuals gain and some lose.

There may be another cost of inflation. If the inflation rate becomes too high, then inflation itself becomes a disruptive force. After World War I in Germany, there was a classic case of hyperinflation. **Hyperinflation** is an accelerating increase in the price level. What cost 1 deutsche mark this morning cost DM 10 by evening. What was DM 10 this evening was DM 100 by morning. What cost DM 100 this morning was DM 1000 by dinner. You can see that under these conditions there would be incentives to spend a lot of time making trades and buying and selling goods. When would there be time to produce? High rates of inflation disrupt the entire economy, and you should not be surprised to hear that the German economy collapsed after a short period of hyperinflation. A high rate of inflation can cause economic, political, and social collapse.

Causes of Inflation

What are the causes of inflation? Runaway or hyperinflation is an extreme form resulting from political or economic instability. The 100 percent per month rate of inflation in Argentina or the trillion percent rate occurring in Germany after World War I is an exceptional but destructive form of inflation. The demand-pull and cost-push inflation that we now experience are more common forms. These lower rates of inflation can also be destructive over time. By using the "rule of 72," we can find how many years it takes for the value of money to fall by half. The "rule of 72" says to divide the inflation rate into the number 72 to estimate the number of years for the value of money to fall by half. This shows that an inflation rate of 6 percent will halve the purchasing power of money in 12 years. The recent inflation history of the United States is shown in Table 17-2.

Demand-pull inflation is described as "too much money chasing too few goods." **Demand-pull inflation** is a rise in the average price level caused by excess demand at full employment. The excess demand increases the average level of prices, which is inflation. Figure 17-1 shows the effect of demand-pull inflation. The full employment level marks the greatest potential output of the economy. As we increase output from zero and start moving along the curve, unemployed resources will be used with little or no competitive pressure on resource cost. There is no need to bid the resources away from alternatives.

Table 17-2   The Rate of Inflation, 1930–2005

Year	Rate of Inflation	Year	Rate of Inflation
1930	−2.53%	1968	4.19
1931	−8.80	1969	5.46
1932	−10.31	1970	5.72
1933	−5.13	1971	4.38
1934	3.35	1972	3.21
1935	2.49	1973	6.22
1936	0.97	1974	11.04
1937	3.61	1975	9.13
1938	−1.86	1976	5.76
1939	−1.42	1977	6.50
1940	0.96	1978	7.59
1941	5.00	1979	11.35
1942	10.66	1980	13.50
1943	6.15	1981	10.32
1944	1.74	1982	6.16
1945	2.28	1983	3.21
1946	8.53	1984	4.32
1947	14.36	1985	3.56
1948	7.77	1986	1.86
1949	−0.97	1987	3.65
1950	0.98	1988	4.14
1951	7.91	1989	4.82
1952	2.19	1990	5.40
1953	0.75	1991	4.21
1954	0.50	1992	3.01
1955	−0.37	1993	2.99
1956	1.50	1994	2.56
1957	3.56	1995	2.83
1958	2.73	1996	2.95
1959	0.69	1997	2.29
1960	1.72	1998	1.56
1961	1.01	1999	2.21
1962	1.00	2000	3.36
1963	1.32	2001	2.85
1964	1.31	2002	1.58
1965	1.61	2003	2.28
1966	2.86%	2004	2.66
1967	3.09	2005	3.38

This table shows the change in the average level of prices. This is a measure of inflation.

Sources: 1930–1957: based on data in *Historical Statistics, Part I, 1970*; 1958–1999 based on data in the *Economic Report of the President, 2000*.
2004, *Economic Report of the President, 2006,* found on the web at http://www.gpoaccess. gov/eop/. All series are for the consumer price index. Used by permission.

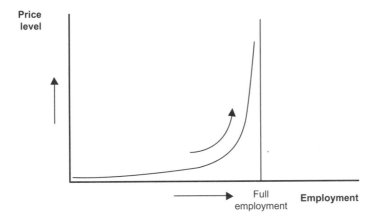

Figure 17-1 Demand-pull Inflation
The closer the economy produces to the full employment level, the higher the resource cost and the higher the average price level.

Consequently, there will be little rise in the price level. As output increases, fewer unemployed resources are available. Further increases in output require higher resource costs, increasing the average level of prices. You can see that the closer we get to full employment, the increased demand for resources will drive up their cost, the output price, and consequently the inflation rate. We should be careful not to adopt policies that push us below the natural rate of unemployment.

Test your understanding of demand-pull inflation by explaining what happens at the full employment level when we *try* to expand output. Physically, the output cannot expand, but resources can be bid from one industry to another. The gain and loss of the resource inputs will offset one another so the output stays constant. The effect of the higher demand for output will be seen only in the higher production costs and vertical rise in the price level. The only result is more inflation. What if the economy were at the full employment level and government tried to buy more goods? This additional demand at full employment would result in demand-pull inflation. This was the situation during the Vietnam period. The government increased spending for the Vietnam action, and at the same time it increased spending for the "war on poverty." The economy was at full employment. We could not produce more. Something had to give. We experienced demand-pull inflation.

Demand-pull inflation *pulls* up the cost of production from an excess demand for resources while cost-push inflation *pushes* up the cost of production from within the productive process. **Cost-push inflation** is a rise in the average price level due to an increase in production costs. Cost-push originates from the supply side of the economy. Monopoly power significantly contributes to cost-push inflation. The monopoly power of labor unions may result in wage increases that inflate the cost of production. The power of monopoly business permits these costs to be passed on to the consumer in the form of higher prices. Once prices go up, labor realizes that its recent wage gain has been eroded, and it again raises wages. The increase in wages again causes prices to rise, and the wage-price spiral repeats itself.

Supply shock is another cause of inflation. **Supply-shock inflation** results from infrequent drastic changes in the production cost of fundamental products. A widespread agricultural disaster such as a drought or freeze may increase food prices and have a widespread impact on average prices. The most visible case of supply shock was the series of OPEC increases in 1970s oil prices. The higher price of oil increased the cost of energy, plastics, and other inputs and resulted in increased production cost in nearly every productive process in the economy. This in turn increased the price of final products and therefore average prices. But these shocks by themselves are not inflation. Inflation is a *continued* rise in prices. Shocks that affect supply cause a one-time change in prices that is not inflation. But these shocks may lead to inflation if they set off cost-push inflation.

Inflation can sometimes occur simply because we expect it to. If consumers believe that the prices of goods are going to rise, they may rush out now and buy before the prices go up. The increase in demand will cause prices to rise so the expectation comes true. Once people start expecting prices to rise, and act upon it by buying more, prices will rise, and **expectations inflation** is the result. Psychology plays an important role in a social science.

We have seen some possible ways in which inflation can be generated — demand-pull, cost-push, shocks, and expectations. Yet there is no one way of looking at inflation that always explains its occurrence. Inflation may result from a combination of causes. The solutions to inflation will in part depend upon the source of the inflationary pressure. We are now ready to begin our discussion of the economy and the forces that cause unemployment and inflation.

▶ Summary

Why are we concerned about unemployment? There are two major reasons. First, unemployment means that resources are unemployed and wasted. The output that could have been produced with those idle resources is lost. The extra output could have been used by someone, and that extra output may have made the society better off. Second, there is the human cost to those suffering the unemployment. They are the ones who go hungry and are homeless. They are the ones whose lives are disrupted by factors that are no fault of their own. This human misery should be avoided. Yet clearly we have not been too successful at achieving this goal.

Inflation too inflicts costs upon society. The major effect is the redistribution of income. There is always the threat, however remote, that inflation can get out of control and literally destroy a society. We can identify various sources of inflation. Demand-pull inflation results from excess demands on the productive capacity of the society. Cost-push inflation originates from monopoly power pushing up the prices of final products. Supply-shock inflation from a sudden increase in production costs results in upward-adjusting prices. Expectations of higher prices may well result in inflation.

If we can identify the causes of unemployment and inflation, can we develop the cures? The answer is left to future chapters. In the next chapter we establish a method to measure the productivity of the economy. We should know where the economy is and where it is going before we attempt to apply economic policy.

▶ Key Concepts

unemployment	full employment
labor force	natural rate of unemployment
unemployment rate	inflation
underemployment	hyperinflation
frictional unemployment	demand-pull inflation
seasonal unemployment	cost-push inflation
cyclical unemployment	supply-shock inflation
structural unemployment	expectations inflation

▶ Discussion Questions

1. How are the population, the labor force, and employment related?
2. Does the unemployment rate measure the amount of unemployment? Explain.
3. Classify the following as frictional, seasonal, cyclical, or structural unemployment.

    a. Aunt Ettie fires her elderberry pickers at the end of the season.

    b. Cousin Clyde lost his job when the sales of his firm and other firms went down.

    c. Cousin Katy got tired of the cold, quit her job in Cleveland last week, and found a new job in Orlando. She starts next month.

    d. Barney went to school to be a buggywhip maker and cannot find a job.

4. What do you believe full employment should be and why?

5. Suppose that inflation is 100 percent per year. What is the impact on the wealthy individual who can afford to save half of income and only spend half of income, compared to the less wealthy individual who must spend all income earned and has to borrow an equal amount as well?

6. How would inflation affect your spending power? Can you avoid the effects of inflation?

7. How can inflation rob your savings?

8. Look again at Table 17-2. What does the negative inflation rate in 1955 mean?

9. What kind of inflation is each of the following?

    a. At full employment, prices go up when everyone tries to buy more.

    b. Prices rise as costs rise.

    c. When people expect prices to rise, they buy more before the prices go up. This extra buying causes the prices to rise.

    d. The inflation rate goes up faster and faster.

    e. A long summer drought substantially reduces agricultural output.

10. What do you believe is the greater evil for you, unemployment or inflation? For the society? Why?

▶ Self-Review

• Fill in the blanks

labor force	Those employed and those unemployed but looking for work make up the _____. The percentage of the labor force that is unemployed is
unemployment rate	measured by the _____. When workers cannot find full-time jobs equal to their
underemployed	skills, they are classified as _____.The
frictional	major types of unemployment are _____,
seasonal, cyclical, structural	_____, _____, and _____.
	People who are voluntarily between jobs compose
frictional	_____ unemployment. Workers laid off
seasonal	during the off season compose _____
	unemployment. When the economy slows down,

cyclical

structural

employment

inflation

hyperinflation

demand-pull, cost-push

supply-shock, expectations

demand-pull

cost-push

supply-shock

expectations

_____ unemployment occurs. When people lack the qualifications for the available jobs, we experience _____ unemployment. We may have a 5 or 6 percent unemployment rate yet some economists may call this full _____. A continued rise in the average level of prices is known as _____. An accelerating increase in the price level is called _____. Other causes of inflation include _____, _____, _____, and _____. Excess demand at full employment may lead to _____ inflation. An increase in production costs may lead to _____ inflation. Sudden increases in production cost of fundamental products results in _____ inflation. People buying more to avoid rising prices causes _____ inflation.

• Multiple choice

1. The unemployment rate is:
   a. the percentage of the population who are unemployed.
   b. the percentage of the labor force who are not able to find work.
   c. made up of workers who have lost their jobs.
   d. none of the above.
2. The unemployment rate may understate the amount of unemployment because:
   a. some unemployed workers become discouraged and leave the labor force.
   b. some people are underemployed.
   c. both a and b.
   d. none of the above.
3. Workers laid off for a predictable part of the year make up:
   a. structural unemployment.
   b. cyclical unemployment.
   c. seasonal unemployment.
   d. frictional unemployment.
4. Cost-push inflation is caused by:
   a. a continued rise in demand at full employment.
   b. rising costs which cause rising prices.
   c. prices rising because they are expected to.
   d. an infrequent and drastic increase in the cost of production of fundamental products.

5. Purchases made now to avoid higher future prices can lead to:
   a. expectations inflation.
   b. demand-pull inflation.
   c. cost-push inflation.
   d. supply-shock inflation.

Answers: 1.b, 2.c, 3.c, 4.b, 5.a.

Chapter 18 GROSS DOMESTIC PRODUCT

Key Topics

microeconomics and macroeconomics

income, output, and employment

gross domestic product

shortcomings of GDP

Goals

distinguish microeconomics and macroeconomics

understand the relation between income, output, and employment

know what gross domestic product is

know what GDP measures and does not measure

Everyone talks about the economy. If the news isn't bad, it's terrible. Sometimes the complaint is inflation and how hard it is just to keep up; other times it is unemployment and the hardships that so many experience. And frequently the problem is inflation and unemployment together, twice as much to talk about. But talking is not the solution. Then what is?

If we understood the economic forces causing unemployment and inflation, perhaps we could find ways of using these forces to promote a more desirable outcome. We now begin an investigation to find what makes the economy function as it does. Then, we can consider what can be done to control the economy.

Up to this point, our emphasis has been on the decision making of the consumer and of the firm. A large part of the first 16 chapters has emphasized the workings of the market process, but so far we have neither discussed the total economic outcome resulting from all the individual market processes nor found a way to measure and evaluate the outcome.

Before an instructor gives you a grade, your progress must be measured. Before we can give the economy a grade, it too must be measured. While it is difficult to develop a fair and accurate grading scale for a classroom situation, imagine the difficulties of developing an evaluation for the economy as a whole. This chapter explores how the amount of output produced in the economy is measured by the gross domestic product. We will see how the concepts of income, output, and employment are also developed as measurements of the economy. And, last, we will discuss the shortcomings of gross domestic product as a measure of the output we produce. However, you should be aware that we have shifted the emphasis of our study of the economy from the grass-roots to a bird's-eye view.

Micro- and Macroeconomics

Microeconomics and macroeconomics are two different views of economics. **Microeconomics** (micro) is the study of the individual parts of the economy. Microeconomics has been the emphasis of 16 chapters, the first half of this text. The focus was on the consumer and the producer. In micro, we discussed one consumer or a group of consumers, one firm or all the firms in the market. The concern was always the demand and supply for either an individual good or a related group of goods, for Wheaties or breakfast cereal in general. The main focus of microeconomics is the market and how the decision process of demanders and suppliers determines the price and quantity in each market.

Macroeconomics (macro) is the study of the economy as a whole. In this chapter we shift to an emphasis on macroeconomics. No longer will the focus be on individual decision makers, but on the collective outcome of all economic decision making. Rather than examine the steel industry, the macroeconomist examines the total economic society of which the steel industry together with all other firms, consumers, and government, is a part. Microeconomics studies the individual buyers and the individual sellers and all buyers and sellers together in a particular market. Macroeconomics studies the total outcome of all markets together.

You can see how macro is different from micro. Each is concerned with the same topics but from different points of view. Micro focuses on the individual parts; macro on the **aggregate**, the total. Let us compare the two. The study of how price is determined in a market is an area of microeconomics. Macroeconomics is concerned with the overall price level, the average price level for all markets together. An increase in the average price level signals inflation in the economy. If one person loses a job, this is an individual, a micro, concern. But if large numbers of people lose jobs, this signals unemployment on the macro level. The amount of employment is related to the amount of output produced. The greater the employment, the greater the output produced. The amount of output produced in a particular market is of interest to a microeconomist. The total amount of output produced in the economy is of interest to the macroeconomist. So we see that the primary concerns of macroeconomics are the aggregate level of prices, employment, and output.

Micro and macro are different but not independent of one another. The sum total of all microeconomic activity becomes the topic of macroeconomics. The behavior of the economy as a whole depends on the behavior of the individual parts. This suggests that to understand macro, all we have to do is somehow add together all of micro. But it is sometimes true that the whole is different from the sum of its parts. In other words, we may not be able to add up the behavior of individuals to explain behavior at the macro level. When we think that the behavior of the whole is the same as the behavior of its parts, we are making the **fallacy of composition**, an error in reasoning. For example, if one driver takes a shortcut to reach a destination more quickly, that driver is likely to succeed. On the other hand, if many drivers attempt to use the same shortcut at the same time, it will be congested, and all will fail to arrive sooner. What is true for one is not true for all.

We can conclude that the relationship among the macro-level variables such as price, output, and employment may not be the same as the relationship among the micro variables with the same names. We cannot use micro models for macro models. This requires that we develop macro models to explain the economy as a whole. Macroeconomics is the emphasis of the remainder of the text. To start our study of macro, we must be able to measure output.

Income, Output, and Employment

Chapter 9 began our study of the micro relation between inputs and output. Now we will expand on that relationship from a macroeconomic view and see that the value of the inputs will equal the value of the output. The circular flow diagram from Chapter 4 is repeated in Figure 18-1. This diagram is a simple macro model representing the entire economy. The top half of the flow involves the production and sale of *output*. The bottom half of the flow represents *income* payments to inputs, the value of inputs. We know that the size of the flow of the top half must be equal to the size of the flow of the bottom half. So the value of the output and the income are identical. Then it will not matter whether we measure the flow of output or the flow of income; either measurement will be

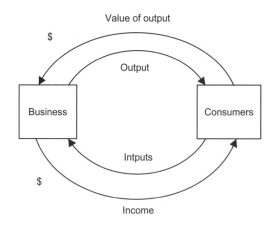

Figure 18-1   Circular Flow; Output Equals Income
This is the circular flow model of the economy. The top half shows the production and sale of output; the bottom half represents income payments to inputs. The value of the output must equal the income it creates.

the same. Before we examine this relation between output and income, we will explain the economic meaning of income.

Income is the money that society earns through production. Production increases output through the use of resources. The income payments to resource owners are rent, wages, interest, and profit and are the returns to land, labor, capital, and entrepreneurship. If you win the lottery, you would not be overly disappointed to know that this money is not income in the economic sense. You would be receiving a transfer of purchasing power from the many losers of the lottery to you. You have not contributed any resources of value to society when you purchased the ticket; society is not rewarding you for any increase in output. So be careful not to confuse income, generated by production, with a transfer of assets, which is just a redistribution of existing purchasing power within the society. Be assured, though, that your lottery winnings spend just as well. But our concern is with finding a way to measure output; and income, in the economic sense, does that.

To produce output, the firm must pay the cost of the inputs. This payment for the resources is the source of income for the resource owners. The price paid for the good goes first to the firm and is the firm's revenue. This money is then distributed among the owners of the raw material, the laborers, the government, and the stockholders or is retained by the business to purchase capital. So the value of the output produced is also a measure of the income earned during the production of the good. Thus output and income are measurements of the same activity.

Another way to think about the relation between output and income is to imagine that $10 trillion of output is sold in the economy. When that output is sold, how much income is created for the sellers? Ten trillion. With $10 trillion of income created, both the output and the income resulting from a productive process are identical. Output and the income that it creates are only different sides of the same coin.

Once the output or income level of society is known, then we also know the employment level of the labor force required to produce this output. So a single number represents the amount of output and income and indicates the employment level of a society. If you know one, you know the others. The name of this single number is gross domestic product.

Gross Domestic Product

Gross domestic product (GDP) is the total *dollar* value of all *final* goods and services produced within a nation's border during a year. GDP is a figure closely watched by economists, the government, private business, the news media, and others because it indicates the level of output in the economy and, by comparison with GDP figures over time, the trend of the economy. Gross domestic product is one measurement of the macro economy.

The definition of GDP stresses that we find the value of all *final* goods. This means that we not count the production of a good more than once. When we count the value of the intermediate products as well as the value of the final product, we are **double counting**. This occurs when the value of steel is counted as output along with the value of automobiles. The value of steel has been counted twice — once in its production and again as a part of the value of the automobiles; the iron ore that went into the steel was counted three times. To avoid double counting, only the value of the final good is used to find GDP. Final goods are those sold at retail. The final value includes all the intermediate production that went into the good; therefore, the sum of all the final values measures the total production of the society.

Next time you go into a store, look at all the goods on the shelves. There is a huge variety, and there are many stores. How can we possibly measure all that is produced by a society? Consider an economy producing just two goods, steamshovels and apples. Table 18-1 shows the output in several successive years. Can you tell from this data how the total output of the economy is

Table 18-1   Output

	Year 1	Year 2	Year 3	Year 4	Year 5
Steamshovels	50	60	50	60	50
Apples	1,000,000	1,100,000	1,200,000	1,000,000	900,000

This table shows the output of an economy producing two goods, steamshovels and apples. The production of the economy is shown for five years.

changing? Compare the output in year 2 to the previous year. More of both goods are produced, so the economy grew. From year 2 to year 3, the output of apples rose, but the number of steamshovels produced decreased. From this information alone, it is not possible to tell whether or not the economy grew. We cannot add apples and steamshovels to find the total output. If we compare year 4 to year 3, again the results are unclear. We have more steamshovels but fewer apples. But by comparing the output in year 5 to year 4, we can see that the output of the economy clearly fell, since the output of both goods fell.

To find the amount of output produced, we cannot simply add the amount produced of one good to the amount produced of another. All goods must be measured in the same unit. The obvious unit of measurement is the dollar. If the amount produced is measured by dollars, it is a simple matter to add together the dollar value of all goods. To find the value for each good, we take the price of the good and multiply by the number of units produced. To find the total value produced, we sum these values for all goods. The result is GDP, which is always expressed in dollars.

Suppose that the price of a steamshovel is $100,000, and the price of an apple is $0.10. To find the value of the output, we take the price of the good times the amount of the good produced for each good and then add. So in year 1 we have $100,000 × 50 + $0.10 × 1,000,000 = $5,100,000. The result of this calculation, GDP, is shown in Table 18-2. To calculate GDP, multiply prices times quantities and add. We can now see that the value of output went up between year 1 and year 2, down between year 2 and year 3, up again between year 3 and year 4, and finally down between year 4 and year 5. There is no question now about what happened to output. We have successfully solved our problem — how to add up all the assorted output of the economy. But by expressing GDP in terms of the dollar, we will find in our next chapter that our solution has created yet another problem.

We have found GDP from an **output approach** by adding up the final value of the total output of the economy. Remember that output and income

Table 18-2   GDP

	Year 1	Year 2	Year 3	Year 4	Year 5
GDP	$5,100,000	$6,110,000	$5,120,000	$6,100,000	$5,090,000

This table shows the gross domestic product for the economy producing steamshovels and apples. We have assumed that the price of a steamshovel is $100,000 and the price of an apple is $.10 and used the data from Table 18-1.

are identical, and so we should also be able to find the same GDP figure by using an income approach. The **income approach** to GDP is found by adding all income received by the factors of production. Rent, wages, interest, and profit sum together to give the identical GDP figure obtained from the output approach. We think of GDP as a measure of both output produced and income earned. In the future, when we mention income do not think of your paycheck — but think of GDP instead.

Expenditure Approach to GDP

A third method of finding GDP is the spending or expenditure approach. This approach divides the economy into four sectors and looks at how much each sector spends. The sectors are consumers, business, government, and foreign. Everything that is produced is purchased by one of these four sectors. That which is not purchased, business "purchases" in inventory. Thus, all production is accounted for as the sum of total spending. The sum of all expenditures by consumers, business, government, and the foreign sector makes up the **expenditure approach** to gross domestic product. First let us consider each sector separately.

Consumers are households buying goods and services for consumption. **Consumption (C)** is the purchase of goods and services by households. We buy food, clothing, entertainment, transportation, and so much more. Purchases of financial securities and other forms of personal "investment" are not counted as consumption since we cannot eat them, live in them, drive them, or in other ways consume them. These purchases are not consumption but merely a transfer of assets between individual consumers or between consumers and business, and are a form of saving.

Business purchases some of the output that it produced. These purchases are capital goods. Expenditures by business for machines, factory buildings, and other plants and equipment, plus expenditures for inventory goods, are called investment. Business is the only sector of the economy that invests in the economic sense. **Investment (I)** means business spending for capital goods plus inventories. Keep in mind that we are discussing the distribution of the pile of new output that has been produced this year, this year's GDP, and that one purchaser is business. Should a farmer's purchase of a 5-year-old tractor count as investment? No, since only newly produced capital goods are part of investment, not used capital goods. The used capital goods were accounted for in investment and GDP in the years in which they were produced. New capital goods may be used either to increase productive capacity or to replace plant and equipment that has worn out. Business expenditures for inventories are also included in investment. Some goods are produced but are not yet sold, or are purchased for the purpose of processing but are not yet processed this year. These goods are inventories and are counted as part of the production of the year they were produced. So investment is purchases of new plant and equipment plus inventories. It does not mean the purchase of stocks and bonds by individuals or business.

Government buys many products. It buys paper, airplanes, ships, typewriters, red tape, and many other items. These items are purchased from business and are part of the production of the economy. The total expenditure by government is called **government spending (G)**. We have accounted for the total spending of the three largest economic sectors — consumers, business, and government. Their total spending is consumption plus investment plus government spending, or C + I + G.

The computation of gross domestic product from the expenditure approach requires that an adjustment be made for the foreign sector. One problem is that some of the goods produced in the United States are exported, purchased by foreign buyers. When we add up the total spending by consumers, business, and government, this total spending will fall short of our total output by the value of the exports. Some of the production was not purchased by us but exported. And when any of our three sectors purchase foreign-produced goods, imports, our total spending will be greater than our total output by the value of the imports. Thus we need to allow for the impact of exports and imports as we calculate the expenditure approach to GDP. To account for the foreign sector, we add the difference between exports and imports, **net exports**, to the total spending of government, consumers, and business. The sum of all the expenditures by consumers, business, and government and the adjustment for the foreign sector, net exports, equals the GDP figure obtained from both the output and the income approach. This expenditure approach will be useful in later chapters. For simplicity, we will leave the foreign sector out of future discussions as the exports minus imports accounts for only a small part of our total spending.

We have seen that there is more than one way to measure the output of the nation. GDP measures the output directly. The expenditure approach measures the total spending on the output. Who receives the money spent? Those who contribute to output receive this spending as income. Since a dollar spent on output results in a dollar of income, the income approach obtains the same GDP figure. We now have a measure of the output of the economy as a whole.

Shortcomings of GDP

The gross domestic product of the United States is over $11 trillion. Some people mistakenly associate GDP with our economic health. They conclude that a large GDP is beneficial. But GDP was never intended to be a measure of economic health — GDP measures only the level of income and output. Even then there are many shortcomings in calculating and interpreting GDP, some of which are discussed here. We start with what is left out of GDP.

Gross domestic product does not include the value of all output. A price must first be established and reported through legitimate markets. If you volunteer your services as an economics tutor, the value of your contribution would not affect GDP since no money changed hands. GDP only measures market activities where there is a price established. Thus the output of housewives is not included in GDP. Also GDP only records reported market values, so anything sold in an underground market is not included. If the Mafia were to have an exceptionally good year it is doubtful that GDP would increase, since such activities are unreported.

What if the price paid for a good does not accurately reflect the opportunity cost of the resources used? Then GDP does not correctly report the value of what is produced. Goods sold under imperfect competition will overstate value, since the price is higher than the average total cost of production. Also, the price of a good is less than the opportunity cost of producing the good for a firm not paying for its pollution. So if we have either imperfect competition or externalities, the prices used to calculate GDP will not reflect the true resource cost and will not measure the true value of the output.

Meaningful comparisons of GDP figures over time are difficult to make. The quality of some goods changes. Medical care today is different from medical care 10 years ago. Television sets have been improved and can play DVDs. And what about cell phones? They did not exist a short time ago. Are we better off because of these improvements? How are these changes measured by GDP? The value from the introduction of new goods and improvements in existing goods may not be accurately captured by the GDP figures.

Gross domestic product should change when output changes. But GDP also changes with inflation. GDP is the sum of the price times the quantity of all final goods. What happens if the prices of goods go up but the quantities remain the same? Gross domestic product would rise, even though there is no change in the amount of output produced. Gross domestic product is affected by changes in prices even when output does not change. Since we want GDP to measure the output produced, the impact of changing prices will undermine our efforts. In the next chapter we will find ways to adjust GDP for inflation.

There are additional complications when we try to compare the GDP of countries with different size populations. One technique used to overcome the problem of population difference is to compare GDP per person, called **per capita GDP**. Take the GDP figure and divide by the population. This will give a measure of output per person. Now we can compare the output per person in Luxembourg, a small European nation, to the output per person in the United States. Table 18-3 shows the comparison with Luxembourg as well as with Japan and Sweden. Comparing GDP from one country to another may lead to different conclusions than if the per capita GDP were compared. The citizens of Luxembourg have more to consume per person than the citizens of the United States. Japan and Sweden have per capita GDPs that are close, and neither is far behind the U.S. in per capita GDP. Per capita GDP can be used in another

Table 18-3 GDP in the United States and Other Countries, 2004

	GDP Millions of $	Population Millions	Per Capita GDP
United States	$11,750,000	295.7	$40,100
Luxembourg	27,270	0.5	58,900
Japan	3,745,000	127.4	29,400
Sweden	255,400	9.0	28,400

The GDP of these countries are vastly different. The GDP of the United States is four hundred and thirty times as large as that of Luxembourg, more than three times as large as Japan's, and forty-five times as large as Sweden's. But the per capita GDP of the United States is about forty-five percent smaller than that of Luxembourg, 35 per cent larger than Japan's, and 40 per cent larger than Sweden's.
Source: The CIA World Fact Book.
Available on the web at: http://www.cia.gov/cia/publications/factbook/index.html

way. When per capita GDP rises over time, we can tell also whether the change in output is keeping up with the change in population.

Even if two countries have the same per capita GDP, that figure does not reflect the distribution of output. Consider two countries with exactly the same output and 10 people each. Both would have the same per capita GDP. Yet the standard of living of the citizens of each country would be dramatically different if the output in one country were equally divided among the people, while in the other country, one person had 90 percent of the output while the other nine people share the remaining 10 percent of the output.

Is a large GDP beneficial? A larger GDP is desirable to the extent that a large GDP means that there is more available to be consumed. So if more consumption is our goal, a larger GDP can support more consumption. But GDP is not a measure of the satisfaction gained by society; it is a measure of the value of the output. Many people enjoy leisure time, but the value of leisure time is not included in GDP. So when people decide to work less and enjoy more leisure, the output of society will fall; yet the society is better off.

Gross domestic product includes the desirable and the undesirable. Some output saves lives; the toxic waste of some output takes lives. GDP just records the dollar value of the output. Certainly there are shortcomings in calculating and interpreting gross domestic product. One number cannot be expected to measure all economic aspects of our economy. No one ever suggested that GDP has to measure everything. All we require is one gross figure that generally estimates the level of income — just in case we want to change it.

▶ Summary

This chapter introduced macroeconomics and established the essential foundation for the study of macro. This foundation is important because we first need to understand how to measure the performance of the economy before we can decide whether the performance should be changed.

We first distinguished microeconomics from macroeconomics. Microeconomics is the study of the individual parts, and macroeconomics is the study of the whole. You learned that we cannot always add up the behavior of the parts to find the behavior of the aggregate. This means that the aggregate relationships must be studied on their own, not just as added-up micro.

We found that output could be viewed as income and that the amount of employment is related to income and output. Thus the measurement of one provides information about the others. We also found a way to measure the

level of output in the economy, GDP. Gross domestic product is an important
concept because of its widespread use. We calculated GDP by three approaches:
output, income, and expenditure.

The final part of this chapter suggests that GDP is a limited concept. It does
not measure the health of the economy but the level of income. Even then, GDP
is not a particularly good measure of the level of income, but as the old saying
goes, it is a whole lot better than whatever is in second place.

Before we seek the cause of the booms and busts in our macro economy, we
will discuss one more measurement, price indexes. These indexes will be useful
because they allow us to measure the price level and inflation. If you know
anyone who has not experienced inflation first hand, be sure to recommend that
they read the next chapter.

▶ Key Concepts

microeconomics
macroeconomics
aggregate
fallacy of composition
income
gross domestic product
double counting
output approach

income approach
expenditure approach
consumption
investment
government spending
net exports
per capita GDP

▶ Discussion Questions

1. Uncle Effron says that economics is economics. It does not matter whether we
   are talking about macro or micro, it's all the same. Explain how macro and
   micro are different.
2. What is wrong with the following statement:
   If one farm doubles its output of oats, the farmer will be better off; therefore,
   if all farms double their output of oats, all farmers will be better off.
3. What does GDP measure? What does GDP not measure?
4. Why not just add up the value of all goods produced to find GDP?
5. Explain why the expenditure approach would yield the same GDP number as the
   income approach. Explain how income and output are the same.
6. Classify the following purchases as consumption, investment, or government
   expenditure:
   a. The purchase of a new family car.

b. Farmer Ted buys a new tractor.

c. Scotty's purchase of 5 pounds of Bar-B-Q ribs for a party.

d. Uncle Sam's purchase of a new aircraft carrier.

e. An increase in business inventories.

7. Uncle Effron says he invested in corporate bonds. Explain to Uncle Effron that he did not invest.

8. Suppose that the sum of expenditure by consumers, business, and government is $100. Exports are $10 and imports are $15. Use the expenditure approach to find GDP.

9. A very ugly shirt is produced this year. If no one buys it, how will it be accounted for in GDP?

▶ Self-Review

• Fill in the blanks

micro	Two major views of economics are _____ and
macro	_____ economics. The study of the individual parts of
microeconomics	the economy is _____. The study of the
macroeconomics	economy as a whole is _____. Our focus
macroeconomics	is now on _____. What society earns
income	through production is called _____. The total income
output	of the economy is equal to the total _____. The total
	dollar value of all final goods and services produced during
gross domestic product	the year is measured by _____.
	The GDP figure can also be found through the
income, expenditure	_____ approach and the _____ approach.
	The income approach adds all income to the resource
wages, interest	owners, rent as well as _____, _____,
profit	and _____. Total spending of the four sectors
expenditure	of the economy yields the _____ approach.
consumption	Purchases by consumers is _____.
	Business spending for new plant and equipment
inventories, investment	plus _____ is known as _____.
government spending	G represents _____. The difference
imports	between exports and _____ adjusts for spending
foreign	by the _____ sector. The calculation and use of
	the GDP figure has many shortcomings yet the figure
	does provide us with a general estimate of the level of
income, output	_____ and _____.

- Multiple choice

1. Microeconomic is the study of:
   a. the history of economics.
   b. the individual parts of the economy.
   c. the economy as a whole.
   d. how the economy should be.
2. The oil tycoon sells the petroleum for $1 million to the refinery, which sells the gasoline for $2 million to the service station, which sells the gasoline to the consumer for $3 million. If this were the total economic activity of this society, GDP is;
   a. $1 million.
   b. $2 million.
   c. $3 million.
   d. $6 million.
3. Which would *not* be included in investment?
   a. An accumulation of inventory in Junk Productions.
   b. Big Piano's purchase of a new delivery truck.
   c. Acme Corporation's purchase of a twenty-year-old factory from Plunko, Inc.
   d. A balloon man's purchase of balloons.
4. If nothing but the quality of goods changed over time, you would expect GDP to:
   a. increase.
   b. decreasse.
   c. remain the same.
   d. cannot be determined.
5. Two countries have the same GDP figure, but country A has twice the population. When comparing per capita GDP, you would expect the per capita GDP of country A to be:
   a. larger.
   b. smaller.
   c. the same.
   d. impossible to say.

Answers: 1.b, 2.c, 3.c, 4.c, 5.b.

| Chapter | 19 | PRICE INDEXES |

Even though inflation has been mild through the 1990's, inflation is one of the most persistent economic problems, and it will be a recurring topic in many of these macroeconomic chapters. Policy makers fear inflation and typically take action to keep inflation low. In this chapter we will develop a method to measure the price level and use this method, a price index, to adjust gross domestic product for the effect of changing prices. In the process, we will have developed a measure of inflation.

When Prices Change

The gross domestic product figure measures the output produced during the year. One of the more useful features of GDP is that it can be compared from year to year. Any difference should show the change in output between the two years. If the GDP figure doubled, we would conclude that output doubled. But this assumes that the only change in the two GDP figures was in output. You will recall from Chapter 18, where GDP is defined, that GDP is the sum of prices times final quantities produced. What if the quantities produced did not change but the *prices* did? GDP would change. GDP measured in dollars changes when prices change even if output remains constant. This makes GDP as it is defined an unreliable measure of the change in output.

If the same level of output were produced for two years, and prices doubled, then the prices of the second year would double the GDP figure. Gross domestic product consequently would double even though the amount of output did not change. We would have paid twice as much for the same quantity of output. Because of the doubled GDP, we would incorrectly conclude that output has doubled in the second year.

The difficulty with measuring GDP in terms of dollars is that prices rise or fall over time. When prices rise, the number of dollars needed to buy a good goes up, while the amount of the good that one dollar will buy goes down. Thus the value of the dollar, what the dollar buys, changes as the prices of goods change. Measuring GDP in dollars means that GDP is measured in units that constantly change. It is like having a speedometer on your car that sometimes says 60 when you are going 40, and sometimes says 20 when you are going 50. This speedometer may not show the true speed of the car. Similarly, the dollar value of GDP may not measure the true level of output of the economy. With the changing value of the dollar, the comparison of GDP from year to year becomes meaningless.

As GDP changes from year to year, part of the change may result from a change in output, but it is likely that some part of the change in GDP is due to a change in price. Since we want to compare only the changes in output produced, we must find and eliminate the part of GDP that changes due to changing prices. The isolation of the change in GDP due to changing prices also provides a method of measuring inflation. To measure the change in prices, we will use a price index.

Constructing a Price Index

A **price index number** records the percentage change in the price of a selected combination of goods compared to the base year.

$$\text{Price index number} = \frac{\text{cost of the market basket, current year}}{\text{cost of the market basket, base year}} \times 100$$

There are several steps in the construction of a price index. For a given year or series of years, called the base year, select a particular bundle of goods and services called a market basket. Then find the cost, the value of that market basket, for several consecutive years. To find the price index number, divide the cost of the market basket in each year, the current year, by the cost of the market basket in the base year and multiply by 100. The multiplication by 100 makes the price index a percentage figure of the cost of the market basket in the base year.

Consider the index numbers in Table 19-1. Let us pick year 3 as the base year, and find that in that year the market basket costs $10. Thus $10 is the base-year cost that we will divide into the cost of the basket for each year under consideration. For year 4, the cost of the basket is $15. Then the index number for year 4 is 150 ($15/$10 × 100). An index number of 150 means that there has been a 50 percent increase in price since the base year for these particular goods. The index number of 200 for year 5 means that the price of the market basket has doubled since the base year. The index number of 300 for year 7 means that price has tripled, and 400 for year 9 means that price has quadrupled since the base year. What is the index number for year 3, the base year? Since year 3 is the current year as well as the base year, $10 is divided by the base-year cost of $10, times 100. The index number for the base year is *always* 100 since the base-year cost is divided into itself as the current-year cost.

Now you have some idea of how to construct a price index. You also know how to interpret a price index. You know that an index of 100 can identify the base year, since the base-year cost is being divided into itself. An index number of 100 also identifies any year in which there has been no change in the market basket price from the base year. Any index number greater than 100 means that the price of the market basket has increased compared to the base year. How much is the increase? An index number over 100 indicates the exact percentage increase in price. An index number of 126 means there has

Table 19-1 Price Index

	Base Year								
	Year 1	Year 2	Year 3	Year 4	Year 5	Year 6	Year 7	Year 8	Year 9
Current cost of market basket	$6	$8	$10	$15	$20	$25	$30	$35	$40
Price index	60	80	100	150	200	250	300	350	400

The price index is calculated by taking the current cost of the market basket in each year and dividing by the cost of the market basket in the base year, here $10 in year 3, and then multiplying by 100. For year 4, the price index is ($15/$10) × 100 = 150.

been a 26 percent increase in price since the base year. A price index is simply a measure of how prices for the contents of a market basket change over time. What if the value of the market basket is lower than in the base year? Then the price index reflects this decrease with an index number under 100. This fall in the index is shown in Table 19-1. Year 3 is still the base year. In year 1 the cost of the market basket is $6. The index number for year 1 is 60, found by $6/$10 × 100. This means that the cost of the market basket was 40 percent lower in year 1 than in the base year.

Note that in the calculation of a price index, only the cost of the goods, the prices, may change. The market basket, which represents the quantities of goods, stays the same. So the price index measures the change in prices of a constant quantity. We will look at two uses for a price index: one as a measurement of the change in prices and the other as an adjustment to eliminate the changes in prices from GDP. Then we can compare GDP over time in a manner that shows only the change in output.

Consumer Price Index

You can construct a price index to measure the change in price through time of any good or group of goods that you wish. For example, you can construct a gasoline price index or one for the ingredients of a bacon, lettuce, and tomato sandwich. There are many price indexes constructed by government and private business. All are constructed in the same manner: base-year cost into current-year cost, times 100. The contents of the market basket will identify the price index. Many indexes measure the price of only a single good such as steel or copper. Other indexes are constructed from a market basket that contains a variety of goods. Two widely known price indexes are the producer price index and the consumer price index. The **producer price index (PPI)** is a measure of the prices of certain goods sold at wholesale and is thought to be a predictor of consumer price movements. Generally, a rise in wholesale prices can be expected to be passed on to consumers. So a rise in wholesale prices may predict a later rise in consumer prices.

The consumer price index is published monthly by the Department of Labor, Bureau of Labor Statistics. Table 19-2 shows the consumer price index since 1930. Notice that the base year is 1982–84. The **consumer price index (CPI)** is calculated by taking the base-year cost of a selected market basket of consumer goods and dividing this cost into the current-year cost of these goods. The CPI is regularly reported by the news media.

Table 19-2   The Consumer Price Index, 1930–2005

Year	Consumer Price Index	Year	Consumer Price Index
1930	16.7	1968	34.8
1931	15.2	1969	36.7
1932	13.6	1970	38.8
1933	12.9	1971	40.5
1934	13.4	1972	41.8
1935	13.7	1973	44.4
1936	13.8	1974	49.3
1937	14.3	1975	53.8
1938	14.1	1976	56.9
1939	13.9	1977	60.6
1940	14.0	1978	65.2
1941	14.7	1979	72.6
1942	16.3	1980	82.4
1943	17.2	1981	90.9
1944	17.6	1982	96.5
1945	18.0	1983	99.6
1946	19.5	1984	103.9
1947	22.3	1985	107.6
1948	24.1	1986	109.6
1949	23.8	1987	113.6
1950	24.1	1988	118.3
1951	26.0	1989	124.0
1952	26.5	1990	130.7
1953	26.7	1991	136.2
1954	26.9	1992	140.3
1955	26.8	1993	144.5
1956	27.2	1994	148.2
1957	28.1	1995	152.4
1958	28.9	1996	156.9
1959	29.1	1997	160.5
1960	29.6	1998	163.0
1961	29.9	1999	166.6
1962	30.2	2000	172.2
1963	30.6	2001	177.1
1964	31.0	2002	179.9
1965	31.5	2003	184.0
1966	32.4	2004	188.9
1967	33.4	2005	195.3

This table shows the consumer price index since 1930. The base year is 1982–1984.

Source: 2000–2005: *The Economic Report of the President, 2006*; found on the web at http://www.gpoacess.gov/eop/
1958–1999: *The Economic Report of the President, 2000*; found on the web at http://bls.gov
1930–1957: *Historical Statistics, Part I, 1970*.
Used by permission.

The CPI is a price index used to measure inflation and deflation in our economy. Inflation is a continued rise in the price level. Inflation does not mean that the prices of all goods are going up. The prices of some goods may go up while the prices of other goods fall. Inflation does mean that the average of all prices, the price level, the CPI, is going up. Inflation also means a fall in the value of a dollar, since each dollar buys less. Do not confuse disinflation, which is a slowdown in the rate of inflation, with deflation. **Deflation** is a continued fall in the price level and an increase in the value of a dollar. Changes in the CPI show that the price level is rising or falling. When the CPI continues to increase, we know that the price level is going up, and inflation is occurring. When the CPI continues to decrease, we know that the price level is going down and that deflation occurs. So the consumer price index is used to detect inflation or deflation, changes in the average level of prices.

Limitations of the CPI

The CPI is an imperfect measure of the price level. How well the consumer price index measures inflation depends on what is included in the market basket. The market basket for the CPI is a combination of nearly 200 goods that the typical urban household might buy. Once a market basket is selected, it will be used for several years. This extended use of the market basket may reduce the reliability of the CPI as a measure of inflation. The reliability is reduced because the market basket may no longer represent what people are actually buying. The combination of goods that consumers buy changes over time, new goods are constantly introduced, and the qualities of existing goods change.

Changes in the market basket are made from time to time to make the consumer price index a more accurate measure of the price level. Then why not select a new market basket every year? The reason is simple. The whole point of calculating a price index is to see how much prices change from year to year with the quantities of goods held fixed. If both prices and quantities change each year, we will not have a measure of how prices alone change. We need a fixed market basket to keep quantities constant so that we can find a measure of the change in prices. Consequently, the price index method requires that the same market basket be used for several years. You can see that the choice of the market basket and the choice of the base year are important for the price index to be a representative measure of the average price level.

On what basis is a base year selected? Prices in all other years will be compared to those in the base year. For this reason, the base year should be a typical year, with few economic disturbances such as war, recession, or inflation. Ideally, the base year should be a year when the economy is running smoothly at full employment with stable prices. If there were substantial unemployment, the combination of goods the "average" consumer buys would be affected. Stable prices indicate that the price level is not going up or down. Consumers are not adjusting their purchases to changing prices, and the market basket is more likely to be representative of consumer purchases. Because the choice of a base year depends on a particular combination of economic conditions, we may have to wait many years for the preferred economic conditions to occur before the base year is changed.

By comparing the CPI from year to year, we have a measure of how much prices are changing. Does this price index accurately measure inflation for you? It depends on whether or not you buy the goods in the market basket. If you are buying goods not included in the market basket, but goods with prices increasing less than the market basket prices, then the price index overstates inflation. Similarly, if you are buying goods with prices increasing faster than the market basket prices, then the price index will understate inflation. No doubt there will be differences in buying patterns for a family with young children and for a retired couple. The CPI provides general evidence of inflation in a society, but the specific impact of inflation is unique to each individual. We have discussed the cost of inflation in Chapter 17.

Real GDP

Another frequently reported price index is the GDP price deflator. The GDP price deflator, or implicit price index as it is also known, is a price index calculated in the same manner as all other price indexes. It shows the percentage change in cost of the market basket from the base year. This market basket is broader than that of the CPI. The market basket for the GDP price deflator contains all final goods and services produced in our economy. This includes goods purchased by business, government, and foreigners as well as the consumer. The market basket for the GDP price deflator is the total output of the economy.

The **GDP price deflator** is a special price index used to convert money GDP into real GDP. Money GDP refers to GDP as we originally defined it. To find **money** or **current GDP**, take the prices times the quantities produced in that year and add. You should be aware that if GDP is not otherwise identified, it usually means money GDP. Real GDP refers to GDP adjusted for changes in price. Real GDP and money GDP are two different concepts. They are related as follows.

$$\text{Real GDP} = \frac{\text{money GDP}}{\text{GDP price deflator}}$$

Real GDP is a measure of output produced by an economy valued in the prices of the base year. To find the real level of output, real GDP, we divide the current level of output, money GDP, by the GDP price deflator index number for the current year. By this division we are removing the price changes from the money GDP figure. The use of this price index to convert money GDP into real GDP allows us to compare real GDP and find how much the output has actually changed from year to year. Remember that it is the change in output that we are seeking.

Table 19-3 shows the application of the GDP price deflator to a five-year series of GDP figures. The money GDP figures incorrectly indicate that output has quadrupled in the five-year time period. The GDP price deflator indicates that the price level has doubled. Real GDP was found by dividing the GDP of each year by the GDP price deflator index number for the year. Remember that an index number is a percentage figure, so to divide by an index number, put the index number in decimal form. For example, an index number of 100 is 1.00, and 125 is 1.25. Table 19-3 shows the adjustment to GDP to account for changing prices. After adjusting for changes in price with the GDP price deflator, we see that output has really only doubled. This is shown by the doubling of real GDP.

Table 19-3   Real GDP

Year	Money GDP	GDP Price Deflator	Real GDP
1	$1,000,000	100	$1,000,000
2	2,000,000	125	1,600,000
3	2,600,000	130	2,000,000
4	3,300,000	150	2,200,000
5	4,000,000	200	2,000,000

To find real GDP, divide money GDP by the GDP price deflator. For year 3, real GDP is $2,000,000 found by $2,600,000/1.30.

Understanding Real GDP

A price index shows the percentage change in price of the market basket since the base year. When you divide the current value of output, GDP, by a price index number, the GDP price deflator discussed in the previous section, you correct the current value of output for the change in price since the base year. Money GDP is price times quantity, which we can write as PQ. The GDP price deflator measures the price level, P. If prices go up, then GDP goes up too. But *real* GDP does not change when prices change since both the numerator (money GDP) and the denominator (GDP price deflator) go up by the same amount.

$$\text{Real GDP} = \frac{\text{money GDP}}{\text{GDP price deflator}} = \frac{\not{P} \times Q}{\not{P}} = Q$$

When price changes, both the P in the numerator and the P in the denominator change by the same amount and cancel out, $\not{P}$, so real GDP, Q, does not change. Real GDP is not affected by a change in price. Thus we see that real GDP is a measure of the quantity of output produced, Q. So if you wish to compare GDP over time to see the direction the economy is taking, be sure that you are comparing real GDP figures that have been adjusted for the change in the price level.

Real GDP is a measure of the amount of output produced. Price changes have already been accounted for in the calculation of real GDP. You should think of real GDP as a measure of the size of the pile of goods and services produced by an economy in a year. It is not a measure of the *value* in terms of prices of the pile of goods but a measure of the *size* of the pile of goods. This is real GDP found by dividing each money GDP by the GDP price deflator. Now the output is valued as it was in the base year, and real GDP can be compared to output in other years.

When we apply the GDP price deflator to money GDP, we are taking the value of each good in the base year and assigning that value to the good in all other years. If the good sells for $1 in the base year, regardless of whether it actually sells for $300 in another year, we assign it a $1 value. We are establishing dollars of constant purchasing power to measure output in all years. We have adjusted for the changing value of the dollar. As a result, real GDP is simply GDP stated in terms of constant dollars. When money GDP changes, you do not know if it is due to a change in price, a change in output, or a combination of both. If real GDP changes, then you know that output has changed. If real GDP doubles, output has doubled; if real GDP falls, output has fallen; if real GDP does not change, then output has remained constant. Thus price indexes adjust for the changing price level and allow more meaningful comparisons between GDP figures.

For the remainder of this text, the term GDP means real GDP. As discussed in Chapter 18, GDP, income, and output are all measures of the same thing. So real GDP is the same as real income and real output. Future use of the term income means real income, and output refers to real output. And just as we converted GDP to real GDP, the spending of each sector of the economy, consumer, business, and government can be expressed in real terms. In future chapters when we talk about consumption or investment or government spending, we will mean those expenditures in real terms. By converting to real terms, we have eliminated the impact of inflation on these measures of spending. You should be aware that this is not the common practice, and when your favorite newscaster talks about GDP, for example, it will be money GDP unless real GDP is specifically mentioned. So if you hear that GDP has doubled, be doubtful about the output of the economy having doubled unless you know it is real GDP.

You can find yet another application for price indexes. There are also concepts known as money salary and real salary. Money salary is the number of dollars in your paycheck; real salary is the purchasing power of your salary in terms of the base-year prices. To find your real salary, divide your money salary by the CPI of that year. Your money salary may double, but will your purchasing power? Not if inflation is 400 percent, as measured by the CPI; then your real salary has fallen in half. It is not just the number of dollars you have that is relevant, it is how much you can buy with those dollars. Inflation erodes purchasing power.

▶ Summary

This chapter has introduced price indexes. The method of constructing a price index requires keeping the quantities of goods fixed and allowing only the prices of the goods to change. In that way we can record the change in the prices of the goods over time. Price indexes are useful in measuring the average price level in the macro economy. Price indexes have the added use of measuring inflation, a continued rise in the average price level over time.

The consumer price index is of special interest since it measures the change in the price of goods that we as consumers typically buy. The consumer price index is widely used as a measure of inflation. The CPI tells us whether or not the typical consumer is now capable of buying more goods or fewer. After all, even if a consumer's income goes up, the gain could be more than wiped out by inflation.

By using another price index, the GDP price deflator, we were able to overcome one of the shortcomings of GDP, our measurement of the output of the economy. By obtaining real GDP, the effect of changing prices is removed and the changes in the amount of output produced can be observed. We can find real output by dividing money GDP by the GDP price deflator. This method gives us a measure of total output where price changes have been eliminated. Any remaining changes reflect only a change in the level of output of the economy. These changes are of vital interest.

The major macro measurement devices have now been discussed. They are GDP, price indexes, and real GDP. Real GDP has provided us with a basis for comparison of output over time. This enables us to use GDP to discover trends and make predictions. If we eventually wish to be able to change GDP, we must first be aware of where GDP is and where it is going.

This chapter did not indicate what determines the level of prices and income. It is one thing to measure the level of income, but quite another to explain why it moves and changes. If we knew what makes the level of income change, we might be able to make it change in the direction we want. The next chapter discusses how the level of income changes over time and suggests the idea that it can be controlled. This idea may seem reasonable to you, but not too long ago it was revolutionary.

▶ Key Concepts

price index number	deflation
producer price index	GDP price deflator
consumer price index	money or current GDP
inflation	real GDP

▶ Discussion Questions

1. What does a price index measure?
2. Suppose that the inflation rate is 10 percent per year. What does this do to the value of a dollar? How is the value of a dollar measured?
3. a. Suppose that payments to retirees and social security recipients go up as the CPI goes up. Will this cause an inflation to get worse?

b. What if union contracts include a clause that causes wages to rise as the CPI rises? What impact might this have on inflation?

c. What if the CPI overstates inflation? If wages are tied to the CPI, won't every increase in the CPI be inflationary? Explain.

4. Uncle Effron says that the CPI is unreliable as a measure of inflation. He kept track of his regular yearly expenditures, and they went up 12 percent over last year, but the CPI shows an inflation rate of 4 percent. Explain to Uncle Effron why the CPI measurement of inflation might be different from his.

5. How does the consumer price index differ from the producer price index? The GDP price deflator?

6. What does real GDP measure? How is real GDP different from money GDP?

7. Suppose you were told that GDP was $100 last year and $120 this year. If the inflation rate were 10 percent, was real GDP higher or lower this year than last? What if the inflation rate were 30 percent?

8. Use Table 19-2. In what years did inflation occur? Deflation? Do your answers agree with the inflation rates given in Table 17-2?

▶ Self-Review

• Fill in the blanks

price index, cost
market basket, base
cost, market basket
current, 100
percentage

base
100
doubled
base

producer price index

consumer price index
fall

money
current

A device used to measure changing prices is a _____. To construct a price index, the _____ of the _____ in the _____ year is divided into the _____ of the _____ in the _____ year, then multiplied by _____. A price index number shows the _____ change in the price of a selected combination of goods compared to a _____ year. The base year index number is always _____. An index number of 200 means that price has _____ since the _____ year. A widely known price index that measures the prices of certain goods sold at wholesale is the _____. An index that measures the change in the price of typical consumer goods and is used as a measure of inflation is the _____. The CPI is also a measure of deflation, a continued _____ in the price level. GDP found by the actual prices times the quantities of the goods produced in the year is _____ or _____ GDP. GDP adjusted for changes in

real, money

GDP price deflator

money, real

real

doubled

prices is _____ GDP. To find real GDP, _____ GDP is divided by the _____. The GDP price deflator is a price index used to convert _____ GDP into _____ GDP. The measure of output produced by an economy valued in the prices of the base year is _____ GDP. When real GDP doubles, output of the economy has _____.

• Multiple choice

1. Year 10 has a price index number of 100. This means that:
   a. the average level of prices is the same as in the base year.
   b. inflation is 100 percent.
   c. prices have increased 10 percent each year since the base year.
   d. none of the above.
2. Deflation is:
   a. a continued fall in the price level.
   b. a rising price index.
   c. a fall in the value of the dollar.
   d. both a and c.
3. If output increases:
   a. prices increase.
   b. real GDP falls.
   c. real GDP stays the same.
   d. real GDP increases.
4. If prices double and nothing else changes, you would expect real GDP to:
   a. decrease.
   b. stay the same.
   c. increase.
   d. not enough information to tell.
5. One problem with a price index is that it uses a market basket of goods representing the purchaser's choices and:
   a. the combination of goods actually purchased changes.
   b. buyers actually buy what is in the market basket.
   c. the market basket changes each year.
   d. no one uses a market basket anymore.

Answers: 1.a, 2.a, 3.d, 4.b, 5.a.

Chapter | 20 | **BUSINESS CYCLES**

Key Topics
> business cycles
> classical economics
> the Great Depression
> Keynes

Goals
> understand that the level of GDP fluctuates
> realize that there are many ways to look at the economy
> recognize that some economic theories have been rejected
> begin a macro model of the economy

When unemployment or inflation seem to get out of hand, people look to the government to do something. Government intervention in the economy is not only accepted but expected. This use of government power may seem obvious to us now, but it was not always so.

The evolving science of economics changed focus and direction during the most disastrous economic times in the history of the United States, the Great Depression of the 1930s. This event shook our confidence in our capitalistic system. Also it was an event that was never supposed to happen. Why were economists so confident that a depression could not occur? How did the depression lead to a new way of thinking about the macro economy? Could such a severe depression happen again? A depression is one part of the business cycle. This chapter examines the mysterious business cycle — the booms and busts in the economy that seem to happen for no apparent reason.

Business Cycles

Business cycles are more-or-less-regular fluctuations in the level of economic activity. These are the up and down phases that accompany the increases or decreases in gross domestic product. Each business cycle goes through four phases: peak, recession, trough, and recovery. These are positions on the cycle and indicate the level of income, output, and employment. Figure 20-1 is a business cycle with the phases identified. The peak is the highest point; the declining period is the recession. A deeper, longer recession is sometimes called a depression. The trough is the lowest point and recovery is the upward swing. Although all business cycles follow the same pattern of peak, recession, trough, and recovery, not all cycles are the same. Some peaks are higher than others, some recessions are longer and more severe, and other variations occur from cycle to cycle. The lower portions of the cycle are usually accompanied by high rates of unemployment. Yet upward movements on the business cycle that reduce unemployment may result in increased inflation.

The term unemployment is frequently used in macroeconomics. We introduced unemployment in Chapter 17. You will recall that unemployment means that there are people looking for a job but are unable to find work at the going wage. There may be work available that they are not trained to do, or there may be work available in other areas of the country. But these people cannot find work that they are capable of doing, that would not require relocating, or that would pay a wage they are willing to accept. Chapter 19 discussed inflation and how it is measured.

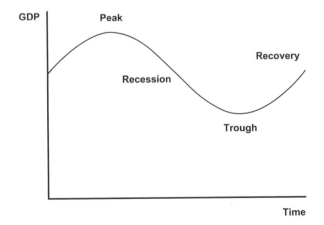

Figure 20-1   Business Cycle
This figure shows the phases of the business cycle. The high point is the peak, the declining portion is the recession, the low point is the trough, and the rising portion is the recovery.

Percent of trend

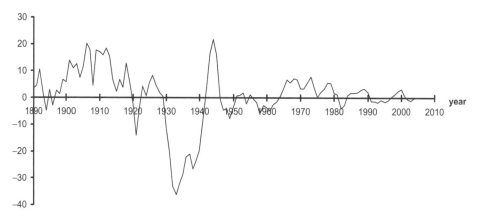

Figure 20-2   American Business Activity Since 1880
This figure records the history of the business cycle of the United States. The level of economic
activity is characterized by the up and down phases shown here.
Source: Based on data from the following sources: 1889–1959: *Historical Statistics, Part I,
1970; 1959–1999 Economic Report of the President, 2000. 2000–2005: Economic Report of the
President, 2006.* Used by permission.

Figure 20-2 shows the history of business cycles in the United States. One
noticeable feature is that the economy peaks during a war and then slides into
a recession afterward. Does this mean that our capitalistic economy cannot
prosper without war? That was the claim of communists and other critics of
capitalism. Their basis was the historical record that you see before you. Within
a few chapters you will have the knowledge to judge the correctness of this
claim yourself.

Theories of Business Cycles

There have been many theories attempting to explain the cause of business
cycles. One early explanation was that the business cycle resulted from
sunspots, those solar flares on the surface of the sun. This theory was based
on an observation that the period between peaks of the business cycle was as
long as the period between the peaks of sunspot activity. Weather, and therefore
agricultural activity, is affected by sunspots, and variations in agricultural output
do lead to variations in the total output produced. But the sunspot theory was
quietly dropped when a more careful investigation of solar activity revealed a
cycle longer than first reported.

Another popular business cycle theory stressed variations in the amount of business inventory. It is difficult for a firm to keep inventories at a constant level. This variation in inventory affects investment, and GDP in turn will vary. The inventory theory, however, has a serious flaw, the fallacy of composition. Just because a situation is true for one business does not mean that the situation is true for all businesses together. While the inventories of one firm are going up, it is likely that those of another firm are going down. These two movements could counteract each other and leave little variation in total inventories. The inventory theory by itself does not explain business cycles; we would still have to explain what causes the cycles in inventories, and that would also explain the cause of the business cycle.

Technological innovations were also suggested as a source of business cycles. At random periods of time, significant inventions have revolutionized a process. Trains, electricity, automobiles, airplanes, and microchips are such major innovations. Their production and use provided a new burst of activity to the economy and greatly increased income, output, and employment. Not only did the invention and production of the auto itself affect the economy, but so did its many spinoffs. The initial invention then required the building of a vast highway system; an oil supply network of producers, refiners, and distributors; motel systems and more to service the new innovation. At some point the production of autos levels off to a replacement level, the highways are built, and spending is only for maintenance. The result is a decline in income, output, and employment until the economy is sparked by the next innovation. Yet it is difficult to explain why more-or-less-regular business cycles would occur using this theory of random innovations. And since we cannot predict the occurrence of the next innovation, the innovation theory is of little value in forecasting the business cycle.

Next we explore another approach to the cause of business cycles and see the radical revolution that changed economic thinking and still influences our thinking today. For this we must go back to the period before the Great Depression.

Classical Economics

Classical economics was the way of thinking that governed economic thought prior to the 1930s. One of its most influential opinions was that the government should stay out of the macro economy. It was acceptable for government to interfere with certain activities on the micro level, such as the regulation of business to encourage more competitive conditions, or the production of public goods like defense or education; but no government interference should occur on the macro level. This hands-off attitude was called ***laissez-faire***. The classical belief was that any government interference on the macro level would make conditions worse, not better. Thus, the government could do the most good in the macro economy by doing the least.

The classical economists followed a *laissez-faire* attitude because they were convinced that the equilibrium outcome of the economy would always be desirable. What would you say is the most desirable level of income for the economy? Full employment. And if you were to ask any classical economist in which direction the economic forces would tend to push the economy, the reply would be the same. The belief was that the economy has a natural tendency to equilibrium at only one level — full employment — the most desirable of all possible outcomes. Thus any recession and period of unemployment would be limited by the very nature of the business cycle. Left to its own devices, the economy would automatically return to full employment. The classical economists relied on various models to support this belief. One of these models is Say's Law; another, market forces.

Say's Law states that supply creates its own demand. The meaning of this statement is that the income paid to resource owners for the use of their resources will be used to purchase the output of producers. In an economy of just one producer, what happens to the income the resource owners receive from selling resources? The income is used to buy the output of the firm. The income is just equal to the value of the output. So supply, the output of the producer, should create a demand, what the resource owners can buy from the producer, of an equal amount. If this is true in an economy with one producer, it was also believed true on a larger scale in the actual economy. In classical economics, production in the economy creates just enough income to purchase the output. The supply creates enough demand to keep the resources employed.

An important question is what would the level of production, supply, be? The classical economists relied on market forces to determine the level of production. They believed that certain market forces automatically guide the economy to an equilibrium level of production at full employment. These market forces are the forces of supply and demand that determine prices, wages, and interest rates. This means that if more was being supplied than demanded, the market forces would adjust prices, wages, and interest rates to make the quantity demanded equal to the quantity supplied.

Consider the impact of prices from the classical point of view. What if the economy were trying to produce more than it was capable of producing because people were trying to buy too much, and the effect was being felt in rising prices? How do we expect people to act in the face of rising prices? We expect them to buy less, of course, which would be the solution needed. And what if the problem were that the economy was producing less than its capacity because people were not buying enough? Prices would fall, and then people would buy more. So it was thought that prices automatically adjust to bring full employment. If society is trying to buy more than can be produced, the result is higher prices. The higher prices reduce the amount purchased. And when sales are slack and output builds up, the falling prices encourage more buying, more production, and as a result, more employment.

In addition to prices, the classical economist relied on wages and interest rates to help prevent any serious fluctuation in the business cycle. Wages are the price of labor in the market for labor while interest is the price of money in the market for money. Because wages and interest rates are prices, they were expected to rise or fall and bring the desired adjustment to the economy. If unemployment exists, the wage would adjust to eliminate the unemployment.

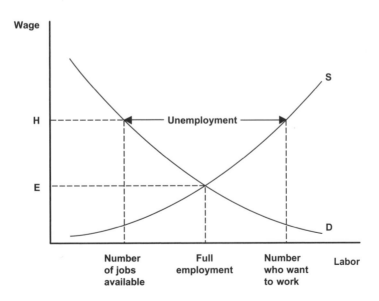

Figure 20-3   Unemployment
At wage H, the quantity supplied of labor is greater than the quantity demanded. Unemployment results until the wage falls to the equilibrium wage, E.

See Figure 20-3. Unemployment results when the amount of labor supplied is greater than the amount of labor demanded at the above-equilibrium wage, H. Thus the number of people willing to work is greater than the number of jobs available — a surplus of labor. If the wage falls, more people will be employed. Notice that the equilibrium wage in the labor market, wage E, brings full employment according to the classical definition, since all those wanting to work at that wage are employed. Similar forces will be at work in the market for money so that the interest rate will reach equilibrium at a rate resulting in full employment. Therefore, equilibrium in all markets is at full employment. Say's Law asserts that by producing at equilibrium, there will be sufficient demand to buy all that is produced. The resulting level of income is in equilibrium at full employment.

The Great Depression

The historical business cycle, Figure 20-2, shows that until the 1930s there were mild fluctuations but certainly nothing as disastrous as what was about to come. The classical economists believed that there must be favorable processes at work and among those were Say's Law and the market forces on price. The quantity of output supplied in the economy would eventually equal the quantity demanded, and a desirable equilibrium at full employment results. If this is where the economy tends naturally, why permit the risk of government interference? The classical economists were insistent that the government keep out of the macro economy. Their concern was that government, for all its good intentions, would interfere with the automatic workings of prices, wages, and interest rates and prevent the economy from reaching full employment. Because of Say's Law and the market forces, the *laissez-faire* attitude was the dominant one as our economy started a serious decline in 1929. This decline was to become known as the Great Depression. The classical response to the condition? Do nothing, for fear that whatever was done would make the economy worse. If left alone, the economy would automatically readjust to full employment.

The American economy did not improve as predicted but became steadily worse. The stock market crash in October 1929 had signaled a new age, an age of poverty and hopelessness, an age of want and joblessness. By 1934, 25 percent of the labor force was unemployed. And most of those who could find work were paid low wages. The collapse of many banks threatened disaster in the banking system, too. People who did not trust the banks tried to withdraw their money. When too many depositors want their money, banks must recall loans from their borrowers. This cannot be done quickly so some banks had to turn people away. This only increased the panic and caused the failure of more banks. The stock market had crashed; there were no jobs, and there was a breakdown of the banking system. The government had done next to nothing. What could be done? To some it seemed the best thing was· to move somewhere else; things could not be any worse there. Yet conditions were the same everywhere. No jobs, no prospects, banks failing — where was the outcome promised by the classical economist?

Even before the Great Depression there had been questions raised about classical economics. By the 1850s, revolution had swept over much of Europe. The seeds of the Russian revolution were already being sown by a German living in England, Karl Marx. Marx argued that capitalism would not function as the classical economist claimed. In reaction to the poverty and misery surrounding him in London, Marx wrote in *Das Kapital* of a classless society where all shared the wealth equally. Marx predicted that one day the capitalistic system would arrive at this classless state. Capitalism could not avoid it; the forces that gave rise to the wealthy class would lead to its own destruction, and the capitalistic system would be replaced by a system of communism. The claim that capitalism itself might be the cause of poverty and that poverty could cause revolution capable of overthrowing the political and economic system was a new and serious challenge to capitalistic thought.

Was this worldwide depression of the 1930s what Karl Marx had predicted in his gloomy assessment of capitalism, *Das Kapital*? Was America doomed to economic failure? The communist solution, that of the overthrow of the political and economic system, became an attractive solution to some as the depression worsened.

Lord Keynes

Classical economics failed to rescue us from the Great Depression. It was apparent to some that doing nothing did not work, that something had to be done. A solution was proposed by the British economist, John Maynard Keynes (Keynes rhymes with plains). Keynes was born in 1883. He was the son of an economist, married to a premier Russian ballerina, a friend of the author Virgina Woolf and the mathematician-philosopher Bertrand Russell. Keynes made a fortune by spending a half-hour in bed each morning speculating in financial markets and was heard to say that his only regret in life was that he had not drunk more champagne. He hardly seemed one to offer clear advice about the inner workings of the economic system. Yet he had studied under Alfred Marshall, the most influential economist at the time, and had clearly learned the classical economics well. Much of Keynes' work is built upon classical economic thought. He had mastered what came before him and was now prepared to extend the boundaries of economic thought. What could Keynes tell us about the economy?

According to Keynes, there was no tendency to the classical equilibrium at full employment. The economy could be in equilibrium at any level of income, including full employment or a deep depression. There is no certainty that the equilibrium level of income, output, and employment will be a desirable one. America was in equilibrium in the 1930s in the most depressed economic condition the nation had ever known, with no tendency to change. We would remain in that condition unless some action was taken to change the equilibrium to a more desirable level of income. For Keynes the key to the depression was a lack of aggregate demand. To support this view, Keynes developed a more accurate description of the inner workings of the economy. In the process, some of the foundations of classical thinking were reexamined.

Keynes found the flaw in Say's Law. Supply does not *necessarily* create an equal amount of demand. You may sell your resources for $1 million, but that does not mean that you will purchase $1 million of production. What if you were to save $1? Saving means not spending. When you do not spend that dollar (and no one else spends it), you leave a dollar's worth of output of some producer unpurchased. This firm will cut back production and as a result reduce output, income, and employment. So although supply is *capable* of creating its own demand, Keynes pointed out that saving can interfere with that outcome. So whatever the level of income resulting in full employment, there may not be enough demand to maintain that income.

Keynes also pointed out that the market mechanisms of prices, wages, and interest rates will tend to be "sticky" on the downward side, not necessarily flexible as claimed by the classical economist. This means that business would tend to let production and consequently employment fall before resorting to lowering prices. The sticky prices are due to imperfections in markets. These imperfections result when markets are not competitive or when the market forces take long periods of time to achieve equilibrium. If the wage were above equilibrium, it might not fall because unions and workers would resist lower wages. Or minimum wage laws imposed by government may prevent a fall in the wage. Since the wage falls slowly, if at all, the labor market will not eliminate unemployment as the classical economists had argued. If interest rates are under the control of large banks, their monopoly power will keep interest rates from falling. So the market forces may fail to bring the favorable economic adjustments expected by the classical economists.

The Keynesian Revolution

It was not clear at the time that Keynes possessed the cure for the Great Depression, but it was clear that the classical solution was not the cure. Keynes offered a revolutionary solution to the Great Depression. He pointed out that in certain situations, and this depression was one, there was no alternative except for deliberate interference by government. Keynes contradicted the entire classical school of economic thought with his recommendation for government intervention in the economy.

Keynes was heard by the highest authorities in his native Britain and in the United States. Although President Roosevelt liked Keynes and found his advice interesting, he also found it too radical. Keynes's solution to the Great Depression was all but ignored. The economy did not recover until the start of World War II in 1939. And in a sense, it was just as Keynes had predicted. Strong action by the government caused the economy to boom. In Chapter 25 we shall see what Keynes suggested that the government do.

A Keynesian view of business cycles is that they are a natural part of the economy. Whatever their cause, they cannot be eliminated, but by government action their impact can be reduced. Keynes recommended one set of policies for the peak period and another for the trough. Keynes sought to reduce the size of the fluctuations in the level of income, in effect to smooth out the business cycle. It is important for us to understand that the Keynesian revolution is a revolution in the truest sense of the word. Keynes introduced new ideas, new concepts, new theories, which represented a fundamental change in the economic way of thinking. These ideas and concepts are now in our media every day; they are ideas and concepts that our grandparents never knew.

Keynes left us with a new way of looking at the economy. We should not think of Keynes as someone who only proposed government intervention, although he did that. His main contribution was in establishing a macro view of the economy. Keynes did not focus on the individual buyers and sellers of the classical economist. He viewed the sum total of the decisions of all buyers and sellers and from that determined the impact on the level of income. Moreover, the idea of understanding what causes the level of income to change so that it can be controlled is central to Keynes's thinking. For the first time we accepted the revolutionary idea that the business cycle can be controlled. When a recession strikes and the economy moves toward a trough, you and I expect the government to do something. To our grandparents and great-grandparents living before Keynes, that thought would have been foreign.

▶ Summary

One of our major observations about the macro economy is that the level of income, output, and employment goes up and down in a cycle. There are many theories of why these business cycles occur. You were introduced to the sunspot, business inventory, and innovation theories. It seems likely that the cycles are a part of the economy and are bound to occur. However, it may be possible to reduce the fluctuations of the business cycle by the use of policy tools developed in later chapters.

The classical economists promoted a *laissez-faire* attitude that did nothing to prevent or correct the Great Depression. Say's Law and the market forces of supply and demand acting on price were among the foundations of classical thinking. The idea that economic tools could be used to reduce the impact of the business cycle originates with Lord Keynes. Keynes was the first economist to provide a model that explained why a depression could occur and to suggest that government intervention could achieve a more desirable equilibrium. Further, Keynes argued that government action could be used to smooth out the previously mysterious business cycle.

In the next chapter we will lay the foundation for determining the equilibrium level of income by discussing how the size of two components of GDP, consumption and investment, are determined.

▶ Key Concepts

business cycle
classical economics
laissez-faire
Say's Law
Keynes

▶ Discussion Questions

1. Uncle Effron does not believe in the business cycle. He says sometimes the economy goes up and sometimes it goes down. Does Uncle Effron correctly conclude there is no business cycle? Explain.
2. What are the phases of the business cycle? What phase are we currently in?
3. Why did the classical economist believe the economy would always return to full employment?
4. What is the meaning of Say's law, and what is the flaw?
5. Keynes believed that markets, particularly the labor market, adjust slowly. How does this belief help to explain unemployment?
6. Interview relatives about their experience in the 1930s. What impact did the depression have on their lives? How did it affect their behavior after the depression?
7. Some economists believe that we can predict business cycles by flipping a fair coin. If we use heads for "GDP rises" and tails for "GDP falls", we would have a suitable model for predicting the movement of GDP. If this view of the economy is correct, how can the economy be controlled? How does this view differ from the Keynesian view?

▶ Self-Review

• Fill in the blanks

business cycles

peak, recession

trough, recovery

sunspot

inventories

innovations

laissez-faire

classical

employment

Say's, supply

demand

supply, demand

prices, wages, interest rates

Keynes

any

saving

Fluctuations in the level of economic activity are called _____. The four phases of the business cycle are the _____, _____, _____, and _____. One theory of business cycles was based on solar activity and is called the _____ theory. Other theories include the level of business _____ and random revolutionary processes or _____. The hands-off or _____ attitude toward the economy was held by the _____ economists. Equilibrium was expected to occur at full _____. One basis for this belief was _____ law, that _____ creates its own _____. Another was the market forces of _____ and _____ which determine _____, _____, and _____. The British economist, John Maynard _____, found that the economy could be in equilibrium at _____ level of income. Also, _____ could prevent supply

fall

government

business cycle

macro

from creating its own demand, and that prices, wages, and interest rates tend to not _____ easily. Keynes, unlike the classical economist, recommended deliberate _____ interference to reduce the fluctuations of the _____. Keynes introduced us to a _____ view of the economy.

• Multiple choice

1. The theory that provides a satisfactory explanation of the business cycle is:
   a. the sunspot theory.
   b. the business inventory theory.
   c. the innovation theory.
   d. none of the above.
2. The classical belief in market forces relied on their effect on all but:
   a. wages.
   b. prices.
   c. government spending.
   d. interest rates.
3. What were the views of Keynes and the classical economists on government intervention in the macro economy?
   a. Keynes favored while the classical economists opposed.
   b. Keynes opposed while the classical economists favored.
   c. Both favored.
   d. Both opposed.
4. If the economy is in a trough, you would expect that the next phase of the business cycle is a:
   a. peak.
   b. recovery.
   c. recession.
   d. none of the above.
5. Why would you expect Say's law to be true?
   a. If more is demanded than is supplied, supply will fall.
   b. If more is supplied than demanded, demand will fall.
   c. The process of supplying creates income equal to the value of what is supplied and that income supports demand.
   d. As demand goes up, the supply will follow.

Answers: 1.d, 2.c, 3.a, 4.b, 5.c.

Module 5 THE LEVEL OF INCOME

The primary goal of this module is to examine how the level of income is determined. There are economic forces at work that establish an equilibrium level of income. We will see how the understanding of these forces has changed. Then we will explore constructive uses of these forces to deal with two persistent economic problems, inflation and unemployment.

The ultimate goal of the chapters in this module and the next is to explain how several macro variables are determined, including the level of national income and output, the interest rate, the price level, and employment. In the simplest view of the macro economy, there are three macro markets. Each market determines a quantity and a price; all three markets are interrelated. There is a market for goods and services that determines the level of output and the price level; there is a market for money that determines the quantity of money and the interest rate, which is the price of money; and there is a market for labor that determines the level of employment and the wage rate.

We can see how these markets are related. One role for money is to allow consumers and business to each carry out their desired purchases. Thus as the amount of money in the money market changes, the demand for goods and services, output, also changes. Changes in the money market affect the demand for output. In a similar fashion, the labor market affects the supply of output. As the labor market changes, the amount of output that can be produced changes, and hence the supply of output changes. This discussion should lead you to think that the micro tools we have developed in the previous modules are useful here. In a way they are. However, the demands and supplies are now for macro-level markets and not the micro, and so we will have to build the aggregate (total) demand and aggregate supply relationships.

The process of building these aggregate demand and supply relationships will be done in steps. We start by looking at how the level of output is determined. Then the money market is brought in. And finally we look at the market for the level of output, including the price. This process is one where we continually build on what we learned previously. Eventually, we will find how the level of income, the price level, the interest rate, and employment are determined. This module will focus on the determination of the level of income. The following module will discuss the money market, and how the money market influences the demand for goods in the market for output.

Chapter 21 involves a close-up look at two important sectors of our economy, consumers and business. The behavior of these sectors helps determine the equilibrium level of income. Chapter 22 examines how the equilibrium level of income is obtained in a world with only two sectors. Chapter 23 introduces the third sector, government, and indicates how the equilibrium level of income is changed by the addition of this sector. Chapter 24 repeats the two previous chapters with a graphical model. To conclude this module, Chapter 25 discusses fiscal policy, one way that the government can act to alter the equilibrium level of income.

Chapter 21 CONSUMPTION AND INVESTMENT

Key Topics

consumption

the marginal propensity to consume

saving

the marginal propensity to save

investment

Goals

uunderstand the determinants of consumption and saving

introduce the marginal propensities to consume and save

understand the primary determinant of investment

We have found that GDP — income — fluctuates along the course of the business cycle. To reduce the fluctuations, we must find what determines the level of income. Once we understand what determines the level of income, we can use this knowledge to find ways to change income.

We know that GDP is made up of consumption, investment, government expenditure, and net exports. Determining the size of each of these components of GDP is essential since we wish to know the size of GDP as well as to explain what causes GDP to change. If we know what makes each component the size it is, we will know the size of GDP. In addition, if we can explain why the components of GDP change, we can explain why GDP changes. The forces that establish the equilibrium level of income will be the subject of the next chapter. In this chapter we will discuss what determines two of the components of GDP, consumption and investment, and what causes them to change.

We start with a simple economy consisting of only two sectors, consumers and business. The government sector will be postponed until Chapter 23. And since net exports are less than 5 percent of economic activity in the United States, we will simplify our model and ignore the influence of net exports on

GDP. However, if we were to study Japan or Great Britain or any one of a number of countries, the foreign sector would be a much larger and more important part of their GDP. Foreign trade will be discussed in Chapters 30 and 31.

In an economy without either a government or foreign sector, the level of income will be determined solely by the amount of consumption and investment. We will examine the sectors of the economy that perform these functions and see how consumption and investment affect the economic performance of the society.

Consumption

The largest part of GDP is consumer expenditure, or consumption, which is currently about 65 percent of GDP. Consumption (C) was defined in Chapter 18 as the yearly total of all purchases of goods and services by consumers. Consumption is more than consumption by an individual household; consumption is an aggregate, a macro concept. Macro is concerned with the total consumption of all consumers. What causes consumption to rise or fall? The main factor is income, real GDP. The direct relation between the level of income and the level of consumption is shown by the **consumption function**. John Maynard Keynes was one of the first to point out this consumption relation. Generally, we expect people to buy more goods and services as income rises. As income rises, so does consumption. As income falls, so does consumption.

Income is an important determinant of the level of consumption. But beware of the fallacy of composition. We are not concluding that aggregate consumption goes up as aggregate income rises just because one person consumes more as income rises. We are concluding that the macroeconomic variable consumption is directly related to the macroeconomic variable income. This is a simple but rather important observation. The level of total income will determine the amount of total consumer spending.

The Marginal Propensity to Consume

Sometimes we wish to know more than just the existing level of consumer spending. We may want to know how consumers react when the income level changes. We have already indicated that as income goes up or down, consumption does also. But by how much does consumption change? The consumption function reveals how much consumption changes as income changes through a new concept, the marginal propensity to consume.

The **marginal propensity to consume (MPC)** is the amount consumption changes when income changes by one dollar. Remember that marginal means "additional" or "extra." Propensity is the inclination or tendency. What is your propensity if someone were to punch you in the nose? Would you tend to turn the other cheek or punch back? What is the propensity of consumers to spend? What will consumers tend to do with an additional dollar of income? What part of that dollar would tend to go into extra consumption? The marginal propensity to consume provides the answer.

$$\text{MPC} = \text{marginal propensity to consume} = \frac{\text{change in consumption}}{\text{change in income}} = \frac{\Delta C}{\Delta Y}$$

The marginal propensity to consume is a marginal concept. It relates changes in consumption, ΔC, to changes in income, ΔY. For example, if consumers receive an extra dollar of income and spend 80 cents more, their marginal propensity to consume would be 80 percent, found by dividing .80 by 1. And if income falls by one dollar and consumers spend 80 cents less, the MPC is still .8, found by dividing the change in consumption, −.80, by the change in income, −1.

Table 21-1   Marginal Propensity to Consume

(1) Income (Y)	(2) Consumption (C)	(3) MPC ($\Delta C/\Delta Y$)
$ 0	$200	
100	260	.60
200	320	.60
300	380	.60
400	440	.60
500	500	.60
600	560	.60
700	620	.60
800	680	.60
900	740	.60
1,000	800	.60
1,100	860	.60
1,200	920	.60
1,300	980	.60

Columns 1 and 2 together show the consumption function.
Column 3 shows the marginal propensity to consume.

Suppose that the data in Table 21-1 were true. The first two columns are the consumption function, income and consumption. The MPC can be easily calculated. The change in income is $100 as Y goes from 0 to 100 in column 1. The change in consumption in column 2 is $60 for this change in income. Thus the MPC is .60 in column 3. Consumption increases by 60 additional dollars, or 60 cents of each additional dollar is spent. As income increases from $100 to $200, consumption increases from $260 to $320, again a change of $60. Thus, the MPC of the second additional $100 is also .60. The MPC tells how many more dollars will be spent when income goes up by one dollar. Of the added dollar of income, what percentage will be spent for added consumption? The answer is called the marginal propensity to consume. What does the consumer do with the remaining income? The remaining income can be either saved or used to pay taxes. Saving is the subject of the next section.

Saving

In the model world we have discussed, there are only three ways that income may be used. Income may be used to buy goods, to save, or to pay taxes. We will postpone discussing taxes until government is included in this model in Chapter 23. The topic we wish to emphasize now is saving.

Saving (S) is that part of income that is not spent for consumption or taxes. In our model, without government or taxes, all income is either spent or saved. Since income is either spent or saved, income equals consumption plus saving, $Y = C + S$. Therefore, if consumption changes with income, then saving must also change with income. When income goes up by one dollar, part of the dollar is consumed. Whatever part of the dollar that is not spent is added to saving. Thus we can expect the level of saving for all people to depend on the level of income for all people. As income goes up, so does the amount saved.

You should recognize that if there is a consumption function, there must also be a saving function. The **saving function** shows that saving increases with the level of income. Recall that consumption also increases with the income level. Thus both the amount of consumption *and* the amount of saving increase as a society produces a higher level of income. With a higher income, a society can afford both to spend more and to save more than before.

When income increases by one dollar, part of that dollar is consumed and the remaining part is saved. As income changes, so does saving. This change in saving has a name. The **marginal propensity to save (MPS)** is the change in saving when income changes by one dollar. The expression for the

MPS is similar to that of the MPC except that the emphasis is on the change
in *saving*.

$$\text{MPS} = \text{marginal propensity to save} = \frac{\text{change in saving}}{\text{change in income}} = \frac{\Delta S}{\Delta Y}$$

When consumers receive an extra dollar of income, and 20 cents goes into
additional saving, the MPS is .20/1 or .20. Recognize that the S in MPS stands
for saving, not spending. The change in spending is represented by consumption,
C, in the MPC.

Since all income is either spent or saved, when income goes up by one
dollar, part of the dollar is spent and the remaining part is saved. All changes
in income must be completely accounted for by the change in consumption and
the change in saving. This means that the sum of the MPC and the MPS must
be 1 or 100 percent of the change in income. When income increases by one
dollar, if the MPC were 80 percent, then the MPS must be 20 percent. Or if
you prefer to think in decimals, the MPC is .80 and the MPS is .20. If the MPC
is 50 percent, then so must be the MPS. If the MPC is 100 percent, meaning
that all extra income is consumed, then the MPS is 0. The MPC + MPS = 100
percent. Thus MPC + MPS = 1.0 in decimal terms.

You will find the saving function, income and saving, in the first two
columns of Table 21-2. From this you can calculate the MPS. As income in
column 1 changes from $1,200 to $1,300, saving in column 2 changes from
$280 to $320. This results in the .40 MPS in column 3. It should be clear that
the MPS had to be .40 if the MPC were already .60 in Table 21-1.

The marginal propensities to consume and save explain how consumers react
to a *change* in income. How will that extra income be divided into changes
in consumption and changes in saving? These changes in consumption, and
therefore saving, are significant because they affect the economic outcome of
society.

A thorough examination of Table 21-3 can clarify the concepts presented
so far in this chapter. Both Tables 21-1 and 21-2 have been combined. Column 1
is the level of total income, the GDP of the economy. Column 2 is consumption.
The first two columns together, income and consumption, are the consumption
function. This shows that consumer spending always increases with the level
of income. Notice that if income is zero, we expect that consumption will
be positive. Even if there is no income, people will consume to live. This
consumption will occur out of past saving or current borrowing. This is a

Table 21-2   Marginal Propensity to Save

(1) Income (Y)	(2) Saving (S)	(3) MPS ($\Delta S/\Delta Y$)
$ 0	$-200	
100	-160	.40
200	-120	.40
300	-80	.40
400	-40	.40
500	0	.40
600	40	.40
700	80	.40
800	120	.40
900	160	.40
1,000	200	.40
1,100	240	.40
1,200	280	.40
1,300	320	.40

Columns 1 and 2 together show the saving function. Column 3 shows the marginal propensity to save.

Table 21-3   MPS and MPC

(1) Income (Y)	(2) Consumption (C)	(3) Saving (S)	(4) MPC ($\Delta C/\Delta Y$)	(5) MPS ($\Delta S/\Delta Y$)
$ 0	$200	$-200		
100	260	-160	.60	.40
200	320	-120	.60	.40
300	380	-80	.60	.40
400	440	-40	.60	.40
500	500	0	.60	.40
600	560	40	.60	.40
700	620	80	.60	.40
800	680	120	.60	.40
900	740	160	.60	.40
1,000	800	200	.60	.40
1,100	860	240	.60	.40
1,200	920	280	.60	.40
1,300	980	320	.60	.40

Here Tables 21-1 and 21-2 are combined. Note that columns 4 and 5 total to 100 percent. Also note that $Y = C + S$, column 2 plus column 3 equals column 1.

form of **dissaving** so current saving will be negative. When we know both the income level and the level of consumption, we can find the level of saving. Saving, column 3, is the difference between columns 1 and 2. Notice also that columns 2 and 3 added together give column 1. This is because consumption and saving together account for all of the income. The income and saving columns, 1 and 3, are the saving function. Observe that at a higher level of income, society can afford to consume more, yet have more left over than before so it can save even more too.

Column 4 in Table 21-3 is the marginal propensity to consume. Column 5 is the marginal propensity to save. The MPC and MPS, added together at each level of income, account for 100 percent of the change in income.

Investment

While investment is the smallest domestic component of GDP, about 15 percent, it is also the most variable. This variation is caused by a complex interaction of economic factors, and is a major cause of the fluctuation in the business cycle. Investment is the purchase of capital goods by business. Business is the only sector of the economy that invests in the economic sense. When consumers "invest," there is a transfer of assets from one individual to another. When you buy a share of stock on the stock market, the ownership of the stock is transferred to you and your money to the previous owner of the stock. This transfer has no impact on the economy. Business investment, however, does have a significant economic impact. When business purchases capital goods beyond replacing worn-out capital goods, the production capabilities of the society have increased. This is shown by the production possibilities curve (Chapter 3) with a movement of the curve to the right, representing economic growth. Our references to investment will always mean the purchase of new capital goods by business.

What causes investment to change? The primary determinant of investment is the interest rate, although there are also several other factors that are important in determining the size of investment. These are business profits, the level of income, and expectations about future economic conditions. But we will focus on how changes in the interest rate affect investment, or investment demand. The amount of capital purchased by business varies *inversely* with the interest rate. Firms usually must borrow to obtain money for investment. So the interest rate, the rate of interest on the borrowed money, will affect the decision of the firm to invest. The higher the interest rate, the less likely the firm is to borrow.

Since the firm pays back the loan from the money generated by the capital, a higher interest rate will require that the capital improvement generate more money than if the interest rate were smaller. If the capital improvement cannot generate the higher interest payments, the project should not be undertaken.

Would your firm borrow money at 12 percent for an investment project that promises a return of 8 percent? Of course not! A project that has a return of 8 percent would be acceptable at a 6 percent or 7 percent interest rate, but not at an interest rate of 9 percent. As the interest rate goes up, fewer and fewer investment projects will have a return high enough to be profitable. Thus the higher the interest rate, the smaller the amount of investment.

Even if the firm has the money on hand and does not have to borrow, the firm may not invest in a capital improvement project. Any investment would have to return more than the firm could earn in interest from an alternative use of the money. One alternative for the firm may be the purchase of bonds. The return on the investment project would have to be greater than the opportunity cost of the money. If your firm has a choice between an investment project that returns 10 percent and a government bond paying 12.5 percent, the firm would be foolish to use its money for the investment project. The higher the interest rate, the less likely the firm can find capital improvement projects paying a rate of return higher than the interest rate it receives by other uses of its money. So again, the higher the interest rate, the smaller the amount of investment the firm will undertake.

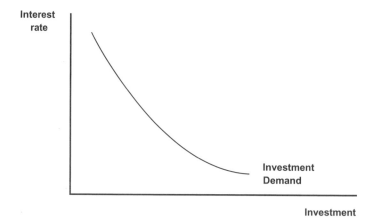

Figure 21-1   Investment Demand
The downward-sloping investment demand curve shows an inverse relation between the interest rate and the amount invested.

If we think of this relationship between investment and the interest rate as investment demand, we see that investment demand follows the law of demand. This inverse relation is shown in Figure 21-1. As the price of investment — the interest rate — rises, the quantity demanded of investment falls.

Because we do not yet have a way in our model to determine the interest rate, we will not immediately use this inverse relationship between the interest rate and the level of investment. When the model is expanded in Chapter 28 to include the interest rate, the relationship between the interest rate and the level of investment can then be applied. For now, recognize that investment does not change with the level of income, as does consumption, but with the interest rate. We will be considering impacts of a change in income in the next chapter; hence investment will remain constant, unaffected by income.

▶ Summary

We have looked at two sectors of the economy, the consumer and business. We have developed a simple model of how two components of GDP, consumption and investment, are determined. The primary determinant of consumption is income. When we understand consumption, we also understand saving. The concepts of the marginal propensity to consume and the marginal propensity to save were also discussed. These marginal concepts are important and will have a major role in Chapter 23.

Investment is the purchase of capital goods by business. We have established that investment spending varies inversely with the interest rate. Investment is for now assumed to be constant since it does not vary with the level of income. We are now prepared to find what determines the equilibrium level of income and what can be done to alter it.

▶ Key Concepts

consumption function
marginal propensity to consume
saving
saving function

marginal propensity to save
dissaving
investment

▶ Discussion Questions

1. What is the consumption function? The saving function?

2. Use the following data to find the MPC and MPS as well as saving.

Income	Consumption	Saving	MPC	MPS
$100	$120	$	–	–
200	190			
300	260			
400	330			
500	400			
600	470			

3. Explain why MPC + MPS = 1. Why Y = C + S.
4. Who invests? What is investment?
5. If buying bonds is not investment, then what is it?
6. Why does investment depend on the interest rate? Is this true when the firm does not have to borrow to invest?

▶ Self-Review

- Fill in the blanks

consumption	The largest component of GDP is _____.
consumption	The _____ function states that consumption
income	is related to the level of _____. As income rises,
rises	consumption _____. As income falls, consumption
falls, direct	_____. This is a _____ relation. The amount that
	consumption changes when income changes by one
marginal propensity to	dollar is the _____.
consume	The MPC is found by dividing the change in
consumption, income	_____ by the change in _____. The
	part of income that is not spent for consumption or
saving, saving	taxes is _____. The _____ function states that
directly, income	saving is _____ related to the level of _____.
	The change in saving when income changes by one
marginal propensity to	dollar is the _____.
save, 1	The sum of the MPC and the MPS is _____ or
100, income	____% of the change in _____. The marginal
change	propensities show what happens to a _____ in
	income. The purchase of capital goods by business
investment	is _____. The primary determinant of
interest rate	investment is the _____. Investment
interest rate	spending varies inversely with the _____.
increases	At lower rates of interest, investment _____.
decreases	At higher rates of interest, investment _____.

- Multiple choice

1. The consumption function directly relates consumption to the level of:
   a. taxes.
   b. income.
   c. wages.
   d. prices.
2. If the marginal propensity to consume were 60 percent, how much would be *saved* of an additional dollar of income?
   a. $1.
   b. $.60.
   c. $.40.
   d. impossible to say.
3. If $75 of an extra $100 is consumed, the marginal propensity to consume is:
   a. 25 percent.
   b. 50 percent.
   c. 75 percent.
   d. 100 percent.
4. As interest rates increase:
   a. consumption increases.
   b. investment increases.
   c. investment decreases.
   d. saving decreases.
5. The marginal propensity to save is:
   a. the change in saving when income changes by $1.
   b. the saving divided by income.
   c. the portion of income going to saving.
   d. saving plus investment.

Answers: 1.b, 2.c, 3.c, 4.c, 5.a.

| Chapter | 22 | **MACRO EQUILIBRIUM**

Key Topics
equilibrium identified
why equilibrium occurs where it does
an alternate view of equilibrium
aggregate supply and demand

Goals
understand where the macro equilibrium occurs and why
find the equilibrium level of income from another point of view
approach the determination of income from supply and demand

This chapter explains how the equilibrium level of income is determined. This is the equilibrium of the macro economy. As you discovered with supply and demand, the idea of equilibrium means a balance of forces. But what are the forces that determine macro equilibrium? What if equilibrium does not occur at a desirable level of income, output, and employment? Once we understand the forces of equilibrium, then we may find ways to control the equilibrium level of income and regulate the business cycle.

Equilibrium Identified in the Macro Model

Imagine a very simple economy made up of just consumers and business. What type of good would each buy? Consumers would buy consumer goods (C represents consumption by consumers) and business would buy capital goods (I represents investment by business). The **total spending** on consumer and capital goods would be the sum of C + I, consumption plus investment. This total spending would make up the total demand in the economy. Who else is left to spend? No one, as both consumer and business spending has been included.

So far we have found total spending. What other concept is needed to obtain the equilibrium level of income? There must be something to balance total spending. As you discovered by your study of GDP, Chapter 18, total spending must be equal to total output. Total spending is C + I, and **total output** is the output of the economy, GDP. Y represents total income, which is also total output. Therefore we know that Y = C + I must be true. Think of it this way. C + I tells how much the society spends; it is total spending. The amount produced is the amount the economy supplies, known as total output, or Y.

Admittedly that is a lot of different titles for one item, but each of us is known by different names and labels (Dr. Smith, Smith, John, student, teacher, son, runner), and we each manage to keep our own identities straight. So it is with total output, and total output is important enough that we make the effort to understand it. Now this information can be combined to form a major observation of the macro economy:

$$Y \qquad = \qquad C + I$$

total output   total spending

or total income

This equality is equilibrium for the economy as a whole. When total output equals total spending, the level of income is at equilibrium with no tendency to change. What else does this equality indicate? Since total output is total income, then total income Y equals spending by the two sectors of a simple economy, consumers and business, resulting in Y = C + I. These are all different but useful ways of looking at the same situation.

The Y = C + I equality determines the equilibrium level of income. When total output and spending are equal or in balance, then the economy is in balance. Here is a potential to regulate and control the overall level of income. In the simple model discussed here the level of total spending will determine the equilibrium level of income. This means that if total spending could be controlled, then so could the level of income. Keynes had discovered the key to the macro economy — total spending.

Why Equilibrium Occurs Where It Does

Let us begin with an investigation of how equilibrium occurs and at the same time obtain a better appreciation of the impact of total spending. Start with Table 22-1. Column 1 represents total output. These are the various levels of production and GDP that the economy *could* be at. But of course the economy can only be at *one* level of income, output, and employment. Which level will it be?

What if total output were at the $100 level in Table 22-1? Would the economy continue to produce at that level? The answer is no. Why not? Look at column 2 showing consumer consumption and at column 3 showing investment. What would be the total spending by consumers and business if the economy were at the $100 level? C + I would be $120 + $20 or a total of $140 of spending. But there is only $100 of output produced. Where will the remaining $40 of output come from? Consumers and business are attempting to buy more than has been produced. A shortage of $40 of output will result ($140 − $100). The inventories that producers have on hand to release to buyers will begin falling. Producers will realize that they could have sold more, given the shortage, if they had had more available. They will begin expanding output for that reason and will also build up reduced inventories. As production in the economy expands, provided that there are idle resources, so does GDP. After all, a penny spent is a penny of income for someone. So the economy will not remain at the $100 level of output. The existing shortage will cause total output, employment, and the level of income to rise to a higher level.

What if income were at the $200 level? Would the economy continue to produce at that level? Again the answer is no. C + I would be $200 + $20 or a total of $220 of spending. Again the consumers and business are attempting to buy more than has been produced. Again, a shortage will exist. Inventories

Table 22-1   Equilibrium Level of Income

(1) Total Output (Y)	(2) Consumption (C)	(3) Investment (I)
$100	$120	$20
200	200	20
300	280	20
400	360	20
500	440	20
600	520	20

This table shows the relationship between the level of income, Y, and consumption and investment. Equilibrium occurs where Y = C + I. In this economy, the equilibrium level of income is at $300.

will be falling. Production will increase. The level of income will not remain at the $200 level, but will rise to a higher level.

What if the economy is producing at the $600 level? Would the economy continue to produce at that level? Once again the answer is no. But this time the reason is different. C + I would be $520 + $20 or a total of $540 of spending. Consumers and business are not buying as much as has been produced. A surplus of $60 will result ($600 − $540). The inventories that producers have on hand will begin piling up. Producers will realize that they are not going to be able to sell as much as they are producing, given the surplus, and will begin reducing output. There is now no need to produce to replace inventories. Inventories are piling up since goods are produced faster than they are being bought under the current surplus condition. So the level of income will not remain at the $600 level of output. The surplus will cause total output, employment, and the level of income to fall to a lower level.

And at the $300 level? Here C + I would be $280 + $20 or a total of $300 of spending. Consumers and business are buying exactly what has been produced. No less. No more. No shortage. No surplus. Would the level of income be stable at that level? The answer is yes. What would happen if the level of income fell to the $200 level? We already know. A shortage would result as consumers and business attempted to purchase more than is produced, driving production up to the $300 level. What would happen if the level of income rose to the $400 level? Again we know. A surplus would result as consumers and business fail to buy as much as had been produced, driving down production to the $300 level.

If the level of income will not expand or contract from the $300 level once it has been reached, and if the economy will automatically move to the $300 level if not already there, then $300 must be the equilibrium or natural tendency of this particular economy. Does this meet our condition of Y = C + I? $300 = $280 + $20. It certainly does.

Yet Y = C + I was supposed to be the same as saying that total spending is equal to total output. Let us see if that is still true. Look at Table 22-2. This is the same table as Table 22-1 except for the inclusion of column 4, total spending. It is a simple process to add together consumption and investment, columns 2 and 3, at each level of output, and obtain the amount of total spending at that level. For example, at the $100 level of income, consumption of $120 and investment of $20 are added together to obtain a total spending of $140.

What happens when total spending is $300? Total output is also $300, and we already found this to be the equilibrium level of income in this simple

Table 22-2   Total Spending Equals Total Output

(1) Total Output (Y)	(2) Consumption (C)	(3) Investment (I)	(4) Total Spending (C + I) (2 + 3)
$100	$120	$20	$140
200	200	20	220
300	280	20	300
400	360	20	380
500	440	20	460
600	520	20	540

This table builds on Table 22-1 by including one more column. The new column is column 4, which was obtained by adding columns 2 and 3. Column 4, total spending, represents the total spending in this economy by business and consumers. Equilibrium occurs where total spending equals total output, where Y equals $300.

economy. What if total spending were greater than total output, as at the $100 level? Then total spending is greater than total output, and the level of income would rise to the $300 level. What if total spending is less than total output, as at the $600 level? Then total spending is less than total output, and the level of income will fall to the $300 level.

What conclusions can be made? If total spending is greater than total output, the level of income will rise. If total spending is less than total output, the level of income will fall. Only if total spending is equal to total output will equilibrium occur. The level of total spending thus determines the equilibrium level of income in the economy.

Another View of Equilibrium

Let us look at equilibrium through another approach. Consider Table 22-3. The only change is that column 3, a saving column, has been added. Recall that all income originates from the production of output. In a capitalistic system, consumers, which all of us ultimately are, own and control the productive resources. When output is produced, the consumers receive the income. What are the options with that income in an economy without a government sector? Only two, consume or save. The total of consumption and saving must equal total income.

Table 22-3   Savings Equals Investment

(1) Total Output (Y)	(2) Consumption (C)	(3) Saving (S)	(4) Investment (I)	(5) Total Spending (C + I)
$100	$120	$–20	$20	$140
200	200	0	20	220
300	280	20	20	300
400	360	40	20	380
500	440	60	20	460
600	520	80	20	540

This table adds another column to Table 22-2, saving, column 3. Saving is that part of total output that is not consumed. Thus column 3 is obtained by subtracting C from Y at each level of income. We are now able to compare saving and investment at each level of income to find the equilibrium level of income where saving equals investment.

Verify that the total of columns 2 + 3 equals column 1. At the $100 level, consumers have $100 for consumption but choose to spend $120. How is this possible? Saving is a negative $20, which indicates that consumers are dissaving, consuming more than they are making, perhaps borrowing or perhaps spending saving earned in the past. Still, consumption and saving add up to total income. At the $600 level, consumers have earned that much income but consumption is only $520. Eighty dollars of income capable of purchasing the remaining output has gone instead into saving.

At this point we can employ a simple but useful model referred to as the bathtub. Consider Figure 22-1. The level of water in the bathtub, representing total income and output, is the equilibrium level of income. Water flowing into the tub through the faucet represents an inflow to the economy. This inflow is investment by business. The drain in the bathtub represents an outflow of the economy, saving. Now consult Table 22-3 for the equilibrium level of income. The equilibrium level is $300, and only at that level of income is investment of $20 equal to saving of $20. Consumer income was $300 but only $280 was consumed. The remaining $20 was saving, leaving a $20 pile of production unpurchased. This normally would create a surplus situation, and the level of income would fall. But we have not yet taken into account the impact of the business sector of the economy. As business purchases $20 of capital, the potential surplus is eliminated and total spending equals total output. Equilibrium results. This is also shown in the bathtub of

Figure 22-2. In other words, when investment equals saving in this simple
economy, what flows in and what flows out of the bathtub are identical,
leaving the level of water undisturbed. If what consumers leave unpurchased
just happens to equal what business does purchase, equilibrium occurs. Saving
equals investment.

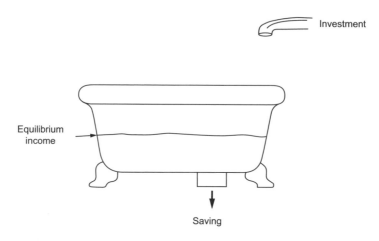

Figure 22-1   The Bathtub
The level of water in the bathtub represents the equilibrium level of income. The faucet represents
an inflow — investment — and the drain represents an outflow — saving.

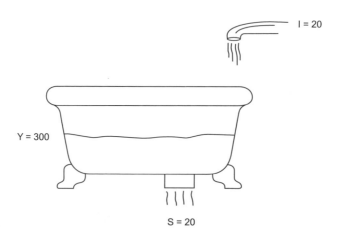

Figure 22-2   Equilibrium
Equilibrium is established at $300 since the inflow of $20 of investment equals the outflow of
$20 of saving.

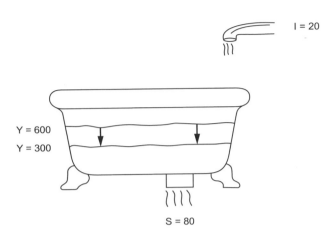

Figure 22-3 Saving Greater than Investment
At an income level of $600, the investment is $20 and saving is $80. Since the outflow is greater than the inflow, the level of income will fall toward equilibrium.

At the $600 level, saving of $80 is greater than investment of $20. Check the bathtub shown in Figure 22-3. More is flowing out than is flowing in so the level of water in the bathtub will fall, as will the level of income. Consumers are purchasing only $520 of output. This $80 of production that consumers have the income to purchase is left in the output pile. Consumers are saving the $80 instead. Therefore a $60 surplus will occur when business only purchases $20 of the surplus production. In the bathtub, $20 of investment flows in, and $80 of saving flows out. Investment is less than saving, and the level of income will fall. This is the expected outcome at this $600 income level, since total spending is less than total output. If what consumers leave unpurchased is not purchased by business, saving is greater than investment, a surplus results, and equilibrium will occur at a lower level of income.

At the $100 level, consumption of $120 leaves dissaving of $20. The bathtub in Figure 22-4 shows the result. Investment of $20 creates a $40 shortage. Twenty dollars of investment flowing into the bathtub and $20 of dissaving flowing into the bathtub, in effect the drain is backing up, causes the level of water in the tub to rise. This is true because total spending exceeds total output. Consumers are attempting to purchase more than is being produced, and this, coupled with investment purchases, creates the $40 shortage. Investment is greater than saving, a shortage results, and equilibrium will occur at a higher level of income.

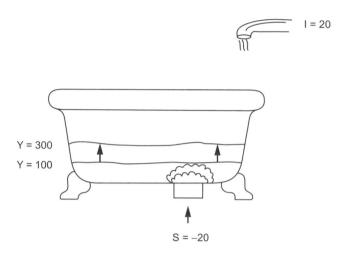

Figure 22-4   Investment Greater than Saving
At the $100 level of income, saving is less than investment. Saving is −$20, showing that
dissaving occurs. The drain in the bathtub is backing up. Since investment of $20 is greater than
saving, the level of income will rise toward equilibrium.

We have established some simple relationships:

If investment is greater than saving, income rises.
If investment equals saving, equilibrium occurs.
If investment is less than saving, income falls.

When we wish to focus on total spending rather than the relationship of
investment to saving, we look at consumption and investment and the relationship
to total output:

If total spending is greater than total output, income rises.
If total spending equals total output, equilibrium occurs.
If total spending is less than total output, income falls.

But through either approach, focusing on total spending or on investment and
saving, we are looking at the same concept, the equilibrium level of income in
the macro economy.

Aggregate Demand and Aggregate Supply

The macro equilibrium we have discussed so far only determines the level of income. We can now extend our idea of equilibrium to include the determination of the price level. To do this, we will consider the market for output.

The market for output consists of a demand for output and a supply of output. **Aggregate demand** is the total demand for output by consumers and business (in a two sector economy) at each price level. **Aggregate supply** is the amount of output produced at each price level.

How are these concepts related to what we have studied earlier in this chapter? Aggregate demand tells how total spending, C + I, changes with the price level. Aggregate supply indicates how total output changes when the price level changes. Up to now, we have not considered how total spending or total output would change with prices. Aggregate demand and aggregate supply both depend on the price of output. In the case of aggregate demand, as the price of output rises, the quantity demanded will fall. As the price falls, a larger quantity will be demanded. For aggregate supply, when the price rises, the quantity supplied will rise. As the price falls, a smaller quantity will be supplied.

Of course there are limits to what can be supplied. At any one time there is just so much labor, just so many machines, and just so much raw material. So at most there can be just so much output. Hence the aggregate supply curve will eventually be vertical at full employment, and output will not increase with price. Before we draw these curves, there is one other concern we ought to think about — what goes on the axes. How will we measure the prices? A

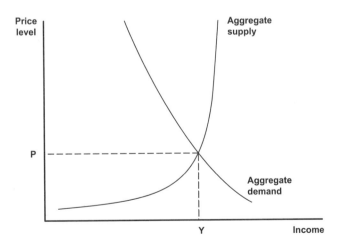

Figure 22-5 Aggregate Supply and Aggregate Demand
The equilibrium price level, P, and equilibrium level of income, Y, can both be determined by the intersection of aggregate supply and aggregate demand.

price index will be used. How is the quantity of output measured? We will use income. The picture of the output market will look as shown in Figure 22-5.

Equilibrium will be determined in this market just as in any market. Recall from Chapter 7 that equilibrium in a market occurs at the intersection of the supply and demand. In Figure 22-5, the equilibrium price is P, and Y is the equilibrium level of income. Thus the equilibrium level of income and the equilibrium price level are determined by the intersection of aggregate demand and aggregate supply.

▶ Summary

We have now found what determines the equilibrium level of income through three different models — total spending, the bathtub, and aggregate supply and aggregate demand.

The total spending model, $Y = C + I$, shows that the level of income is determined where total spending equals total output. If total spending increases, the equilibrium level of income increases; if total spending decreases, the equilibrium level of income decreases. The bathtub shows that there are forces that push the level of income to where investment equals saving, the equilibrium level of income in a two-sector economy. If investment is greater than saving, the level of income will rise to equilibrium. If investment is less than saving, the level of income will fall to equilibrium. Thus in this two-sector model, when saving and investment are not equal, there are forces changing the level of income. In the aggregate supply and aggregate demand model, both the price level and the level of income are found by the intersection of aggregate demand and aggregate supply.

All three of the models give the same conclusion. If I increases, total spending, $C + I$, rises and income rises. If I increases, more flows into the bathtub and income rises. If I increases, aggregate demand, $C + I$, rises, and income rises.

Our next stage of understanding is to investigate what changes the level of equilibrium. What determines why equilibrium occurs at one level of income, production, and employment, and not at another? Through our tables, we found why equilibrium occurred at $300. Could equilibrium possibly be changed to another level of income, such as $200 or $500? This is an entirely new problem. To add more realism, the next chapter will introduce the third sector of the economy, government, into our equilibrium models. We will also encounter a few surprises, one of which is called the multiplier.

▶ Key Concepts

total spending
total output
equilibrium
aggregate demand
aggregate supply

▶ Discussion Questions

1. What is total spending?
2. Define the differences between total spending, total output, and total income.
3. Uncle Effron believes that there is only one possible level of income where equilibrium occurs in the economy. Is he right? Explain.
4. If total spending is greater than total output, explain why the level of income rises.
5. What will happen to the level of income if
   a. investment is less than saving.
   b. total spending equals total output.
   c. total spending is greater than total output.
   d. investment is greater than saving.
   e. total spending is less than total output.
   f. investment equals saving.
6. Suppose that the income level, Y, is less than equilibrium. What will happen to Y? To inventories? If Y is greater than equilibrium, what will happen to Y? To inventories? Do you see why the inventory theory of business cycles was thought possible? But do inventory cycles cause business cycles or it is the other way around?
7. If there is an increase in investment, what happens to aggregate demand? The level of income? The price level? What if the economy is already at the full employment level of output?
8. Suppose that aggregate demand rises. What will happen to inventories? What if aggregate demand falls. What will happen to inventories?

▶ Self-Review

• Fill in the blanks

	The total spending in a simple two sector economy
consumption, investment	is the sum of _____ and _____.
	The equilibrium level of income occurs where

total output	total spending is equal to _____. Here
Y	$C + I =$ _____. If total spending is greater than total
rise	output, the level of income will ____. If total spending
total output, income	is less than _____, the level of _____
fall	will ____. An alternate view of equilibrium is to
saving	consider the relation of investment to _____. If
rises	investment is greater than saving, income ____. If
saving, equilibrium	investment equals _____, _____ occurs.
saving	And if investment is less than _____, income
falls	_____. The total demand for output is known
aggregate	as _____ demand. The amount of output
aggregate supply	produced at each price level is _____.
	In the market for output, the intersection of aggregate
aggregate supply	demand and _____ determines both
price, income	the _____ level and the level of _____.

• Multiple choice

1. Find the true statement:
   a. Total output and total spending are always equal.
   b. Total output and total spending are never equal.
   c. Total output and total income are always equal.
   d. none of the above.
2. When total output is greater than total spending, then:
   a. inventories rise, firms reduce production, and income falls.
   b. inventories fall, firms increase production, and income rises.
   c. inventories rise, firms increase production, and income falls.
   d. inventories fall, firms reduce production, and income rises.
3. At $Y = 200$, you would expect:

Y	C	I
100	100	50
200	175	50
300	250	50
400	325	50
500	400	50

   a. Y to rise.
   b. Y to rise to 400.
   c. Y to fall.
   d. no change in Y.

4. Total output and total income:
   a. are the same.
   b. measure different sides of the same activity.
   c. are two different names for the same concept.
   d. all of the above.
5. If the price level is above the intersection of aggregate supply and aggregated demand, you would expect:
   a. the amount produced to be greater than the amount demanded, inventories to rise, and prices to fall.
   b. the amount produced to be greater than the amount demanded, inventories to fall, and prices to fall.
   c. the amount produced to be less than the amount demanded, inventories to fall, and prices to rise.
   d. the amount produced to be less than the amount demanded, inventories to fall, and prices to fall.

Answers: 1.c, 2.a, 3.a, 4.d, 5.a.

$$\boxed{\text{Chapter } \boxed{23}} \quad \textbf{GOVERNMENT}$$

Key Topics
> taxes
> government spending
> equilibrium
> income multiplier

Goals
> understand the role and economic impact of government
> understand the income multiplier process

We have found how equilibrium is determined in a simple two-sector economy. But what if that equilibrium is not a desirable one? What if the level of consumption and investment is not sufficient to bring forth an equilibrium at full employment? Then we must investigate the Keynesian proposal for deliberate government interference. Now we will allow more realism in our model and expand it to include a third sector, that of government.

The spending decisions of consumers and business are made for reasons other than obtaining a desirable macro equilibrium. There is no reason to expect that consumers and business will spend the amount necessary to achieve and maintain full employment. During a recession, the government could make the necessary adjustments to total spending and expand the level of income to the full employment level. One solution is for government to adjust taxes and its own spending to reduce the fluctuations in the business cycle. For government to carry out this role successfully, we must find how much the level of income changes when government spending changes. The relation between the change in government expenditure and the change in income will be explained by introducing the multiplier — a unique phenomenon. This introduction to the income multiplier reveals a little of the underlying complexities of the economy.

Before we discuss government spending, we will first examine the government's source of income, taxes.

Taxes

As the saying goes, taxes, like death, are certain. Taxes are paid by both consumers and business. However, we will focus mainly on how taxes affect consumer behavior. Before consumers make any consumption or saving decision, taxes are taken out of their income. Thus the consumption function introduced in Chapter 21 must be altered. When there are taxes, the consumer makes the consumption decision based on disposable income, where **disposable income** is income after taxes. This is true for the individual consumer as well as all consumers together at the macro level. Total tax collections are subtracted from income to yield disposable income. Disposable income can be either spent or saved by consumers. The impact of taxes is to reduce the income available for spending and therefore lower consumption. Similarly, saving will also be lower at each level of income because part of the income that would be saved now goes for taxes.

The consumption function describes how consumption changes when income changes. This information is summarized in the marginal propensity to consume, which is the change in consumption due to a change in income. The marginal propensity to consume has the same interpretation that it had in Chapter 21, except that we are now concerned with disposable income rather than income. With taxes, the MPC now tells the change in consumption due to a change in disposable income. So if disposable income changes by one dollar, consumption changes by the MPC. The main difference in the consumption function is that it now depends on disposable income rather than income.

We will assume that the amount of taxes collected does not depend on the level of income. Even if, as is most likely true, tax collections rise with income, our conclusions about income determination will not be significantly changed. To simplify the discussion, we make the assumption that total tax collections do not change with the level of income. But what impact will taxes have on the economy? Taxes act to reduce the amount available for spending and so reduce the equilibrium level of income.

There are many kinds of taxes on individuals, but all have the same effect of reducing consumption. As long as the consumer does not save every added dollar of income, an increase in taxes will cause consumption to fall. If the consumer saves every extra dollar of income, an increase in taxes will make only saving fall. In every other case, part of the money paid in higher taxes may come from saving, but the remainder will come out of consumption.

A reduction in taxes will have the opposite effect on consumption. Lower taxes are like an increase in income — suddenly there is more disposable income. Some of the increase in income that would have been tax payments may go into saving, but part will go into additional consumption. Thus a change in taxes will have an effect on consumption and also, as we know, on the level of income. Taxes have the identical effect on investment as on consumption. An increase in taxes reduces investment; a reduction in taxes increases investment. Taxes have the potential to change the level of income, as does government spending.

Government Spending

How is the federal budget prepared? The amount of revenue that will be generated from taxes is estimated, and government spending decisions are made. In some cases there are projects that were started in earlier years that require payment to continue — perhaps the purchase of aircraft carriers, or the building of dams or highways, or the provision of welfare benefits. There will be new projects to fund, like special space missions or research projects on energy. When the spending is totaled, it can be compared to the tax revenue. If the revenue is less than spending, a deficit occurs. If the revenue is greater than spending, a surplus results. The impact on the economy of the deficit or surplus is examined (we will learn how to do this in Chapter 25). If the deficit is too large, the budget may be adjusted either by raising taxes or lowering spending. Similarly, if the surplus is too large, expenditures may be increased or taxes lowered.

Government expenditures have the same impact on the economy as consumer consumption or business investment. An increase in any one serves to speed up the economy; a reduction in any one serves to slow down the economy. In the three-sector economy, the aggregate demand relates C + I + G and the price level, where G represents government spending. As government spending increases, so do aggregate demand and the equilibrium level of income; as government spending decreases, so do aggregate demand and the equilibrium level of income. Now aggregate demand is the total spending of the economy including government.

Note that the business and consumer sectors cannot spend at will. Investment is dependent on the level of interest, and consumption is dependent on the level of income. This is not true of the government sector. Most government spending is independent of both the interest rate and income. Thus the interest rate and level of income do not keep the government from spending more. However, government too encounters opportunity cost, which will be discussed in Chapter 25.

Government spending can be used as an economic tool. An increase in government spending increases aggregate demand. If consumers, business, and government were each spending $100 and then government increases its spending by another $100, then aggregate demand will increase from $300 to $400. What the government purchases, or the reasons for its purchase, make no difference in the impact of its spending. Simply the fact that government has increased spending will increase total spending and therefore the level of aggregate demand. Similarly, a decrease in government spending will reduce the level of aggregate demand.

The ability of the government to tax provides another economic tool. An increase in taxes on consumers will reduce consumption and therefore aggregate demand. The same impact results from an increase in taxes on business. A reduction in taxes on consumers will increase consumption, and a reduction in taxes on business will increase investment. Either reduction in taxes will increase spending and aggregate demand. Thus the ability of the government to tax or spend will affect aggregate demand and the direction of the economy. The use of this ability has policy implications discussed in Chapter 25.

Do not assume that if government increases spending by $1, taxes will increase by $1. That would be the balanced budget approach of a classical economist. The decision to tax and the decision to spend by government can be made independently. Spending can be increased by $1 and taxes can remain the same.

Equilibrium Again

We now see that government action can change aggregate demand. The government affects the macro economy in two ways, through taxation and through spending. From these actions, we can discover the impact of government on the equilibrium level of income. We now examine what happens to the level of income if taxes are changed or if government expenditures are changed.

In the previous chapter you saw a comparison between the level of income in the economy and the level of water in a bathtub. Consider an economy with no taxes or government expenditure, and the level of income is at equilibrium.

The water level in the bathtub is neither rising nor falling. The inflow from investment is exactly equal to the outflow of saving. Suppose now that the government imposes a tax, T, but spends nothing. What will happen to the level of income? The impact of an increase in taxation is illustrated by the bathtub in Figure 23-1. The level of income will fall. This is because taxes are a drain on the economy in the same manner as saving. The drain is opened farther so the water level in the tub falls. But the tub will not completely empty. As the tub empties, the outflow will slow down, and finally the outflow will be equal to the inflow and equilibrium will be established again, but at a lower level in the tub.

Why does the outflow slow down? The answer involves the saving outflow. Saving depends on the level of income, and saving will fall as the level of income falls. So the size of the outflow, saving plus taxes, will fall as income falls. As income falls, because the outflow is bigger than the inflow, the outflow gets smaller and will continue to decrease until the outflow and inflow are again equal. Once the outflow, S + T, and inflow, I, are equal, income will not change and so saving and taxes will not change, and a new, lower equilibrium is established. Thus the increase in taxes reduces the equilibrium level of income.

Can you predict the result of a fall in taxes? When taxes fall, the outflow in the bathtub is reduced. Hence the level of income rises. As the level of income rises, the outflow will increase because saving increases with income. The level of income will reach a new, higher equilibrium when taxes fall.

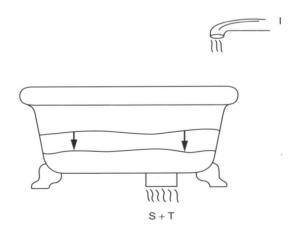

Figure 23-1   An Increase in Taxes
An increase in taxes is a drain on the level of income, causing the equilibrium level of income to fall.

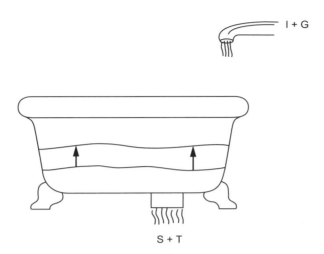

Figure 23-2 An Increase in Government Spending
Government spending is an inflow and increases the equilibrium level of income.

Now, consider an economy with no taxes or government spending, and the level of income is at equilibrium. What if the government begins to spend? What will happen to the level of income? Government expenditure, G, is an inflow to the economy. Therefore the inflow into the tub is increased, and the water level rises as in Figure 23-2. Should you call the plumber or rely on the economist? Will the tub overflow? Assuming sufficient productive capacity in the economy, no. Again the size of the outflow will depend on the level of income because saving, an outflow, depends on the level of income. As income goes up, the outflow, saving, also goes up and will continue to go up until the outflow and inflow are just equal. Equilibrium results at a higher level of income. Thus the increase in government spending causes the level of income to rise. If government spending falls, however, the level of income will fall. You should try to explain why the equilibrium level falls when government spending falls. Figure 23-3 shows equilibrium occurring when the inflow in a three-sector economy, I + G, equal the outflow, S + T. The impact of a change in taxes or government expenditure on the level of income has now been determined.

The conclusions reached in Chapter 22 are still valid here. When aggregate demand equals aggregate supply, the economy will be in equilibrium. The only difference is that G is now included in the aggregate demand that relates C + I + G to the price level. It is easy to see that if government spending

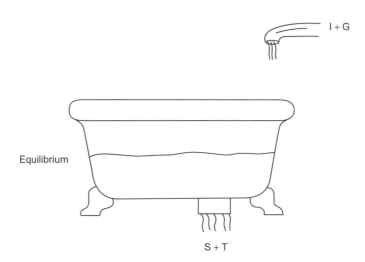

Figure 23-3   Equilibrium
Equilibrium occurs where the inflow, I + G, equals the outflow, S + T.

increases, so will G and aggregate demand. And if taxes increase, either C or I or both will fall and will cause aggregate demand to fall. We know that if aggregate quantity demanded is greater than aggregate quantity supplied, the equilibrium price level rises, and if aggregate quantity demanded is less, then the equilibrium price level falls. Thus government expenditure and taxation affect the level of income through their impact on aggregate demand.

We have seen the impact of government on the equilibrium level of income through three models. If G increases, total spending, C + I + G, rises and income rises. If G increases, more water flows into the bathtub, and income rises. If G increases, aggregate demand, C + I + G, rises, and income rises.

The Income Multiplier

Suppose that government spending increases by $100. What will happen to income? It will go up by $100 since income, or Y, equals C + I + G and G just went up by $100. But now an amazing process starts. Since Y has gone up, consumption will rise because C rises as Y rises. But since Y = C + I + G, and C just went up, so must Y. Thus Y goes up again, and the process starts over. This is the multiplier effect of a change in spending.

The **income multiplier** means that any initial change in spending results in a greater change to total income. An *initial* change in spending can be caused by any increase or decrease in spending by consumers, business, or government. This means that any one of the sectors can start the multiplier process by changing its level of spending. We know that total spending is equal to income and that when spending changes so will the level of income. We would normally expect that as spending increases by $100, so would the level of income. But the income multiplier states that the level of income will change by *more* than the initial change in spending. By how much does the level of income change? By the initial change in spending times the multiplier. But what is the multiplier? The multiplier is simply a number that, as the name implies, is multiplied times the initial change in spending to find the change in the total level of income. Let us apply this information to an example.

If any sector of the economy were initially to increase spending by $100, we are aware that the income level will also change because spending is income. But the multiplier principle tells us that the change in income will be greater than the original change in spending. If the multiplier is 4, then the change in total income will be a $400 increase. The $400 increase was found by multiplying the multiplier of 4 times the initial $100 increase in spending. In this case, if any sector increases spending by $100, income in the economy increases by $400. If a sector were to increase spending by $200, then income would increase by $800. In this example the change in income is always four times the initial change in spending. Carefully note that the multiplier works in both directions. If spending were to initially *fall* by $50, then income would *fall* by four times, or $200. This means that if total income were $1,000 before the $50 reduction in spending, total income is now $800.

How did we find the size of the multiplier, 4, in our example, and how can we find it in any situation? The income multiplier is the reciprocal of the marginal propensity to save. Reciprocal is just the MPS in fraction form turned upside down. In our example, the marginal propensity to save must have been 25 percent. Twenty-five percent is the fraction 1/4, which when turned upside down (finding the reciprocal), is 4/1 or 4. The income multiplier is 4 when the MPS is 25 percent. The income multiplier is also 4 when the marginal propensity to consume is 75 percent. That is because the MPC and the MPS add up to 100 percent, so if the MPC is 75 percent, the MPS is 25 percent, and the income multiplier is 4. A close observation of Table 23-1 should clarify the relationship between the MPC, the MPS, and the income multiplier. The marginal propensity to save determines the size of the income multiplier. The smaller the MPS, the greater the size of the income multiplier, as you may have noticed in the table.

Table 23-1 The Income Multiplier

MPC	MPS	Multiplier
1/2 or .50	1/2 or .50	2
2/3 or .67	1/3 or .33	3
7/10 or .70	3/10 or .30	3.33
3/4 or .75	1/4 or .25	4
8/10 or .80	2/10 or .20	5
9/10 or .90	1/10 or .10	10

This table shows the relationship of the marginal propensity to consume, the marginal propensity to save, and the income multiplier. The multiplier is the reciprocal of the MPS. Recall that the MPS and MPC add to 1.

How does the marginal propensity to save determine the size of the income multiplier? The answer to this question takes a little thought. First let us consider what happens when income is spent. Persons receiving the additional income will place some into saving and the remainder into consumption. So not only does the initial spending create income for consumers, but some of this income is respent and creates yet more income for other consumers. And what will these other consumers do with their additional income? Some of their additional income will find its way into additional saving but the remainder will be spent on additional consumption. This creates even more income. We are seeing a chain reaction set off by the initial change in spending. You can see why the income multiplier is sometimes referred to as the consumer respending effect. Now recognize that the less income that enters into saving (the smaller the MPS), the more that is respent, and the greater this respending effect, the larger is the income multiplier.

The Multiplier Process

If we consider the initial change in spending to be $100 and the MPS to be 20 percent, hence a multiplier of 5, Table 23-2 illustrates the sequence of events in the multiplier process. You will have a better understanding of the multiplier principle if you carefully examine this table. Column 1, change in income, shows the amount of income that is created through each round of the multiplier. Column 2, change in consumption, shows the effect of the marginal propensity to consume. This is the amount of the additional income that is respent in each round. In the first round when consumers have received 100

Table 23-2   Multiplier Effect of $100 Change in Spending

Round	(1) Change in Income	(2) Change in Consumption	(3) Change in Saving
1	$100.00	$80.00	$20.00
2	80.00	64.00	16.00
3	64.00	51.20	12.80
4	51.20	40.96	10.24
5	40.96	32.77	8.19
6	32.77	26.21	6.56
7	26.21	20.97	5.24
8	20.97	16.78	4.19
9	16.78	13.42	3.36
10	13.42	10.74	2.68
Other rounds			
Summed	53.69	42.95	10.74
TOTAL	$500.00	$400.00	$100.00

This table shows the change in income that is generated by the multiplier process after a $100 initial change in spending. The MPC is .80, and the multiplier is 5. You can see that the multiplier process has expanded income by $500 from the $100 injection.

additional dollars of income, they chose to consume an extra $80. We know this to be true since the MPC is 80 percent. This $80 of respending creates $80 of additional income for consumers and starts round 2. Column 3, change in saving, shows the effect of the marginal propensity to save and the amount of additional income that is saved in each round of the multiplier. This saving does not enter the next round of income creation since it is not respent. In the first round, consumers have received $100 of additional income, but the MPS of 20 percent determines that $20 enters saving. Only the $80 is respent and continues to round 2. The last figure in column 1 records the total of new income created by the initial change in spending. The multiplier of 5 (reciprocal of the MPS of 20 percent), times the initial $100 increase in spending, results in the creation of this $500 increase in income.

The amount of saving withdrawn in each round eventually limits the potential change to total income. The amount of new income that goes into additional saving is income that will not go to the next round of spending. Thus less and less additional income is created in each round, and some of that still "leaks" into saving, until there are no more additions to income to be respent, and the multiplier effect is concluded. Observe in Table 23-2 that saving increased in total by $100. This $100 increase in saving is equal to the $100 initial change in spending. The multiplier effect is ended when the original $100 of spending has all leaked into saving and there can be no more respending effect. Yet observe that consumption increased by $400 as well as the $100 original increase in spending. During the multiplier process, $500 of spending and income that did not exist before is created. So the equilibrium level of income, as well as output and employment, is increased by more than the initial change in spending.

The multiplier establishes an upper limit on the change in income. The upper limit is calculated by multiplying the initial change in spending by the multiplier. In our example, income cannot increase by more than $500 with an initial change in spending of $100. This full impact of the multiplier can be achieved only if there are no leakages, except the predicted saving, in each round. In our model, we have assumed that each consumer has the same MPS. If some consumers save more, the income generated for the next round will not be as great as it might have been, and these additional leakages would reduce the full impact of the multiplier. Also, the multiplier process takes time. The income multiplier originates from consumer respending. This respending and its effect will only be felt after a lag in time. Thus we cannot expect that the full change in income will occur right away, and it may never occur due to additional leakages. But the important point is that the multiplier process exists and does magnify any initial change in spending.

If government intends to increase the level of *income* by $100, an increase of $100 of government *spending* ignores the income multiplier. The multiplier would significantly increase the impact of the $100 change in spending. This could result in too large a change to total income and perhaps contribute to inflationary pressure. We must recognize that there are economic forces at work, such as the multiplier, and we must take these forces into account when considering any adjustment to the economy.

Automatic Stabilizers

There are mechanisms already in place in the macro economy that will tend to move the level of income toward the full employment level and help to "smooth out" the business cycle. These mechanisms automatically change aggregate demand in the right direction at the right time. These mechanisms are called **automatic stabilizers**. No action need be taken on the part of government for these mechanisms to function appropriately. Two prominent examples of these stabilizers are unemployment compensation and the progressive income tax structure. Workers pay to the government, through their employers, money for unemployment benefits. During a period of full employment, these contributions reduce disposable income, spending, and aggregate demand to help offset inflationary pressures.

The opposite effect occurs during a recession. When an unemployed person loses income, normally he or she must reduce spending. This reduction in spending causes the income of someone else to fall, and the multiplier process begins to contract the level of income. However, unemployment payments to the individual mean that the reduction in spending will be less, and the multiplier process that reduces income will not be as great. Thus, the level of income will not fall as far as it would if there were no unemployment benefits. You can see that unemployment collections and payments act as an automatically controlled flow to help even out fluctuations in the business cycle.

A progressive income tax also has a stabilizing effect on the economy. With a progressive tax, the percentage of income paid in taxes rises as income rises. When the level of income increases and becomes an inflationary threat, the higher income moves people into higher tax brackets with higher tax payments. With less disposable income than otherwise, spending and aggregate demand will be somewhat reduced. And when the level of income falls during a recession, people are moved into lower tax brackets and contribute less in tax payments. They are left with more purchasing power than they would have had otherwise, and the fall in aggregate demand is partially offset.

Automatic stabilizers cause the level of income to move toward full employment and help to counteract the business cycle. So even if the government does nothing, there are automatic forces that will move the level of income in the direction of full employment. But by themselves, these stabilizers cannot change aggregate demand by the necessary amount to obtain full employment. There may be times when deliberate government action is needed.

▶ Summary

Government, consumer, and business spending determine the equilibrium level of income. We have examined two impacts of government — taxation and expenditure. To finance expenditure, the government collects taxes. Taxes affect consumption as well as investment. Because the consumer must pay taxes, the consumer has less income to spend on consumption, so consumption falls. A major impact of taxes is to reduce consumption and thus reduce total spending. Government takes the taxes collected and contributes to total spending. Taxes influence the spending of business and consumers and reduce aggregate demand, while government spending increases aggregate demand. These are two significant influences of government. The equilibrium level of income was again established in this model, which now includes the government. The aggregate demand of the three sectors, C + I + G at each price level, determines equilibrium.

The income multiplier tells us that if there is an increase in spending, the equilibrium level of income will rise by a multiple of the increase in spending. If there is a decrease in spending, the equilibrium level of income will fall by a multiple of the decrease in spending. The size of the income multiplier depends on the marginal propensity to save. The smaller the MPS, the larger the income multiplier. The multiplier is an important concept that will be used in the following chapters. The next chapter develops the Keynesian Cross, a graph, to illustrate the equilibrium level of income.

▶ Key Concepts

disposable income
taxes
government spending
equilibrium
income multiplier
automatic stabilizers

▶ Discussion Questions

1. The Full Employment Act of 1946 made the federal government responsible for maintaining full employment. We were concerned with sliding back into another depression. How did this contrast with the attitude toward government involvement in the macro economy prior to the Great Depression?
2. What is the effect of an increase in taxes on aggregate demand? A decrease in taxes? An increase in government spending? A decrease?
3. Suppose that government spending goes up in the bathtub model so that I + G is greater than S + T. The level of income will rise. Why will the level of income stop rising and achieve a higher equilibrium?
4. Suppose that all consumers try to save more. What will happen to the level of income and saving?

5. Consumption, C, is determined by consumers following their best interest. Investment, I, is determined by businesses following their best interest. Yet C + I could leave us at less than full employment. Apply the fallacy of composition. What can the government do to look after the best interest of society?

6. Assume the MPS is 1/3 and fill in the blanks.

   a. The multiplier is _____.

   b. If government increases spending by $10, the level of income rises by

   _____.

   c. If the equilibrium level of income was $100, it is now

   _____.

   d. Suppose that you want the level of income to go up by $600. Government spending should change by _____.

7. Uncle Effron finds this talk of an income multiplier ridiculous. He says it is hard enough to add to his income, and it certainly does not multiply. Explain the income multiplier to Uncle Effron.

8. Drop a tennis ball. What happens after the initial bounce? How does the total up and down distance of the bouncing ball compare to the initial bounce? How is the motion of the ball like the multiplier?

9. Suppose that the MPC is 1 (the reciprocal of the MPS = 0 is infinity). Work through the multiplier process. How much extra income could be generated by a one dollar increase in G?

10. a. Suppose that a consumer has an income of $10,000 per year and the income tax rate is 10 percent. How much will the consumer pay in taxes? How much is left for consumption?

    b. Suppose now that the consumer's income goes up to $20,000. How much does the consumer pay in taxes? How much is left for consumption?

    c. What if, when the consumer's income goes up to $20,000, the tax rate is increased to 20 percent — how much tax would the consumer pay now? What impact does the higher tax rate have on disposable income?

    d. What impact would the higher tax rate on higher income have on aggregate demand compared to a constant tax rate?

▶ Self-Review

- Fill in the blanks

taxes, increase
decrease
increases

The level of consumption and therefore income is affected by _____. Lower taxes _____ consumption and higher taxes _____ consumption. Government expenditure _____ income and a reduction in

reduces

S + T, C + I + G

supply

income multiplier

number

MPS, multiplied

consumers

business, government

income, larger

automatic stabilizers

unemployment

income tax

government spending _____ income. In a three sector economy, equilibrium occurs where I + G equals _____, or aggregate demand of _____ intersects aggregate _____. A greater change in total income may occur due to an initial change in spending as a result of the _____. The multiplier is simply a _____. We find the multiplier by taking the reciprocal of the _____. This number is then _____ times any initial change in spending by _____, or _____ or _____. The result is the change in total _____. The smaller the MPS, the _____ the income multiplier. Mechanisms that automatically move aggregate demand toward full employment are known as _____. Two examples of automatic stabilizers are _____ compensation and the progressive _____.

● Multiple choice

1. Taxes cause consumers to save _____ at each level of income.
   a. less
   b. more
   c. the same amount
   d. not enough information to tell
2. Automatic stabilizers have the impact of:
   a. lowering income.
   b. raising income.
   c. causing income to rise by less or fall by less.
   d. forcing the business cycle to go into a recession.
3. If the government decreases expenditure but does not change taxes, you would expect the equilibrium level of income to:
   a. rise.
   b. fall.
   c. not change.
   d. not change but the price level would rise.
4. An increase in income causes:
   a. consumption to increase which then increases income.
   b. consumption to fall which then decreases income.
   c. investment to rise which then increases income.
   d. government spending to rise which then increases income.

5. If the MPS is 1/3 and government reduces expenditure by $100, how much will income change?
   a. $300.
   b. $100.
   c. −$300.
   d. −$100.

Answers: 1.a, 2.c, 3.b, 4.a, 5.c.

Chapter | 24 | **THE KEYNESIAN CROSS**

Key Topics
  the consumption and investment function
  the equilibrium level of income
  government expenditure and taxes
  equilibrium again
  the income multiplier
  equilibrium using saving and investment
  total spending and saving and investment

Goals
  find equilibrium level of income in a graphical model

This chapter summarizes the income determination problem graphically. Since the substance of this chapter has already been covered, this chapter need not be read unless the graphical emphasis is desired.

In Chapter 18 we saw how to measure the performance of the economy. One important concept defined there was gross domestic product (GDP). It is one thing to define the concept; it is another to ask what determines the level of GDP. Once we know how GDP is determined, we will know what can be done to make GDP change. So if GDP starts to go in a direction that is not desirable, there may be ways to correct its movement.

In this chapter several concepts are reviewed. First is consumption, and second is investment. Equilibrium GDP (what the actual level of GDP is) will then be discussed. The model will then be expanded to include the government, and equilibrium will be revisited. Impacts on GDP of changes in government spending will then be examined. All of this is done by use of graphs to illustrate the words.

The Consumption Function and Investment Function

The sum of consumer spending, business investment, government expenditure and exports minus imports is gross domestic product. Yet if we are to understand what makes the GDP what it is, we must understand what makes each of the components what they are. For simplicity the net export sector will be ignored, and a discussion of business investment and government spending are temporarily postponed.

We studied the consumption function in Chapter 21. It was suggested that the consumption of the society depended upon the income of the society and that as income goes up so will consumption. Table 24-1 illustrates that idea. The analysis is made easier by drawing a graph of this information. The level of real income (Y) will be plotted on the horizontal axis and the corresponding consumption will be plotted vertically. Thus in Figure 24-1, if Y is zero, C is 40. If Y is 100, C is 120. When Y is 200, so is C. As this process is continued, several points on the consumption function can be found. If these points are connected, the consumption function results and looks as shown in Figure 24-1.

In Chapter 21, the marginal propensity to consume was discussed. The marginal propensity to consume is the change in consumption divided by the change in income, MPC = $\Delta C/\Delta Y$. What is the MPC in the previous example? Note that as Y goes from 0 to 100, the change in Y is 100 units. The resulting change in C is 120 − 40 or 80. The MPC is the ratio of the change in C, 80,

Table 24-1   The Consumption Function

Y	C
0	40
100	120
200	200
300	280
400	360
500	440
600	520
700	600
800	680

As the level of income goes up, so does the amount consumed by the society. Note too that if income is zero, consumption is still positive.

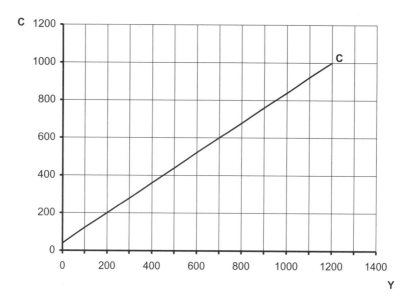

Figure 24-1   The Consumption Function
The consumption function shows how consumption varies as income varies. At an income
of zero, consumption is 40. If income is 100, consumption is 120. As income rises, so does
consumption. In this graph you can also see that the MPC is .8 since as income goes up by 100,
consumption goes up by 80.

to the change in Y, 100, or 80/100 or .8. Does the MPC stay constant in this
example or change? If income goes from 100 to 200, the change in Y is 100. The
corresponding change in C is 80 (260 − 180). Thus the MPC = 80/100 = .8. If
this process is continued for all levels of income shown, the MPC is always .8.
Will the MPC always be constant? A more likely prospect is that the MPC will
fall as the income rises. Such a prospect is easy to graph, but the calculation
of the MPC becomes more difficult. So for our purposes, it will suffice to
consider a consumption function with a constant MPC. What have we learned
so far? We know that there is a relationship between Y and C showing what
happens to C at each level of Y. This is one piece of information that will be
needed in the calculation of the equilibrium level of income.

Now business investment will be discussed. Investment involves several
important activities. When a business expands its plant capacity, investment
has occurred. If a firm increases its inventory of unsold goods, investment has
occurred. For our purposes, the simplest assumption is that investment (I) does
not depend on Y. Thus investment is the same for all levels of Y. This is the

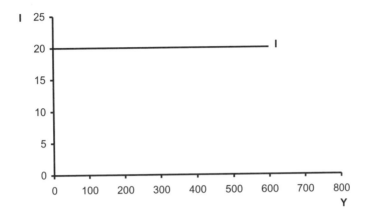

Figure 24-2   Investment

Investment is assumed to not vary as the level of income varies. Thus investment is the same amount at each level of income. Here, investment is 20.

investment function shown in Figure 24-2. At every Y, I is the same. For the purpose of illustration, it will be assumed that $I = 20$. Now the question of the equilibrium level of income can be addressed.

The Equilibrium Level of Income

When this chapter started we mentioned that to determine the level of income, the various components of income had to be understood. This has been done. Both C and I have been discussed. The next step is to discuss what we mean by equilibrium and how it can be represented by potential equilibria, which is all possible equilibrium points. After that, total spending, $C + I$, will be found. Then the equilibrium level of income can be determined by putting total spending together with the potential equilibria.

To start with, the notion of equilibrium is that of a balance of forces. What the forces on Y are must be determined. The forces on Y will involve inventories. If the amount actually produced is greater than total spending by persons and business, then inventories will rise. The firms will sooner or later find it desirable to cut back the amount produced. The point is that because the amount of inventories on hand is either too large or too small, the level of income will change. There would be a force on Y. Thus there would not be a balance of forces on Y, so Y could not be at equilibrium. An equilibrium Y means that Y will not be changing. This argument will be repeated later;

be sure to watch for it. Also note that the forces will drive Y back to the equilibrium level of income so that the equilibrium is a stable equilibrium.

The next matter of interest is how we can draw a graph of the equilibrium condition. This will be done in Figure 24-3. Recall that according to the GDP accounts $Y = C + I$ (in this world without government) must hold. We will take this to define equilibrium. Thus no matter what Y is, if it is to be an equilibrium Y, then $Y = C + I$ must hold. To graph this relationship, we will put Y on the horizontal axis, and $C + I$ on the vertical axis. Note that how much C actually is or how much I actually is, is not of interest. The question is: if Y is equilibrium, how much must C and I be together so $Y = C + I$? So if $Y = 0$, $C + I = 0$. If $Y = 100$, then $C + I = 100$. If $Y = 1000$, then $C + I = 1000$. In fact no matter what Y is, $C + I$ must be the same if Y is to be an equilibrium Y. This is the line of potential equilibria.

Note that the line of potential equilibria shows an interesting feature in Figure 24-4. The line through the origin cuts the angle between the two axes exactly in half. The line makes a 45° (45 degree) angle with either the Y axis or the $C + I$ axis. Thus the line is also called the 45° line. Another useful feature

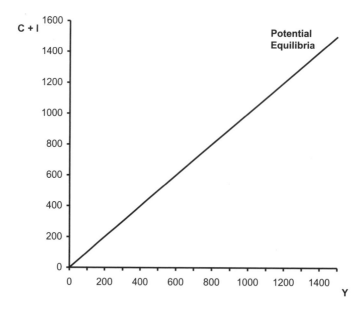

Figure 24-3   Potential Equilibria
Potential equilibria is all possible points where equilibrium could occur. Since equilibrium occurs when $Y = C + I$, we are looking for the points where $Y = C + I$. If $Y = 0$, then $C + I = 0$. If $Y = 1000$, then $C + I = 1000$.

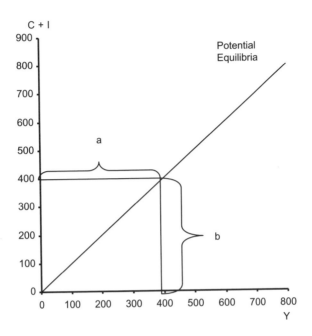

Figure 24-4   Features of Potential Equilibria

Potential equilibria has two features. First, it forms a 45 degree angle with either the Y axis or the C + I axis. Second, the distance a equals the distance b. Distance a is Y and distance b is C + I . For equilibrium, Y = C + I.

of the 45° line is the following. Since Y = C + I at each point on the line, then along the line, the horizontal distance a is exactly the same length as the vertical distance b. This is because the length a is Y, and the vertical distance b is C + I. This 45° line, **potential equilibria**, represents the combinations of Y and C + I where equilibrium could potentially occur. This is a graph of Y = C + I, the condition which must hold at equilibrium. The potential equilibria line shows how much is produced at each level of income. But where is equilibrium? To answer that question, the actual amount of consumption and investment is discussed next.

To find the actual total spending (consumption plus investment) consumption must be added to investment. To carry out this procedure, both the consumption function and the investment function will be put on the same graph in Figure 24-5. The idea now is to add these two together. So at each Y, the amount of consumption will be added to the amount of investment. At Y = 0, total spending would be 40 + 20 (consumption at Y = 0 is 40 and I = 20). If Y = 100, then C + I = 120 + 20. If this process is continued for each Y, the outcome is the line of total spending in Figure 24-6. This graph shows the total amount of consumption plus investment which would actually occur at each level of income. Thus the graph shows the total spending at each Y. Now the equilibrium level of income can be found.

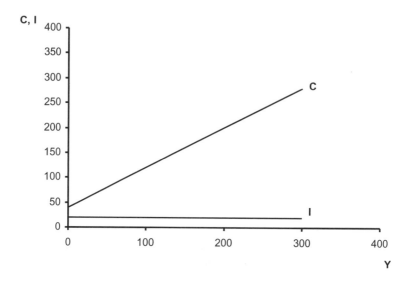

Figure 24-5   C and I
The consumption function and the investment function are both shown on the same graph.

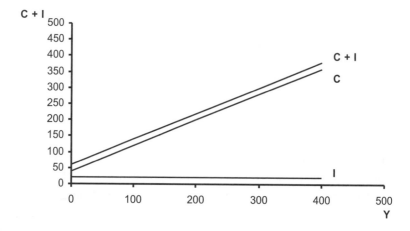

Figure 24-6   Total Spending
Total spending is found by adding together consumption and investment. At each Y the amount of C is added to the amount of I and total spending results.

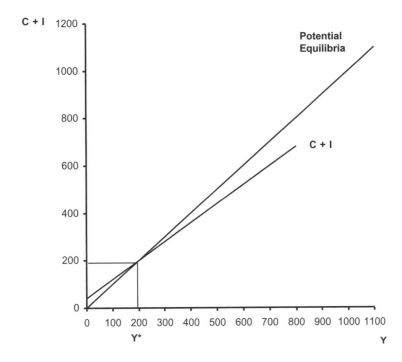

Figure 24-7   Equilibrium
Equilibrium will occur where the potential equilibrium line and the total spending line
$C + I$ intersect. The equilibrium level of income is Y^*.

The potential equilibria line must be put together with the $C + I$, the total
spending line, in Figure 24-7. Now you can see why this is called the Keynesian
Cross. Where would the equilibrium level of income be? If you guessed where
the lines cross, you would be right. Why? First of all, at that level of income,
Y^*, (called Y star), total spending, $C + I$, equals income Y^*, so the definition of
equilibrium is satisfied. But this is not very informative. What forces the level
of income to be at Y^*? If Y^* is the equilibrium level of income, there must
be forces which cause the level of income to move back to Y^* if the level of
income is first moved away from Y^*.

Suppose that the level of income were at Y_1 in Figure 24-8. What would
cause the level of income to change? If the level of income is Y_1, then the
output of the economy is Y_1. It is appropriate to think of Y as the amount of
output of the economy. Of course, as you know, if Y measures output, it also
measures income. Further, the amount that is purchased is $C + I$ at Y_1. These
amounts can be compared. Y_1 is easily identified on the horizontal axis. By the

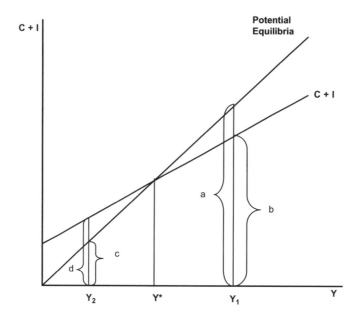

Figure 24-8 Why Equilibrium Occurs at Y*
Equilibrium cannot occur at Y_1 since the output, a, is larger than total spending, b. Soon firms cut back production, and Y falls. At Y_2, output, c, is less than total spending, d. Soon firms increase production, and Y rises. Equilibrium can only occur where total spending and potential equilibria cross.

feature of the potential equilibria line, Y_1 is also the vertical distance a to the potential equilibria line. The total spending is the distance b to the C + I line at Y_1. It is easy to see that the amount produced, Y_1, is greater than the total spending, C + I. What happens to the unsold production? It adds to inventories. These are not inventories the firm expected to hold. If this continues, the firms will soon be holding too much in the way of inventories and will cut back production. Cutting back production means that the amount produced, Y, must fall. So Y is not at rest, and Y_1 is not equilibrium. This conclusion will hold as long as Y is greater than Y^*.

What if the level of income is less than Y^*, at Y_2 in Figure 24-8? In that case, the total output of the economy is Y_2 and can be represented by the vertical distance c. The total spending is C + I at Y_2. This is represented by the vertical distance d. Since the total spending is more than total output, inventories will fall. Firms will increase production and thus output or GDP. So Y will rise, and since Y is moving, Y_2 is not equilibrium. Again, this conclusion will hold for any Y below Y^*.

It should be clear now why the equilibrium level of income is at the point where the C + I (total spending) crosses the potential equilibria line. Here total spending and total output are equal. Note too that there is a way to change the equilibrium level of income. If it is possible to cause either consumer or business to alter spending, then Y^* would change. There will be an opportunity to expand this discussion after government is introduced. That is the next topic.

Government Expenditure and Taxes

There are two ways that the government can affect the actual level of income. First is by spending. Second is through the collection of taxes. Government expenditure and taxation will be discussed and then the question of the equilibrium level of income will be reconsidered. If government spending (G) is constant for all Y, it would look as shown in Figure 24-9.

How do taxes enter the calculation of the equilibrium level of income? When a tax is imposed, the basic impact is to reduce the amount that the consumer can spend or save. The simplifying assumption is that taxes (T) are constant. Thus if Y is the level of income, then Y − T is available for consumption or saving. This Y − T is disposable income. Now consumption depends on Y − T rather than Y. The impact of this alteration is to slightly change the way the consumption function appears. The consumption function in Figure 24-10 shifts down since at each Y, C must be lower after taxes than before.

Figure 24-9 Government Spending
Government spending is assumed to be constant at 50. Thus it is the same at all levels of income.

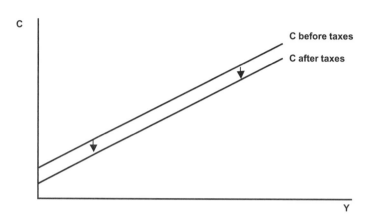

Figure 24-10   The Impact of Taxes on Consumption
Taxes reduce the amount of income that the consumer can spend. At each level of income, the amount of consumption will be less than without the tax. Thus the consumption function will shift down at each level of income.

Table 24-2   The Consumption Function with Taxes

Consumption without Taxes		Consumption with Taxes		
Y	C	Y	C	T
0	40	0	24	20
100	120	100	104	20
200	200	200	184	20
300	280	300	264	20
400	360	400	344	20
500	440	500	424	20
600	520	600	504	20
700	600	700	584	20
800	680	800	664	20

When taxes of 20 are included, then at each level of income the consumers have less to spend. Hence consumption goes down by the MPC, .8, times the tax.

The impact of taxes on consumption are also reported in Table 24-2. Here you can see that at each level of income, the consumption is less than it was before the tax. Note that the consumption has fallen by $16 at each level of income. The amount of income the consumer could spend went down by $20 due to the tax. Consumption falls by $16 because the MPC is .8. So for every $1 decrease in disposable income, consumption falls by $.80. If the taxes fall mainly on consumption and do not affect investment decisions, then all of the effects of the tax have been captured. We are now ready to proceed to equilibrium.

Equilibrium Again

The question now is what impact does the introduction of the government have in the calculation of the equilibrium level of income? Much can be learned from our previous effort. When equilibrium was found before there were two concepts that were needed. First was the potential equilibria line and second was the total spending line. These concepts will be taken up in that order.

To get the potential equilibria line, an equilibrium condition is needed. Again the equilibrium condition for this expanded economy will be taken from the components of GDP. In this case equilibrium occurs if $Y = C + I + G$. Thus to find the potential equilibria line, the points where $Y = C + I + G$ holds must be isolated. Where does this occur? Recall again that the question is not what would $C + I + G$ be at each Y, but rather given Y what must $C + I + G$ be so that $Y = C + I + G$. So if $Y = 0$, $C + I + G = 0$ must be. If $Y = 100$, $C + I + G = 100$ must also hold. Does this sound familiar? We have done this before! In fact, the potential equilibria line looks just as it did in the case where there was only consumption and investment. It is the 45° line. It is shown in Figure 24-11.

Now the total spending line will be developed. Again the line of total spending should tell the total amount actually spent at each level of Y. Total spending consists of the spending by consumers (after taxes) plus business investment plus government expenditure. So at each Y the amount of C must be added to the amount of investment plus government expenditure. The three lines (C, I and G) are shown in Figure 24-12. Now to get total spending at each Y, we need to add $C + I + G$ at each Y. So if G is 50, and investment is 20, and the after tax consumption function is as reported in Table 24-2, then at $Y = 0$, $C + I + G = 94$. If $Y = 100$, then $C + I + G = 174$. If we continue for all Y, the total spending line $C + I + G$ can be determined. This is shown by Figure 24-13.

Now the equilibrium level of income can be obtained by putting together the potential equilibria line with the total spending line. Again the equilibrium will occur at Y^*. Why? Figure 24-14 shows that at the level of income Y^*, total spending, $C + I + G$, equals Y^*, so the definition of equilibrium is satisfied. But again this is not very informative. What forces the level of income to be

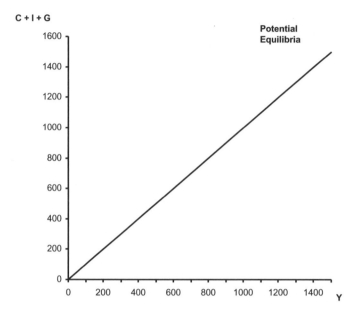

Figure 24-11   Potential Equilibria
Potential equilibria is all possible points where equilibrium could occur. Since equilibrium occurs when $Y = C + I + G$, we are looking for the points where $Y = C + I + G$. If $Y = 0$, then $C + I + G = 0$. If $Y = 1000$, then $C + I + G = 1000$.

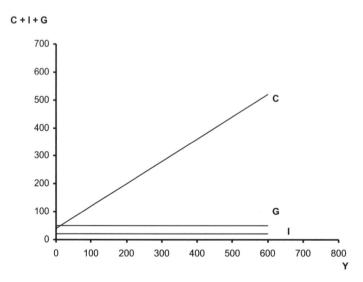

Figure 24-12   C, I and G
Consumption is again shown as a line which rises with income. Investment is constant at 20 and government spending is constant at 50.

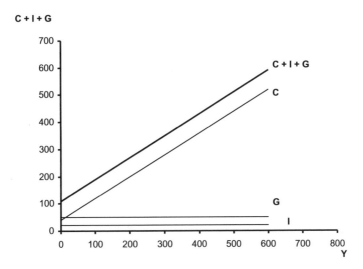

Figure 24-13   Total Spending

Total spending is found by adding together consumption, investment and government spending. At each Y the amount of C, I and G are added together and total spending results.

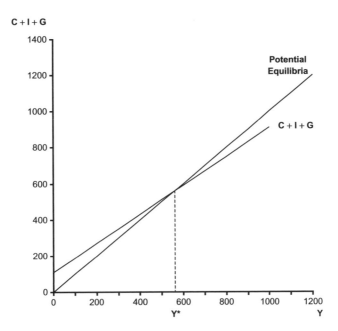

Figure 24-14   Equilibrium with Government

Equilibrium will occur where the potential equilibrium line and the total spending line C+I+G intersect. The equilibrium level of income is Y*.

at Y^*? If Y^* is the equilibrium level of income, there must be forces which cause the level of income to move back to Y^* if the level of income is first moved away from Y^*.

Suppose that the level of income were at Y_1 in Figure 24-15. What would cause the level of income to change? If the level of income is Y_1, then the output of the economy is Y_1. Further, the amount that is purchased is $C + I + G$ at Y_1. These amounts can be compared. Y_1 is easily identified on the horizontal axis. By the feature of the potential equilibria line, Y_1 is also the vertical distance a to the potential equilibria line. The total spending is the distance b to the $C + I + G$ line at Y_1. It is easy to see that the amount produced, Y_1, is greater than the total spending, $C + I + G$. What happens to the unsold production? It adds to inventories. These are not inventories the firm expected to hold. If this continues, the firms will soon be holding too much in the way of inventories and will cut back production. Cutting back production means that the amount produced, Y, must fall. So Y is not at rest; Y_1 is not equilibrium. This conclusion will hold as long as Y is greater than Y^*.

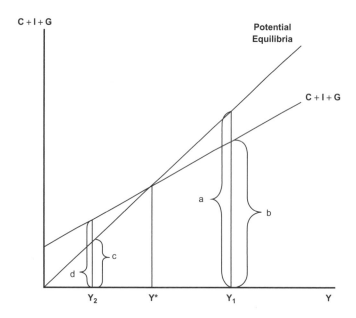

Figure 24-15   Why Equilibrium Occurs at Y^*
Equilibrium cannot occur at Y_1 since the output, a, is larger than total spending, b. Soon firms cut back production, and Y falls. At Y_2, output, c, is less than total spending, d. Soon firms increase production, and Y rises. Equilibrium can only occur where total spending and potential equilibria cross.

What if the level of income is less than Y^*, at Y_2 in Figure 24-15? In this case, the total output of the economy is Y_2 and can be represented by the vertical length c. The total spending is $C + I + G$ at Y_2. This is represented by the vertical length d. Since the total spending is more than total output, inventories will fall. Firms will increase production and thus output or GDP. So Y will rise, and since Y is moving, Y_2 is not equilibrium. Again, this conclusion will hold for any Y below Y^*.

It should be clear now why the equilibrium level of income is at the point where the $C + I + G$ (total spending) crosses the potential equilibria line. Here total spending is equal total output. Note too that there is a way to change the equilibrium level of income, through government expenditure and taxation.

Now that we have a model of income determination, some interesting questions may be asked. For example what would happen to the equilibrium level of income if G went up by 50? In the next section this and questions of similar interest will be addressed.

The Income Multiplier

One important question is the following. Suppose that the government decided it wanted to raise the equilibrium level of income. By how much should it raise G in order to make Y rise by 100? The answer involves the income multiplier, a concept studied in Chapter 23.

As you learned before, if G goes up there will be a multiplied change in Y. Recall that the income multiplier is the reciprocal of the marginal propensity to save. The impact of the multiplier can be seen in Figure 24-16. Start with the potential equilibria and the $C + I + G$ line. Before a change in government spending, the equilibrium level of income is at Y_1^*. Suppose that G rises by ΔG to G'. The impact is to raise $C + I + G$ vertically by the distance ΔG to $C + I + G'$. The impact on the equilibrium level of income is to raise it to Y_2^*. The change in income is $Y_2^* - Y_1^*$. The increase in the level of income is found by multiplying the multiplier by the change in government spending.

Suppose we use the multiplier concept to help us answer the question we initially raised: what if a change in income of 100 is desired? By how much should G change? In order to answer the question, the MPS must be known. Suppose that the MPS is 1/5. First the income multiplier will be determined. The reciprocal of an MPS of 1/5 is 5/1 or 5. Thus the multiplier is 5. We know that every extra dollar the government spends change Y by 5. How many dollars must government spend to make income go up by 100? The answer

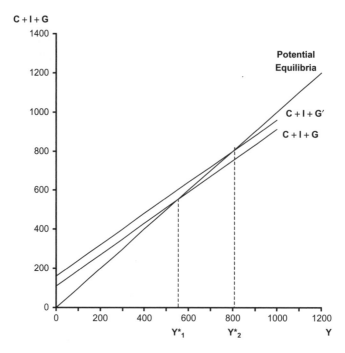

Figure 24-16   The Multiplier
A change in G from G to G' causes the total spending to shift up. Thus the equilibrium level of
income will rise from Y_1^* to Y_2^*. The change in income will be equal to the change in G times the
multiplier.

is 20. You can check by multiplying the change in G, 20, by the multiplier,
5, to get the desired change in income, 100. Thus if G is increased by 20, Y
will rise by 100! And indeed if G had been increased by 100, Y would have
increased by 500.

Note that the multiplier process could be initiated by other sectors. For
example, a change in I would have exactly the same impact as a change in
G. In fact, investment and government spending have exactly the same income
multiplier. So far we have learned that changes in income can be obtained from
changes in G or I. And that a change in G or I yields a multiplied effect on Y.
The use of these tools in economic policy will be taken up in the next chapter.

Equilibrium Using Saving and Investment

The entire analysis which has just been completed could have been carried out
from another point of view. Up to now the analysis has been done from the

point of view of consumption. The analysis will be done over from the point of view of saving (S). To carry out this task the saving function will be needed. Note too that the governmental sector will be ignored temporarily.

Recall that consumption depends on income. Further, consumers may either consume or save their income. Thus saving must also depend on income. Note that as income rises saving will rise as long as MPC is less than one. Why is that true? If income goes up and not all of that is consumed, then saving must also go up. Thus as Y rises, so must S. By how much does saving go up if Y rises by one dollar? The answer is whatever is not spent; the amount spent is MPC. Thus the increase in saving is the change in income minus the change in consumption or 1 – MPC. This amount is called the marginal propensity to save or MPS which was discussed in Chapter 21. The MPS answers the question how much does saving rise if income goes up by one dollar. Note too that if consumption is positive at zero income and consumption plus saving add up to income, then S must be negative by the exact amount that C is positive. We may conclude that the saving function looks as shown in Figure 24-17.

Now to complete the equilibrium discussion, an equilibrium condition is needed. In our earlier effort the equilibrium $Y = C + I$ was used. Now the equilibrium condition needs to be written in terms of saving. This can be done since all income is either spent or saved, and $Y = C + S$ holds. Since $Y = C + S$ and $Y = C + I$, the conclusion is that $C + S = C + I$ must hold at equilibrium. The C on each side of the equality cancels so at equilibrium $S = I$ must hold. The equilibrium condition is now $S = I$. All of this should remind you of the discussion of the bathtub in Chapter 22.

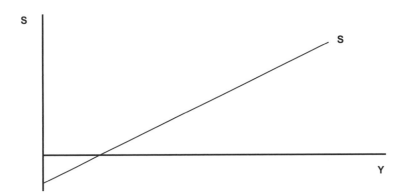

Figure 24-17   The Saving Function
The amount consumers save will rise as the level of income rises.

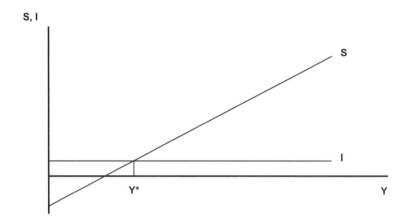

Figure 24-18   Equilibrium
Equilibrium will occur where saving and investment are equal. Thus the equilibrium level of income is Y^*.

To find the equilibrium level of income, all that is now needed is the I curve. As you recall, investment was assumed to be constant. Thus when saving and investment are put together, they look as shown in Figure 24-18. Equilibrium occurs at the level of income where the two curves intersect, Y^*. Of course this has to be since it satisfies the equilibrium condition $S = I$. Are there forces which would not be in balance if Y were not at Y^*? What if Y were above Y^*, at Y_1 in Figure 24-19? At Y_1 the amount saved, distance a, is greater than the amount invested, distance b. Saving is a withdrawal from income. Investment is an injection to income. Thus with saving greater than investment the withdrawals are greater than the injections and there must be a decrease in Y. So Y would fall.

What if Y were less than Y^*, at Y_2 in Figure 24-19? In that case the amount invested, distance c, is greater than the amount saved, distance d. There is a gain in income and income must rise. So in either case if income were above or below Y^*, there would be forces which would automatically move the level of income toward Y^*. Thus Y^* satisfies our definition of what an equilibrium should be.

What if the government sector is reintroduced? The place to start is with the consumer. Consumers now have an alternative way to use their income. They may spend, save, and pay taxes. Thus $Y = C + S + T$ must hold. Further recall that at equilibrium $Y = C + I + G$ has to hold. Thus the equilibrium condition with government can now be obtained since $Y = C + S + T$ and

$Y = C + I + G$, then $C + S + T = C + I + G$ must hold. Again the C's cancel out, hence $S + T = I + G$ holds at equilibrium. The graph necessary to determine equilibrium is easily obtained. I and G were both assumed constant. So their sum will also be a constant in Figure 24-20. Note that because taxes are taken

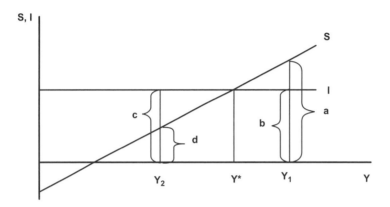

Figure 24-19   Why Equilibrium Occurs Where S = I
Equilibrium cannot occur at the level of income Y_1 since at that Y, the amount saved and withdrawn from income, distance a, is greater than the injection of investment, distance b. Thus the level of income must fall. At Y_2, the investment, distance c, an injection, is greater than the withdrawal of saving, distance d. Hence the level of income will rise. Thus if we are not at Y^*, there are forces which would push the level of income to Y^*, the equilibrium level of income.

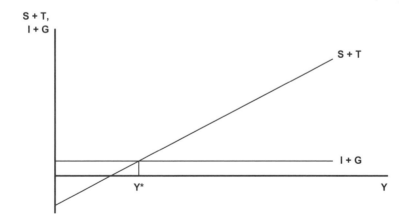

Figure 24-20   Equilibrium with Government
Equilibrium will occur where saving plus taxes equals investment plus government spending. Thus the equilibrium level of income is Y^*.

out of income before the saving occurs, S will be lower at every level of income because of the tax. We assume that S has been adjusted for this impact. To obtain S + T, the constant T must be added to the S function at each Y. This will result in a new curve parallel to the original S curve and exactly T units above the old S curve in Figure 24-20. And where is equilibrium? Again at the level of income where S + T and I + G cross. Why should this be true? Of course this has to be since it satisfies the equilibrium condition S + T = I + G. But in what sense are there forces that would not be in balance if Y were not at Y^*? What if Y were above Y^*, at Y_1 in Figure 24-21. At Y_1, the amount saved and paid in taxes, distance a, is greater than the amount invested and spent by government, distance b. Saving and taxes are a withdrawal from income. Investment plus government expenditure is an injection to income. Thus with saving greater than investment the withdrawals are greater that the injections and there must be a decrease in Y. So Y would fall.

What if Y were less than Y^* as at Y_2 in Figure 24-21? In that case the amount invested and spent by government, distance c, is greater than the amount saved and taxed, distance d. Thus there is a gain in income and income must rise. So in either case if income were above or below Y^*, there would be forces which would automatically move the level of income toward Y^*. Thus Y^* satisfies our definition of what an equilibrium should be.

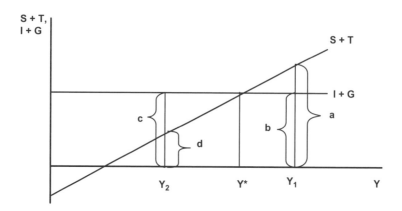

Figure 24-21   Why Equilibrium Occurs Where S + T = I + G
Equilibrium cannot occur at the level of income Y_1 since at that Y, the amount saved and withdrawn from income, distance a, is greater than the injection of investment, distance b. Thus the level of income must fall. At Y_2, the investment, distance c, an injection, is greater than the withdrawal of saving, distance d. Hence the level of income will rise. Thus if we are not at Y^*, there are forces which would push the level of income to Y^*, the equilibrium level of income.

The equilibrium level of income is again determined. Note that if I or G rises, so will the equilibrium Y. If T rises, we see that the equilibrium Y would fall. All this is in accord with our earlier efforts. Moreover, the analysis concerning the relationship of the change in G or I and the change in Y, the multiplier analysis, still holds.

Total Spending and Saving and Investment

It may seem to you that you have been studying two separate and distinct models for income determination. One model is the C + I + G or total spending model; the second is the saving and investment model. In fact both are essentially the same model and whatever the equilibrium level of income is in one model, it will be the same in the other model. If the two graphs are placed in a line vertically, they would line up as shown in Figure 24-22. Note that I and G are the same in both pictures, and the consumption and savings are closely related in that if you know one, the other can be found. The information needed to generate equilibrium can be used to determine the equilibrium in the other model too. Thus the two models are not different but are different ways of looking at the same model.

▶ Summary

In this chapter much ground has been covered. In particular a theory has been developed which explains why the level of real income is where it is and also tells us what to do if a change in the level of income is desired. Further it is clear that each change in G or I generates a greater change in income. Finally we have discovered an alternative way to view the income determination process through savings. These technical issues are important not only because they help us understand the world around us but also because they form the basis of fiscal policy. That is the topic of the next chapter.

▶ Key Concepts

potential equilibria

▶ Discussion Questions

1. Compare the Keynesian Cross and the bathtub model.

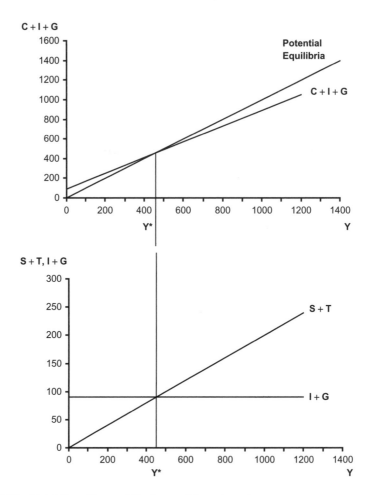

Figure 24-22   Total Spending and Saving and Investment
When the equilibrium level of income is found using saving and investment, the bottom half of
this graph, we will get the same level of income as when we use the total spending approach
in the top half of the graph. Thus we have not discussed two separate approaches to income
determination; they both use the same information and provide the same outcome.

2. Suppose that the marginal propensity to consume increases. What will happen
   to the equilibrium level of income?
3. If taxes increase, what will happen to the equilibrium level of income?
4. Explain why potential equilibria is a 45° line.
5. Assume that the MPC is 1 so that every extra dollar of income would be spent.
   What problem will this cause for the Keynesian Cross model?
6. Uncle Effron says that there cannot be two different models of equilibrium
   output. Is he right?

▶ **Self-Review**

• Fill in the blanks

consumption	The consumption function shows how _____
income	changes as _____ varies. Potential equilibria shows
	combinations of Y and total spending so that they are
equal, equilibrium	_____. At the _____,
level of income	there is no pressure to cause income to change.
C + I or C + I + G	Equilibrium occurs where _____ crosses
potential equilibria	_____. If total spending is greater
rise	than income, then income will _____. If total spending
fall	is less than income, then income will _____. If saving
	plus taxes are greater than investment plus government,
fall	then income will _____. If saving plus taxes are
	less than investment plus government, then income will
rise	_____.

• Multiple choice

1. If C + I + G is greater than Y, then:
   a. inventories fall and Y falls.
   b. inventories rise and Y falls.
   c. inventories fall and Y rises.
   d. inventories rise and Y rises.
2. Potential equilibria occurs where:
   a. Y = C + S + T.
   b. C = Y + I.
   c. I + T = S + G.
   d. Y = C + I + G.
3. If there is an increase in G, then:
   a. Y rises by the same amount as G rises.
   b. Y falls by the same amount as G rises.
   c. Y rises by more than G rises.
   d. Y rises by less than G rises.
4. If the new intersection of the 45° line and C + I + G is beyond the current equilibrium level of income, equilibrium level of income will:
   a. rise.
   b. fall.
   c. stay the same.
   d. impossible to say.

5. If G rises, then:
   a. total spending rises in the Keynesian model and I + G rises in the saving and
      investment model and equilibrium Y rises.
   b. total spending falls in the Keynesian model and I + G rises in the saving and
      investment model and equilibrium Y rises.
   c. total spending rises in the Keynesian model and I + G falls in the saving and
      investment model and equilibrium Y rises.
   d. total spending rises in the Keynesian model and I + G rises in the saving and
      investment model and equilibrium Y falls.

Answers: 1.c, 2.d, 3.c, 4.a, 5.a.

Chapter 25 | FISCAL POLICY

Key Topics

what fiscal policy is

how fiscal policy works

evaluation of fiscal policy

the national debt

Goals

understand what fiscal policy is

understand the strengths and weaknesses of fiscal policy

assess the costs and burdens of the national debt

We are now ready to discuss the first of our two major policy tools. These are the instruments that the government can use to regulate the economy. This chapter will explain the tools of fiscal policy, while the tools of monetary policy will be explained in Chapter 27. Fiscal policy and monetary policy are the major tools for the regulation of the business cycle, and if fiscal and monetary policies do not perform satisfactorily, then we must develop alternatives. Some alternative policies will be considered in Chapter 29. We are now prepared to examine the advice given by John Maynard Keynes during the Great Depression.

What Fiscal Policy Is

The government performs many tasks in our economy. It regulates various industries. It reallocates resources by taxing some individuals and then giving the tax revenue to others. Government is a producer of goods and services. It establishes and protects private property rights through the legal system and maintains the money supply. Another critical task that the government undertakes is called **stabilization policy**. The objective of stabilization policy is to smooth out the up and down pattern of the business cycle. The government may deliberately choose to take steps to make the level of income less variable. Fiscal policy is one form of stabilization policy. Fiscal policy involves changes in the size of government spending and tax collections. Either of these changes alters the government budget. **Fiscal policy** is the use of the federal budget as an economic tool to stabilize the economy.

Who administers fiscal policy? Fiscal policy is administered by the president and Congress. These administrative and legislative branches of the government determine the federal budget. There are two sides to the federal budget. First is the inflow, which is tax collections. Second is the outflow, which is government spending. We conclude that fiscal policy involves the ability of the government to tax and to spend, and thus use the federal budget to affect aggregate demand, and hence GDP.

How Fiscal Policy Works

We saw in Chapter 23 that a change in either government spending, G, or taxation, T, changes the level of aggregate demand. Aggregate demand increases with an increase in government expenditure and falls with an increase in taxes. We now have two tools, spending and taxation, that can be applied to either unemployment or inflation. What if the economy is performing at a low level of income, and the result is unacceptable amounts of unemployment? Government could apply the appropriate adjustments to spending and taxation and increase aggregate demand, $C + I + G$ at each price level, to the desired amount. By raising G, $C + I + G$ would rise and so would income, Y, since $Y = C + I + G$. Thus an increase in government spending increases aggregate demand, and the equilibrium level of income. Or, as an alternative to an increase in government spending, taxes could be reduced. This would leave more spending power in the hands of consumers and/or business and increase aggregate demand. Or, an increase in spending *and* a reduction in taxes could be combined. These are expansionary fiscal policies, intended to increase the level of income. In this manner, fiscal policy could be used to increase the equilibrium level of income and reduce unemployment.

Suppose that we know the level of employment representing full employment. This level of employment will be able to produce a certain level of output that we will call the full employment level of output. You should realize that the equilibrium level of output and the full employment level of output are two different concepts. The full employment level of output is what should be, and the equilibrium is what is. Now we can understand what the government could do to achieve equilibrium at full employment. For example, suppose that the equilibrium level is less than the full employment level. Then we would want to increase the equilibrium level of income and therefore employment. What action could the government take to make the level of income rise? It could increase spending or lower taxes.

The government could also apply fiscal policy tools when the equilibrium level of income is greater than the full employment level of income. In this case, there is inflationary pressure due to too much spending. Changes in spending, taxation, or a combination of both could again be employed. A reduction in government spending is an appropriate fiscal policy choice to reduce total spending and inflationary pressure. An increase in taxation can be used to reduce consumption, or investment, or both. Thus an increase in taxes reduces total spending and, with the same impact as decreased government spending, reduces inflationary pressure. A reduction in government spending and an increase in taxes can also be combined to combat inflationary pressure. These are contractionary fiscal policies, intended to decrease the level of income. To carry out either expansionary or contractionary fiscal policy successfully, the government needs to know how much to change spending or taxes.

How much should government change spending or taxes to achieve equilibrium at full employment? The easy way to find the answer is to use the income multiplier. Suppose that the level of income is $5 trillion and that the full employment level of income is $5.2 trillion. How much should government increase spending to raise the equilibrium level of income to full employment? The desired change in income is $200 billion. If we know the MPS, we can find the desired change in government spending. If the MPS is .25, the multiplier is 4. Then the government should increase spending by $50 billion. The multiplier of 4 times the $50 billion increase in government spending would increase income by the desired $200 billion. The income multiplier allows us to find the change in government spending needed to cause a specific change in the level of income. What if the economy were at the $5 trillion level of income, and we wish to reduce the level by $200 billion? If government were to reduce spending by $50 billion, total spending would fall by $50 billion, and the level of income would fall by the desired $200 billion.

The application of fiscal policy through the federal budget results in a countercyclical budget. This means that when aggregate demand is rising and increasing equilibrium beyond the full employment level, fiscal policy tools can be used to reduce aggregate demand. And when aggregate demand is falling below the level needed to maintain full employment, fiscal policy can be used to counteract this trend. Fiscal policy applied against the trend of the business cycle offsets the cycle to create more stability in the business cycle pattern.

The Federal Budget

A budget has two flows, the inflow and the outflow. The inflow to the federal budget is tax collections, and the outflow is the amount of government spending. What if tax collections are equal to government spending? Only in this case will the budget be balanced. A **balanced budget** results when tax collections and government spending are equal. When the budget is not balanced, the budget is either a surplus or a deficit. A **surplus budget** results when the government collects more in taxes than it spends. When government spends more than it collects in taxes, the result is a **deficit budget**.

Fiscal policy is applied through the federal budget. Fiscal policy tools are summarized in Table 25-1. Assuming a balanced budget, a reduction in government spending and/or an increase in taxes would result in a surplus budget and a reduction of inflationary pressures. An increase in government spending and/or a reduction in taxes would result in a deficit budget and an increase in output and employment.

We now see what Keynes wanted the government to do during the Great Depression. The equilibrium level of income was below full employment, so an increase in aggregate demand was needed to increase income to the full employment level. An increase in government spending was needed. Keynes argued vigorously for increased government spending, but Congress and the president were both unwilling. An increase in government spending would result in a deficit budget, which was not a solution that either the Congress or the president would accept. However, the Roosevelt administration did finance public work programs causing small deficits, which were considered scandalous

Table 25-1   Fiscal Policy

	Raise Y	Lower Y
G	raise	lower
T	lower	raise
Budget	deficit	surplus

G is government spending and T is taxes. When either G or T changes, the level of income, Y, changes. Also a change in G or T will change a balanced budget to a deficit or surplus.

at the time. It was inconceivable in the 1930s that the government should interfere in the macro economy, and for it to run the size of deficit needed to overcome the depression might have startled even Keynes. The necessary increase in government spending finally did take place during World War II, but for political reasons, not economic. Yet the result of the wartime spending confirmed Keynes's theory. If government spending had increased earlier, could we have avoided the Great Depression?

Evaluation of Fiscal Policy

Is fiscal policy effective in achieving full employment? We have seen that there are business cycles and that we are not always at full employment. Why don't we just apply fiscal policy, reach full employment, and then use fiscal policy to stay there? First, we have only rough estimates of the equilibrium level of income and can only roughly estimate the full employment level of income. Too, we have only estimates of the size of the MPS, so we do not know the income multiplier with certainty. And there are additional difficulties with applying fiscal policy.

Although the federal budget may be countercyclical, state and local budgets tend to reinforce the trend of the business cycle. State and local officials face great pressure to balance the budget. Many states are prohibited by their constitutions from having a deficit. When inflation occurs, local spending should be reduced. Instead, the surplus that the inflation brings from increased tax collections is spent. This increase in spending reinforces inflationary pressure. When income falls, so do local tax collections, so spending is reduced to balance the local budget. This reduction in spending reduces aggregate demand and contributes to the unemployment trend. Since government expenditure includes state and local as well as federal expenditures, federal policy may be counteracted.

By its very nature, fiscal policy does not work on the economy in general but through its effects on certain groups and geographic areas. When taxes are imposed or eliminated, or existing taxes raised or lowered, certain individuals will bear more costs or receive more benefits than others. A change in government spending must focus on some specific project. The closing down of an army base or shipyard is often met with resentment by those associated with it or located in the affected region. The construction of a dam or a hospital most greatly benefits those in a specific geographic area. Fiscal policy has an uneven effect on the population and regions.

Significant difficulties in the use of fiscal policy arise from the administration of fiscal policy through a political process. What makes good economics and what makes good politics may be radically different. Since the federal budget is controlled by elected officials, and government spending and taxation compose the budget, political realities interfere with the use of fiscal policy. Politically, fiscal policy leans more toward expansionary policy, raising aggregate demand by lowering taxes or increasing government spending. These are popular means for attracting votes. Normally it is political suicide to increase taxes or reduce government spending. Successful campaigns for elected offices are usually not run on promises of higher taxes or a reduction of spending on local projects. Some projects cannot be stopped in midstream, and most government commitments are long term. The question of where to reduce spending is a difficult one. So even if the economic situation calls for a reduction in government spending or an increase in taxes, these policies may not be enacted.

Time lags are another political problem with fiscal policy. First it may take some time before the president and the Congress realize that some policy action is needed, perhaps an increase in government spending. Then it takes time to formulate the policy, as the Congress will have to hold hearings and develop legislation. Both houses of Congress have to pass the legislation and add the funding to the next budget. And when the money is spent, it will take time for the multiplier to work and the policy to be felt in the economy. So there can be substantial lags between when the policy is needed and the time the policy is felt in the economy. By that time, there may have been a change in consumption or investment so that the opposite fiscal policy is required. Constant adjustments in fiscal policy might be needed to achieve full employment. You can see that achieving full employment is not an easy task. Do not expect economics to be an exact science. We should be suspicious of those who tell us that full employment can be easily achieved and maintained.

Perspectives on Fiscal Policy

The choice of fiscal tools influences the degree of government involvement in the economy. If government spending for goods is increased to enact an expansionary policy, then the government has more control over resource use. More resources would flow into the production of public goods. If instead taxes were reduced on business, individuals, or both, then there would be more private spending and more resources would flow into the private sector. More resources would be allocated into television sets rather than roads, into cars rather than tanks. During a contractionary policy, a reduction in government spending, rather than an increase in taxes, would lessen government influence and permit more private decision making. Conservatives may favor less government spending and lower taxes because they feel that every time the government acts, the role of the government in the economy grows but never gets smaller. For those who favor a smaller share of the economy controlled by the government and a larger share controlled by private firms and individuals, this constant growth by the government is a threat.

How has government spending changed over time? Look at Figure 25-1 showing the share of GDP that is government expenditure for goods and services for all levels of government. You can see that government expenditure is related to wars. The large peak after 1940 is due to World War II. The peak after 1950 is due to the Korean war. The bump in the late 1960s is because of Vietnam. The chart also suggests that since 1950, government spending as a percentage of GDP has not changed substantially.

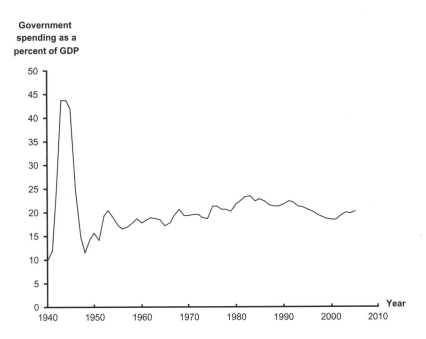

Figure 25-1 Government Spending as a Percentage of GDP, 1940–2005
Spending by all levels of government for goods and services reached its peak during World War II and then fell. It rose again in the 1950s and has not changed substantially.
Source: *Economic Report of the President, 2005.* Found on the web at: http://www.gpoaccess. gov/eop. Used by permission.

Does the government in fact make fiscal policy? Are the decisions of how much to spend and how much money to collect in taxes really made in light of their economic impact? Or are they the outcome of a complicated political process that has little concern for the economic impact? After all, despite the best efforts of Keynes, President Roosevelt believed in balanced budgets and did not try fiscal policy during the Great Depression. Our escape from the Great Depression seemed due to World War II and not to deliberate fiscal policy. Except for a tax cut in the Kennedy administration and one under Reagan, there are few cases where the government consciously attempted fiscal policy, and those cases tend to be tax policy rather than expenditure. The reason is that Congress can more easily agree to change taxes since there will be a similar impact on all congressional districts. But controlling spending means that it is likely that some districts will be harder hit than others. Thus it is harder to get a consensus on spending levels than on taxation. This view of fiscal policy is that all the talk about policy is fine, but when is the government going to start actively making decisions about the amount to spend and tax based on the economic impacts of the budget? In other words, it may be that deliberate use of fiscal policy is rarely tried by the government.

The National Debt

One of the effects of fiscal policy that you may have noticed is that the government may not be able to stabilize the economy and balance the budget at the same time. Every time the government runs a deficit — spends more than it collects in taxes — the national debt goes up. The **national debt** is the outstanding government debt created when the government deficit spends. The national debt is also commonly referred to as the federal or public debt. How can the government spend more than it collects? Just as individuals can spend more than they earn, the government too can go into debt. The national debt is all the outstanding government bills, bonds, and notes issued by the U.S. Treasury and for the most part held by ordinary citizens, banks, or insurance companies.

The Keynesian view of the debt was that it should not be a problem. In the peak years of the business cycle, the government would run surpluses, while in trough times deficits would occur. Presumably these two would nearly balance out, and no substantial debt would accumulate.

In previous years all the debt seems to do is go up. Table 25-2 shows that there has not been a surplus or balanced budget between 1970 and 1998. The

Table 25-2   Federal Deficit and Surplus 1955–2005

Year	Surplus or Deficit Billions	Year	Surplus or Deficit Billions
1955	−$3.0	1981	−79.0
1956	3.9	1982	−128.0
1957	3.4	1983	−207.8
1958	−2.8	1984	−185.4
1959	−12.8	1985	−212.3
1960	.3	1986	−221.2
1961	−3.3	1987	−149.7
1962	−7.1	1988	−155.2
1963	−4.8	1989	−152.6
1964	−5.9	1990	−221.1
1965	−1.4	1991	−269.3
1966	−3.7	1992	−290.3
1967	−8.6	1993	−255.1
1968	−25.2	1994	−203.2
1969	3.2	1995	−164.0
1970	−2.8	1996	−107.5
1971	−23.0	1997	−21.9
1972	−23.4	1998	69.2
1973	−14.9	1999	125.5
1974	−6.1	2000	236.2
1975	−53.2	2001	128.2
1976	−73.7	2002	−157.8
1977	−53.7	2003	−377.6
1978	−59.2	2004	−412.1
1979	−40.7	2005	−426.6
1980	−73.8		

We can see that Federal spending has exceeded Federal revenues in every year from 1970 to 1997. The deficit resumed in 2002.

Source: *Economic Report of the President, 2005*. Found on the web at: http://www.gpoaccess.gov/eop. Used by permission.

size of the debt is frequently an important political issue. What do we mean by a large debt? How can we decide whether the debt is large or not? One measure is to compare the debt to GDP, our national income and ability to pay the debt. In Figure 25-2, you can see that the debt as a percentage of GDP has declined steadily from 1946 to 1981. That means that GDP has grown far faster than the debt. In the last few years, the debt as a percentage of GDP has started to

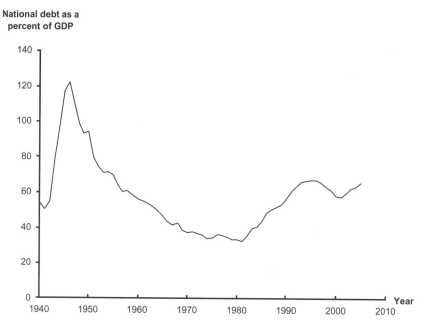

Figure 25-2   National Debt as a Percentage of GDP, 1940–2005
The national debt as a percentage of GDP reached its peak during World War II. Since that time until 1982, this percentage has fallen. In 1982 this percentage started to rise and is still growing. This graph shows that up to 1982, GDP has grown far faster than the government debt.
Source: *Economic Report of the President, 2005*. Found on the web at: http://www.gpoaccess. gov.eop/. Used by permission.

rise. Does this mean that we should worry? If we were not worried about the percentage of debt to GDP in the 1950s and 1960s when the percentage was higher than now, should we worry now?

The national debt is a measure of how much we as a nation have borrowed from ourselves. Some people are opposed to a debt in principle. Because it is called "debt," many people feel that a large national debt is bad. They commit the fallacy of composition in assuming that what they think is bad for them personally is also bad for the government. A more useful approach would be to weigh the costs and benefits of the public debt.

One benefit of the debt is that people hold the debt as a part of their savings. People holding the national debt chose this as the most desirable form of saving for them. The existence of a national debt provides a low-risk form of saving, as secure as the government itself.

Another benefit of increasing the debt is that higher levels of employment may be generated. For example, the national debt increased dramatically during World War II. Not only did the vast increase in government spending help win the war, it was the step needed to rescue us from the Great Depression. This increase in government spending was the solution proposed by Keynes, not done when and for the purpose that he recommended, but done later and for a noneconomic purpose. Yet the result was the same. The rapid increase in deficit spending was sufficient to increase aggregate demand and therefore the level of income, output, and employment to eliminate the depression completely, although not erasing it from the memory of those who agonized through it. If deficit spending can reduce unemployment and the associated personal and economic difficulties that accompany it, then this is to be considered a benefit of deficit spending and the national debt.

We are asking whether the benefits to society generated by a deficit are worth the cost of the deficit. In the case of World War II, the citizens of the United States almost unanimously supported the expenditure because the benefits of winning the war were far greater than the cost of the deficits. These choices are not always so easy to make. When faced with a high level of unemployment and no war, society cannot always find government expenditures that we would all agree are worth the cost of the deficit. The value of the various government programs depends on who is doing the evaluation. Some may find human service programs their first priority while others may strongly support national defense. Thus some do not favor extending human services, since the benefits are not perceived to be great enough, while others refuse to support more defense on the same grounds. It is not easy to calculate the benefits and costs when there is disagreement on the value of the programs. And unless agreements are reached by Congress, sufficient spending to end a recession will not be forthcoming.

Costs and Burdens of the Debt

One of the potential costs of the national debt is that the funds the government borrows have other uses. As a borrower of money, the government competes with the private sector for funds. When the government obtains these funds, they are spent on new goods for consumption by the society, such as for defense or roads. This removes the funds and the resources from the private sector. An increase in the national debt results in the production of more public goods at the expense of private goods. For those who favor a larger private sector, this aspect of the debt imposes costs.

The interest payment on the debt also imposes costs on society. The government obtains its funds for deficit spending from the sale of government securities. The incentive to purchase the securities is provided by the interest rate paid to the purchaser. Not only does the sale of these securities increase the national debt, but the interest payment due the owners of these securities becomes a part of government spending and an additional burden of the debt. There are two reasons why this interest payment may change. First is the size of the debt. The larger the debt, the larger the interest payment. The second reason is the interest rate. The higher the interest rate, the higher the interest payment. How does this interest payment compare to GDP? Figure 25-3 shows the interest payment as a percentage of GDP. Because of high interest rates in the late 1970s, the interest payment as a percentage of GDP increased. As interest rates fell in the 1990's, the interest payment as a percentage of GDP decreased.

Why should there be concern over the interest payment on the national debt? The immediate result of deficit spending is seen as interest rates are driven

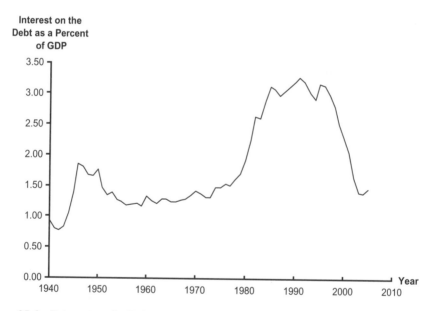

Figure 25-3   Interest on the Debt as a Percentage of GDP, 1940–2005
The interest on the debt has been a relatively small part of GDP. Since the 1970s, higher interest rates have caused the interest to become a larger part of GDP. As interest rates fell in the 1990's, so did the interest payments as a percentage of GDP.
Source: *Economic Report of the President, 2005*. Found on the web at: http://www.gpoaccess. gov/eop. Used by permission.

up as government competes for funds. Higher interest rates in turn choke off expansion in the construction and manufacturing industries and reduce business spending. This **crowding-out effect** reduces investment.

Another concern is that the interest payment is a part of government expenditure. The government, in bidding resources away from the private sector, drives up the interest rate and its own interest payment. So the greater the interest payment, the larger will be government spending, the larger will be the deficit, and the larger will be the debt. As the interest payment on the debt goes up, the government must spend less on other areas if it intends to not increase the deficit. Thus one concern over the national debt is that the interest payment may become a substantial portion of the federal budget and force the government to reduce other expenditures.

Who bears the burden of the debt? An increase in the debt stems from an increase in the government's role in the economy. Perhaps there is a war or some other crisis requiring government action. In effect, we are sliding along our production possibilities curve, producing more public goods and fewer private goods. Government borrowing does not shift the production possibilities outward. Thus the burden of the debt is paid by the current population because there are fewer private goods available for consumption and more of the current resources flow into the government sector. Yet not everyone would consider a larger government sector to be a burden.

But who will have to pay back the debt? The answer is future generations. We might think that by borrowing now and having our children or grandchildren pay it back is unfair to them. But what if they never pay it back? Our grandchildren borrow from their grandchildren. Still, the debt may have costs as well as benefits. Some grandchildren will pay taxes to pay the interest on the debt. Other grandchildren, who are holders of the debt, will receive those interest payments as income. Thus the debt may redistribute income within a future generation.

The size of the national debt is an important political issue. Yet there are few economic grounds for concern over the size of the debt alone. An economic evaluation of the debt requires a weighing of the benefits of the debt against its costs. Deficits have occurred and the benefits are socially desired outcomes such as roads or schools, increased employment, and a larger supply of securities for savings. These deficits also impose costs. For those who favor less government, the costs include the replacement of private investment by government spending, the increase in interest payments by government, and the increased role of the government in the economy.

▶ Summary

Fiscal policy involves the use of the governmental tools of spending and taxation in a deliberate attempt to stabilize the business cycle. Fiscal policy can be either expansionary to reduce unemployment or contractionary to reduce inflation. The principle of fiscal policy is that changes in government spending or taxation will directly change the level of aggregate demand and therefore the equilibrium level of income. An increase in government spending or a reduction in taxes increases aggregate demand and the level of income. A reduction in government spending or an increase in taxes lowers aggregate demand and the level of income.

One reason why full employment may seem so easy to obtain is that the model we have developed here is very simple. If we make the model more like the real world, the problem of controlling the level of income becomes even more difficult.

Politicians have been criticized for too enthusiastically following expansionary fiscal policy. It is too tempting to win votes with projects and concessions to the home voters. First and foremost, the federal budget is a budget, and there will be political difficulties involved in bending it to the purposes of achieving economic goals.

Now that we are ready to conclude this module, do you have the answer to our initial question in Chapter 20: Does capitalism need war for survival? It is not war that makes the business cycle boom, it is an increase in aggregate demand. Aggregate demand does increase with government wartime spending. But it is not necessary to fight a war to bring the economy to full employment. Aggregate demand could also be increased by additional government spending for purposes more beneficial than war. Keynes was correct in that a lack of aggregate demand was the cause of the Great Depression. The ability to control aggregate demand is essential in being able to control the equilibrium level of income. The use of fiscal policy is one solution to controlling aggregate demand and thus GDP. In the next module a second tool for stabilizing the economy, monetary policy, will be considered.

▶ Key Concepts

stabilization policy   balanced budget
fiscal policy   surplus budget
change in taxes   deficit budget

change in government spending   national debt

crowding-out effect

▶ Discussion Questions

1. What options does the government have for a contractionary fiscal policy?
2. How is the equilibrium level of income different from the full employment level of income? Explain.
3. Depending on the size of the inflow and the size of the outflow, what are possible outcomes for the federal budget?
4. If the government runs a deficit budget, what happens to the level of income? Explain. What did Keynes recommend for the Great Depression? Why would this have been an effective policy?
5. Fiscal policy can be used to reduce the fluctuations of the business cycle. What drawbacks are there to fiscal policy?
6. Uncle Effron is offended by the size of the national debt. He says if anyone, including business, ran a debt like that, they would be bankrupt, and that the government is in trouble because of the debt. Is he right? Why or why not?
7. How does the national debt affect interest rates and investment?
8. Look at Figure 25-2. For the period 1950-1980, which went up faster, GDP or the national debt?
9. Was war the only way out of the Great Depression?

▶ Self-Review

- Fill in the blanks

fiscal policy

president, Congress

spending

taxes

income, government spending

taxes

demand, decrease

increase

income

balanced

The use of the federal budget to stabilize the economy is _____. Fiscal policy is administered by the _____ and _____ and affects aggregate demand through the ability of the government to change government _____ and _____. To increase aggregate demand and the level of _____, increase _____ and/or lower _____. To decrease aggregate _____ and the level of income, _____ government spending and/or _____ taxes. The size of the _____ multiplier will also be important. When tax collections and government spending are equal, the budget is _____. When government collects more than it spends, we

surplus
more, deficit

national debt
deficit
costs, benefits

have a _____ budget. When government spends _____ than it collects, we have a _____ budget. The outstanding government debt is called the _____. The national debt is a result of _____ spending. As in any circumstance, there are both _____ and _____ associated with the national debt.

• Multiple choice

1. If the equilibrium level of employment is below full employment, you would expect:
   a. an increase in government expenditure.
   b. a decrease in government expenditure.
   c. a decrease in taxes.
   d. either a or c or both.

2. In an inflation period, the appropriate fiscal policy is to:
   a. increase government spending and increase taxes.
   b. increase government spending and decrease taxes.
   c. decrease government spending and increase taxes.
   d. decrease government spending and decrease taxes.

3. Suppose that the MPS is 1/5 and the equilibrium level of income is $200 below full employment. By how much should G change?
   a. $200.
   b. $1000.
   c. $40.
   d. $100.

4. A surplus budget means:
   a. tax collections equal government spending.
   b. tax collections are greater than government spending.
   c. tax collections are less than government spending.
   d. there is not enough information to tell.

5. The potential cost of a larger debt includes:
   a. the production of more public goods and fewer private goods.
   b. the large interest payments required by a large debt.
   c. the increase in interest rates and smaller investment that may occur.
   d. all of the above.

Answers: 1.d, 2.c, 3.c, 4.b, 5.d.

Module | 6 | MONEY

In the previous module, we saw how the level of income, the real gross domestic product, is determined. Yet nowhere in that discussion did we refer to money. This module will introduce money and show how money affects the level of income. You probably think that relating money to the level of income should be a simple matter. After all, to increase the level of income, we only need to have more money. While the conclusion is correct, the mechanism by which money affects the level of income is more roundabout. We will soon explain the process that links money and income. But by now you should suspect that money and income are two different things, and indeed they are. We will try to make that distinction clear in the next few chapters.

In the previous module, we indicated that the macro economy could be viewed as three interrelated markets. The first is the market for goods and services. We now know that this market consists of the aggregate demand and aggregate supply. Together, they determine the price level and level of output. The second market is the market for money. In this market, the demand and supply of money determine the price of money, which is the interest rate, and the quantity of money. The current module focuses on the money market. We will see how the money market affects the aggregate demand in the market for goods and services. The third market is the labor market, which is linked to the market for output. After completing this module, you will have seen how the three main macro markets work and how they are interrelated. This provides an understanding of how the macro economy works.

Money is a particularly slippery subject. We use money every day, but we rarely stop to think about why we have it or what it does for us. If we are to understand money and how it affects the level of income and prices, we must understand some basic issues. What is money? What services does money provide? Where does our money come from? And how does money affect income and prices? This module is particularly important since it will be devoted to that universal but little understood topic, money.

This module has the following order. We start Chapter 26 with a discussion of what money is and the role it plays. This chapter also explains how money can be created or destroyed. Chapter 27 contains a description of the Federal Reserve System, which is the central bank of the United States. We also discuss the tools and methods our central bank has for controlling the money supply. Chapter 28 links with material discussed in Module 4 and shows how money affects the level of income. The market for money plays a prominent role in this chapter. Chapter 28 summarizes how money can be used as a stabilizing force on the business cycle. The topic of money concludes our description of the macro economy begun in Chapter 17. We will apply the macro model to a discussion of stabilization policies in Chapter 29. There we will discuss the trade-off between unemployment and inflation, and the modern problem of stagflation, which is a combination of both unemployment and inflation. Chapter 29 also highlights some of the various schools of economic thought and indicates how these schools approach stagflation.

The next module will introduce the idea of trade. There we will discuss the significance of trade and the problems that some believe can occur with international trade. But for now we will concentrate on money. There can be little doubt that money is a popular topic. Much of our daily discussion revolves around money and income. It is time we develop a solid understanding of money and its relationship to income.

Chapter | 26 | MONEY

Key Topics

what is money
fractional reserves
the creation of money
the money multiplier

Goals

understand what money is
understand money creation and the multiple expansion process

Money, money, money. It may not be everything, but it keeps the world going around. You are in for a few surprises. Money isn't just what you think it is; however, money is what you think it is. Puzzled? Although we use money every day, we rarely think about it except when we wonder where it all went and how we can get more. Who creates money in our society? Certainly not the government. Is gold part of our money supply? Certainly not. How is money destroyed? Wait a minute! Destroy money? Well, just what is money, anyway?

First, let us see exactly what money is, what functions money performs, and what forms it takes. Then, how is money created? Remember that what is created can also be destroyed. We will follow the process of the creation and destruction of money.

What Is Money?

Money is by no means a modern concept. Every society eventually develops some form of money. Can you imagine cows as money? You can take them with you, but only with some inconvenience. And how do you make change for a cow? Obviously some goods perform better as money than others. How can money be recognized? Money has been gold, silver, coins, paper, beads, woodpecker scalps, nails, rocks, pelts, and even cigarettes. What is common among all these and many other varied forms of money? They all serve the same function, that of a medium of exchange.

Money as a medium of exchange replaces the **barter system**, that of one good being directly traded for another. What if, under a barter system, you wish to trade this economics textbook for a pizza? First, you must find someone who has the pizza that you want (with or without anchovies); second, that person must be willing to trade the pizza; third, the person must be willing to trade for an economics text; and, fourth, the person must be willing to trade for your particular economics text. Only if all these conditions are met will the barter be completed. A lot of time and effort will be used in finding this special set of circumstances.

The barter system is too clumsy to work efficiently. It fails to encourage and promote specialization in production by the individuals of a society. (We will see the advantages of specialization in Chapter 30.) The use of money as a medium of exchange streamlines and simplifies exchange. First, it is only necessary to find someone who wishes to buy the textbook. Then, cash in hand, find someone who wishes to sell your favorite pizza. All very neat and tidy. The condition that the textbook meets the approval of the pizza owner, and vice versa, is avoided.

A major function of money is that it serves as a medium of exchange. A **medium of exchange** is anything that can be used to buy goods and services. Why are you willing to accept money from someone? Because you know that someone else is willing to accept it from you. You and the pizza owner were confident that the money is "good," that it is capable of buying goods and services from someone else. Therefore it is acceptable. Money is acceptable in exchange and for payment of debt as long as everyone believes that it will continue to be accepted by someone else. When "money" is no longer acceptable in exchange, it no longer is money because it no longer serves as a medium of exchange. An item that fails to serve as a medium of exchange is not money because it does not perform one of the primary functions of money.

A second function of money is that it serves as a standard of value. A **standard of value** is a function of money that permits people to measure the values of different goods. Value is usually compared in terms of money. The value of this textbook is measured in money (both you and the bookstore agreed on this), and the value of the pizza is also measured in terms of money. The dollar is a common measurement of value in our society. Not all forms of money serve as a satisfactory measure of value. What if prices were announced in terms of cows? Since not all cows are the same, the price of a pizza might be different depending on which cows were offered.

Another function of money is that it serves as a store of value. A **store of value** allows people who have money now to spend it at a later time. For this reason there is no necessity to spend your money immediately; you may postpone spending it now and spend it sometime in the future. In this way money is a claim on future goods and services. Any form of money that holds its value over time could satisfy this function of money. Gold seems to hold its value well, but some goods do not. You might save a cow for a year or two. But what if your parents set aside a cow when you were born to pay for your college education?

Money also serves as a measure of debt. A debt is a promise to pay sometime in the future. And how is the amount of this debt measured? In money. **Measure of debt** is a function of money that records the amount of money to be paid in the future. If someone promises to pay back a loan in a year, you would like to be sure that you are being paid back what you are owed. If the debtor promises to pay you back in different cows, how can you be sure that you are getting paid enough? How can the debtor be sure not to pay too much?

Thus **money** serves as a medium of exchange and also functions as a standard of value, a store of value, and a measure of debt. Anything that is money performs these functions for a society.

What Counts as Money?

What serves as money in the United States? Ask someone to describe the money supply. They are sure to name coins and paper money. Paper money is also known as Federal Reserve notes since that is what is written across the top of each bill. Coins and the paper together are **currency**. Only currency that is in circulation counts as money. "In circulation" means in the hands of the general public, whether in a cookie jar or a cash register. Currency in a bank is not considered to be money. A bank embezzler therefore increases the money supply, at least until caught, because the currency in circulation is increased. Yet currency in circulation is only a small part of our total supply of money — less than a third. Most of our money supply is made up of demand deposits, what you call a checking account. A demand deposit is the bank's IOU. The bank owes the money to anyone holding a check drawn on the account. The check serves as a medium of exchange, making demand deposits money. We also count as money other checkable deposits on which checks can be written such as NOW accounts (negotiable order of withdrawal) at banks and savings and loans.

Because there are other forms of money, though less serviceable as a medium of exchange (such as passbook savings accounts, certificates of deposit, and marketable liquid Treasury obligations), economists are having difficulty defining and measuring the total money supply. What is counted as money depends on the ease with which the "money" can be spent. Consider passbook savings accounts. You cannot use your savings passbook to purchase a new car, but you can visit your bank and convert your passbook into — what? Why, currency or a check. So for our purposes, we will not consider savings accounts to be money. By our narrow definition, the **money supply** consists of currency in circulation and any checkable deposits. This is money narrowly defined, M1. M1 is our form of money serving readily as a medium of exchange. The broader definitions of money include those forms that primarily serve as a store of value. M2 is more broadly defined and adds savings deposits to the M1 forms of money. M3 includes certificates of deposit. There are more than a dozen classifications of money, but because M1 is the most widely used definition of money, all future references to the money supply will mean the M1 definition.

If you take a dollar to a bank and ask for what backs the dollar, you will get another paper dollar, or perhaps a silver dollar, or possibly 10 dimes, or 20 nickels, or even 100 pennies. These are all equivalent to the dollar you brought in. There is nothing behind the dollar but trust and faith. Money is not backed by gold or silver or anything. The worth of the dollar is only in what we can buy with it.

Fractional Reserves

There is a story that banks began when people with excess cash and wealth wanted to deposit these assets where they would be safe. The goldsmith had the facilities to keep his own gold safe and permitted others to deposit their assets, too. The enterprising goldsmith soon discovered that when a person deposited money, that money frequently stayed in the shop for some time. Further, when the depositor came to reclaim the money, the smith could give the depositor any similar coins of the same value, and the depositor would never know. Just as long as the smith had the money required, there would be no problem. These observations led the smith to realize that on any one day, he needed to have only a fraction of the total deposits on hand. There was rarely a call for a large part of the deposits at any one time. Soon the smith began to see the wisdom of lending out part of the deposits and holding the remainder for the depositors making withdrawals. Of course he would charge interest on the loans and so make some profit for himself.

Whether precisely true or not, this is a story of how the modern banking system got its start. The only problem was that sometimes the bank did not hold enough cash and its depositors would demand more than it had available. Since the bank had the remainder out on loan, it could not honor its depositors' claims. If all its depositors would demand their cash, the bank would be forced out of business, and the depositors would lose their assets. This behavior, together with some dishonest practices, led to the regulation of banks by the government.

Banks in the United States originally operated under state charter. It was not until the 1863 National Banking Act that the federal government began chartering banks. In 1913 the Federal Reserve Act established a central banking system. The Federal Reserve will be discussed in more detail later. For now it is enough to understand that the Federal Reserve requires banks to hold a certain fraction of their deposits in reserves. This is known as the fractional reserve system. A **fractional reserve system** requires that banks hold a percentage of their deposits as reserves. If banks were required to hold all deposits in reserve, then clearly they would have no money to loan out and would be unable to earn income themselves. Banks are permitted to make loans as long as a portion of the total deposits are held in reserve. Anything not held in reserve can be loaned out. Because of a fractional reserve system, banks can create money. They do not create paper money or coins, they create checking accounts. Since checking accounts are a part of the money supply, the banks create money. How do they do it?

The Creation of Money

Who creates and destroys money? Not the government as is commonly thought, but the commercial banking system. Any bank that accepts checkable deposits is a commercial bank. Commercial banks are privately owned and profit-seeking businesses. Money is created when banks make loans. Money is destroyed when loans are paid back. The process is as simple as that, but it requires further explanation. If you go to a bank and ask to see the money, you might be shown the money in the bank vault. This could be a substantial sum, but it is only a small part of the total money held by the bank. Banks have money that exists only in their books. This money is the list of accounts that they owe their depositors and must pay out when the depositor demands it by writing a check. Can these amounts really be money? When a depositor writes a check, the check serves as a medium of exchange and is therefore money. These checkable deposits are the major form of money that the bank holds.

When someone takes a loan from a bank, the bank records the borrower's name in its list of accounts and credits the individual with a checkable deposit of the amount of the loan. What did it cost the bank? Nothing. Well, maybe only a few bytes of memory. Are we certain that the checkable deposit of this newly created loan is money? Certainly, since checkable deposits are money and now checkable deposits and hence the money supply have increased. The borrower may now make a purchase with a check. Or the borrower may cash the check and take currency out of the vault instead. Now there is more currency in circulation than before. Whether the purchase is made by check or currency, money is created when banks make loans.

Banks are limited in their ability to create money. A reserve requirement is imposed by the Federal Reserve upon the deposits of a bank. The **reserve requirement** is the percentage of its deposits that a bank must keep on deposit with the Federal Reserve or as cash in the bank vault. The amount of its deposits that a bank is required to hold in reserve are **required reserves**. The bank cannot make loans with these required reserves. Any money that a bank has over and above its required reserves is its **excess reserves**. A bank is free to make loans with its excess reserves. If a bank does not have any excess reserves, it cannot legally make loans.

Let us apply the reserve requirement, required reserves, and excess reserves to an example to see the money creation process. Assume that Bank A has $1,000 in excess reserves. Suppose that all other banks have zero excess reserves, so that there is only $1,000 in excess reserves in the banking system. If the reserve requirement is 20 percent, this means that a bank must keep 20 percent of any new deposit in required reserves. The remaining amount of its new deposit is the excess reserves of the bank. Suppose that an aspiring tennis pro, Fred Fudge, comes to Bank A to get a $1,000 loan for new rackets. Since he is creditworthy, his request for a loan is granted. The bank opens a checkable deposit for Fred for $1,000. The money supply has gone up by $1,000. Why? There is an additional $1,000 checkable deposit in Bank A that did not exist before. Thus the money supply has increased by $1,000. Fred will spend the whole $1,000 with one check. What happens to the check? Fred takes it to the Plastic Sporting Goods Store and gives the check to the store in return for some rackets. The store deposits the check in Bank B. Note that Bank A now has no excess reserves left to loan and so the loan officer goes fishing. But the story has just begun.

Bank B must keep 20 percent of its new $1,000 deposit in required reserves, $200, but it is free to lend out the remaining $800 of new excess reserves. When the $800 is borrowed and spent, the process begins all over again. Suppose that Madeline applies to Bank B for a loan of $800 to buy a coat from the Fuzzy Coat Company. Bank B opens a checkable deposit for Madeline for $800. Madeline buys the coat and pays with a check. The coat store deposits the check in Bank C. Now Bank B has no excess reserves, and Bank B has added an additional $800 to the money supply.

What can Bank C do? It has a new deposit of $800, and it must keep 20 percent of that in reserve. Thus it must keep $160 in reserve and is free to loan out the remainder. Bank C now has $640 in excess reserves. Suppose that Sam comes into Bank C to borrow $640 for a deluxe electric fly swatter. Sam gets a checkable deposit for $640, and $640 is added to the money supply. The Fly Swatter Shoppe deposits Sam's check in its bank, Bank D. With the addition of $640 to the Fly Swatter Shoppe's checking account, the checkable deposits at Bank C decrease by $640. Deposits increase by $640 at Bank D. Bank D must keep 20 percent in reserve, but is free to loan out the excess reserves.

You can see that as each bank receives a new deposit through the loan process, the amount of excess reserves becomes 20 percent smaller. Sooner or later the excess reserves will approach zero, and the loan process must stop. The total addition to the money supply that this process is capable of generating is shown in Table 26-1. There is the $1,000 created when Bank A made the initial loan. Then there is the additional $800 loaned by Bank B. As more loans are made in the banking system, the money supply increases. A total of $2,440 has been created by banks A, B, and C. The next bank will bring the total to $2,952. How much will the total addition to the money supply be? The answer is $5,000.

The Money Multiplier

Notice that any one individual bank can only create money up to the amount of its excess reserves. But notice that something very different happens when you observe not a single bank but the banking system as a whole. All banks

Table 26-1   Multiple Expansion of the Money Supply

Bank	Deposits	Required Reserves	Excess Reserves
A			$1,000
B	$1,000	$200	800
C	800	160	640
D	640	128	512
Other banks			
summed	2,560	512	2,048
Total	$5,000	$1,000	

Bank A has $1,000 in excess reserves. The money supply increases by $1,000 when Bank A opens
a $1,000 checkable deposit to make a loan. The $1,000 is spent and is deposited in Bank B. This
$1,000 deposit is shown in the deposit column. Bank B now has $800 in excess reserves (the reserve
requirement is 20 percent). Again the money supply goes up, now by $800 when Bank B opens
a $800 checkable deposit to make a loan. The $800 is spent and the deposit is shown in Bank
C. The process continues until there are no excess reserves to loan out. The total increase in the
money supply will be $5,000, which is found by taking the money multiplier times the initial excess
reserves, 5 × $1,000 = $5,000.

together can create money because when a loan is made, the excess reserves
of one bank are redeposited, and a portion becomes excess reserves for another
bank. What is a decrease in reserves for one bank becomes an increase for
another. As money is loaned from one bank and flows into another bank and
the process is repeated again and again, the banking system as a whole can
multiply the original excess reserves by five times, as in Table 26-1. This is a
multiplier process similar to that in Chapter 23. In this situation, though, we
call it the money, or deposit, multiplier.

The potential change in the money supply can be found by taking the
reciprocal of the reserve requirement and multiplying by the initial excess
reserves. Since 20 percent is the same as 1/5, the reciprocal of 20 percent is
5. The change in the money supply is five times the initial excess reserves
of $1,000, or $5,000. This is the money multiplier formula. The change in
the money supply is the reciprocal of the reserve requirement times the initial
excess reserves.

With the **money multiplier**, any initial change in bank excess reserves will
result in a multiple change to the total money supply. The money multiplier
is the reciprocal of the reserve requirement. This money multiplier process
can be summarized as follows. Start with the initial excess reserves. To find
excess reserves, subtract required reserves (which are deposits times the reserve
requirement) from the reserves. The excess reserves can all be loaned out.

These dollars will eventually be deposited in a bank. That bank is required to hold part of the deposit as reserves but can loan out the rest. It can loan out the deposit minus the reserves required for that deposit. Each round generates more loans and more demand deposits. This is the money multiplier process. The size of the money multiplier is found by taking the reciprocal of the reserve requirement, in this case 20 percent or 1/5, for a multiplier of 5. The end result is that the total money supply has expanded by $5,000, or five times the initial $1,000 in excess reserves.

How does the reserve requirement determine the size of the money multiplier? The required reserves are the amount of a new deposit that *cannot* be loaned out, spent, and then redeposited to continue the effect of the money multiplier. Eventually, the $1,000 in excess reserves leaks into and becomes the $1,000 total of required reserves in Table 26-1. Then there are no more excess reserves to continue the next round of money creation. But, eventually, each dollar of the original $1,000 in excess reserves supports $5 of new checkable deposits.

When the banking system experiences an initial change in reserves, the resulting excess reserves are available for lending. The lending by one bank creates more money because the bank creates a checkable deposit when the loan is made. The checkable deposit is money. When the loan is spent, this spending is deposited in another bank. This deposit becomes reserves that will support more loans, and the process continues. What happens when loans are paid back? If money is created when banks make loans, money is destroyed when loans are paid back. When loans are paid back, deposits are in effect reduced in one bank to pay off the loan in another bank, and this process is repeated from bank to bank. The total amount of deposits is reduced in the banking system, and the total amount of the money supply is reduced. Thus the money multiplier also works in reverse to cause a multiple contraction of the money supply. It does not matter whether the change in the excess reserves was positive or negative; the money supply will change in either case. If there are positive excess reserves, then the money supply will increase, while if the excess reserves are negative, the money supply will decrease, always by a multiple amount.

The effect of an increase in excess reserves is that it makes it possible for the money supply to expand. But successful efforts to change the money supply by changing excess reserves requires that people come to the bank to get loans. If there is no demand for loans, the excess reserves will not cause the money supply to increase. Further, if in the multiple expansion process some of the money is not redeposited in a bank but is held in cash, the multiple expansion will not continue for the money held as cash. Thus the change in the money supply will be affected by the amount of money that leaks out of the process into cash holdings. The money multiplier process provides an upper limit on the increase in the money supply. This upper limit depends on the initial excess reserves and the reserve requirement. In our example, with excess reserves of $1,000 and a reserve requirement of 20 percent, no more than $5,000 could be created by the banking system. Of course, less than $5,000 will be created if not all excess reserves are borrowed or there are cash leakages.

Control of the money supply requires the ability to increase excess reserves or decrease excess reserves. In the next chapter you will see how excess reserves can be changed so that the money supply can be controlled. You may be surprised to know that nearly every day some effort may be made to change the excess reserves in the banking system.

▶ Summary

A way to think of money is in terms of the functions it provides. Money is a medium of exchange, a store of value, a standard of value, and a measure of debt. The M1 definition of money is currency in circulation plus all checkable deposits. A large part of the money supply is created by the multiple expansion of bank deposits. A fractional reserve banking system makes possible this multiple expansion process. When one bank makes a loan of its excess reserves, the money is eventually deposited in another bank. That bank is required to keep only a portion of that deposit on reserve and can loan out the remainder. This process generates a multiple expansion of the money supply. This money multiplier is the change in bank deposits that can be generated by a dollar of initial excess reserves, and is the reciprocal of the reserve requirement.

The ability of banks to create money is limited by the Federal Reserve. The reserve requirement provides one mechanism for controlling the size of the money supply. The limitation of the money supply keeps money scarce and maintains its value. The tools that control the money supply will be the topic covered in the next chapter.

▶ Key Concepts

barter system
medium of exchange

money supply
fractional reserve system

standard of value

store of value

measure of debt

money

currency

reserve requirement

required reserves

excess reserves

money multiplier

▶ Discussion Questions

1. "Time is money." By avoiding barter, what scarce commodity does money make less scarce?
2. If someone were to say that money is only a figment of your imagination, would you tend to agree or disagree? Why? What makes money valuable? What backs money?
3. Explain why tomatoes would not make a good money.
4. Cigarettes served as money in World War II prisoner-of-war camps. Can you describe how cigarettes could serve the functions of money?
5. Can money satisfactorily perform the functions of money during a hyperinflation?
6. Which of the following would be counted as part of the M1 money supply?
   a. coins in a piggy bank
   b. U.S. savings bonds
   c. $10 in Fred's checking account
   d. a roll of dimes in the bank vault
   e. $50 in Elsie's passbook savings account
7. Uncle Effron says that banks do not create money. Explain to Uncle Effron the money creation process.
8. What if there were a 100 percent reserve requirement. What would the money multiplier be? How would this affect the multiple expansion process?
9. Suppose that Bank X has $100 in deposits, reserves of $20, and the reserve requirement is 10 percent.
   a. How much are required reserves?
   b. How much excess reserves does the bank have?
   c. How much can the bank loan out?
   d. By how much will Bank X increase the money supply?
   e. By how much will the banking system increase the money supply?

▶ Self-Review

- Fill in the blanks

barter
medium of exchange

standard of value

store of value
measure of debt
circulation

demand

M1

fractional
banks

reserve requirement

required reserves

excess reserves
excess reserves

money multiplier
reserve requirement

The trading of one good directly for another is known as _____. Money replaces the barter system since money serves as a _____. When money measures the values of different goods, it serves as a _____. Money also permits spending to be postponed to the future as a _____, and records the amount to be paid back in the future as a _____. The money supply consists of currency in _____ and checkable deposits. Checkable deposits are _____ deposits and other accounts on which checks can be written. This is the narrow definition of money known as _____. Banks must hold a fraction of their deposits in reserve and thus operate under a _____ reserve system. Money is created and destroyed by commercial _____. The percentage of its deposits that a bank must keep in reserve is the _____. The amount of its deposits that a bank is required to hold in reserve is the _____. Any money that a bank has over and above its required reserves is its _____. To create money, a bank must have _____. A change in excess reserves can cause a multiple change to the total money supply by the _____. The money multiplier is the reciprocal of the _____.

• Multiple choice

1. A medium of exchange:
   a. is anything that can be used to buy goods and services.
   b. is essential to a barter system.
   c. is used instead of money.
   d. all of the above.
2. When we compare two goods in terms of price, money is performing its function as a:
   a. medium of exchange.
   b. store of value.
   c. standard of value.
   d. standard of deferred payment.

3. The M2 definition of money adds _____ to M1.
   a. certificates of deposit
   b. savings deposits
   c. $10,000 bills
   d. nothing
4. When a bank with excess reserves makes a loan, the money supply increases because:
   a. the loan is part of the money supply.
   b. the bank sets up a checkable deposit for the amount of the loan, and checkable deposits are part of the money supply.
   c. the bank prints money to give to the loan customer.
   d. the loan makes money productive.
5. If the money multiplier is 4, the reserve requirement must be:
   a. 10 percent.
   b. 15 percent.
   c. 20 percent.
   d. 25 percent.

Answers: 1.a, 2.c, 3.b, 4.b, 5.d.

Chapter | 27 | MONETARY TOOLS

Key Topics

the Federal Reserve System

tools of the Fed

Goals

introduce the Federal Reserve System

develop the tools needed to control the money supply

understand how the tools can be used to control the money supply

The commercial banking system alone has the ability to create and destroy money. This ability in turn is regulated by the government. Consequently, money becomes an economic tool for regulation of the business cycle. You will discover the use of money as an economic tool in this chapter and the next. Here, we will investigate the powers of the Federal Reserve System. The Federal Reserve affects the money supply essentially by use of the reserve requirement, the discount rate, and open market operations. These three major tools of the Federal Reserve are discussed in this chapter. Two of the three tools affect the size of the money supply by altering the amount of excess reserves in the banking system. The third tool has an indirect impact on the money supply by acting as a signal of the Fed's desires and intentions. When we refer to the "Fed," we mean the Federal Reserve, not the FBI. But to some, the Federal Reserve is at least as mysterious and powerful as the FBI.

The Federal Reserve System

The Federal Reserve System was established by Congress in 1913 to bring stability to the banking industry. When the Fed was established, it was hoped that it could prevent or at least reduce the impact of financial panic and bank failures. But if the Great Depression was a test of the ability of the Fed to achieve those goals, the Fed was a failure. Since the depression, the banking industry has changed, and the job of the Fed has changed, too. Its primary function now is to control the money supply. The Federal Reserve also has other roles, which include operating a check clearinghouse, regulating and overseeing commercial banks and bank-like institutions, providing currency, and serving as banker for both government and commercial banks.

The Federal Reserve is a central bank, but, unlike the central banks of most governments, it is independent of the administration and Congress. That means that the Fed can act in the way it believes best obtains economic stability. The Federal Reserve operates on three levels. There is the administering Board of Governors, the 12 Federal Reserve district banks, and the commercial member banks.

The Board of Governors is made up of seven members. Each is appointed to a 14-year term by the president of the United States, subject to the approval of the Senate. The term is as long as it is in order to isolate the Board from political pressures. The term is nonrenewable, so that an individual appointed to the Board need not be concerned with cultivating political favor to gain reappointment. The terms are staggered, so that one governor is appointed every two years. The president appoints the chairman of the Board of Governors. The Board's job is to oversee the operations of the Fed and to set policy. One of the more important committees responsible to the Board of Governors is the Federal Open Market Committee. The Open Market Committee is made up of the seven Board members plus five of the district bank presidents. This committee is responsible for open market operations. We will have much to say about open market operations in this chapter.

Most actual operations of the Fed are carried out by the district banks. The Federal Reserve Act of 1913 divides the country into 12 districts and establishes a district bank in each. Figure 27-1 shows the district boundaries and the corresponding district banks. Each district bank carries out the policy directives of the Board of Governors. The New York Federal Reserve Bank has the added responsibility of carrying out open market operations under the direction of the Open Market Committee. The banks that are members of the Fed are shareholders in their district bank. Which banks are member banks? Only commercial banks. Yet not all commercial banks belong to the Fed. Only those banks with a federal charter, usually identified with a "national" or "federal" in their name — about twenty-five percent of all banks —

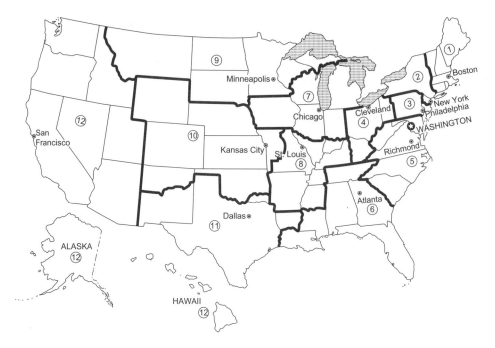

Figure 27-1   Federal Reserve Districts
There are 12 Federal Reserve districts, each with a district bank.
Source: *Federal Reserve Bulletin.* Used by permission.

are required to join the Federal Reserve System. State chartered banks are given a choice. Of the 7,700 banks, less than 2,900 belong to the Fed. Yet this minority of banks are the largest banks and control a large part of total bank reserves.

Since 1980, the Fed has had authority over any institution that offers a checkable deposit. This authority extends beyond the membership of the Fed to all banks and bank-like institutions such as savings and loans and credit unions. The fact that the Fed has the power to regulate all of these institutions means that it has better control of the money supply than it had before 1980.

Our interest in the Federal Reserve is in its ability to regulate the money supply through the banking system, so we will concentrate on this specific power of the Fed. The Fed has three tools for this purpose. First is the reserve requirement, second is the discount rate, and third is open market operations. We will discuss each of these starting with the reserve requirement.

Changing the Reserve Requirement

A rarely used but extremely powerful tool of the Federal Reserve is its ability to change the reserve requirement. The reserve requirement is the percentage of their deposits that banks must keep in reserves. The reserve requirement was introduced in the last chapter; now we see that the Fed determines its size. The required reserves cannot be loaned. These reserves must be in the bank's own vault or on deposit in the district bank of the Federal Reserve System.

What is the impact of a reduction in the reserve requirement? Banks immediately have more excess reserves. Any reduction in the reserve requirement means that a smaller percentage of their deposits must be held as reserves. Some reserves that were once required now automatically become excess reserves. As these excess reserves are loaned out, money is created, and the money multiplier process is initiated. We see that decreasing the reserve requirement increases the money supply.

And what is the impact of an increase in the reserve requirement? When the reserve requirement is increased, an increased percentage of the bank's deposits must be held in reserve. This means that some money that once would have been excess reserves instead becomes required reserves. The ability of banks to loan money is reduced and the rate of growth of the money supply is restricted.

When the reserve requirement changes, not only are excess reserves affected, but the size of the money multiplier is also changed. Since the money multiplier is the reciprocal of the reserve requirement, a reduction in the reserve requirement increases the size of the money multiplier. If the reserve requirement falls from 20 percent to 10 percent, the multiplier increases from 5 to 10. If the reserve requirement is increased, the money multiplier falls. Thus there are two effects associated with changing the reserve requirement. If, for example, the reserve requirement is reduced, the amount of required reserves falls, causing excess reserves to increase; but in addition, the money multiplier increases, so that any additional excess reserves will generate a greater amount of additional money. Even small changes in the reserve requirement will have a substantial effect on the banking industry and the money supply. You can see why the Fed rarely applies a change in the reserve requirement. The Fed has no desire to shock the economy and possibly send it into a recession. Consequently, the Fed will more frequently resort to other tools. The discount rate and open market operations have a less dramatic effect on the money supply but are still capable of achieving the monetary goals of the Fed.

Discount Rate Policy

Another tool available to the Fed is the discount rate. This tool is not as powerful as a change in the reserve requirement. The **discount rate** is the interest rate that banks pay on money borrowed from the Federal Reserve System. The discount rate obtained its name from the method used by the Fed of discounting the interest in advance. For example, when a commercial bank borrows $100 discounted at 10 percent interest, the commercial bank receives $90 and must pay back $100. This borrowing from the Fed is considered to be a privilege and not a right, and the Fed can reject a bank's request to borrow. Banks are encouraged to borrow from other banks before resorting to borrowing from the Fed.

What impact does a change in the discount rate have on the money supply? The main impact is as a signal of the intentions of the Federal Reserve System. If the Fed wishes to discourage borrowing, it has the option of raising the discount rate, which makes it more expensive for commercial banks to borrow. An increase in the discount rate sends a signal to the banks that they should not let their excess reserves fall so far that they might have to borrow from the Fed. Banks become more careful about making loans and the impact of the money multiplier is reduced. Every dollar left in excess reserves means fewer dollars created by the banking system. If, however, the Fed wants to encourage banks to become more aggressive in making loans and creating money, the discount rate is lowered. The Fed is signaling the member banks that it is acceptable to borrow if necessary.

However, banks tend to prefer borrowing from one another than to draw attention upon themselves by borrowing from the Fed. The interest rate that banks charge one another for overnight borrowing is called the federal funds rate. An immediate objective of the Fed is to use monetary policy to change the federal funds rate.

Do not confuse the discount rate, which the Fed charges its commercial banks for borrowing, with the prime rate, the interest rate that the commercial banks charge their favored borrowers. Large corporations such as General Motors carry less risk as a borrower than do you or I and therefore are charged a lower interest rate, the prime rate. In the next chapter we will see that the federal funds rate, the prime rate, and other rates in turn will be affected by the actions of the Fed, including its use of the discount rate.

Open Market Operations

The tool used most frequently by the Federal Reserve to change the money supply is open market operations. Open market operations are under the control of the Federal Open Market Committee, an advisory committee to the Board of Governors. This committee meets about once a month and recommends an open market policy. What is an open market operation, and how does it affect the money supply? An **open market operation** is the purchase or sale of negotiable government securities in the open market by the Federal Reserve. The **open market** is the exchange where federal government securities are traded, just like the stock market. Negotiable means that anyone can buy and sell these government securities, just like a stock. The government securities have been issued by the U.S. Treasury and include Treasury bills, bonds, and notes. You may recognize that these are the securities that make up the national debt. The only part of the national debt that is not negotiable is U.S. savings bonds. Savings bonds cannot be sold to someone else but must be redeemed by the owner or the estate of the deceased owner. The other securities are negotiable and are traded on the open market. We will simply refer to these negotiable securities as bonds.

Anyone may buy or sell government bonds on the open market, including private citizens and businesses (remember that banks are businesses) as well as the Fed. And we know that any time excess reserves enter the banking system, there may be a multiple expansion of the money supply. An open market operation will generate excess reserves. Here is how: when the Fed decides to *buy* on the open market, the Fed receives the bond and increases bank reserves in exchange. The Fed pays by a check drawn on itself. If the bonds are purchased from an individual, the individual gives up the bonds and receives the Fed's check in return. Eventually, the check is deposited in a bank, and the bank has new reserves, some of which are excess reserves. Now the banking system can begin the multiple expansion process. There is also the same change in the money supply if the Fed purchases the bonds from a bank. Then the bank receives a check in exchange for its bonds. The bank presents the check to the Fed and now has more reserves. Thus the bank has exchanged the government bond for reserves. These reserves are all excess reserves, and the multiple expansion process begins.

Recognize that the Fed's check is not money. The Fed cannot create money — only commercial banks can. The Fed is increasing excess reserves in the banking system. And when the banks make loans, money is created.

If the Fed decides to slow down the rate of growth of money, the Fed will *sell* in the open market. When the Fed sells in the open market, then the individuals or businesses get the bonds and the Fed gets the money. The Fed releases the bond in exchange for a check. The check is drawn from a bank and results in a fall in bank reserves and a multiple contraction of the total money supply. The money used to pay for the bonds comes out of bank reserves. If the banks have no excess reserves, they will have to reduce loans, and thus the money supply. So open market operations can be used to control excess reserves and eventually the size of the money supply. When the Fed buys in the open market, it in effect pumps up bank reserves; when the Fed sells in the open market, it skims off bank reserves. The purchase and sale of government bonds by the Federal Reserve System through the open market is an effective way for the Fed to regulate the money supply.

Bond Prices and Interest Rates

You might wonder how the Fed is able to buy and sell bonds if no one is willing to sell or buy from the Fed. The key to the success of the Fed in the open market is that there is an inverse relationship between bond prices and interest rates. When bond prices go up, the effective, or actual, interest rate goes down. The reason is that there is a difference between the face value of the bond — what is printed on it — and the actual price of the bond determined by the interaction of supply and demand in the open market. Also, there is a difference between the interest rate printed on the bond and the effective rate of interest — the yield — on the money actually spent on the bond.

What if, for example, a bond has a face value of $100 at a 5 percent rate of interest? Then whoever owns the bond receives $5 per year, which is 5 percent of $100. The face value and interest rate printed on the bond determine what the owner will receive in interest. But the real price of the bond and the effective interest rate may be different from what is printed on the bond. What if the owner had paid only $50 for the bond? The owner still receives $5 per year, but $5 is 10 percent of the $50 price paid for the bond, for an effective interest rate of 10 percent. If the same bond had been purchased

Table 27-1   Monetary Tools

	More $	Fewer $
Reserve Requirement	lower	raise
Discount Rate	lower	raise
Open Market Operation	buy	sell

This table show how the monetary tools can be applied and their effect on the money supply.

for $500, again the owner would receive $5 a year. But $5 is only 1 percent of the $500 spent. The bond price is higher, but the effective interest rate is lower, just as when the bond price was lower, the effective interest rate was higher. So we see that there is an inverse relation between bond prices and interest rates.

When the Fed chooses to buy in the open market, how do we know there will be sellers? When the Fed buys in the open market, the number of buyers is increased. The increase in the number of buyers increases the market demand for the bonds and drives up the competitive price. At higher prices, and consequently lower interest rates, the Fed will find ready sellers. When the Fed chooses to sell in the open market, how do we know there will be buyers? As the Fed dumps bonds in the market, the supply of bonds increases, and the price is driven down. The lower price means higher effective interest rates. Higher interest rates increase the incentive for investors to purchase. Whether the Fed is buying or selling in the open market, its actions automatically obtain cooperation from the public through the effects on bond prices and interest rates.

The rule for open market operations is this: the Open Market Committee buys bonds to increase the money supply and sells bonds to decrease the money supply. This tool is the most frequently used and flexible tool of the Federal Reserve System. The Fed can change from buy one day, to sell the next. Even the amount can be easily varied in the open market to speed up or slow down the Fed's policies. The final control over the money supply rests with the Federal Reserve System.

The monetary tools are summarized in Table 27-1. We have seen that the use of the reserve requirement, the discount rate, and open market operations provide the Federal Reserve with the means of regulating the growth of the money supply. The next chapter establishes why it is so important that there be control over the ability of banks to create and destroy money.

▶ Summary

The Federal Reserve is the central bank of the United States. It is composed of a Board of Governors, 12 district banks, and the member banks. The Fed controls the money supply.

The three major tools employed by the Federal Reserve to control the money supply are the reserve requirement, the discount rate, and open market operations. A change in the reserve requirement is rarely used because it has rather substantial impacts on the money supply and indicates a dramatic shift in Federal Reserve policy. The discount rate is largely used to signal the intentions of the Fed. The most flexible and frequently used tool is open market operations. This tool is used on a monthly basis and can be used to increase or decrease the growth of the money supply.

These monetary tools of the Fed — changes in the reserve requirement, the discount rate, and open market operations — can be applied to the regulation of the money supply and the business cycle. But first we must establish the connection between the money supply and the level of income. In the next chapter we will discuss how changes in the money supply affect the level of income. The fact that money can be used to alter the business cycle means that the Federal Reserve administers an important economic tool, monetary policy. That is also the subject of the next chapter.

▶ Key Concepts

Federal Reserve
reserve requirement
discount rate
open market operation
open market

▶ Discussion Questions

1. What are the monetary tools of the Federal Reserve?
2. How does changing the reserve requirement affect the money supply?
3. What is the discount rate? How do changes in the discount rate signal the intentions of the Fed?
4. Uncle Effron says that open market operations have no effect on the money supply. After all, the Fed and someone merely exchange bonds and money. How can excess reserves change? Explain to Uncle Effron.

5. Suppose that Bank X has $100 in deposits, reserves of $10, and the reserve requirement is 10 percent. Suppose that now the Fed buys a $100 bond from the bank.
   a. What happens to reserves?
   b. What happens to excess reserves?
   c. How much can the bank loan out?
   d. What will be the total increase in the money supply?
6. How can the Fed be sure that it can buy or sell bonds when it wants? Explain.

▶ **Self-Review**

• Fill in the blanks

Federal Reserve	Our money supply is controlled by the _____ System. The Federal Reserve is administered by its Board of
Governors	_____. The major monetary tools
reserve requirement	of the Fed are the _____,
discount rate	the _____, and
open market operations	_____. Decreasing
increases	the reserve requirement _____ the money supply. An increase in the reserve requirement
decreases	_____ the money supply. A change in the reserve requirement also changes the size of
money	the _____ multiplier. The interest rate banks pay on money borrowed from the Fed is the
discount rate	_____. An expansion in the money
reduction	supply can be encouraged by a _____ in the discount rate, while a contraction in the money
increase	supply can be encouraged by an _____ in the discount rate. Negotiable government securities
open market	are traded in the _____. A purchase or sale by the Fed in the open market is called an
open market operation	_____. To increase the
buy	money supply, the Fed will _____ in the open market. To reduce the growth of money, the Fed will
sell	_____ in the open market. The inverse relation
interest rates	between bond prices and _____ assists the Fed in achieving its open market objectives.

- **Multiple choice**

1. Changing the discount rate means that the:
   a. banks change the interest rate they charge their best customers.
   b. banks change the interest rate they charge on home mortgages.
   c. Fed changes the interest rate it charges its member banks to borrow.
   d. Fed changes the reserve requirement.
2. If the Fed wished to increase the money supply by $500 and the reserve requirement was 20 percent, it would have to provide excess reserves of:
   a. $10.
   b. $100.
   c. $5.
   d. $1000.
3. If the Fed wants to increase the money supply, it should:
   a. buy bonds in the open market.
   b. sell bonds in the open market.
   c. raise the reserve requirement.
   d. raise the discount rate.
4. The Federal Reserve is:
   a. a commercial bank.
   b. a central bank.
   c. a public bank.
   d. not a bank.
5. A decrease in the reserve requirement:
   a. means more reserves must be held.
   b. means some money held as excess reserves become required reserves.
   c. increases the money multiplier.
   d. all of the above.

Answers: 1.c, 2.b, 3.a, 4.b, 5.c.

Chapter | 28 | MONEY AND THE LEVEL OF INCOME

Key Topics

the money market
money and income
the link from money to income
monetary policy
evaluation of monetary policy

Goals

recognize the difference between money and income
understand the impact of changes in the money supply on the interest rate
understand how money affects the level of income
evaluate monetary policy

All this talk about money, and we still have not seen how money affects the level of income. This chapter establishes the link between money and the level of national income. We will start with a discussion of the demand for money. Then we will review our work on the money supply. By putting money demand and money supply together, we will determine the interest rate. The interest rate will determine the level of investment. And investment, as we know, affects the level of income. This linkage is important because it allows us to understand how changes in the money supply affect the level of income. We will then see how the Federal Reserve's ability to control the money supply can be used to change the level of income. The result will be monetary policy, another stabilization policy tool in addition to fiscal policy. Your own employment possibilities and the purchasing power of your money will be affected by the actions of the Federal Reserve on the business cycle.

The Money Market

We are about to discuss the market for money. Since there is a demand for money and a supply of money, there is a market for money. The market for money determines both the price and the quantity of money. In this case the price of money is the interest rate, and the quantity of money is the money supply.

Why do people demand or hold money? People hold money because they expect to spend it. Holding money means having the money in currency or in a checkable deposit. What is the alternative to holding money? Money can be converted into interest-earning assets, such as bonds. But money in bonds is not so easily spent. So why do people hold bonds? The basic reason is that they want to earn interest on the money that they do not intend to spend soon. They want to earn interest on their savings. The main motivation for holding bonds is to earn more interest than a checkable deposit pays, interest sacrificed by holding money. When the interest rate is high, you would expect people to hold more bonds and less money. The opportunity cost of holding money, the forgone interest, is now high. But if the interest rate is low, you would expect people to hold fewer bonds and more money.

The opportunity cost of holding money is the sacrificed interest from interest-earning assets. Thus we should expect the quantity of money demanded to vary inversely with the interest rate. When the interest rate is high, the quantity of money demanded will be low. When the interest rate is low, the quantity of money demanded will be high. This relationship is shown in Figure 28-1, where the interest rate is measured on the vertical axis and the quantity of money is measured on the horizontal axis. You can see that as the interest rate rises, the quantity demanded falls, and the quantity demanded rises as the interest rate falls. The amount of money people hold varies inversely with the interest rate.

We have now established the demand for money. **Money demand** tells how much money people will hold in currency and checkable deposits at each interest rate. What about the supply of money? The money supply is the M1 definition and is controlled by the Federal Reserve. As you saw in the last chapter, the money supply can be altered by changing excess reserves. To summarize what we learned there, the money supply can be expanded or contracted by the reserve requirement, the discount rate, or open market operations. The size of the money supply did not vary with the interest rate. We will consider the relation between the money supply and interest rate to be constant and to look as shown in Figure 28-2. The money supply does not change when the interest rate changes.

Now we can put the money supply and money demand together to form the money market. This is done in Figure 28-3. Here the price of money — the rate of interest — is determined. Where is the equilibrium interest rate? If you said at i_e, the intersection of money supply and money demand, you would be

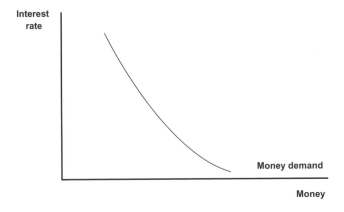

Figure 28-1   Money Demand
The amount of money that people hold depends on the interest rate. At a higher rate of interest, people would rather hold more interest-bearing assets. At a lower rate of interest, more money will be held.

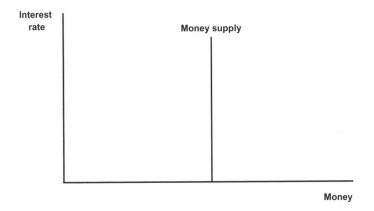

Figure 28-2   Money Supply
In our discussion, the money supply does not depend on the interest rate. Therefore, the money supply will be vertical at a level determined by the Federal Reserve.

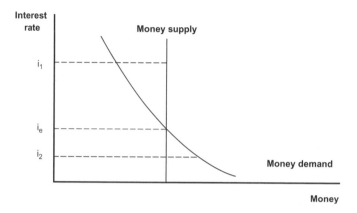

Figure 28-3   Money Market
Interest rate i_1 causes a surplus of money, and the interest rate falls to i_e. At i_2 there is a shortage of money, and the interest rate rises to i_e. Equilibrium will occur at the intersection of money demand and money supply at i_e. This market determines the interest rate.

correct. But why is this true? Suppose that the interest rate were at i_1 above the equilibrium rate. What would happen? The amount of money supplied is greater than the amount of money people want to hold in currency or in their checking deposits. People will try to buy the high-interest bonds and, as a result, increase their price. Recall from the last chapter that the interest rate on bonds is inversely related to the price of bonds. When the price of bonds rises, this means that the interest rate must fall. So any time the interest rate is above the equilibrium rate, there will be a force that pushes the interest rate down.

What happens when the interest rate is at i_2 below the equilibrium rate? Then there is an excess demand for money. This means that people do not want to hold bonds and are trying to sell them. But the only way they can get others to hold the bonds is to lower the price of the bonds. Thus the interest rate rises. Whenever the interest rate is below the equilibrium rate, the market will cause the interest rate to rise.

The money market works just like any other market. We can think of money as just another good, such as popcorn, baby rattles, or bottle brushes, with its own supply and demand. But of course money is not just any other good; it is a good that serves as a medium of exchange, a standard of value, a store of value, and a measure of debt.

Now we can understand what happens to interest rates when the Federal Reserve changes the size of the money supply. If the Fed increases the money supply, the money supply curve will shift to the right as shown in Figure 28-4. This causes the equilibrium interest rate to fall. If the Fed decreases the money supply, the money supply curve will shift to the left as shown in Figure 28-5, and this causes the equilibrium interest rate to rise. One impact of changes in the size of the money supply is on the interest rate. Changes in the money supply will also ultimately affect the level of income. But first we should understand that there is a difference between money and income.

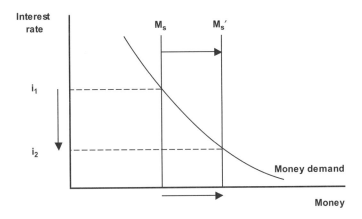

Figure 28-4   Increase in the Money Supply
When the Fed acts to increase the money supply, the interest rate falls.

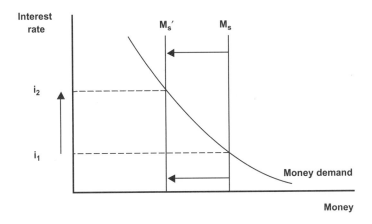

Figure 28-5   Decrease in the Money Supply
When the Fed acts to decrease the money supply, the interest rate rises.

Money and Income

Economists carefully distinguish between the concepts of money and income. They are not the same thing. If you are to understand how money affects income, you must understand the difference. The problem is that in everyday language, money and income are used almost interchangeably. And worse yet, we measure income in money terms. But they have different meanings for an economist. Your income is a measure of what you could buy with what you earn. For the society, income is gross domestic product. Money, on the other hand, is checkable deposits and currency in circulation. We frequently say that the reason we do not do something, like buy a new Porsche, is because we do not have enough money. But there is plenty of money; the real problem is that we did not have enough income.

To see the difference between money and income, consider a fully employed world where the only difference from the current one is that everyone has twice as much money. Would everyone be able to buy twice as much? Since there is no change in the amount of output produced, there is not twice as much to buy. So what happens? The prices of goods will be bid up until we can each buy no more than before. The amount of income, what was produced, did not double, but only the amount of money doubled. Thus, even if we had more money, we still might not be able to buy a Porsche if the increase in the amount of money caused a greater increase in prices. What we really need is more income, a larger part of the total output produced — a Porsche! We can see that money and income are two different things, and we must carefully distinguish between them. Although money and income are different, the money supply can be used to change the level of income. How does this happen? That is the topic of the next section.

The Link from Money to Income

In the last chapter we discussed the tools used by the Federal Reserve to change the money supply. We now know how the money supply and money demand determine the interest rate. However, we still do not know how money can affect the level of income. The impact of changes in the money supply that we have so far determined is that the money supply affects the interest rate. This change in the interest rate can in turn change the level of income through its effect on investment. Consumer spending is also affected by changes in the interest rate. As the interest rate goes up, consumers borrow less and consumer spending falls. When the interest rate goes down, consumer spending will rise. For simplicity, we will focus only on how business spending is affected by the interest rate.

Remember that investment means purchases by business for new plants and equipment and inventories. Investment does not mean consumers buying securities. You should recognize, however, that money demand is related to consumers buying securities. If consumers buy securities, they are not holding money. An alternative way to think of buying bonds is as saving. When consumers buy bonds, they are not consuming, and they are not spending. Hence they must be saving. Thus we should think of buying bonds as a form of saving. In any case it is not investment.

Recall our conclusion from Chapter 21 that the level of investment depends on the rate of interest. In that chapter we determined that an increase in the interest rate would decrease the level of investment, and a decrease in the interest rate would increase the level of investment. Changes in the interest rate will have an impact on the level of investment and therefore on the level of income.

We may summarize the impact of a change in the money supply on the level of income as follows. As the money supply increases, the interest rate falls, the level of investment rises, aggregate demand rises, and so does the level of income. As the money supply decreases, the interest rate rises, the level of investment falls, aggregate demand falls, and so does the level of income. These relationships are illustrated in Figure 28-6 and Figure 28-7. We now see how the money supply affects the level of income. The relationship we have described here is not a direct link from money to income, but it is a linkage that passes through the interest rate to investment, to aggregate demand, and then to the level of income. It should be evident now that the Federal Reserve can influence the level of income and the business cycle, since the Fed can change the money supply by changing excess reserves.

Monetary Policy

The Federal Reserve administers what is known as monetary policy, another form of stabilization policy. **Monetary policy** is the use of monetary tools by the Federal Reserve System to influence the money supply and interest rates in order to stabilize the business cycle. We know that the Federal Reserve has

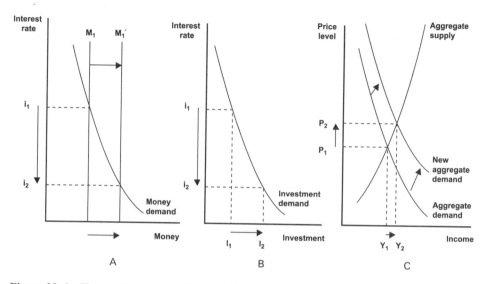

Figure 28-6   How an Increase in Money Affects the Level of Income
When the Fed increases the money supply, the interest rate will fall in panel A. The result of the
fall in the interest rate is more investment in panel B. The increase in the level of investment will
cause aggregate demand to rise in panel C and the level of income to rise.

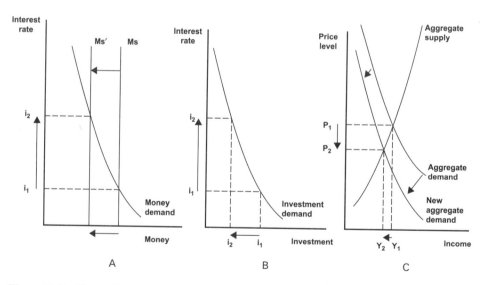

Figure 28-7   How a Decrease in Money Affects the Level of Income
When the Fed decreases the money supply, the interest rate will rise in panel A. The result of the
rise in the interest rate is less investment in panel B. The decrease in the level of investment will
cause aggregate demand to fall in panel C and the level of income to fall.

three major tools to affect the supply of money and interest rates. These tools are the reserve requirement, the discount rate, and open market operations.

Now we are able to combine our knowledge of the monetary tools and the effect of money on the level of income. The Federal Reserve uses monetary policy to adjust the excess reserves in the banking system to control the money supply and interest rates. Monetary policy is largely open market operations. When the Fed buys bonds in the open market, this increases demand for the bonds. This increased demand drives up the market price of the bonds. The higher price of the bonds results in a lower interest yield on these government securities. This reduction in interest rates for government securities reduces the competition for money. This means that the interest rates that business must offer to compete for money also fall. Since business can obtain the funds for expansion at lower rates of interest, more investment will occur and aggregate demand will increase. The result of the Fed's purchases in the open market has been an increase in the money supply, lower interest rates, more borrowing and investment, and an increase in aggregate demand and the level of income. This was the objective of the Fed in its open market purchases. We have seen how there will be securities for the Fed to buy when it wants to buy. The increase in demand by the Fed drives up the price of the bonds until selling to the Fed becomes attractive.

When the Fed sells in the open market, the price of bonds is driven down as the Fed dumps bonds in the market. The lower prices result in higher interest yields. The Fed will continue to dump, prices will continue to fall, and the effective interest yield will rise until the bonds are more attractive than the option of spending. While selling in the open market the Fed has reduced bank reserves and also increased interest rates throughout all money markets. This is because business competes with the government for savings and must increase interest rates to attract lenders. This reduces business borrowing and investment. The Fed has reduced aggregate demand and the level of income as a result of selling in the open market.

The Federal Reserve usually pursues a monetary policy against the direction of the business cycle. So if the economy is moving too fast and generating inflationary pressure, the Fed will slow down the rate of growth of the money supply. When the economy is moving too slowly and generating unemployment, the Fed will speed up the growth of the money supply. Thus the Fed generally follows a countercyclical policy. It is sometimes said that the Federal Reserve "leans against the wind."

Evaluation of Monetary Policy

The purpose of monetary policy is to stabilize the level of income, which is a purpose shared with fiscal policy. Fiscal policy employs a direct link between government expenditure or taxes and the level of income. We recognize that the monetary tools work indirectly on the level of income.

We have also seen that the Federal Reserve has been designed to be isolated as much as possible from the political pressures that plague much of fiscal policy. Also, by being free to function outside of the political process, the Fed can more quickly respond to economic needs. The Board of Governors can usually reach an agreement and enact policy well before the Congress and the administrative branch. And monetary tools, especially the frequently used open market operations, may produce an impact well before fiscal measures, such as a change in taxes, can be felt. This is an advantage of monetary policy.

Another advantage of monetary policy is its flexibility. Monetary policy can be changed at any time by simply reversing the open market operation. This flexibility does not exist for fiscal policy. The budget is made once a year, and although spending does occur all through the year, it is difficult to alter the spending once it has been legislated by Congress.

There is also a belief that under some circumstances, one stabilization policy is better than another. For instance, it is thought that in a depression, fiscal policy is a more certain way to cure unemployment than monetary policy. Why is this? For monetary policy to work, there has to be a multiple expansion of the money supply. That can only occur if banks loan out their excess reserves. In a depression, banks may become particularly conservative in making loans. Banks may believe that loans to support business expansion are certain to be defaulted if business is not selling its output. And what firm would want to go into debt if it could not see a sufficient market for its product? So not only will banks be reluctant to make loans, but there will not be a large demand for loans. Thus, increasing the excess reserves may not have an impact on the level of income. It won't if the extra reserves are not borrowed to support extra purchases. This belief is summarized in the saying, "You can lead a horse to water, but you cannot make it drink." The idea is that you can make excess reserves available, but you cannot force people to borrow or the banks to make loans. The Fed may make all the conditions right for a major expansion of the money supply and an increase in the level of income, but the result depends upon the cooperation of the public. However, with fiscal policy, the government can spend and increase income without the cooperation of the public.

In the case of inflation, there is a belief that monetary policy works better than fiscal policy. The basic idea is that even if government decreases its demand for output, the output may now be demanded by another sector. Thus, we will not get as strong a decrease in aggregate demand if fiscal policy is used. But if monetary policy is used, every sector will be forced to face higher interest rates, and the demand for output will certainly fall. This means that during inflation, there is some incentive to use monetary policy. And to reduce inflation, it is not necessary for the Fed to secure public cooperation. The Fed can clamp down on the money supply without question. As a last and effective measure, the Fed can raise reserve requirements.

The adjustment of the money supply so that the level of income is maintained near full employment is no easy task. We should be suspicious of those who say that monetary policy is the solution to all our problems.

▶ Summary

This chapter has discussed how money affects the level of income. Money and income are not the same thing. Income is gross domestic product, and money is checkable accounts plus currency in circulation. Money affects the level of income in a roundabout manner. The supply and demand for money together determine the interest rate. The interest rate determines the amount of investment. Investment is one part of aggregate demand. And aggregate demand together with the aggregate supply determine the level of income. Thus, as the money supply is changed by the Federal Reserve, the interest rate will change, the amount of investment will change, aggregate demand will change, and so will the level of income. Monetary policy is the use of monetary tools by the Fed to stabilize the level of income. Money itself becomes a tool to control the business cycle.

We have now completed our study of money. Is money all that you thought it was? Or more? There were probably a few surprises. Next we return to the problems of unemployment and inflation. We will see that these two problems may be related and that monetary and fiscal policies that try to combat both problems may not work as well as we would like. Other possible alternatives to stabilization policy will be discussed in the next chapter.

▶ Key Concepts

money demand
money supply
link from money to income
monetary policy

▶ Discussion Questions

1. Explain why the quantity of money demanded decreases as the interest rate rises. What are people doing with the money? What else could they do with their money?
2. Uncle Effron says there is no money market; banks set interest rates. Is he right? What happens if a bank sets an interest rate that is too high? Too low?
3. Distinguish money demand from investment.
4. What is the link between the money supply and the level of income?
5. Uncle Effron says that the relationship between money and the level of income is easy to see. More money is more income. Do you agree? Explain.
6. The King of Parkerville called you for economic advice. He says that he was talking to the peasants and that they complained of too little money in the kingdom. The king wants to double the money supply. If the king does double the money supply, what impact would you expect on output? On prices? What would you advise?
7. How can the Fed change the money supply? What is the purpose of monetary policy?
8. What are advantages of monetary policy? Disadvantages?
9. Might it have helped during the Great Depression to send out bombers loaded with money?

▶ Self-Review

• Fill in the blanks

interest rate
Federal Reserve

interest rate
GDP
income

The amount of money people hold varies inversely with the _____. The supply of money is determined by actions of the _____. Money supply and money demand determine the price of money, the _____. While money means currency in circulation and checkable deposits, income refers to real _____. The link between money and _____ is roundabout. As the

falls	money supply increases, the interest rate _____, the level
rises, rises	of investment _____, aggregate demand _____, and the
rises	level of income _____. As the money supply decreases,
rises, falls	the interest rate _____, investment _____, aggregate
falls, falls	demand _____, and the level of income _____. The
	use of monetary tools by the Fed to stabilize the economy
monetary policy	is known as _____. To increase real GDP,
lower, lower	the Fed could _____ the reserve requirement, _____ the
buy	discount rate, or _____ in the open market.

• Multiple choice

1. An increase in the money supply causes:
   a. interest rates to fall, investment to increase, and income to rise.
   b. interest rates to rise, investment to decrease, and income to fall.
   c. interest rates to rise, investment to increase, and income to fall.
   d. interest rates to fall, investment to decrease, and income to rise.

2. When the Fed buys bonds in the open market, there is:
   a. a money multiplier effect on the money supply.
   b. a change in the discount rate.
   c. monetary policy aimed at inflation.
   d. a reduction in the money supply.

3. If the Fed wants to increase the level of income, it should:
   a. increase the money supply.
   b. decrease the money supply.
   c. increase the interest rate.
   d. decrease excess reserves.

4. During an inflation period, the appropriate monetary policy is to:
   a. increase the reserve requirement, increase the discount rate, and buy in the open market.
   b. decrease the reserve requirement, increase the discount rate, and sell in the open market.
   c. decrease the reserve requirement, decrease the discount rate, and buy in the open market.
   d. increase the reserve requirement, increase the discount rate, and sell in the open market.

5. Monetary policy is favored in inflationary times because:
   a. reductions in the money supply cause interest rates to rise, which causes aggregate demand to fall.
   b. the Fed directly controls prices.

c. monetary policy is not flexible.

d. increases in the money supply help keep interest rates and costs down and thus keeps prices from rising.

Answers: 1.a, 2.a, 3.a, 4.d, 5.a.

Chapter 29 ECONOMIC POLICY

Key Topics
  economic goals
  Phillips curve and stagflation
  policy failure
  other schools of thought
  goal trade-offs

Goals
  re-examine macro goals and potential policies
  recognize that under stagflation, traditional policies may fail
  examine other schools of economic thought
  realize that policy has an opportunity cost

As an evolving science, economics has generated various schools of thought. There is a controversy within economics as to which policy tools are capable of regulating the business cycle. The public is concerned with the policy choices since the public is so vitally affected by the outcome of these controversies. Our purpose here is to clarify some of the issues and present an overview of the policy choices available. We have discussed the major tools of stabilization policy, fiscal and monetary policy, at length. We have also indicated various shortcomings of these tools. There are those who believe that the basic philosophies of fiscal and monetary policy are in error and recommend reforms in our approach to stabilization policy.

Policy starts with goals. Before we can decide what tools to use and how to use them, we must decide what goals to achieve. We begin this chapter with a discussion of alternative goals that might be chosen for an economy. Next we will introduce a problem of the modern economy, stagflation. We will then discuss the impact of monetary and fiscal policy on stagflation. We will briefly review classical and Keynesian economics. We next investigate some alternative approaches to policy, including monetarism, supply-side economics, and rational expectations. Our exclusion of any economic philosophy by no means indicates a lack of merit, only that we lack space for a complete review of current philosophies. We do not seek to recommend or condemn any approach to the business cycle but to summarize the rational for the alternatives. Finally, we return to the general problem of policy choice and observe that goals do trade off.

Economic Goals

There are many goals that may be important for an economy. The most common form of debate in economics is over the appropriate goals. In Chapter 4 we discussed possible goals. That list of goals is reproduced here for convenience:

1. Economic growth
2. Efficiency
3. Economic freedom
4. Equitable distribution of income
5. Clean environment
6. Full employment
7. Price stability

As you may well understand, for each individual some goals are more important than others. And we should not be surprised if the goals conflict. If all goals cannot be achieved at the same time, we should determine which goals we strongly wish to achieve and which may be of lesser importance. Recall the discussion in Chapter 2 about positive and normative statements. Positive statements are those that can be tested to see if they are true. A statement such as "fiscal policy can be used to raise the level of income" is a positive statement. On the other hand, the statement that "fiscal policy should be used rather than monetary policy" is a normative statement. Normative issues involve value judgments and arise in deciding which goals to pursue. There is no test we can apply to decide which goal is most important. As long as more of one goal requires giving up some amount of another goal, we must choose among the goals. The determination of which goals to pursue is a normative issue.

We know that if the economic goals trade off, then normative statements about the value of the goals will be needed to decide what goals to pursue and what economic policy to follow. In the next section, we will discuss how the two goals of price stability and full employment trade off.

Phillips Curve

Suppose that we look at the price level and the level of unemployment together. How are these two related? So far, we have assumed that our difficulties with the business cycle might be either unemployment *or* inflation, but certainly not both. Keynes suggested the solution to only one problem during the Great Depression, how to reduce unemployment. He was not concerned that his solution would cause inflation. Yet it appears that unemployment and inflation may trade off. One is the opportunity cost of the other. This trade-off is illustrated by the Phillips curve in Figure 29-1.

The **Phillips curve** shows the inverse relation between unemployment and inflation. When unemployment goes down, inflation tends to go up. When inflation goes down, unemployment tends to go up. This relationship is a major thorn in the side of policy makers. It means that we cannot expect to achieve full employment and low inflation at the same time. There is a trade-off between the two. Less of one means more of the other. We cannot make economic policy just by looking at the impact of the policy on employment. The policy will also affect the rate of inflation. Nor can we simply make policy to reduce inflation; any effort to reduce inflation will affect the level of employment. So

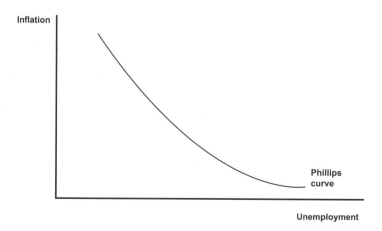

Figure 29-1   The Phillips Curve
The Phillips curve shows the trade-off between inflation and unemployment.

the making of economic policy is more difficult than originally thought. We cannot make policy to just achieve full employment or make policy to just reduce inflation. When policy is made, we must look at how the policy will affect both employment and inflation.

You can see that a movement down the Phillips curve shows a lower rate of inflation while at the same time a higher rate of unemployment. With a little thought, this is a logical outcome. As aggregate demand is reduced, inflationary pressures are reduced. However, as aggregate demand is reduced, the business cycle slides downward and unemployment increases. Measures taken to reduce inflation result in a higher rate of unemployment. If unemployment is considered the greater evil, then increases in aggregate demand will reduce the rate of unemployment. At the same time, the rate of inflation is increased due to the increased demand for limited production. If unemployment and inflation are actually trade-offs, then monetary and fiscal policy can only change aggregate demand and allow us to select our position on the Phillips curve. In effect, we pursue a policy to reduce either unemployment *or* inflation, but realize that the price paid will be higher levels of the other. Fiscal and monetary policy become single-purpose tools incapable of reducing unemployment and inflation at the same time.

Stagflation

There is another aspect of the Phillips relationship that is troublesome. The curve does not stay in the same place. It seems to move over time. Figure 29-2 shows the outward shift of the Phillips curve to the right. This outward shift of the Phillips curve represents stagflation. **Stagflation** is undesirable rates of both unemployment and inflation at the same time. When the Phillips curve shifts to the right, both the unemployment and the inflation rates increase. In the 1950s the inflation rate averaged 2 percent, and the unemployment rate 4.5 percent. But since then, there have been increasingly higher rates of both unemployment and inflation. We did not get more inflation and at the same time less unemployment; rather, we got more of both. Although more recently, both unemployment and inflation have been low.

What causes the Phillips curve to shift is not entirely clear. One explanation is that the economy becomes less competitive. Wages and prices become less sensitive to market forces, and can be affected by labor and business. Labor can more easily keep wages going up and firms can make prices rise to cover the higher cost. But the higher prices soon cause buying to fall, production to fall,

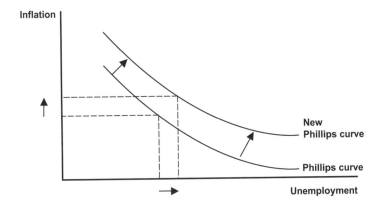

Figure 29-2   Stagflation: Phillips Curve
The outward shift of the Phillips curve shows more of both unemployment and inflation. This condition is called stagflation.

and unemployment to rise. Yet the labor still employed causes wages to go up even more and the process continues.

Another explanation for a shift in the Phillips curve is a decline in labor productivity. Labor productivity links the labor cost and the price of output. If the wage goes up faster than labor productivity, firms can only recover the higher cost through higher output prices. Thus, when labor productivity slows, so that wages go up faster than productivity, firms are forced to raise the price of output, sell less, and lay off workers. The increase in inflation and unemployment moves the Phillips curve outward.

Changes external to our economy may shift the Phillips curve. The most obvious example is the 1973 OPEC increase in the price of oil. The impact was a widespread increase in the cost of energy and all oil-based products. This increased the cost of nearly every industry and consequently the price of output. The resulting reduction in the quantity demanded increased unemployment. This meant that there was more inflation and even more unemployment.

Other explanations have been given for stagflation, including the increased natural rate of unemployment, the inflationary expectations of labor and producers, and the effects of government regulation. For example, when the minimum wage increases, both inflation and unemployment increase. Whatever the explanation for stagflation, the fact that the Phillips curve shifts causes policy problems. When the Phillips curve was first discovered, it was thought to be evidence of the trade-off between unemployment and inflation. But once

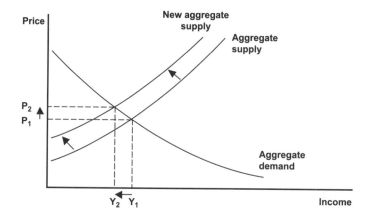

Figure 29-3   Stagflation: Aggregate Demand and Supply
When the aggregate supply curve shifts left, we can have an increase in the price level and a decrease in output — stagflation.

we see that the Phillips curve moves, it becomes apparent that we can have more of both.

Stagflation can also be illustrated with the tools of aggregate supply and aggregate demand. In Figure 29-3, the aggregate supply has decreased, possibly due to a decrease in labor productivity. The decrease in aggregate supply causes the price level to rise at the same time that income falls. And as income falls that means output and employment fall. The result: more unemployment and inflation.

Policy Failure

Can either fiscal or monetary policy be used to reduce unemployment and inflation at the same time? Consider fiscal policy. When faced with unemployment, the usual process is to increase government spending or lower taxes. This would cause the aggregate demand to shift to the right. While unemployment would fall, inflation would rise. What if we consider monetary policy? If we reduce the money supply to fight inflation, we decrease aggregate demand. This has the desired effect of reducing prices, but will cause unemployment to rise. This monetary policy was used against the inflation of the late 1970s and early 1980s and resulted in a severe recession.

Stagflation presents problems beyond the scope of monetary and fiscal policy. Neither of these policies can reduce both unemployment and inflation.

Overcoming the joint problem of unemployment and inflation is more difficult than is attacking either problem alone. New stabilization policy will be required to make the Phillips curve shift inward, reducing both inflation and unemployment. What other alternatives could we pursue? A move in the aggregate supply curve to the right would be desirable. Policies aimed at moving the aggregate supply curve are called supply-side policies. More will be said about this alternative soon.

Why do we want to be able to explain the shift in the Phillips curve? The reason is that we would like to design policies that would move the Phillips curve inward. Any steps taken to reduce inflation, for example, will leave inflation at a still unacceptable level while increasing unemployment from an undesirable to a yet more undesirable level. There is a need for policy tools capable of reducing stagflation. An inward movement of the Phillips curve would reduce *both* unemployment and inflation at the same time. If we do not understand what causes the Phillips curve to move, we can treat the symptoms of more unemployment and more inflation, but not the root cause of the problem. As it stands, there is no theory explaining stagflation that the majority of economists agree is correct. In that case, rather than try to treat the reason for the shift of the Phillips curve, we will explore the treatment of the symptoms.

Classical, Keynesian, and Monetarist

There is more than one approach to economic problems. In this text we have provided a view that a large number of economists would agree with. But numbers alone should not persuade you. At one point in time, much of what we have presented here was the minority view. When Keynes was writing, he was nearly alone, and now his view is a predominant one. Just because many people agree with a view does not make it the best. There are other ways to look at the economy, and we now present some of them. We begin with the classical and Keynesian schools of thought and then follow the development of three modern schools — monetarism, supply-side economics, and rational expectations.

The classical economist, as you may recall from Chapter 20, believed that the economy would always achieve equilibrium at full employment. There was never any need for stabilization policy since the economy would automatically achieve full employment. This point of view was badly shaken in the depression of the 1930s. At that time the economy showed no signs of coming out of the depression, and it became clear that some form of government intervention would be necessary. The view that intervention in the economy would be desirable was put forth by Keynes. He argued that if the private sector — consumers and business together — could not provide sufficient demand to achieve full employment, then the government should increase aggregate demand so that the economy would return to the desired level of employment. At that point, the economy would again be on its own and the role of the government would be reduced.

Those believing in **Keynesian economics** were of the opinion that the economy could be fine tuned using the fiscal and monetary tools. The economy could be controlled. It was not long before flaws were found in the theory. Some believed that fiscal policy does not affect the level of income or the price level. Rather, the main impact of fiscal policy is to increase or decrease the role of government in the economy. Whenever the government increases spending by one dollar, there is a one dollar reduction in spending by business. If the government decreases spending by one dollar, there is a one dollar increase in business spending. The only policy tool left was a form of monetary policy. The economists believing this view are called monetarists.

The basis of monetarism is a classical equation called the **equation of exchange**. It is useful in explaining the quantity theory of money. The equation of exchange is

$$MV = PQ$$

where M represents the money supply, and V is the velocity of circulation, P is the price level, and Q is the quantity of real output. The **velocity of circulation** is the number of times a dollar is spent in buying the final output of the economy in a year. If the output of the economy is $50 and the money supply is $5, then each dollar is spent an average of 10 times during the year. The velocity of circulation would be 10. MV, M times V, therefore represents the total spending. Total spending is the number of dollars times the number of times each dollar is spent. With our figures, the total spending is $5 × 10, or $50. PQ, P times Q, is the total output of society, money GDP. We have returned to the circular flow model where total spending equals total output.

The equation of exchange shows us that the money supply can be used to influence the level of income and the price level. The monetarist believed that V did not change quickly and was relatively constant. Thus an increase in M would increase P or Q, or both. If we were at less than full employment, an increase in M would make both P and Q rise. If we were at full employment, where Q is as large as it can get, an increase in M would only increase P.

Thus inflation could occur only if there were a continued increase in the money supply at full employment. The monetarist had taken a definition used by the classical economists and transformed it into a theory. **Monetarists** believe that only changes in the money supply affect output or prices. The monetarists prefer that the Federal Reserve drop its role as policymaker. Because of lags between the time that we see policy is needed and the time that the policy is felt in the economy, monetary policy and fiscal policy are destabilizing. The Federal Reserve should only maintain a steady growth in the money supply matching the growth of labor productivity.

These two theories, Keynesianism and monetarism, were in competition as a basis for policy. There was a split among economists about which led to better policy. The issue was never settled. New economic problems arose that neither could adequately solve.

One problem was inflation. The Keynesians argued for a decrease in aggregate demand led by a cut in government spending or an increase in taxes. The monetarists concluded that the appropriate policy tool would be a reduction of the money supply. If inflation is predominately demand-pull in our society, then it should be clear that stabilization policies, either monetary or fiscal policy, can be quite effective. For example, it is within the power of the Federal Reserve to clamp down on the money supply and aggregate demand. On the other hand, neither fiscal nor monetary policy is effective against the monopoly power that contributes to cost-push inflation. It is not clear what part of our inflation is demand-pull and what part is cost-push. Neither demand-pull nor cost-push seem to explain every inflation. And worse yet, sometimes we have both high unemployment and high inflation.

There were times when neither the Keynesians nor the monetarists could explain why the economy was working as it did. The most difficult problem was stagflation. For both the Keynesian and the monetarist, the conditions under which inflation would occur would be full employment. So how could there be inflation at less than full employment? The supply-siders believed they had an answer.

Supply Side and Rational Expectations

The focus of both Keynes and the monetarists was aggregate demand. **Supply-side economics** emphasizes the importance of policy action on the aggregate supply curve. The supply-siders noted that, by shifting the aggregate supply curve to the left, Figure 29-3, it was possible to explain why inflation and unemployment occurred at the same time. This shift would cause the price level to rise and the level of output to fall. The way to reduce both unemployment and inflation, therefore, would be to make the supply curve shift to the right. This could be accomplished by inducing people to work more. Thus tax rates should fall so that the workers could keep a larger part of their earned income. This would induce greater work effort and increase aggregate supply.

Figure 29-4 shows the Laffer curve, a fundamental basis of supply-side philosophy. The Laffer curve indicates a reduction in tax collections at high tax rates. The curve shows that as tax rates increase from zero, the taxes collected at first rise, and then as the tax rate approaches 100 percent, the taxes collected fall. If the economy were at point A on the curve, a decrease in tax rates would cause a movement to the left, to B, and tax collections would increase. The idea is that lower tax rates will result in increased productivity through an increased incentive to work and therefore higher tax collections.

Supply-side policies were favored in the early 1980s. But before these policies could be put to work, the Federal Reserve reduced the money supply to choke off inflation. And just as the Phillips curve predicted, there was an increase in unemployment. In fact unemployment was the worst it had been since the Great Depression. The inflation slowly declined, the economy recovered, and the level of employment improved. During the same period, there had been a revival of classical thought. This time it went by the name of rational expectations.

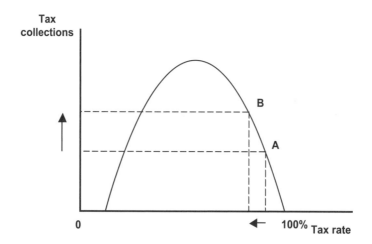

Figure 29-4   The Laffer Curve
If tax rates are high, we can achieve higher tax collections by reducing the tax rate and increasing the incentive to work.

Rational expectations is the belief that people adjust to expected actions by the government so that when the action actually occurs, its effect has already been accounted for in the market. Rational expectations is a modern version of the classical school of thought, so much so that it is sometimes called the new classicalism. Both share the belief that government intervention in the economy can accomplish no good. Both believe that equilibrium occurs at the natural rate of unemployment. Any attempt to increase output beyond the natural rate of unemployment will fail to produce benefits, but costs may result.

Rational expectationists claim that decision makers, including consumers, business, and labor, use all possible information to advance or protect their own self-interest. This information includes anticipating changes in government policy and the effects of the policy on the economy. Everyone expects fiscal or monetary policy to be applied to expand or contract the economy as needed and the effects of the policy are predictable.

For example, people expect the Federal Reserve to take measures to increase the money supply to expand the level of output. But this expectation will cancel out the possible benefits of the government policy. Workers realize that this policy will increase aggregate demand and cause both output and prices to rise. Workers know from experience that when prices rise and if they make no adjustment, their real income will decrease. Workers have had that happen before and, according to rational expectations, people don't consistently make the same mistakes; rather, they adjust. So workers anticipating higher prices and lower real income would demand higher wages and cancel out even a temporary increase in output. The increase in output would not occur, certainly not above the natural rate of unemployment, but the price level would rise — an undesirable effect of the government policy.

Under rational expectations, as long as people know that government will take some action, they will form expectations and adjust to account for the action. What if the policy is a complete surprise? The policy will have an impact but only for a short time — only until people realize what happened and then make adjustments. And if government policy turns out to be other than what people rationally expect, for example, a contractionary policy during a recession, how could it be a good economic policy? The conclusion by rational expectations is that it will do no good to use monetary and fiscal policy. Thus the economy maintains a level of output consistent with the natural rate of unemployment, and all those who want to work at the going wage are employed. The economy stays at full employment.

However, there are flaws in the theory of rational expectations. According to its supporters, workers expecting lower prices would automatically push to reduce wages to reduce unemployment. This seems unlikely. Also, it is difficult to believe that people can anticipate and respond to monetary and fiscal policy. Most people have never ever heard of these terms. And if equilibrium occurs at the natural rate of unemployment, how does rational expectations explain the Great Depression?

As you can see, there are many different philosophies in economics. There is not just one correct theory of the macro economy. Economics is both art and science. And as the economy grows and changes, there are even more opportunities for new ideas. Economics is an evolving science.

Goal Trade-Offs

We have seen the trade-off between price stability and full employment. Are there trade-offs between other economic goals? Consider efficiency and an equitable distribution of income. We know that perfect competition will allocate resources efficiently. What kind of income distribution results? A competitive process pays those who are productive. Who could argue that such payments are not equitable? Yet some who are productive may be more lucky than productive. Consider the situation of two actors auditioning for the same role in a Broadway play. The actor getting the role may have a long run on Broadway, which will provide opportunities for other shows and possibly even a Hollywood contract. The actor who does not get the part may end up without an acting career. Yet it is also possible that these two actors are nearly equal in talent. Why should only one reap huge rewards?

There are other cases where luck affects the distribution of income. Can we be sure that some people born to rich parents would have achieved the level of income they now have if they had been born to poorer parents? And what about two athletes equally skilled? One is a football player while the other is smaller and plays squash instead. The football player may make a fortune while the squash player makes a living selling light bulbs. The only real difference between them is their size. There are factors in a competitive economic system in addition to productivity that determine how much one person will be paid. There is no assurance that a competitive system will reward in an equitable fashion even if our definition of equity is based on productivity. So to the extent that we choose perfect competition for its efficiency, we may be trading off some degree of equity.

We have pointed out the trade-off between unemployment and inflation and the trade-off between efficiency and an equitable distribution of income. You can be sure that there are trade-offs between other economic goals as well. It will not be possible to achieve all goals at the same time. Thus it is essential to decide which goals are the most important. You already realize that all individuals will not agree on the choice of goals. A normative choice among goals cannot be avoided. Even in the late 1970s when unemployment and inflation were both serious, there was loud debate among economists about which problem should be addressed first. So the trade-off among goals is an important consideration that enters into any policy discussion. By now you should be well aware of the emphasis that economists place on trade-offs.

▶ Summary

We started this chapter with a list of possible economic goals for our society. There are trade-offs among the goals. All of the goals may be desirable, but we quickly learned that the goals of full employment and stable prices may conflict. This trade-off was shown in the Phillips curve. We cannot just try to end one economic problem. To ease one problem is likely to make another worse. There may be times when we get more of both unemployment and inflation, and stagflation occurs. The tools of monetary policy and fiscal policy are of little help against stagflation.

There are various schools of thought with different strategies for ending a given economic problem. Besides the Keynesians, there are monetarists who believe that the money supply is the main policy tool. Monetarists believe that a constant rate of growth in the money supply will be a better policy than will trying to push against every fluctuation in the business cycle. The supply-side school believes that we cannot ignore the effects of the aggregate supply curve. There may be times when adjusting the supply curve is the only effective policy, such as against stagflation. The rational expectations school believes that the only way a stabilization policy can have an impact is if the policy is a complete surprise. Rational expectationists conclude that government policy is not needed because the economy always returns to full employment. You can see why the rational expectations school is thought of as the new classical school.

Regardless of the economic school, the fact is that the goals trade off. Hence there is a normative decision that must be made, namely, which goal is most important and should be pursued first. There will be great debate over which goal should be most important. You cannot afford to be left out of that debate, for its outcome will affect much of what happens in your life.

In the next module we shift our emphasis to the significance of trade both within our society and with the global society.

▶ Key Concepts

Phillips curve   velocity of circulation
stagflation   monetarists
classical economists   supply-side economists
Keynesian economists   rational expectations
equation of exchange

▶ Discussion Questions

1. What are the major economic goals for our society?
2. Explain why inflation and unemployment trade off.
3. What is stagflation? How does the Phillips curve show stagflation?
4. What is the proper role for economic policy according to the classical economists? How does this view differ from that of the rational expectations economists?
5. What is the equation of exchange? What is the relationship of the money supply to the value of output (PQ) in the equation of exchange?
6. What policy prescriptions do the monetarists pursue?
7. How do supply-side economists plan to overcome stagflation?
8. How do Keynesian economists differ from classical or rational expectations economists? Monetarists? Supply-siders?
9. Uncle Effron says that there are too many different kinds of economists, and that they never agree. Why are there so many differing schools of thought?

▶ Self-Review

• Fill in the blanks

	One difficulty in selecting economic policy is that
trade off	economic goals _____. The trade-off between
inflation, inverse	unemployment and _____ is an _____ relation
Phillips	and is illustrated by the _____ curve. Undesirable
	rates of both inflation and unemployment are known
stagflation	as _____. A shift of the Phillips curve to the
right	_____ indicates stagflation. Stagflation can also be

left	shown by a shift in the aggregate supply curve to the _____. Fiscal and monetary policy do not shift the
on the curve	Phillips curve but move us _____. Thus we
inflation	can lower unemployment or _____, but only by
increasing	_____ the other. Monetarists use the equation of
exchange, money	_____ to explain the quantity theory of _____.
MV, PQ	The equation of exchange is _____ = _____. V
velocity of circulation	represents the _____, the
dollar	number of times a _____ is spent in buying the
output	final _____ of the economy. Monetarists prefer
constant	a _____ rate of growth in the money supply
equal to	_____ the growth of labor productivity. The school
	of thought that emphasizes the importance of policy
supply-side	action on the aggregate supply curve is _____
	economics. The supply-side solution for stagflation
increase	is to _____ aggregate supply. The belief that
	people adjust to expected actions by the government is
rational expectations	_____.

- Multiple choice

1. The Phillips curve shows a trade-off between:
   a. growth and efficiency.
   b. unemployment and growth.
   c. inflation and unemployment.
   d. efficiency and inflation.
2. With the use of aggregate supply and demand, stagflation is demonstrated by:
   a. a decrease in aggregate supply.
   b. a decrease in aggregate demand.
   c. an increase in aggregate demand.
   d. an increase in aggregate supply.
3. A possible explanation for stagflation is:
   a. a decline in labor productivity.
   b. a reduction in the level of competition in the economy.
   c. a change external to our economy such as rising oil prices.
   d. all of the above.
4. A monetarist believes:
   a. the only workable policy tool is monetary policy.
   b. money is income.
   c. government spending affects the level of income.
   d. increases in the money supply reduce the level of income.

5. Rational expectations means that:
    a. any expectation is rational depending on your point of view.
    b. people adjust to expected actions by the government so that the effect of the action is accounted for in the market.
    c. all economic actions are rational.
    d. everyone does the same thing.

Answers: 1.c, 2.a, 3.d, 4.a, 5.b.

Module 7 TRADE

So far we have been content to look at a world with only one country. If you were living in a country like Japan or Great Britain, this view of the world would bother you a great deal. If you lived in either of those countries, you would be aware that some countries do not have the resources that we have in the United States. Japan has to import almost all its raw material. There is almost no oil or coal in Japan, and little iron ore. Without imports, there would be little production in Japan. Without imports, there would be no exports. Similar facts hold for Great Britain and many other countries. So if you lived in one of those countries, you would recognize that trade would be an important part of all economic activity. But because you live in the United States, and we have a large variety of resources, trade may not seem so great a concern for us. Yet in some ways we are now starting to understand the importance of trade. By the 1970s we had become dependent on foreign oil sources. When those countries cut off our oil supply, we suddenly realized how important trade is and that we are not and cannot be independent of other countries. International trade has become a more and more essential part of our economy. The volume of trade grows every year, and it is important for us to understand trade. This module is about trade.

We are going to learn that whether two individuals or two nations trade, both sides can gain. Indeed, in a situation of free trade, neither side loses if trade occurs. We wish to do away with the belief that one person gains in trade only at the loss of another. The potential for both sides to gain from trade is a significant point studied in this module. The secret to gains from trade is not in each producer being more efficient at producing his or her own good. This is what is commonly, but mistakenly, thought. The amazing fact you will find is that both sides can gain from trade even if one is the more efficient producer of both goods.

Actually you already know quite a bit about the importance of trade. After all, trade between two people is not too much different from trade between two nations. The main difference is that when two of us trade, we have the same currency. Trade between nations may require exchanging one currency for another.

This module contains two chapters. Chapter 30 provides the case for free trade. Free trade is beneficial to both trading parties. The gains from free trade are first examined in a world without money. Chapter 31 expands the discussion of trade to international trade in a world with money. The case for barriers to trade is also discussed there. When you have completed this module, you should recognize that there are times when the gains from trade are great and that free trade among nations should occur. There may also be times when international trade imposes costs that may make barriers to trade desirable.

Chapter 30 | TRADE WITHOUT MONEY

Key Topics
  absolute advantage
  comparative advantage

Goals
  understand gains from trade

So far, our concern has been with the production, distribution, and consumption within one country. We well know that the world consists of more than one country and that trade between countries frequently makes the news. However, the idea of trade does not apply just to countries; trade occurs between individuals, too. You are already familiar with the idea of trade. As a child you may have traded baseball cards, comic books, or stickers, or played one of the many board games that are designed around the idea of trade — Monopoly is the most famous of these. And now nearly every day you trade your money for goods and services. So you are already acquainted with trade. We will now have a closer look at this universal activity.

In this chapter, we will ignore the complicating fact that there are many different currencies. We will first consider a world without money. To discover the gains from trade, we begin with the idea of absolute advantage. Absolute advantage will then be distinguished from comparative advantage. In the next chapter you can apply this knowledge of trade to a world with money and become better acquainted with the process of international trade.

Absolute Advantage

Let us start with two countries (or individuals), both producing the same two goods. The countries are Cal and Oh, and they each produce oranges and glass. The oranges of one country cannot be distinguished from the oranges of the

Table 30-1   Absolute Advantage, One Good

	Oranges	Glass
Cal	10	1 ton
Oh	5	2 ton

This table shows the amount of each good each country can produce with the same amount of resources. Cal has the absolute advantage in oranges and Oh in glass.

other country, and similarly for glass. The opportunities for trade are apparent since one country is superior in the production of oranges and the other in glass. Each country has an absolute advantage. **Absolute advantage** means the ability of a country to produce a larger quantity of a good with the same amount of resources as another country. The country's absolute advantage may be due to the nature of its resources or to its production skills.

Suppose that we are given the information from Table 30-1 about production in each of our two countries. The first country, Cal, can produce 10 oranges or 1 ton of glass using a given amount of inputs. The second country, Oh, can produce 5 oranges or 2 tons of glass with the same amount of resources. Cal has an absolute advantage in oranges, and Oh has an absolute advantage in glass. Cal can produce 10 oranges compared to 5 for Oh, while Oh can produce 2 tons of glass compared to 1 for Cal. Obviously Cal would choose to specialize in the production of oranges and Oh in the production of glass. The question is, can these countries gain by trading?

Suppose that 3 oranges trade for 1 ton of glass. What if the people of Oh use their resources to produce 2 tons of glass and then trade their glass to the people of Cal for oranges? Oh would get 6 oranges back. The people of Oh would be 1 orange ahead, since if they did not trade with Cal, at best they could have produced only 5 oranges with the same amount of resources. The people of Cal are also better off having produced oranges. They traded 6 oranges but gained 2 tons of glass. So they now have 2 tons of glass and the remaining 4 oranges. If they did not trade with Oh, the resources used to produce 10 oranges produce but 1 ton of glass instead. So Cal is 1 ton of glass and 4 oranges ahead compared to if it had not produced oranges and traded.

This example suggests that both countries gain by trade. Observe that there is no reason to expect the gain to be shared equally. But both countries have more than if they had not specialized and traded. By specializing in the production of one good, and then trading, each country can have more than by producing both goods itself. In the example given here, this result is not too surprising. After all, Cal is the more efficient producer of oranges, and Oh is the more efficient producer of glass. What about a situation where one country is more efficient in the production of all goods, and therefore has the absolute advantage in both? This means that the other country has no absolute advantage. Will specialization and trade make sense then?

Comparative Advantage

Suppose that we have the same two countries as before but that conditions have changed somewhat. Cal is able to produce 10 oranges or 2 tons of glass with a given amount of resources. Oh can produce 3 oranges or 1 ton of glass. Look at Table 30-2. You can see that Cal has an absolute advantage in producing *both* oranges and glass. Will specialization and trade still occur? It is not so obvious now. Suppose that the terms of trade, the rate at which oranges trade for glass, is 4 oranges for 1 ton of glass. What about Oh? Although it has no absolute advantage, if Oh produces a ton of glass it could trade the glass for 4 oranges. It would have 1 orange more than if it had produced oranges. Oh would be ahead. What about Cal? Cal, being the more efficient producer of both oranges and glass, would not seem able to gain from trade. Yet when Cal produces 5 oranges, it gives up 1 ton of glass. It could exchange 4 of those oranges for 1 ton of glass and be 1 orange ahead. So specialization and trade still make sense even when one country has an absolute advantage in the production of both goods.

The possibilities for trade are not determined by how efficiently a good can be produced. What matters is the opportunity cost of producing each good. A country has a **comparative advantage** in the production of a good if its opportunity cost for the good is less than the opportunity cost for the same good in another country. Table 30-3 shows that the opportunity cost of glass in

Table 30-2   Absolute Advantage, Two Goods

	Oranges	Glass
Cal	10	2 ton
Oh	3	1 ton

This table shows the amount of each good each country can produce with the same amount of resources. Cal has the absolute advantage in both oranges and glass.

terms of oranges is 5 for Cal (Cal gives up 10 oranges to get 2 tons of glass) and 3 for Oh (Oh gives up only 3 oranges to get 1 ton of glass). These different opportunity costs make possible gains from trade. Relatively, compared to Cal, Oh is the more efficient producer of glass. Oh gives up fewer oranges than Cal to obtain 1 ton of glass. Notice that Oh does not have an absolute advantage, but a comparative advantage in glass production. Oh sacrifices fewer oranges, 3, than Cal, 5, to obtain a unit of glass.

Since Oh has the comparative advantage in the production of glass, Cal will have the comparative advantage in the production of oranges. Table 30-4 shows that the opportunity cost to Cal of producing an orange is 1/5 of a ton of glass, for Oh, 1/3 of a ton of glass. Since 1/5 of a ton of glass is less of a sacrifice than 1/3, Cal sacrifices less glass to produce oranges than Oh. Relatively, compared to Oh, Cal is the more efficient producer of oranges. We see that since Oh has the comparative advantage in glass, and Cal in oranges, there is the possibility for specialization and trade, and the potential of gains from trade.

So it is not absolute advantage but comparative advantage that is the key to specialization and trade. What matters is not which producer can make the

Table 30-3 *Comparative Advantage, Glass

Opportunity cost of producing 1 ton of glass	
Cal	5 oranges
*Oh	3 oranges

This table shows the amount of oranges that each country must give up to produce 1 ton of glass. These opportunity costs are based on the production data in Table 30-2. Since Oh has to give up fewer oranges than Cal, Oh has the comparative advantage in producing glass.

Table 30-4 *Comparative Advantage, Oranges

Opportunity cost of producing 1 orange	
*Cal	1/5 ton of glass
Oh	1/3 ton of glass

This table shows the amount of glass each country must give up to produce one orange. These opportunity costs are based on the production data in Table 30-2. Since Cal has to give up less glass than Oh, Cal has the comparative advantage in producing oranges.

good more cheaply, but which can make the good *relatively* more cheaply. The opportunity cost for one producer must be compared to the opportunity cost for the other. Comparative advantage is less obvious than is absolute advantage but is the factor determining specialization and trade. Whether or not trade occurs depends on the opportunity cost, not on how many resources go into the production of a good. A good may require a larger amount of resources in one country and still be produced for trade. The country would specialize in that good if the opportunity cost is lower than for the other country. So even if one producer is less efficient in all production, there still remains the opportunity for both to benefit from trade. Keep in mind that the principle of comparative advantage applies equally to individuals as it does to nations. It tells individuals what to specialize in and trade, and nations what to import and export.

Potential for Trade

Examples of absolute advantage are plentiful. Suppose that there is a person who can make excellent furniture and another who can fix cars. It seems reasonable that the one who can fix cars will fix the cars for both and that the furniture maker will make the furniture for both. Examples of comparative advantage also abound. What if one person can make furniture and fix cars better than the other? Will the one do both jobs? The answer is no. Each person will specialize in the activity in which he or she has a comparative advantage. Both parties gain by this arrangement, and both can have more with trade than if they did not specialize. So the fact that people choose careers and specialize in that activity is due to comparative advantage. Comparative advantage, specialization, and trade make the output of the society larger than it would have been without trade.

Notice, however, that trade between Cal and Oh will only occur if the terms of trade of oranges for glass falls between the opportunity costs. In Table 30-2, the opportunity cost of 1 ton of glass is 5 oranges for Cal, and the opportunity cost of 1 ton of glass is 3 oranges for Oh. The terms of trade for 1 ton of glass must be between 5 and 3 oranges. In our example, 1 ton of glass trades for 4 oranges, thus the terms of trade for a ton of glass is between 5 and 3 oranges, and trade occurs.

What if the terms of trade were not between the two opportunity costs? In that case both countries would want to produce the same good, and trade would not occur. Suppose that 6 oranges trade for 1 ton of glass. Now what? What will Cal produce? Cal will want to produce glass and trade for oranges since it can get 6 oranges by trading while it could only get 5 if it did not trade. Oh, on the other hand, will also want to produce glass since it can get 6 oranges by trading but only 3 if it does not trade. So everyone will want to produce glass and no one will be producing oranges. How can trade occur if everyone wants to produce glass? There will be no oranges to trade. Thus the potential for trade depends on the terms of trade as well as the opportunity costs.

Production Possibilities

Comparative advantage can be illustrated graphically. Each country has certain possibilities for production. These possibilities can be represented by the production possibilities curve introduced in Chapter 3. First we will obtain the individual production possibilities for each country, Cal and Oh, producing without trade.

To obtain the production possibilities, we start where all resources are used to produce oranges, decrease orange production, and find the amount of glass that can be produced for each amount of oranges given up. Suppose that we know that if Cal uses all its resources to produce oranges, it can produce 100 oranges. Further, suppose that Cal has to give up 10 oranges to get 2 tons of glass. Suppose that we decrease orange production by 10 to 90. How many tons of glass can Cal produce? According to the opportunity cost, Cal can produce 2 tons of glass. Two tons of glass and 90 oranges becomes a point on Cal's production possibilities. If we further reduce orange production by 10 more to 80, glass production will increase by 2 more tons to 4 tons. As we continue reducing orange production by 10 at a time, glass production will rise by 2 tons for each reduction of 10 oranges. When all resources are shifted over to the production of glass, Cal will be able to produce 20 tons of glass and no oranges. The result is a straight-line production possibilities for the country Cal, as shown in Figure 30-1.

The same process can be used to find the production possibilities for Oh. Assume that Oh can produce 3 oranges or 1 ton of glass and that the largest possible orange production in Oh is 30 oranges. The production possibilities for Oh is shown in Figure 30-2. Note that if all resources are used to produce glass, Oh can produce 10 tons.

We now want to find the production possibilities with trade in a world made up of Cal and Oh. What is the total production that can be obtained when both countries combine their output? The world production possibilities is shown in Figure 30-3. To determine the world production possibilities, we add the production possibilities of the two countries together. How are production possibilities curves added?

Suppose that we start with the production possibilities for each country and find the total orange production. If all resources are used to produce oranges, 100 oranges are produced by Cal and 30 by Oh. The total production will be 130 oranges. But what is the opportunity cost? We are about to take resources

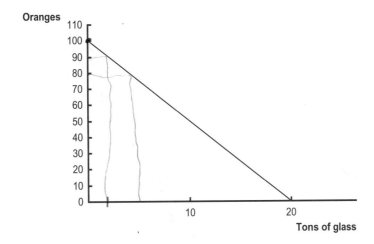

Figure 30-1 Production possibilities for Cal
This graph shows the production possibilities for Cal in oranges and glass.

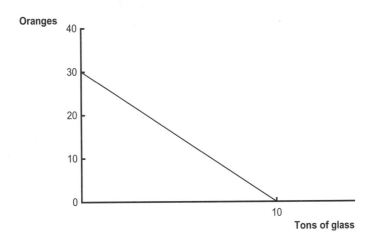

Figure 30-2 Production Possibilities for Oh
This graph shows the production possibilities for Oh in oranges and glass.

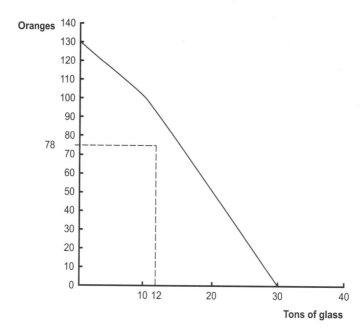

Figure 30-3   World Production Possibilities with Trade
The world production possibilities shows that both countries can have more with specialization
and trade than without.

out of the production of oranges and put them into the production of glass. We
want to get the most glass possible for our oranges. Thus we will take resources
out of orange production where we can get the most glass. So we should take
resources out of orange production in Oh because we can get 1 ton of glass by
spending only 3 oranges while in Cal we would have to spend 5 oranges to get
one ton of glass. We will continue taking resources out of orange production in
Oh until there are no more resources producing oranges in Oh. At that point we
will have a world production of 100 oranges and 10 tons of glass.

The rule we use to obtain the world production possibilities is to reduce the
production of a good in the country that could provide the largest amount of the
other good and to continue the reduction until the country produces no more
of that good. Then our only choice will be to take resources out of production
of the good in the other country, in this case orange production in Cal. Now
to get each added ton of glass, we will have to reduce orange production by
5. This process will continue until we have no resources producing oranges
in either country, and only glass is produced. Now we will have 30 tons of

glass. This is reasonable, since if all resources are used to produce glass in Oh, 10 tons can be produced; while if all resources are used to produce glass in Cal, 20 tons can be produced. A total of 30 tons of glass can be produced by both countries combined.

Now that we have the world production possibilities, what does it show? Suppose that no trade occurs. Then the best that each country can do is choose some combination of oranges and glass on its individual production possibilities. Suppose that Cal chooses 60 oranges and 8 tons of glass and that Oh chooses 18 oranges and 4 tons of glass. Without trade, neither can have more of both goods. And with trade? With trade, the world production possibilities becomes feasible. Note that the choice made by each country individually gives a total of 78 oranges and 12 tons of glass. This choice without trade is inside the world production possibilities. Thus trade allows both countries to consume more than if no trade occurs.

▶ Summary

The possibilities for trade have been the topic of this chapter. You learned that if for some good each country has an absolute advantage — the ability to produce a good more cheaply than another — then trade makes sense. But the surprising lesson is that even if one country can produce both goods more cheaply than another, there still may be gains from trade. In this case, comparative advantage — the ability to produce relatively more cheaply in terms of opportunity cost — will determine if trade should occur. It is not the absolute advantage but the comparative advantage that is important.

By specializing and trading, two countries can have more of each good than without trade. Specialization and trade allow the amount of consumption in the world to increase. The case for specialization and trade is impressive. But could there ever be situations where this case could be dismissed? Would we ever wish to forgo the gains from trade? In the next chapter we will consider the case where money is required for trade. We will also consider whether there are times when barriers to trade may be desirable.

▶ Key Concepts

absolute advantage
comparative advantage

▶ Discussion Questions

1. Cousin Sue grows asparagus. She hates asparagus. Why would she grow it?
2. Attorney Blankstare is a successful lawyer. He also types flawlessly at 100 words per minute. Should attorney Blankstare hire a typist who can only type 80 words per minute or continue doing both the legal work and the typing? Explain what economic principle is involved.
3. Uncle Effron does not believe in comparative advantage. He says that when you can produce with fewer resources, there is no need to trade. Is he right? Explain comparative advantage to Uncle Effron.
4. Comparative advantage does not depend on the terms of trade, yet the terms of trade may determine that trade does not occur even when there is a comparative advantage. Explain.
5. How does the world production possibilities in Figure 30-3 show that gains from trade are possible?

▶ Self-Review

• Fill in the blanks

absolute advantage

absolute
trade
still

comparative advantage

comparative

comparative
other
relatively
opportunity

gains

The ability to produce a larger quantity of a good with the same amount of resources is called the _____. When one producer has an absolute advantage in good A and the other producer has an absolute advantage in good B, you would expect each to specialize in the _____ advantage and _____. But what if one producer has the absolute advantage in both goods? Trade is _____ possible. When the opportunity cost of a good is less than the opportunity cost for the same good by the other party, the first party has a _____ in the production of the good. The key to specialization and trade is _____ advantage. When a producer has a comparative advantage in the production of one good, the other producer has a _____ advantage in the production of the _____ good. What is important is which producer can make the good _____ more cheaply in terms of the _____ cost. The combined production possibilities curve for two countries shows the possibility of _____ from trade.

• Multiple choice

1. Suppose that country A can produce 3 tons of sweet potatoes or 6 tons of turnips with a given amount of resources. Country B can produce 2 tons of sweet potatoes or 4 tons of turnips with the same resources.
   a. Country A has an absolute advantage in sweet potatoes.
   b. Country B has an absolute advantage in turnips.
   c. Country A has an absolute advantage in both goods.
   d. Country B has an absolute advantage in both goods.

2. Comparative advantage means:
   a. one country has a lower opportunity cost for a good than another country.
   b. what one country has to give up to get a unit of the good is less than what another country has to give up.
   c. both a and b.
   d. none of the above.

3. Cindy and Sue are best friends and decide to work together over the summer to earn money. Cindy can wash four dogs or weed one garden in an hour. Sue can wash six dogs or weed two gardens in an hour. Who has the comparative advantage in which good?
   a. Cindy has a comparative advantage in weeding.
   b. Sue has a comparative advantage in both.
   c. Sue has a comparative advantage in washing dogs.
   d. Cindy has a comparative advantage in washing dogs.

4. The opportunity cost of a tomato is 3 beans for country A and 4 beans for country B. Which country has the comparative advantage in tomatoes?
   a. Country A.
   b. Country B.
   c. Neither has a comparative advantage.
   d. Not enough information to tell.

5. If country X can produce a good using less resources than country Y, then country X has:
   a. a comparative advantage in the good.
   b. an absolute advantage in the good.
   c. both a comparative advantage and an absolute advantage in the good.
   d. no advantage in either good.

Answers: 1.c, 2.c, 3.d, 4.a, 5.b.

Chapter | 31 | TRADE WITH MONEY

Key Topics

foreign exchange rate

foreign exchange market

balance of payments

barriers to trade

free trade versus protectionism

Goals

understand how the price of a currency is determined

understand the balance of payments

discuss any advantages to restricting free trade

Trade is a universal activity whether conducted on an individual or a national level. There are, however, two special considerations of international trade. One is that since each nation maintains its own currency, international trade requires that a foreign exchange market be established for currencies. Second, there are the issues involving barriers to trade. Does it ever make sense to limit the number of cars we import from Japan? Should we require U.S. citizens to pay a higher price for Canadian products than for the same product made in the United States? There is much concern over the protection of domestic American industries. We should take the time to understand the economic aspects of international trade.

Foreign Exchange Rate

When you buy a Jaguar, an auto made in Great Britain, how is the transaction made? You go to your local Jaguar dealer and order the car. To purchase the car, you write a check and give it to the dealer. And you drive the car home. The dealer has to pay the manufacturer for the car. The check you gave the dealer is in dollars. But the manufacturer will require the currency of Great Britain for payment, pounds (£). After all, if the manufacturer receives dollars, what good are they to him? He cannot use the dollars to pay his costs in Great Britain. The dealer will go to a bank and use your dollars to buy pounds. The question is, How many pounds will the dealer be able to buy? The answer depends on the exchange rate. The **exchange rate** is the price of one currency in terms of another.

The exchange rate equates the number of pounds that can be bought for one dollar. You can see that the price the dealer charges for the Jaguar will partially depend on the exchange rate. The price of the car from the manufacturer will depend on the manufacturer's local conditions such as the price of raw materials and the price of labor and capital as well as demand. These conditions determine the number of pounds the manufacturer requires. But as the exchange rate changes, the number of dollars you need to give to the dealer will change. This is because the number of pounds you can buy with your dollars — the exchange rate — varies from day to day.

Whether or not you are able to buy the car will depend on the price you have to pay. You will pay in dollars, which are then converted into pounds. The manufacturer requires some given number of pounds. The number of pounds you can get for a dollar will determine how many dollars you have to pay. So if a Jaguar costs £50,000, and each dollar buys £1, the cost to you is $50,000. But if it takes $1.50 to buy £1, the same £50,000 Jaguar will cost $75,000. When you can get more pounds for your dollar, you are more willing to buy the Jaguar than if you get fewer pounds for your dollar. Changes in the exchange rate will make the car less or more expensive for you. One important thing to understand is how the exchange rate is determined.

Foreign Exchange Market

The exchange rate is determined in a market. There are many people in the United States who want to buy goods manufactured in Great Britain. They will all need pounds to make the trade. They will be willing to give up dollars to get pounds. On the other hand, all those in Great Britain who want to buy goods made in the United States will need dollars and are willing to give up pounds to get dollars. This demand and supply for currencies establishes a foreign exchange market.

We will look at the currency market from the viewpoint of the United States. We are demanders of pounds. We want pounds to buy British goods

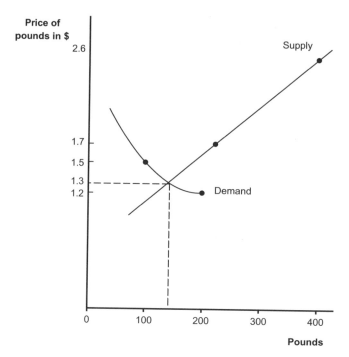

Figure 31-1   The Market for Pounds
The demand for pounds is the demand by those in the United States wanting pounds to buy British goods. The supply of pounds is provided by those in Great Britain who want to give up pounds to get dollars to buy goods in the United States. The exchange rate, the number of dollars needed to buy a pound, is determined by the intersection of the supply and demand.

or for travel to Britain. People in Great Britain are suppliers of pounds. They want to purchase goods from the United States or travel in this country. The currency market is shown by Figure 31-1. On the horizontal axis, we measure pounds. On the vertical axis, we measure the number of dollars we have to give up to get a pound, or dollars per pound. The demand curve is our demand for pounds. The demand curve says that if each pound costs $1.50, we will only want £100. If each pound costs $1.20, then we will want £200, and so on. The supply curve is the number of pounds the British are willing to give up to get dollars for the purpose of trade. It says that if the price of pounds is $2.60 per pound, then £400 will be supplied. If the price is $1.70, then the British will only be willing to supply £225. The intersection of the demand and supply determines the exchange rate, the number of dollars we have to give up to get a pound. The exchange rate established here is $1.30 a pound.

We can now ask what happens to the exchange rate when there is an increase in demand for British products. The result is an increase in demand for pounds, and the price of the pound will rise as shown in Figure 31-2. So it takes more dollars to buy one pound than before. To get the same good, we will have to pay more, not because the good costs more to produce, but because the amount we have to pay to get a pound has gone up. This also means that one pound now buys more dollars than before. So the price of dollars has gone down.

What if there is a reduction in the supply of pounds as shown in Figure 31-3? This might be caused by a reduction in the demand for American goods by the British. Remember that less purchasing by the British results in a smaller supply of pounds in the market. In that case, pounds become more scarce, and the price of the pound goes up. Again we have to pay more for the goods we want to import from Great Britain.

The exchange rate changes from day to day and is determined by the interaction of supply and demand. This market method of determining the exchange rate is called a floating exchange rate system and is used to determine exchange rates in world markets. While most currencies are allowed to float in the free market, there are times when nations may participate in the market for the purpose of changing the exchange rate. For example, a nation may purchase its own currency to prop up its price. Active government participation means that the foreign exchange market is no longer a free market but is a managed float or "dirty" float.

Balance of Payments

To understand how floating exchange rates affect international trade, we need to examine the accounts of the transactions. Each country keeps an account of its international trade. The international accounts are made up of three parts. First there is the **current account**, which essentially records the value of what is sold to other countries, the exports, minus the value of what is bought from other countries, the imports. The second part of the accounts is called the **capital account**, which records the flow of money from one country to another for the purpose of buying financial assets. Some individuals in foreign countries buy stocks or bonds in American corporations. They may even buy a whole company. And of course there is a similar flow of money from the United States to other countries. The capital account of the United States records the inflow minus the outflow of money for buying financial assets. The third part of the international accounts is called the **official settlements account**. This account includes the movements of cash from one country to another or the movement of credit from one central bank to another. This account also records changes in the government's reserves of foreign currencies.

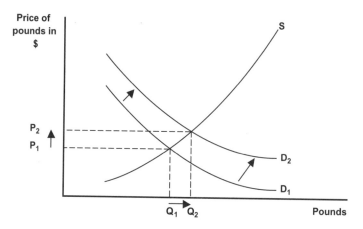

Figure 31-2   An Increase in the Demand for Pounds
When the demand for pounds increases, there is an increase in the exchange rate. The number of dollars needed to buy one pound is increased.

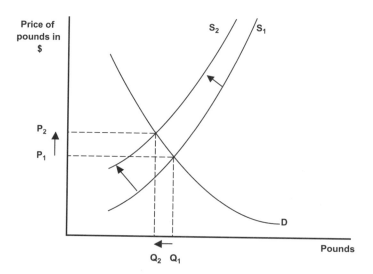

Figure 31-3   A Decrease in the Supply of Pounds
When the supply of pounds decreases, there is an increase in the exchange rate. The number of dollars needed to buy one pound is increased.

The three international accounts record all the international transactions in and out of a country. Note that every one of these transactions went through the foreign exchange market. For example, some number of pounds were traded for some number of dollars. All those dollars were used by British citizens to buy U.S. goods or securities (our exports and capital inflow) or were held by citizens or by the government as part of reserves. All the pounds were used by U.S. citizens to buy British goods and securities (our imports and capital outflow) or were held by citizens or by the government as part of reserves. When the quantity supplied equals the quantity demanded in the foreign exchange market, the total value of the inflow (the dollar value of our imports, capital outflows, and the change in holdings of foreign currencies) must equal the value of the outflow (the dollar value of our exports, capital inflows, and the change in foreign holdings of our currency). The difference between them is zero. The international accounts *always* balance. Then what is the balance-of-payments problem?

The news headlines frequently report that the balance of payments is the worst ever. **Balance of payments** is the sum of the current account and the capital account. If this sum is positive, there is a surplus balance of payments, and if negative, a deficit. Floating exchange rates are thought to correct both a balance-of-payments deficit or surplus. A closely related concept is the **balance of trade**, which refers to the difference in the value of what we export and what we import. If the value of what we import is greater than the value of what we export, then there is a balance-of-trade deficit. When the value of our exports exceeds the value of our imports, there is a balance-of-trade surplus.

Suppose that there are two countries, Cal and Oh, trading with one another. Suppose that they can both produce oranges and glass, and that Cal specializes in oranges and Oh in glass. What if Cal starts to run a balance-of-payments deficit because of a decrease in Oh's demand for Cal's oranges? That means that the value of the glass that Cal imports is now greater than the value of the oranges it exports. What will happen to the exchange rate? Since there is a reduced demand for Cal's oranges, there is a decrease in demand for Cal's currency, oscars. The price of the oscar to the people of Oh falls, making Cal's oranges less expensive. This increases the quantity demanded for Cal's oranges by the people of Oh, which in turn increases the amount of Cal's exports and eliminates Cal's balance of payments deficit. Further, since the amount that people in Oh pay for an oscar is smaller, the amount that people in Cal pay for Oh's currency is higher, causing the people in Cal to pay more for Oh's glass. This reduces Oh's exports of glass, and any balance-of-payments surplus for

Oh also disappears. The floating exchange rate eliminates a deficit or surplus. There is a balance of payments. This is the major reason why floating exchange rates are used.

The floating exchange rate system may not immediately eliminate a deficit or surplus. But over time the floating exchange rate will apply pressure on the imbalance of payments, which will cause the imbalance to disappear. During the time of the imbalance, the other international accounts will also be out of balance. For example, suppose that we import more than we export so we have a deficit in the current account. That means that we are buying pounds and using the pounds to buy British goods. The British are buying dollars and not using the dollars to buy our goods. But they are using the dollars to invest in the United States. Thus the capital account of the United States will show a surplus. The current account and the capital account together will exactly offset the official settlements account. Again, there will eventually be a balance of payments.

Barriers to Trade

One of the more frequent arguments against free trade is that when we allow trade to occur, someone loses a job. The auto industry is an example. A major complaint against imported autos is that they steal jobs from American workers. Arguments of this nature usually conclude by recommending some kind of barrier to trade. Does this mean that we should prevent autos from being imported? We will evaluate two common barriers to trade, tariffs and quotas, before discussing the issue of free trade versus protectionism.

One reason why foreign goods can be easily sold in this country is that they may be less expensive than the same good made in the United States. One way to reduce the amount of the foreign good sold in the United States is to raise the price of the foreign good when it is sold in this country. This can be accomplished by a tariff. A **tariff** is a tax on imports. By taxing imports, we raise the price of the imports but do not change the price of the goods produced by our own workers. That gives the domestically produced good an advantage in competing against the now relatively more expensive foreign good. The impact of a tariff is shown in Figure 31-4. By putting a tax on the imported good, the supply of that good is reduced. That means that the price will rise and the quantity demanded will decrease. Less will be bought of the foreign good. We see that a tariff can be used to protect domestic industries.

Domestic industries can be protected in another way. Rather than raise the price of imports by a tariff, it is possible to reduce the imports by use of a

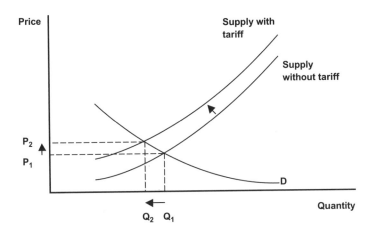

Figure 31-4   Tariff

A tariff is a tax imposed on an import. The effect is to increase the price at each quantity, which causes the supply curve to shift left. The equilibrium price of the import will rise from P_1 to P_2, and the quantity of the import will fall from Q_1 to Q_2.

quota. A **quota** is a restriction on the amount of a particular good that can be imported. The quota, by restricting the amount that the foreign producer can sell in the United States, leaves less competition for the domestic producer and consequently higher prices for the domestic good. An important impact of a quota is to raise the price of the imported good. So when a quota is imposed on Japanese autos, consumers will be willing to bid up the price of the few Japanese autos that are allowed into this country. Since the price of a substitute has increased, demand for domestic autos increases and so does the price.

A quota has an impact similar to a tariff. How a quota affects a market is shown in Figure 31-5. The quota is set at a quantity less than the market equilibrium. The impact is to limit the quantity to the quota amount and raise the price in the market to P_2. You can see that the impact of the tariff and the quota are similar. Both result in less competition to the domestic producer and higher prices to the consumer of the good, both domestic and imported.

Free Trade versus Protectionism

Let us return to the question of restricting the flow of goods from another country. On the face of it, this reduction of imports seems ridiculous. Why should we turn away goods that are cheaper than those we can produce

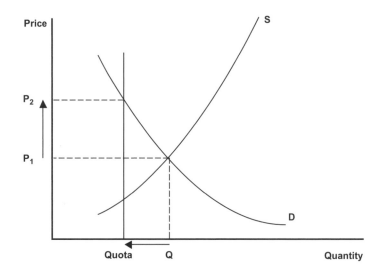

Figure 31-5   Quota
A quota is a restriction on the amount that can be imported. The impact is to reduce the quantity
of the import that can be sold, which raises the price of the imported good from P_1 to P_2.

ourselves? And why should we use up our resources to produce a good that
could have been imported more cheaply? But there may be times when such
actions are desired. We will see that there are frequently economic or political
reasons given for one country to try to block or at least reduce the flow of
imports from another country.

An important reason for barriers to trade involves the reallocation of
resources that must occur when free trade begins. As you learned in the last
chapter, free trade is desirable since the total production of the countries will
be greater with specialization and trade than without. But suppose that before
trade occurs, each country is producing some of each good. Then when trade
starts, each country specializes in the production of one good. So if the country
Cal is to specialize in the production of oranges and reduce glass production,
the question is how to get the workers and other resources in the glass industry
into the orange groves. There will be some glass workers who do not want to
work in the orange industry. They are proud of their skill as glass makers and
do not want to become orange producers or move to Oh. You can see that there
can be problems with achieving specialization. In determining the comparative
advantage, we assumed that all resources were perfectly mobile. That means
that if one industry declined, the workers would easily and quickly move into

another industry. If workers and other resources do not respond to the decline of an industry that way, then the cost of specialization was underestimated, and some of the gains from trade are reduced. If these costs are high enough, then it may make sense to impose barriers to trade.

The need for barriers to trade may be greater if the industry to be protected is considered important for national security. For example, there is an argument that we do not want to become dependent on foreign energy supplies or foreign steel supplies because our ability to defend ourselves depends crucially on the availability of these goods. This means that we need to protect these domestic industries even if we could obtain these commodities more cheaply from foreign sources. So another reason for barriers to trade is to protect industries that are important for national security. One problem is that many, if not all, industries can make the claim that they are important for national security.

There is another case where barriers to trade may be desirable. Suppose that Cal is not now producing oranges but that Cal would have a comparative advantage in orange production if it did. It would probably take some time for Cal to develop its orange-producing industry. In the meantime, Cal would not be able to achieve profitable production unless its price were protected from foreign competition. To allow Cal the time needed to develop the industry, a tariff or quota could be used to protect the developing industry. The main problem with providing protection to developing industries is that, once the protection is in place, it is politically difficult to remove. The protected industry has an interest in seeing the protection maintained.

The existence of goals other than more consumption may reduce the desirability of trade and argue in favor of barriers to trade. The gains from trade are important because the gains mean that each person could potentially have more for consumption. But what if more output were not the only goal for the economy? What if more output of the good in which we have a comparative advantage also means more pollution? Do we necessarily want to encourage free trade if to do so means to destroy our environment?

Another reason for protectionism is that sometimes one country can afford to sell its product more cheaply abroad than the importing country can produce it due to factors other than comparative advantage. For example, if a foreign government subsidizes the production of a good, then our domestic producers may not be able to compete if they do not get a subsidy. If we value the continued output of the domestic industry, we will erect barriers to trade to reduce the flow of this artificially cheaper import. Yet it may be difficult to detect when one country is subsidizing the production of a good for trade. So it will be difficult to know when to impose barriers for this case. We should also note that if we act to protect our industries, other nations may erect barriers against our exports in retaliation. Thus efforts to protect our domestic industries may lead to hardship for our exporting industries.

You should be skeptical if you hear people argue for barriers to trade as protection from "cheap" foreign labor. The argument goes like this. If we are to compete with the foreign-produced good, we will have to lower our wages to their level. Then our standard of living will fall to their level. The error of this argument is that it ignores the fact that other inputs besides labor are used in the production of a good. It may be true that labor is less expensive in other countries. But that means that other resources, such as capital, may be less expensive here. Hence we would expect the domestic producer to be using the "cheap" capital to substitute for the more expensive labor, while the foreign producer will be using the "cheap" labor to substitute for the more expensive capital. So there is no reason to believe that the cost of production must necessarily be higher in this country because the cost of labor is higher.

Further, the productivity of labor may be higher in the United States because of the use of capital, and American labor may earn its higher wage with greater output per person. If, for example, a worker in Hong Kong gets $4 per day to produce shirts but can only produce 16, the labor cost is 25 cents per shirt. If an American worker gets $40 per day but produces 200 shirts, the labor cost is 20 cents per shirt. With higher labor productivity, the labor cost per unit of output may actually be less than the labor cost per unit of output in the foreign country. But, nevertheless, as you learned in the previous chapter, it is not the cost of the resources that determines who produces the goods but rather the comparative advantage.

You should now be aware that although there are gains from trade, the gains may be offset by other considerations. Whether or not barriers are imposed will depend, in part, on how strong the political forces are on each side. Those favoring protectionism are usually those in the industry with much at stake. This will be a small group with high individual costs if protectionism does not occur. Those opposing protectionism usually represent consumers who may benefit from lower prices if protectionism does not occur. There will be a large number opposing protection but with only a small benefit per individual. It is not surprising that the small group with high individual costs lobbies hard to generate political pressure for protectionism. But the decision to protect or not should depend on the total value of these costs and benefits. If the costs of protectionism outweigh the benefits to society, then we should not have barriers to trade. We can conclude that there may be times when barriers to trade are needed. On the other hand, there are also times when barriers are proposed and should be rejected.

▶ Summary

This chapter has emphasized two aspects of international trade. First is that to carry out foreign trade, there must be a market for foreign exchange. The foreign exchange market will affect how much trade will occur. Floating exchange rates should help to improve balance-of-payments deficits.

A second important aspect of international trade is that there may be times when barriers to free trade are needed. Barriers may be erected to protect employment in some domestic industry or to allow a developing industry to get started. Barriers may also be used to reduce our dependence on foreign sources of materials that are essential for national defense. Barriers may also be desirable if a country is artificially reducing the price of its good in the international market by using a government subsidy. On the other hand, a reason you may hear for barriers, which you should reject, is that without a barrier, the competition of "cheap" foreign labor will cause us to reduce our wages and standard of living in this country.

International trade is becoming a more important part of our daily life. In the past we have been able to ignore the impact of foreign trade on our level of income, employment, and prices. But as the world becomes more of a global society, the role of international trade will become larger and more important.

▶ Key Concepts

exchange rate	balance of payments
foreign exchange market	balance of trade
current account	tariffs
capital account	quotas
official settlements account	

▶ Discussion Questions

1. Explain how the exchange rate is determined.
2. What will happen to the exchange rate (dollars per pound) if:
   a. more British decide to vacation in Las Vegas?

  b. Americans increase their demand for English toffee?

  c. there is a reduction in demand for U.S. cars in Britain?

  d. Americans traveling in Britain reduce their purchases of British antiques?

3. Determine the international account in which to record each transaction:

  a. The purchase of steel from Japan.

  b. The purchase of the U.S. company Moregrow Feed by Japanese investors.

  c. The purchase of British pounds by the U.S. government.

  d. The purchase of stock by a U.S. citizen in Oil of Araby, an Egyptian company.

4. What is the difference between the balance of trade and the balance of payments?

5. Explain how the floating exchange rate helps to achieve a balance of payments.

6. Explain the impact of a quota and a tariff.

7. Uncle Effron favors a quota on foreign-built autos. He says that foreign workers take jobs from American workers. How is he right? How is he wrong? What role does comparative advantage play? Are you more willing to agree with Uncle Effron if the good is oil rather than cars? Why or why not?

▶ Self-Review

  • Fill in the blanks

exchange	The price of one currency in terms of another is called the _____ rate. The exchange rate is determined by the interaction of the
supply, demand currency or foreign exchange	_____ and the _____ for currencies in a _____ market.
current, capital official settlements	The international accounts are made up of the _____ account, the _____ account, and the _____ account.
current	The account that records the difference between the value of the imports and the exports is the _____ account. The flow of money from one country to another to buy financial assets is
capital	recorded in the _____ account. Movement of cash and credit between countries are recorded
official settlements	in the _____ account.
balance	The international accounts always _____.
balance of payments	The sum of the current account and the capital account is the _____. If this

surplus

deficit

balance of trade

deficit

surplus

tariff

quota

sum is positive, we have a balance of payments _____. If this sum is negative, we have a balance of payments _____. The difference in the value of what we export and what we import is the _____. If the value of imports is greater than the value of the exports, we have a balance of trade _____. When the value of the exports exceeds the value of the imports, we have a balance of trade _____. A tax imposed on imports is a _____. A restriction on the amount of a particular good that can be imported is an import _____.

• Multiple choice

1. The exchange rate is:
   a. how much you get when you take something back to the store for exchange.
   b. the price of one currency in terms of another.
   c. the amount the currency dealer charges for his services.
   d. what it cost to buy a new Jaguar.
2. If the number of dollars required to buy a pound goes down, you would expect:
   a. U.S. imports from Great Britain to rise.
   b. U.S. imports from Great Britain to fall.
   c. U.S. imports from Great Britain to stay the same.
   d. The number of Japanese cars imported into the U.S. to rise.
3. If we have a floating exchange rate system, then:
   a. exchange rates are determined in a market.
   b. the government sets the exchange rate.
   c. the banks set the exchange rate.
   d. currency dealers set the exchange rate.
4. Which of the following would be a transaction recorded in the current account:
   a. The purchase of a foreign-produced good by an American citizen.
   b. The purchase of a foreign currency by a government.
   c. The purchase of a U.S. corporation's stock by a foreign citizen.
   d. all of the above.
5. The impact of a quota or a tariff is to:
   a. raise the price of the imported good.
   b. reduce the quantity imported.

c. give the domestically produced good an advantage in the market.
d. all of the above.

Answers: 1.b, 2.a, 3.a, 4.a, 5.d.

Module $\boxed{8}$ CONCLUSION

You have completed this text, and your first economics course is nearly over. What may seem the conclusion is just the beginning. You are now equipped with ideas that will help you understand the economic aspects of the world. You should not be afraid to use these ideas. You will have plenty of opportunities in your lifetime. There will always be economic problems. You will be affected by both the problems and the policy solutions. As the policy debates rage, you cannot afford to stand idly by. To choose among the alternatives, you must understand what the debate is about and what the costs and benefits are likely to be, and for whom. So the course may be over, but your use of this knowledge is just beginning.

Ten years from now what will you remember from this course? We doubt that most students will recall the precise definition of marginal cost or GDP. So what have you gained that you can use for a lifetime? There were many important lessons, and we will summarize some of them for you now.

The fundamental problem that economics addresses is scarcity. The fact that resources and the resulting output are scarce means that choices must be made. Economics is about choice. People, firms, and governments make choices. One of the fundamental lessons of economics is that when making a choice, one must find the alternatives. What else could be done? And what is the opportunity cost of each alternative?

An important lesson has been one on the economic way of thinking, recognizing costs and benefits and understanding that there are trade-offs. For an economist, making a choice involves weighing the costs and benefits of each alternative. You should by now realize that whenever there is a benefit, there is also a cost. Whenever someone tries to convince you that everyone will benefit from some action, you can be sure that somewhere there is a hidden cost. There is no such thing as a free anything. When making a choice, this weighing of costs and benefits is essential and becomes the basis of choice.

We have seen that every economy must allocate its scarce resources, and to allocate resources means to answer the three questions concerning choices about what to produce, about how to produce, and about who will get the output. We have emphasized the market process that capitalistic societies use to answer these three questions. We have also examined economic systems other than capitalism as well as a variety of market structures.

Our society allocates resources and goods through markets. By now you should have a basic understanding of the market process. Every time there is a discussion centering on a scarce good to be allocated, you should think of who demands it and who supplies it. Of course you should then think in terms of a market and the equilibrium price. Not all markets are perfectly competitive, and not all goods can be analyzed using these tools. But you will be amazed at how much of what goes on in the world can be explained using the simple tools of supply and demand.

We know that the perfectly competitive firm will allocate resources efficiently by producing a level of output where cost per unit is smallest. No other market structure will do the same. The advantage of competition is its efficiency. But there are other economic goals in addition to efficiency. We also know that markets determine income, and the amount of income we make may depend on factors in addition to productivity. Since a market may fail to produce the socially desired quantity of a good, there are times when the government will be involved in allocating resources. Choices between market forces allocating resources and the government allocating resources require careful consideration of the trade-offs.

Another important lesson is that the marginal (extra or additional) unit is the important unit. When deciding how much to produce, we proceeded on a one-unit-at-a-time basis. For each unit we asked about the cost of the unit and the revenue of the unit. We did not ask what happened to the total or the average; rather we took a marginal approach. Thinking marginally is important when trying to achieve the maximum profit. And in any decision-making process, finding the best alternative requires marginal thinking. You should be aware that marginal thinking is a valuable economic tool.

Equilibrium is a central idea in both microeconomics and macroeconomics. There are forces which push markets and the economy toward equilibrium. We can use our knowledge of these forces to tell us how the economy will behave and enlist these forces to change the behavior.

We have seen the problems that unemployment and inflation impose on society, and we have seen that an understanding of the economy can lead to the development of tools to stabilize the economy. That realization did not come easily and it took a Great Depression to make us see the importance of understanding the forces determining the equilibrium level of income.

You should now recognize that the federal budget as well as the money supply can be used to control the business cycle. The two have different links to the level of income and prices, but either tool can be used to regulate the economy. Of course in a period of stagflation, when the levels of unemployment and inflation are both high, other tools may be needed.

We have seen that unemployment and inflation trade off. In fact, no matter what goals we select to pursue, the goals will trade off. To get more of one goal will require getting less of some other goal. Thus we have to choose which goals are more important. Once the goals are chosen, you should be aware that there are many different views of the correct policy to follow. The difference between the policy prescriptions is due to the fact that various economists have different goals and different methods for achieving those goals. If your goals or methods differ from theirs, then you will want to find economists and politicians with goals and methods nearer your own.

A last important lesson is that there are substantial gains possible from trade. When two parties, whether individuals or nations, trade freely, both gain. This is true even if one can produce all goods more cheaply than another. Gains from trade exist regardless of how efficient or inefficient the participants are.

There are no doubt other lessons that you have learned from this course. There is no need now to summarize every chapter. Rather, we are looking for the big picture. There is a theme that runs through each of these important lessons: Scarcity, a fundamental fact, requires choice and results in opportunity cost. This is what economics is about. We are back to where we started. Economics is defined as ... .

GLOSSARY

A

Absolute Advantage is the ability of a country to produce a larger quantity of a good with the same amount of resources as another country.

Aggregate means the sum total.

Aggregate Demand is the total demand for output by consumers, business, and government at each price level.

Aggregate Supply is the total amount of output produced at each price level.

Allocate means to distribute, as in the case of scarce resources or scarce goods.

Allocation of Resources or **Resource Allocation** answers the following questions:

1. *What* goods will be produced and in what quantities?
2. *How* will resources be combined to produce the goods?
3. *For whom* are the goods produced? How much of each good will each consumer get?

Antitrust legislation is aimed at reducing monopoly power.

Assumptions are the simplifying device.

Automatic Stabilizers, such as unemployment compensation and the progressive income tax structure, tend to move the level of income toward the full employment level and help "smooth out" the business cycle.

Average Fixed Cost (AFC) is the total fixed cost divided by the number of units produced. The result is the fixed cost per unit of output. The expression for AFC follows:

$$\text{AFC} = \text{average fixed cost} = \frac{\text{total fixed cost}}{\text{quantity of output}} = \frac{\text{TFC}}{Q}$$

Average-Marginal Relation specifies that if the marginal is greater than the average, the average will rise; and if the marginal is less than the average, the average will fall.

Average Total Cost (ATC) is total cost divided by the level of output. ATC is found by the following expression:

$$\text{ATC} = \text{average total cost} = \frac{\text{total cost}}{\text{quantity of output}} = \frac{\text{TC}}{\text{Q}}$$

Average Variable Cost (AVC) is the total variable cost divided by the level of output. The expression for AVC follows:

$$\text{AVC} = \text{average variable cost} = \frac{\text{total variable cost}}{\text{quantity of output}} = \frac{\text{TVC}}{\text{Q}}$$

B

Balance of Payments is the sum of the current account and the capital account from the international payments account. If this sum is positive, there is a surplus balance of payments, and if negative, a deficit.

Balance of Trade is the difference in the value of what we export and what we import. If the value of what we import is greater than the value of what we export, then there is a balance-of-trade deficit. When the value of our exports exceeds the value of our imports, there is a balance-of-trade surplus.

Balanced Budget results when tax collections and government spending are equal.

Barriers to Entry are factors that keep firms from entering the market when there are incentives for them to enter.

Barter System is a method of trade without money where one good is directly exchanged for another.

Break-even Points are the points of intersection between demand and the average total cost. Any production level between the two break-even points yields an economic profit.

Business Cycles are more-or-less-regular fluctuations in the level of economic activity. These are the up and down phases that accompany the increases or decreases in gross domestic product. Each business cycle goes through four phases: peak, recession, trough, and recovery.

C

Capital is a man-made tool of production; it is a good that has been produced for use in the production of other goods. Capital is a scarce resource.

Capital Account is the international account that records the flow of money from one country to another for the purpose of buying financial assets.

Capitalism is an economic system where the individuals own and control the resources.

Cartel is a group of firms acting as one — in effect a monopoly — to determine the profit maximizing level of output and price.

Change in Demand is a shift of the whole demand curve and occurs when a determinant of demand changes.

Change in Quantity Demanded is a movement along the demand curve and occurs when the price of the good changes.

Change in Quantity Supplied is a movement along the supply curve and occurs when the price of the good changes.

Change in Supply is a shift of the whole supply curve and occurs when a determinant of supply changes.

Circular Flow is a macro model showing the flows of income and product between consumers and business.

Classical Economists believe that the economy will always achieve equilibrium at full employment.

Coefficient of Price Elasticity greater than one indicates elastic demand. A coefficient of price elasticity equal to one indicates unitary elasticity. A coefficient of price elasticity less than one indicates inelastic demand.

$$\text{coefficient of price elasticity of demand } = \frac{\% \text{ change in quantity demanded}}{\% \text{ change in price}}$$

Communism is an economic system identified by public — government — ownership of resources.

Comparative Advantage means a country can produce a good with a lower opportunity cost than the opportunity cost for the same good in another country.

Complements are goods such that if you purchase more (less) of one, you purchase more (less) of the other.

Conclusion is drawn from a model and is a prediction of behavior.

Consumer Price Index (CPI) records the percentage change in the price of a selected number of consumer goods compared to a base year.

Consumption (C) is the purchase of goods and services by households.

Consumption Function is the direct relation between income and consumption that tells the amount of consumption at each level of income.

Cost-Push Inflation is a rise in the average price level due to an increase in production costs. Cost-push originates from the supply side of the economy.

Crowding-Out Effect occurs when deficit spending by government increases interest rates and reduces investment.

Currency is the portion of our money supply consisting of coins and Federal Reserve notes.

Current GDP See *money GDP*

Current Account is the international account that essentially records the value of what is sold to foreign countries, the exports, minus the value of what is bought from other countries, the imports.

Cyclical Unemployment occurs when the economy slows down and there are more unemployed people than there are available jobs.

D

Deficit Budget occurs when government spends more than it collects in taxes.

Definition gives a name to an idea.

Deflation is a continued fall in the price level and an increase in the value of a dollar.

Demand is a list or schedule of the quantities of a particular good that a buyer would be willing and able to buy at alternative prices.

Demand-Pull Inflation is a rise in the average price level caused by excess demand at full employment. The excess demand increases the average level of prices, which is inflation.

Determinants of Demand, including a change in taste for a good, a change in income, an expectation of a change in the price of a good, or a change in the price of a related good, are capable of shifting the demand curve.

Determinants of Price Elasticity of Demand include whether the buyer views the good as a luxury or necessity, the availability of acceptable substitutes, and how large a part of the budget the purchase is for the buyer.

Determinants of Supply are changes in nature, the cost of production, the price of other goods, and expectations of a change in price, all of which are capable of shifting the supply curve.

Differentiated Product is one where the consumer can distinguish one firm's output from another firm's output.

Discount Rate is the interest rate that banks pay on money borrowed from the Federal Reserve System.

Disposable Income is income after taxes and can be either spent or saved by consumers.

Dissaving consumers are consuming more than they are making, either borrowing or spending past saving.

Double Counting occurs when we count the value of the intermediate products as well as the value of the final product in GDP.

E

Easy Entry is the absence of entry barriers in a market. Easy entry results in more firms and less control over price; more barriers to entry result in fewer firms and more control over price.

Economic Loss occurs when total cost exceeds total revenue.

Economic Profit occurs when total revenue exceeds total cost. The revenue of the firm more than covers all opportunity cost. After paying the explicit cost and accounting for the implicit cost, the firm has revenue left over. This remaining revenue is economic profit.

Economics is a social science that studies how society chooses to allocate its scarce resources, which have alternative uses, to provide goods and services for present and future consumption.

Economic System is the process used by each society to allocate resources.

Economies of Scale cause the average total cost to decline in the long run as the productive capacity of the firm increases and are a basis for natural monopoly.

Efficient Allocation of Resources occurs when a good is produced at the lowest possible opportunity cost. This means as few of society's scarce resources as possible are used up, leaving resources free to be used in the production of other goods. A firm produces efficiently at the level of output corresponding to the lowest point on the average total cost curve.

Elastic Demand occurs if the coefficient of elasticity is greater than one. This means that buyers are relatively responsive to a change in the price of the good.

Elasticity See *price elasticity of demand.*

Entrepreneurship is the organizational force that combines the other factors of production — land, labor, and capital — and transforms them into the desired output. Entrepreneurship is a scarce resource.

Equation of Exchange says that the money supply times the velocity of circulation equals price times output, or $MV = PQ$.

Equilibrium is a balance of forces.

Equilibrium Point occurs at the intersection of the market supply and the market demand curves.

Excess Reserves are any reserves that a bank has over and above its required reserves. A bank is free to make loans with its excess reserves.

Exchange Rate is the price of one currency in terms of another.

Expectations Inflation occurs when people expect prices to rise and act upon the expectation by buying more. Prices will rise as a result.

Expenditure Approach to gross domestic product is the sum of all spending by consumers, business, government, and net exports.

Explicit Costs are the money costs of producing the product.

Externalities occur when the cost to society of production differs from the cost to the producer.

F

Fallacy of Composition is an error in thinking that assumes that the behavior of the whole is the same as the behavior of its parts.

Fiscal Policy is the use of the federal budget as an economic tool to stabilize the economy.

Fixed Factors of production are the inputs that cannot be increased during the short-run productive process.

Fractional Reserve System requires that banks hold a percentage of their deposits as reserves.

Free Good is a good with zero opportunity cost, which means that you can have all you want without giving up anything else.

Frictional Unemployment includes those people in the process of relocating from one job to another.

Full Employment is defined at some level of unemployment. The exact percentage of unemployment that marks full employment is open to debate.

G

GDP Price Deflator is a special price index used to convert money GDP into real GDP.

Good is anything that satisfies a want.

Government Spending (G) is the total expenditure by government.

Gross Domestic Product (GDP) is the total dollar value of all final goods and services produced within a nation's border during a year.

H

Hyperinflation is an accelerating increase in the average price level.

I

Implicit Costs are the opportunity costs of owner-owned resources which are used in production, and for which no money is paid.

Income is the money society earns through productive processes. The payments to resource owners are rent, wages, interest, and profit and are the returns to land, labor, capital, and entrepreneurship.

Income Approach to GDP is found by adding all income received by the resource owners.

Income Effect of a change in price measures the change in consumption of a good because of the change in purchasing power when the price changed.

Income Multiplier means that any initial change in spending results in a greater change to total income. The income multiplier is the reciprocal of the marginal propensity to save.

Inelastic Demand occurs if the coefficient of elasticity is less than one. This means that buyers are not so responsive to a change in the price of a good.

Inferior Good is a good for which demand decreases as income increases.

Inflation is a continued rise in the average level of prices.

Investment (I) represents business spending for capital goods plus inventories. Business is the only sector of the economy that invests in the economic sense.

K

Keynesian Economists believe that the economy can be fine tuned using the fiscal and monetary tools.

Kinked Demand is a model of oligopolistic behavior.

L

Labor is human effort, both physical and mental. Labor is a scarce resource.

Labor Force consists of those employed and those unemployed but looking for work.

Laissez-Faire is the classical attitude that the government should leave the macro economy alone.

Land is land itself and anything that grows on it or can be taken from it — the "natural resources." Land is a scarce resource.

Law of Demand states that there is an inverse relationship between the price of a good and the quantity demanded of that good.

Law of Diminishing Returns states that as an increasing amount of a variable factor is added to a fixed factor, the marginal product of the variable factor will eventually fall.

Law of Increasing Costs states that as society obtains an extra unit of one good, ever-increasing amounts of the other good must be sacrificed.

Law of Supply states that a direct relation exists between the price of a good and quantity supplied of that good.

Long Run is a period of time in which all inputs to the productive process are variable.

M

Macroeconomics (macro) is the study of the economy as a whole.

Marginal Cost (MC) is the change in total cost as one more unit of output is produced. It is the additional or extra cost of producing another unit. The expression for marginal cost follows:

$$MC = \text{marginal cost} = \frac{\text{change in total cost}}{\text{change in quantity of output}} = \frac{\Delta TC}{\Delta Q}$$

Marginal Input Cost (MIC) is the change in total cost due to the hiring of another unit of a variable input.

Marginal Product (MP) is the change in total product as one more unit of variable input is added to a productive process.

Marginal Profit is the change in total profit when one more unit is produced and sold.

Marginal Propensity to Consume (MPC) is the amount by which consumption changes when income changes by one dollar. The expression for MPC follows:

$$MPC = \text{marginal propensity to consume} = \frac{\text{change in consumption}}{\text{change in income}} = \frac{\Delta C}{\Delta Y}$$

Marginal Propensity to Save (MPS) is the change in saving when income changes by one dollar. The expression for MPS follows:

$$\text{MPS} = \text{marginal propensity to save} = \frac{\text{change in saving}}{\text{change in income}} = \frac{\Delta S}{\Delta Y}$$

Marginal Revenue (MR) is the change in total revenue as one more unit is produced and sold. Marginal revenue answers the question, What is the extra revenue from the sale of one more unit of output? The following is the expression for marginal revenue:

$$\text{MR} = \text{marginal revenue} = \frac{\text{change in total revenue}}{\text{change in output}} = \frac{\Delta TR}{\Delta Q}$$

Marginal Revenue Product (MRP) is the change in total revenue due to the use of another unit of the variable input.

Market is a situation where buyers and sellers meet to negotiate price and to trade.

Market Power is the ability to control price. When a firm changes the price of its good, not only will it affect its own revenue, but it may affect the revenue of other firms as well.

Market Structure refers to the elements of market organization that affect the behavior of the firms. Three elements identify the market structure: the number of firms in the market, freedom of entry and exit, and the degree to which the product is standardized.

Measure of Debt is a function of money that records the amount of money to be paid in the future.

Medium of Exchange is anything that is generally accepted in exchange for goods and services. Medium of exchange is a function of money.

Microeconomics (micro) is the study of the individual parts of the economy.

Misallocation of Resources occurs when a good is produced at other than the lowest point on the average total cost curve.

Model is a simplification of reality.

Monetarists believe only changes in the money supply affect output or prices.

Monetary Policy is the use of monetary tools by the Federal Reserve System to influence the money supply and interest rates to stabilize the business cycle.

Money serves as a medium of exchange and also functions as a standard of value, a store of value, and a measure of debt. Anything that is money performs these functions in a society.

Money or Current GDP is the GDP figure without adjustment for changes in price.

Money Demand tells how much money people will hold in currency or in checkable deposits at each interest rate.

Money Multiplier is the multiple change in the total money supply resulting from any initial change in bank excess reserves. The money multiplier is the reciprocal of the reserve requirement.

Money Supply in the narrow M1 definition consists of currency in circulation and any checkable deposits.

Monopolistic Competition is characterized by a market structure that has many sellers, a differentiated product, and easy entry.

Monopoly is a market structure where there is a single seller, no acceptable substitutes for the product, and entry into the market is restricted. The firm faces the same downward-sloping demand as the market because the firm is the market.

Multiplier See *income multiplier* or *money multiplier.*

N

National Debt is the outstanding government debt created when the government spends more than it collects in taxes. The national debt is also commonly referred to as the federal or public debt.

Natural Monopoly is characterized by a market that is large enough to support only one firm of an efficient size.

Natural Rate of Unemployment is frictional plus structural unemployment.

Net Exports is the difference between exports and imports and accounts for the foreign sector in the expenditure approach to GDP.

Normal Good is a good for which demand increases as income increases.

Normal Profit results when total revenue equals total cost. A normal profit is also called a zero economic profit. This means that the firm exactly covers its opportunity cost.

Normative models express value judgments that prescribe how the world should be.

O

Official Settlements Account is the international account that includes the movements of cash from one country to another or the movement of credit from one central bank to another, and records changes in the government's reserves of foreign currencies.

Oligopoly is a market structure of just a few sellers, usually protected by barriers to entry, for a product that is either standardized or differentiated.

Open Market is the exchange where negotiable government securities are traded, just like the stock market.

Open Market Operation is the purchase or sale of negotiable government securities in the open market by the Federal Reserve.

Opportunity Cost is the value of the foregone alternative — what you give up when you get something.

Output Approach to gross domestic product. See *gross domestic product.*

P

Per Capita GDP is GDP per person. To find per capita GDP, divide GDP by the population.

Perfectly Competitive Market is a market structure characterized by many firms, a standardized product, and easy entry. When a market is competitive, no firm has control over price.

Perfectly Elastic Demand occurs if the coefficient of elasticity is some number divided by zero. No matter how many units are bought, the price stays the same.

Perfectly Inelastic Demand occurs if the coefficient of elasticity is zero. No matter what the change in price, the quantity demanded does not respond.

Phillips Curve shows the inverse relation between unemployment and inflation. The outward shift of the Phillips curve shows stagflation.

Positive economic models are models that describe.

Potential Equilibria are the combinations of Y and C + I (or C + I + G) where equilibrium could possibly occur, where Y = C + I (or Y = C + I + G).

Price is what the buyer gives up to get another unit of a good.

Price Elasticity of Demand measures the responsiveness of the quantity demanded to a change in price.

Price Index Number records the percentage change in the price of a selected combination of goods compared to the base year. The price index number is a measure of the average price level. The expression for a price index number follows:

$$\text{price index number} = \frac{\text{cost of the market basket, current year}}{\text{cost of the market basket, base year}} \times 100$$

Price Leadership is the practice of all oligopoly firms uniformly increasing price after an increase in price by the industry leader. The price leader may be the most powerful firm or simply one taking the position by custom.

Producer Price Index (PPI) is a measure of the prices of certain goods sold at wholesale and is thought to be a predictor of consumer price movements.

Production Possibilities model shows all possible combinations of two different outputs that the society is capable of producing.

Profit is total revenue minus total cost.

Profit Maximization means making the greatest possible amount of profit.

Profit Maximization Point (input) is the point of intersection of the marginal input cost with the marginal revenue product. The level of input that this point represents is the profit maximizing level of input.

Profit Maximization Point (output) is the point of intersection of the marginal cost with the marginal revenue. The level of output that this point represents is the profit maximizing level of output.

Public Goods are goods that we consume collectively; that is, goods for which an increase in your consumption does not require me to decrease mine.

Q

Quantity Demanded is the amount a buyer is willing and able to buy at a specific price.

Quantity Supplied tells the amount that a seller is willing and able to produce at a specific price.

Quota is a restriction on the amount of a particular good that can be imported.

R

Rational Expectations is the belief that people adjust to expected actions by the government so that, when the action actually occurs, its effect has already been accounted for in the market.

Real GDP is a measure of output produced by an economy valued in the prices of the base year. To find the real level of output, real GDP, divide the current level of output, money GDP, by the GDP price deflator index number for the current year:

$$\text{real GDP} = \frac{\text{money GDP}}{\text{GDP price deflator}}$$

Required Reserves are the amount of its deposits that a bank is required to hold in reserve and not lend out.

Reserve Requirement is the percentage of its deposits that a bank must keep in reserve as required by the Federal Reserve.

Resources are the so-called factors of production or means of production. These resources can be classified as land, labor, capital, and entrepreneurship.

S

Saving (S) is that part of income that is not spent for consumption or taxes.

Saving Function is the direct relation between income and saving that tells how much is saved at each level of income.

Say's Law states that supply creates its own demand. The meaning of this statement is that the money paid to resource owners for the use of their resources will be used to purchase the output of producers.

Scarcity is the basic economic problem of unlimited wants competing for limited resources.

Seasonal Unemployment occurs when workers are laid off during the off season.

Shortage exists whenever the quantity demanded is larger than the quantity supplied at the going price.

Short Run is a period of time in which at least one of the factors of production is fixed.

Shutdown Decision tells the firm to stop production if its revenue does not cover its variable cost.

Shutdown Point is the lowest point on the average variable cost curve.

Socialism is an economic system that favors a combination of private and public ownership of resources.

Social Science uses the scientific method to study human behavior.

Stabilization Policy is any action taken by the government to smooth out the business cycle and includes both monetary and fiscal policies.

Stagflation is undesirable rates of both unemployment and inflation together. An outward shift of the Phillips curve shows stagflation.

Standard of Value is a function of money that permits people to measure and compare the values of different goods.

Standardized Product is one where the consumer cannot distinguish one firm's output from another firm's output. The products seem identical.

Store of Value is a function of money that allows people who have money now to spend it at a later time.

Structural Unemployment occurs when there are many people unemployed while there are many jobs available, but the unemployed lack the necessary qualifications for the jobs.

Substitutes are goods such that if you buy more (less) of one, you buy less (more) of the other.

Substitution Effect of a change in price measures the change in consumption of a good because the good becomes a less or more attractive substitute for other goods.

Supply is the list or schedule of alternative prices and the amount of the product that the seller is willing and able to offer for sale at each price.

Supply-Shock Inflation is inflation that results from infrequent drastic changes in production cost of fundamental products.

Supply-Side Economics is a view that emphasizes the importance of policy action on the aggregate supply curve.

Surplus is the condition that occurs when the quantity supplied exceeds the quantity demanded at the going price.

Surplus Budget is a budget that results when the government collects more in taxes than it spends.

T

Tariffs are taxes imposed on imports.

Technology is the knowledge required to turn inputs into output.

Total Cost (TC) is the sum of the fixed cost and the variable cost at each level of output.

Total Fixed Cost (TFC) is the cost that does not change with the level of output. This means that the total fixed cost remains the same, or constant, whether zero or an infinite amount of output is produced. Total fixed cost is not related to the level of production.

Total Output is the amount produced by the economy, real GDP.

Total Product (TP) is the total output produced by the inputs of a firm.

Total Revenue (TR) is the money the firm collects by selling the good (price times quantity sold).

Total Spending is the amount spent by all sectors of the economy, $C + I + G$ ($C + I$ in a two-sector economy).

Total Variable Cost (TVC) are those costs that change with the level of output.

U

Underemployment occurs when workers can find only part-time employment or jobs not utilizing their skills.

Unemployment exists when people are looking for a job, but they are unable to find work at the going wage.

Unemployment Rate for the United States measures the percentage of the labor force who are not able to find employment.

Unitary Elasticity means that the percentage change in quantity demanded will be the same as the percentage change in price.

V

Variable Factors of production, or variable inputs, are those inputs that can be increased during production.

Velocity of Circulation is the number of times a dollar is spent in a year in buying the final output of the economy.

INDEX

F

N